Democracy and Goodness

D0840088

Citizens, political leaders, and scholars invoke the term "democracy" to describe present-day states without grasping its roots or prospects in theory or practice. This book clarifies the political discourse about democracy by identifying how its primary focus is human activity, not consent. It points out how democracy is neither self-legitimating nor self-justifying and so requires critical, ethical discourse to address its ongoing problems, such as inequality and exclusion. Wallach pinpoints how democracy has historically depended on notions of goodness to ratify its power. The book analyses pivotal concepts of democratic ethics such as "virtue," "representation," "civil rightness," "legitimacy," and "human rights," and looks at them as practical versions of goodness that have adapted democracy to new constellations of power in history. Wallach notes how democratic ethics should never be reduced to power or moral ideals. Historical understanding needs to come first to highlight the potentials and prospects of democratic citizenship.

John R. Wallach is Professor of Political Science at Hunter College and The Graduate Center of The City University of New York. Previously, a Liberal Arts Fellow in Political Science at Harvard Law School and a recipient of a National Endowment for the Humanities Fellowship for College and University Teachers. He is the author of *The Platonic Political Art: A Study of Critical Reason and Democracy* (2001) and co-editor of *Athenian Political Thought and the Reconstruction of American Democracy*, with J. Peter Euben and Josiah Ober (1994).

Democracy and Goodness

A Historicist Political Theory

John R. Wallach

Hunter College and The Graduate Center, The City University of New York

CAMBRIDGE
UNIVERSITY PRESS

CAMBRIDGE
UNIVERSITY PRESS

University Printing House, Cambridge CB2 8BS, United Kingdom

One Liberty Plaza, 20th Floor, New York, NY 10006, USA

477 Williamstown Road, Port Melbourne, VIC 3207, Australia

314–321, 3rd Floor, Plot 3, Splendor Forum, Jasola District Centre, New Delhi – 110025, India

79 Anson Road, #06-04/06, Singapore 079906

Cambridge University Press is part of the University of Cambridge.

It furthers the University's mission by disseminating knowledge in the pursuit of education, learning, and research at the highest international levels of excellence.

www.cambridge.org
Information on this title: www.cambridge.org/9781108422574
DOI: 10.1017/9781108524971

First published 2018

Printed in the United States of America by Sheridan Books, Inc.

A catalogue record for this publication is available from the British Library.

Library of Congress Cataloging-in-Publication Data

Names: Wallach, John R., author.
Title: Democracy and goodness : a historicist political theory / John R. Wallach, Hunter College, The City University of New York.
Description: Cambridge, United Kingdom ; New York, NY, USA : Cambridge University Press, 2018. | Includes bibliographical references and index.
Identifiers: LCCN 2017042276| ISBN 9781108422574 (hardback : alk. paper) | ISBN 9781108435567 (paperback : alk. paper)
Subjects: LCSH: Democracy—Moral and ethical aspects. | Common good. | Political ethics.
Classification: LCC JC423 .W284 2018 | DDC 172—dc23 LC record available at https://lccn.loc.gov/2017042276

ISBN 978-1-108-42257-4 Hardback
ISBN 978-1-108-43556-7 Paperback

To
Sophia (b. 1993) and David (b. 1995)
the best of my future

Contents

Preface

The seeds of this book were sown decades ago, in my puzzlement about the extent to which many searing practical and conceptual issues were conspicuously absent in the work of much political theory about democracy, and my dismay about the skewed, ignorant, and unproductive debates in American politics that keep citizens and leaders (intentionally or not) misunderstanding one another. Since then, the seeds have just developed; they still pertain to much contemporary political theory and the grim politics of the present.

In the academy, political theorists, political philosophers, and political scientists talk past each other; they attend mostly to self-contained discourses of ethics, epistemology or power, and fail to diagnose the political crises that warrant their aid – attending more to the meaning of autonomy or rights or the vileness of their systemic foes than the actions taken by citizens and their putative agents. In the political world, politicians and journalists continue to use obsolete and misleading labels of left, center, and right, liberalism, conservatism, and radicalism – vestigial political terms forged in the wake of the French Revolution – to divide the complex amalgam of political discourse into manageable categories and terrains for their own interests. Although the political misunderstandings that have resulted surely aren't principally responsible for current political movements toward civil wars, greater social and economic inequality, suicidal ecological politics, technological innovation that degrades humanistic education – not to mention the other abuses of power – they haven't helped much either. Those self-placed on a moral high ground embrace principles and values without attending to their practical use or the knowledge that informs them; progressive critics of political life often minimize the ethical and emotional motivations of political actors, excusing male and female workers of the world for not promoting more extensive social democracy in the societies where they live.

In this context, the need to understand how the dynamic interaction of ethics and power drives political life becomes secondary to the professional and personal interests of true believers in one creed or another, one constellation of power or another. As a result, we pay insufficient attention to how the sparks ignited by the ethics–power dynamic drive political life. This particularly has been the case since many academics sought shelter after the political brutalities of the 1960s and 1970s. The tide has turned somewhat recently as the costs of silence have become more difficult to bear. Academics now seriously wonder how a world of such wealth and knowledge has come to such a pass, and they should if they take democracy seriously. More practical democrats or Democrats no longer ignore the large swaths of voters who support shameless politicians promoting arguably anti-democratic political programs. One cannot fail to notice the millions of dollars and work of powerful organizations designed to make voters do their bidding, and yet to disregard the act of voting mocks the freedom and equality that inhabit democracy's heart.

This book addresses the dynamic of ethics and power – rather than "morality" or "political reality" – because inattention to this irreducible dynamic has infected our understanding and practice of democracy. Democracy is never perfect; democracy is always *in media res*; democracies always exhibit conflict – as do all political orders. As a result, democracies need ethical justification for the way in which they would make democracy more powerful and effective – if, in fact, that is what citizens want. I hold not only that this is what democratic citizens fundamentally want but also that it comprises the path toward better lives for the vast majority of human beings.

To make this interpretation of democracy an intelligible, desirable direction for the future, we need to understand much better than we do the backgrounds of power and ethics in history that carve the paths democracies have taken. We need a historicist understanding of democratic ethics to sustain democracy as a good and workable political order now and for the years ahead. This kind of understanding is not the kind of discourse that one readily finds in narrower studies of politics or public discourse that attract popular attention in the news and popular or professional journals and books, which focus on the immorality or ignorance of elites and the general populace. Recognizing and interpreting the dynamic of ethics and power in political action is the work in which political theorists ought to engage on behalf of the reading public and our political worlds. This kind of pursuit has animated the best political theories. I want this work to be worthy of that tradition.

Acknowledgments

I am grateful to the National Endowment for the Humanities, which financially supported my work on versions and pieces of this project in 2003–4, 2006, and 2012. In the middle and final stages of the project, I received pivotal financial help from the Professional Staff Congress of the City University of New York and presidential funds from Hunter College. Genuine thanks also go to the following universities and associated seminars and individuals who invited me to present segments of this book and with whom I had valuable exchanges: The City University of New York/ Graduate Center; Columbia University; The New School University; University of California, Santa Cruz/Cowell College; Universidad Carlos III de Madrid; University of London; University of Pennsylvania. As a result of each of these occasions, this project improved.

I hereby publicly thank persons who steered me away from misleading paths, corrected my faulty claims, and encouraged me to plug ahead. While this book is still not what it might be, it has assumed the form I am best able to craft so as to fulfill the imagined design of my endeavor. In addition to the inspirational students I taught at Hunter College and The Graduate Center of The City University of New York while composing this book, I want to single out for thanks two long-time mentors, one assistant, and a number of friends and colleagues without whom this book would not have come to fruition. During the book's gestational period, I was encouraged by Sheldon Wolin. As it began to take shape I had the good fortune of receiving unsparing criticisms, constructive advice, and friendly support from Raymond Geuss, whose careful thinking about my work has made me a better political theorist. Caroline Sigler worked as an editorial assistant for me in the later stages of manuscript-editing, helping me hone the book to its right size, shape, and focus.

I am greatly indebted to the insight, knowledge, judgment, and support for this project given me by the following (alphabetically listed) individuals (a list which omits the anonymous reviewers for Cambridge University Press – the most helpful of all): Talal Asad, Ryan Balot, Harry Beskind, Thomas Carothers, Richard Dagger, Kyriakos Demetriou, Mary

G. Dietz, J. Peter Euben, Jill Frank, Timothy Kaufman-Osborn, Melissa Lane, Kirstie McClure, Josiah Ober, Hanna Pitkin, Michele Press, Kurt A. Raaflaub, Corey Robin, Mary L. Shanley, Quentin Skinner, Rogers M. Smith, Amanda L. Thornton, Nadia Urbinati, and Richard A. Wilson.

Finally, I want to thank Abirami Ulaganathan, along with her bench of copy editors and typesetters at MPS, and most notably John Haslam and his staff at Cambridge University Press, for guiding this project from manuscript to book.

Introduction

When Woodrow Wilson announced to the American Congress about one hundred years ago that the United States needed to fight in World War I on behalf of "all mankind ... to make the world safe for democracy," he probably thought his audience knew what he meant by "democracy." But he elaborated later in his speech that "democracy" was a form of government in which the people had an effective voice in their government – unlike the autocratic government of the German State and more like the governments of France, the United Kingdom, and the United States.[1] Even as all three countries politically subordinated women, colonized and dominated non-white countries, and the United States (with Wilson's help) subjugated African Americans, "democracy" was understood to be "good," a virtuous exemplar of self-government. Since then, the meaning of democracy has justified dubious invasions of small countries and large, diminishing its moral authority and implicit goodness. Although a word's meaning is not reducible to its use, "democracy" now lacks a rosy aura and has more of a descriptive than evaluative meaning (although radical critics invoke "democracy" as the signpost of their critique). Its meaning is used ubiquitously to describe modern, liberal-capitalist republics – which are not *per se* democracies in which the people exercise authoritative political power. As a result, the meaning of "democracy" has become increasingly murky, its goodness subject to question. To be sure, the meaning and merit of democracy has been disputed since its introduction in ancient Athens and again when it favorably reentered popular political discourse in the early nineteenth century. Then, it described the emergence of republican constitutions that housed the economic engine of capitalism, the political de-authorization of public (i.e., Christian) religion, and the conceptual affirmation of equal rights for all. While the framers of the American constitution took

---

[1] Woodrow Wilson, *War Messages*, 65th Cong., 1st Sess. Senate Doc. No. 5 Serial No. 7264, Washington, D.C., 1917 (April 2). Cf. Wilson's "14 Points" for a post-war settlement, enunciated in a speech to Congress on January 8, 1918.

pains to differentiate the American republic from a "democracy" in *The Federalist* (1787), fifty years later the United States was commonly called a democracy.[2] Democracy's meaning these days is opaque, but it can be clarified. And because the word has such powerful and widespread resonance now, 2,500 years ago after its Athenian birth, we need to address carefully what it means as a linguistic and political term, and what makes its practice signify goodness.[3]

I shall not argue for its correct philosophical lineage or its primary theoretical features. I shall not assert an authoritative, architecturally sufficient meaning for democracy. Yet, for that meaning to stay close to its roots, it denotes a political work in progress, undertaken by a particular *demos* (a political people) that exercises *kratos* (in Attic Greek, forceful power). Its meaning changes as the makeup and actions of the *demos* in question evolve. Democracy by its very nature is *in media res*, always called upon to act, to address the uncertainty of the future so as to cohere with its present character.[4] That does not mean that only ancient Athenian democracy – especially given its utilization of slaves and subordination of women – can count as a true or genuine democracy or, on the opposite pole, that anything goes. Etymology and historical origins yield no single, dominant authority over linguistic and political usage, and it would be foolhardy to forbid the use of "democracy" to describe twenty-first-century societies that do not mimic the direct democracy of ancient Athens. But political discourse still should resist abuse, and it can indicate how a particular constitutional framework, social structure, or public policy is more or less democratic – roughly understood as promoting or inhibiting demotic agency – the political authority of the

---

[2] Madison defined democracy reasonably well, even if he took pains to reject it as a political model for the United States. In *The Federalist*, No. 10, he states, "Democracy [is] a Society, consisting of a small number of citizens, who assemble and administer the Government in person." This definition was also used by Rousseau in *Du Contrat Social* (III.iv), when he criticized "democracy" for conflating executive and legislative powers (even as he based his ideal social contract society on authoritative, ethical, and astute political participation by all citizens). Of course, democracies by definition need not be small; Madison referred to them to improve the persuasive authority of his design for the American "republic." For the emergence of "democracy" as the moniker for the American republic, see Hanson (1985).

[3] A brief, perceptive account of the historical course of its usage appears in Dunn (2005). For a much different, French account of "democracy" as a concept for radical politics, see Ranciere (2006 (2005)).

[4] In this respect, democracy should be understood more as an *explanandum* than an *explanans* – that is, *not* a self-subsisting entity that needs explanation but a term potentially used to explain a political phenomenon. I take this important point from Raymond Geuss. I do not strictly follow it here because of my interest in dominant, conventional uses of the term, hazy as they may be in relation to its etymologically precise meaning in ancient Athens.

people understood as the many more than the few.[5] And if we concur with Aristotle's definition of democracy, as I do in this instance, it is the many who are not rich, since if the many are rich they would value wealth over and against democracy's principal values of freedom and equality.[6]

The problem raised in this book, however, is not primarily semantic, terminological, or rhetorical. It concerns the relation between democracy, as a kind of political power, and goodness, as a kind of political ethic. It defines and illustrates a political relationship between power and ethics, intentionally burdening them with historical valence and weight. In this vein, I assign "activity" as the necessary but insufficient feature of democracy, and prior to democracy's definition in theory. Even if human activity is imperfect, it must be the principally generative force for democracy. If democracy is read as fully encapsulated in "theory," then *action* becomes secondary – which undermines the participatory, actual, and fundamental elements of democratic life. Of course, if democracy is reduced wholly to practicality, it becomes merely a particular manifestation of power – as Plato's Thrasymachus identified it in the first book of Plato's *Republic* (338e) as one iteration of political orders that render justice as the interest of the stronger (338c).[7] If democracy is a work in progress, it must work on behalf of practical goals, and those goals must resonate beyond the majority that advances them – to keep the defeated minority an active participant in democracy as a collectivity, even if it will never practically enact the interests of all and so falls short of embodying perfect political justice. This requires a kind of constructive ethics and mode of conduct that transcends individual interests. It operates on the horizon of activity and power, offering immediately justifications and legitimations for answers to questions about what democracies ought to do in pursuing their flexible constituent elements of freedom and equality (freedom to do what? equality on behalf of what?).

Working with "democracy" as an ongoing activity whose meaning is constituted by politics and history, the book's argument possesses ... two structural features. First, *democracy is not inherently or sufficiently self-legitimating*. Second, *democracy is not inherently self-justifying or self-explanatory*. Having the politically authorized people (i.e., the *demos*) rule (i.e., exercise authoritative *kratos*) may work out well, but

---

[5] Here, its meaning may emerge through democracy's negation. If a political order or practice *ipso facto* prevents or subverts democracy – as is the case with dictatorships, tyrannies, oligarchies, demagogic subversions of constitutional norms, fascisms, etc. – they, by definition, are anti-democratic.

[6] Aristotle, *Politics*, IV.4.

[7] Because Thrasymachus's statement begs the question of *what* is politically "stronger" and *who* or *what* is the ethical or political agent of strength, his attempt to define justice fails.

it also may not. The sheer exercise of power by the *demos* (or whatever one takes to be a current equivalent) is generally good for a citizenry, for it enables them to act. But on behalf of what should the *demos* act? toward what goal? with what justifiable consequences or relationship to its historical identity, insofar as *democracy* is always a *political* entity that at least minimally honors freedom and equality? Democracies require leaders who would help articulate these practices without undermining the power or virtue of the *demos*.[8] But democratic leaders and citizens require complementary ethics to justify their proposed courses of action, even as such ethics may endanger as well as enhance democracy.[9] For if one makes ethical standards fixed compasses for answering these questions, in response to perceived imperfections of the virtue or power of the *demos*, or simply relies on its extant ability to exercise *kratos*, that unduly constrains the meaning of democracy or its practical potential. In an age when "democracy" is ubiquitous, how democracies might become ethically legitimate, how democracy and goodness may become allies rather than opponents, is not well understood.

This scheme hardly settles questions about the meaning of democracy or how to understand it better. "Democracy" signifies very different political phenomena for radicals, liberals, and conservatives – each of whom may claim it as their friend (if understood "correctly") – and may assume different forms depending on irreducible world-views and historical contexts. For example, democratic skeptics, those with sour views of human nature and exalted views of philosophy (typically political conservatives or liberals), may have representative governments impose severe practical limits on authoritative democratic agency. Democratic visionaries, typically on the political left, alternatively may endow the power of the *demos* or democratic politics with a kind of political wisdom

[8] I do not explore the *logos* or *ergon* of democratic leadership in a sustained way in this book. However, the book's argument informs it. For democratic leadership presupposes an imperfectly democratic society, the challenges of practical, political reason, and coordination with the political ethics of the society leaders would lead. On the importance of political prudence, see the work of Dunn (1990), etc. For recent accounts of democratic leadership, see Keohane (2010) and Kane and Patapan (2014). For basic issues of democratic leadership in America, see Alexis de Tocqueville's classic work, *Democracy in America*. Genuine political conservatives (e.g., Aristotle, Walter Lippmann, Straussians, not congressional Republicans) seek leaders who can rationally and morally control the narrow-minded and overly emotional members of the *demos*. Most radical democrats envision leadership as an epiphenomenal problem the need for which, with luck, will diminish in historical time.

[9] While "morality" cannot be bad because we understand it as inherently good, ethics may be bad or good, since they need not be approved by all. Thus, Herodotus noted non-judgmentally the ethics (*ethea*) of different societies (*Histories*, II.30.5, etc.).

and virtue that it does not *automatically* have.[10] This epistemological binary has morphed into different substantive perspectives on democracy. Critical discussions of political ethics and democracy since World War II, 1989, and 2001 have tended either (1) to dismiss substantive ethical standards for democracy as anti-democratic, politically dangerous, or irrelevant (democratists, poststructuralists, Marxists, and analytical realists); (2) to endorse ethical standards designed to constrain democracy because of its constitutive imperfections (conservatives, from Burke to Strauss); (3) to marginalize ethical standards of democracy for fear that democracy cannot tolerate their projection into the political realm (liberal theorists, from Locke to Habermas), or (4) to downplay the role of power in constituting democratic ethics (virtue ethics, communitarians, and capability theorists). From the perspective offered here, notions of virtue or goodness are either overly inflated or mistakenly ignored in relation to democracy – with the political right *overemphasizing* the importance of ethics for political understanding and the political left anxious about ethical concepts hardening into hierarchies that limit freedom or equality, *underemphasizing* the political importance of ethics. The political left typically fails to engage the actual political ethics and sentiments of voters, whereas the political right tends to exploit them while failing to attend to the actual sources of political problems. In turn, academic and journalistic studies of politics deny the centrality of the dynamic of ethics and power in constituting politics and our social world on behalf of misguided notions of a science of politics or the self-evidence of facticity.

The failure to understand the constitutive interdependence and potential complementary of ethics and power for democratic societies has vitiated political discourse and occluded prospects for accommodating democracy and goodness in political theory and political life. A major reason for the general *cul de sac* derived from the four aforementioned intellectual perspectives has been disregard of the historical dimension … By attending to links between political histories of power and ethics in (mostly) Western democracies, the book charts a way out of this intellectual *aporia*.

---

[10] This was the case with John Dewey, when he sought, for the sake of political inspiration, to define democracy not only as a form of government but as "a way of life" and inherently moral. See his "Creative Democracy: The Task Before Us." Thus: "democracy is a moral ideal and so far as it becomes a fact it is a moral fact" (see Dewey 1985 (1939), 226–8).

By reading democracy more closely in relation to activity and its historical logics, this temporal account of democratic ethics cuts against the grain of professional political theory that is mostly fueled by dismissal of history for one reason or another and encouraged by the anti-historical drift of technological changes and globalization. And yet it is history that bears much of the responsibility for presenting the dramas of politics and democracy. History records actions taken amid an ongoing dynamic, a moving river whose direction can be changed by its parts. *Political* actions address practical obstacles and pursue practical hopes; they compose the essential superstructure of social life. If one understands what has historically generated the disconnect between ethics and power – which exists in every society that falls short of perfect justice – then we can address usefully the ongoing tension all democratic societies experience between *democracy*, as an agency of popular power, and *goodness*, as the horizon of political action and discursive source of its legitimacy as an ongoing combination of ethics and power.

The focus on goodness as the overarching framework for understanding democracy avoids moralistic traps and lends itself to considerations of power. In Attic Greek, the adjectival form of virtue or excellence (*arete*) is "good" (*agathos*), and Plato's effort to define the good simply turned the adjective into a noun (*ho agathos*) and conjoined it with the virtue of justice (*dikaiosune*) – thereby linking ethical quality and power in his concept of justice. But that concept was decidedly ideal (as well as critical), and subsequent treatments of "virtue" had smaller or dubious political components. Thus, "virtue ethics" today refers more to questions about moral character than to politics. "Goodness," by contrast, has mostly a practical and ethical ring to it; it better suits the array of terms through history that have justified democratic conduct. As such, it signifies the linkage within all political judgments between considerations of ethics and power – as well as how ethics always have a power dimension, whether by means of religion or an enforced code of conduct – and how justifiable political power needs an ethical dimension to promote coordinated action among citizens.

The *historicist* political theory offered in this book promotes a kind of hermeneutic loop between the present, past, and future in ways that depart from received views of historicism. For example, the arguments offered here are admittedly contingent and spring from considerations that mark current democratic life. They do not rely on a belief in "fused" horizons that presume the immediate or eventual accommodation of conflicting beliefs and interests over time.[11] I turn to history for crucial

---

[11] The belief that historical interpretations properly may manifest "fused" horizons was claimed by Gadamer (1975 (1960), 269–74).

antecedents, most of which are not appreciated today. But the historicist perspective employed here avoids determinist views of power in action or nihilistic rejections of ethical values for persons and collectivities.[12] Nor do I adopt science or *techne* of history that directly informs political understanding. The historicism I deploy emphasizes the centrality of action to democracy and notes how that (1) draws on ethical guideposts that transcend power understood either as a potentiality or coercive force (*bia* or *kratos*) and (2) depends on a context of practical (albeit politically indeterminate) possibility.[13] By rooting politics in the lives and genealogies of individuals and institutions, this historicist perspective on politics deflates the moralistic or philosophically fixed dimensions of political ideals or so-called empiricism as a sufficient basis for democratic judgment. An immediate criticism is simply to condemn historicism as relativist, but that presupposes an authoritative standpoint or reason or religion which I prefer to bracket for the sake of democratic understanding (and discuss further in Chapter 1).

The book's argument develops incrementally, with theoretical claims, historical evidence, and political interpretation. But throughout it finds that democracy and goodness are best served when they are neither collapsed into one another nor categorically opposed. It notes how these poles are constructed but potentially avoided amid historical conflicts about democratic ethics that have sought to foster a politics of goodness. In this regard, the book does not address the discourse of political leaders who have disingenuously instrumentalized democracy for their own political gain – whether dictators or demagogues. *Democracy and Goodness* addresses particular ethical standards that have become ingrained in democratic life – even as their value and meaning are regularly contested. The versions of goodness discussed hardly exhaust a list of democratic virtues or practices; rather, they portray moments when conceptions of a democratic good are crucially formed in relation to particular societies, from antiquity to the present. They are *virtue*; *representation*; *civil rightness* (a neologism for equal opportunity to succeed according to merit); *legitimacy*; and *human rights*. They retain birthmarks and salience for

---

[12] See Popper (1957 (1936)) and Strauss (1953). Wilhelm Dilthey conceptualized historicism as a human science in the late nineteenth century, as an encapsulation of historical experience in the trajectory of time (see Dilthey 2002 (1910)). His concept of historicism will be discussed in Chapter 1.

[13] In Attic Greek, the English "power" could be rendered as *dunamis* – which meant "potential" for Aristotle (vs. "actual") but had a more coercive element in earlier Greek political discourse (thus, *dunatoi* referred to dominant politicians) – or as dominant, if not coercive, force (*bia* or *kratos*), each of which has a distinctive, ugly character in Aeschylus' *Prometheus Bound*.

contemporary democratic ethics. Need it be said, various other concepts are extremely important – such as community, obligation, self-interest (properly understood), authority, voting, the rule of law, religion, tradition, and so on, or, negatively, racism, sexism, imperialism, logocentrism, etc. But the ones I have chosen have clear, distinctive corollaries of ethics and power. They notably took hold amid different historical constellations but resonate politically today.

The book addresses interested citizens and professional political theorists who are open to more historical perspectives on political thought and action than currently are available. More particularly, it concerns political discourse about the merits of ethics and power in considering public policy – illustrated by the gaps between, e.g., David Brooks, Paul Krugman, Gail Collins, or Noam Chomsky – by interpreting their historical roots in political thought and action, as a means of illuminating the practical and conceptual dimensions of politics – so as to enhance political judgment that connects thought and action, addressing problems of collective life. The argument of the book is threefold. First, it argues for the major value of historical understanding for democracy in general and particularly democratic ethics. Second, it shows the enduring value of *differentiating* democracy from standards of goodness for political action while *maintaining* a dialectical and complementary relationship between democratic practice and ethical standards of action. Third, it identifies selected ethical ideas and their roots in specific historical periods as gauntlets through which democratic ethics have been centrally constituted for us. The aim is neither to fetishize the past nor to marginalize its significance but rather to illustrate how historical understanding can enhance democratic activity as a politically free and egalitarian conjuncture of ethics and power. Then, we may think about political action in a democratic society not as a matter of how to apply a principle in practice or react to putative accounts of the practically real or theoretically necessary, but as how to draw on histories and theories so as better to participate in and shape the life of an ongoing society. In what follows, I focus on distinct historical moments in which democracy found new ways to justify its existence. Invariably, they exhibit political dimensions that are mostly hidden from contemporary view. Under the rubric of "goodness," they collect around political moments in different societies.

The first chapter, "Historicizing Democratic Ethics," presents the book's approach in constructing arguments about democracy and goodness. Over and against "consent," it identifies the importance of "activity" for democracy as a public practice and the pivotal role of "history" for constituting that activity. Rather than determining that activity, I argue that the kind of historicism employed here is needed to avoid being blindsided by politics. The role given to history is not as a set of shackles but as practical constituents of political freedom. In making this argument, I briefly note alternative views of historical meaning since the liberal revolutions of the late eighteenth century, but argue for the benefits of a historicist approach for understanding democratic ethics by pointing out how mostly ahistorical political perspectives provide insufficient critical tools for understanding democracy and its complements of goodness.

Chapters 2–6 offer accounts of my view of principal, extant components of democratic ethics in political life, embarking on a journey that begins in the present, turns to the past, and returns to the present. The second chapter, "Democracy and Virtue in Ancient Athens," opens with reflections on contemporary conundrums about the importance of "character" for politics – specifically the extent to which it is to be understood in terms of moral behavior (a matter of internal choice) or power (a matter of external constraint). It notes how political decisions invariably involve historical trajectories that inform the political conjuncture of ethics and power. It then turns to the first major democracy and pinpoints its chief features, explaining the nature of the *demos* as a judge for the exercise of power, how Athenian democratic politics invoked standards of virtue or goodness (*arête*) to justify public decisions, though criticized by dramatists, sophists, and philosophers. This argument challenges conventional views of Athenian democracy and its critics, ancient and modern, with regard to the relationship between democracy and virtue in classical Athens.

The third chapter, "Representation as a Political Virtue and the Formation of Liberal Democracy," provides a historical commentary on the crisis of political representation in contemporary democracies. Beginning with notation of low-level voter turnouts, the absence of trust in official politicians, the abundant but distorted distribution of money in politics (particularly in the United States since the Supreme Court's major decision of 2010, *Citizens United*), and the political problems of the more direct means of referenda, this chapter turns to the beginnings of liberal democracy, when representation acquired the status of a political virtue – the first time that a modern society that would identify its constitutional structure as democratic. This means that the chapter conventionally makes a big historical leap from ancient Greece to seventeenth-century Europe.[14] Against views that see representation as either anti-democratic or as the salvation for democracy, this chapter argues

---

[14] This may seem to reinforce the distinction between "the ancients" and "the moderns" (which, however, became significant earlier, with Machiavelli and the Renaissance), but I do not place any interpretive significance in that contrast when rendered as anything more than an ideal-typical construct (see Wallach 2016).

that political representation in democratic republics produces paradoxical results: expansion of the rights of the modern *demos* with diminished
power for individual citizens. It analyzes the way representation was initially designed to make modern democracy politically virtuous but notes
its problematic effects in the England/Great Britain, the United States,
and France – historically and now, particularly in an era when populist
politics have cast doubt on the authority of representative institutions.[15]

With the simultaneous advent of liberal, secular, representative democracy and capitalism as engine of modern economic life, the need emerged
for an ethic in civil society that would be available to all, compatible with
criteria that accommodated the hierarchies of large-scale organizations,
and in accord with a secular version of social virtue – i.e., merit. That
ethic came to be called "equal opportunity," more a legal and political
standard than a coherent concept or social goal. Born in the nineteenth
century as a goal sought by male workers, women, and subordinate races,
it remains salient today as a legal and political standard – in relation to
questions about affirmative action, political hope, or the market ethics of
neoliberalism. It offers an accepted discipline for virtuous behavior for the
implicit conventions of putatively non-political competition. Chapter 4,
"Civil Rightness: A Virtuous Discipline for the Modern *Demos*," invokes
a neologism to view the combination of equal opportunity and merit as
a kind of goodness that ambiguously conflates equality, liberty, and inequality amid the putatively democratic context of modern civil societies.

The term legitimacy became salient for critical political discourse in
the late seventeenth and eighteenth centuries, as England, England's
American colonies, and France justified changes in their constitutional
structures. But the term only became politically prominent in the twentieth century, with attempts to accommodate democratic ethics to the
political form of the nation-state. Max Weber set the standard for its
meaning, as a citizenry's acceptance of rule by governing authorities. But
with harsh political contests in many contemporary states – because of,
e.g., civil wars, weak public support, non-political motivations for acceptance of rulers, and transnational currents of power (see Marx, Foucault,
Wolin), its meaning has become politicized. Chapter 5, "Democracy
and Legitimacy: Popular Justification of States Amid Contemporary
Globalization" addresses current crises of political legitimacy, explains
its changed meaning since Weber, and shows how its meaning and use
have acquired new dimensions. These have become extremely hard to
determine amid the upsurge of critiques of conventionally legitimate

---

[15] See the acute, concise analysis of post-war populism by Mueller (2016) and the important survey of post-war populist politics by Judis (2016).

institutions (to different degrees) by both democratic revolts (the Arab Spring; the Bernie Sanders campaign); right-wing Populist discontent in Western Europe, and the angry, self-centered, cynical, and celebrity politics of the candidacy and presidency of Donald Trump.

Since its authorization by the General Assembly of the United Nations in 1948, human rights (it oft has been noted) have become the *lingua franca* of international political ethics. As such, they are officially and unofficially linked to democracy. But just as the meaning of democracy has been obscured by the size and power of states, so too has the meaning of human rights: as a discourse of humanity, it is universalistic and trans-political; as a practical discourse of rights, it requires enactment by local political groups if it functions as more than a global projection of ethical desires and non-governmental organizations. Human rights assert the moral equality of all human beings to get our attention without addressing the vastly unequal political conditions in which they live. These constitutive components of human rights destabilize its conceptual character and practical acuity. But whether human rights reflects the approaches of rights, capabilities, or political movements, a discourse of human rights will continue to assume a prominent role in today's political discourse – regionally or globally – because of the transnational character of so many political problems – such as the repercussions of war, capitalism, and global warming. Chapter 6, "Human Rights and Democracy," explains how the discourse of human rights *may* supplement civil rights and promote democracy in non-arbitrary ways, but I also argue that it cannot usefully address global political problems unless its discursive limits are duly recognized in theory and practice and its practical purpose enacted by NGOs or political groups is actually hinged to democracy.

This project's focus on the principal links among democracy and goodness, understood in a historicist vein, covers an amount of historical and theoretical ground not usually allowed for one book. Recognizing the hazards of this enterprise, the author has tried to avoid getting lost in intellectual rabbit holes while attending carefully to relevant events, texts, and interpretations that pertain to the questions at hand.

1   Historicizing Democratic Ethics

> [M]y work will have served its purpose well enough if it is judged useful by those who want to have a clear view of what happened in the past and what – the human condition being what it is – can be expected to happen again some time in the future in similar or much the same ways.
>
> *Thucydides*[1]

1.1   The Problematic

Despite the many efforts to fashion accounts of democratic ethics, no author has composed a book of note with the subject in its main title for nearly one hundred years.[2] This creates a problem for an argument that "historicizes" democratic ethics, since we may not be sure about what is being historicized. This historicist account of democratic ethics relates democracies to legitimating conceptions of goodness in historical time. This chapter provides a lens for reading the subsequent, substantive chapters about specific kinds of goodness that have signified goodness for democracies – by historicizing democracy as an activity; explaining how this focus reveals gaps in democratic understanding offered by three dominant perspectives in political theory; comparing the historicism deployed here to other kinds of historicism; indicating how it is not undermined by the charge of relativism, and then directly linking the value of historicist understanding to comprehending democratic ethics.

My use of "democracy" stems from its Greek origins, namely, *demos*: the organized, politically authoritative people, mostly comprised of the

---

[1] Thucydides, *The War of the Peloponnesians and the Athenians*, Jeremy Mynot, trans. and ed. (Cambridge: Cambridge University Press, 2013), I.20.4.

[2] The closest contributions we have are Tocqueville's *Democracy in America*, written in French for the French in the 1830s and a relatively nousy account of democratic ethics by Louis F. Post, in the spirit of Henry George (to whom the book is dedicated), first published in 1903 (Post 1916 (1903)). John Dewey wrote thousands of pages on various dimensions of the topics from the 1880s to the 1930s, but he never directly addressed the subject outside of an early article taking to task the work of Sir Henry Maine (Dewey 1969 (1888), 227–49).

middle and lower classes (made up in Athens of shopkeepers, artisans, small farmers, and workers), and *kratos*, their exercise of dominant political power in society, a word coined in the fifth century.[3] Because of the deep-seated meaning of *politeia* in ancient Greece, *demokratia* signified both a form of government and an *ethos*. Without the expectation of political activity as a part of the responsibility of citizenship – which yielded practical benefits – their political order could not have functioned.[4] There are no directly comparable democracies and have not been any since the time of the ancient Athenians that have assigned the intensity and extent of political responsibilities to the *demos* (cramped or enlarged) of the Athenian democracy.[5] When "democracy" was reintroduced as a practically meaningful political term in the eighteenth century, it had been relegated to the position of an authorizing agent to representatives and republican government. Conventional political discourse regularly refers to advanced, capitalist, constitutional societies as democracies to greater or lesser degrees – simply by virtue of participating in relatively fair, competitive electoral processes open to most adults (more difficult to do in the United States if you're poor, black, or belong to an otherwise suspect class) in order to sanction legally empowered future actions of public officials (who may or may not act consistently with their pledges made to voters during their campaigns for office). In these terms, there is no dispute that the political system of the United States is a democracy relative to Russia, China, and North Korea. But insofar as the "consent" of a majority of adults for the laws passed by their public officials rarely occurs, the current definition of democracy operates mostly as a rhetorical trope and

---

[3] We should recall, however, that even in the Homeric poems there was an unusually interactive relationship between the leaders and the people (Haubold 2000).

[4] M. I. Finley emphasizes the practical benefits of the Athenians' political system (Finley 1984). Since Greek societies were regarded as flawed political referent points for historical instruction until the early eighteenth century, overshadowed by Rome, a comparison with Roman "popular power" makes sense. Romans referred to their *populus* as "the people," but this group did not comprise all of the citizens with political rights (e.g., not the upper classes) and did not exercise authoritative political power. When Roman popular assemblies acted, it was at the behest of a tribune in relation to legislation he episodically had the power to propose (and eventually was subject to veto by higher powers) (see Beard 2015; Lintott 2003).

[5] In today's media-saturated societies, one might think otherwise. But it is well-known that only between 55 and 60 percent of eligible voters actually have voted in recent American presidential elections, which translates into less than 30 percent affirmative support for the winner. This is less than the percentage of adults voting in the principal elections for leaders in European states, but the differences are not huge, 10–15 percent. See the Pew Center's data: www.pewresearch.org/fact-tank/2016/08/02/u-s-voter-turnout-trails-most-developed-countries/ (accessed April 7, 2017).

reflects the inadequacy of our political terminology.[6] As a result, by the twentieth century, the notions of democracy as a form of government and an ethos had been either artificially isolated or confusingly combined.

This justifies my adherence to the initial meaning and use of the word democracy as empowered, politically authoritative *activity* of the people. Whether or not this activity primarily concerns the common good, private interests or official, governmental actions depends on the character of the citizenry and collectivity, enabling the provisional definition to be elastic. Regardless of how large, institutionally regulated, or capitalistically fueled a democracy may be, this definition may apply to it.[7] I offer no criteria for ranking societies over time as more or less democratic, better or worse according the character of their activity, or more or less obligated to accept refugees and immigrants.[8] Instead, I define demotic power as essentially dependent on widespread political activity for its effectiveness and use it as a critical concept for understanding democracy in post-Athenian politics. This definition importantly differs from the standard liberal conception of democracy as dependent on consent, which values belief over action and stemmed not only from a critique of tyranny and despotism but also from the desire to neutralize the social value of different religious faiths as ways of life for fear of the disruptive influence of allowing them to be publicly expressed.[9]

[6] Journalists and many empirical democratic theorists and scholars of comparative politics persistently use "democracy" to identify most advanced, capitalist societies of the West. For examples of the latter, see the work of Robert A. Dahl and Samuel P. Huntington, each of whom was a President of the American Political Science Association in the last third of the twentieth century.

[7] That doesn't make its practical meaning any easier to define. A current ethical and political issue illustrating the difficulty of defining the *demos* today has raised the political temperature of European states and the United States, namely, the extent to which these countries: have political obligations to immigrants and refugees, depend on the labor of undocumented migrants, and have difficulty responding to new claims of immigrants and refugees for political residency because of perceived threats to the integral operation of the political system – especially given the state's dependency on the economic labor of workers who live thousands of miles away.

[8] Relative to ancient Athens, therefore, accounting for its slaves, metics, and politically subordinated women, one could say that modern "democracies" have not been more democratic than the Athenian version – at least until slavery was abolished, women received the vote, and segregation was outlawed. The United States and the United Kingdom could warrant the term democratic in the 1920s (or 1965 in the United States, given Jim Crow segregation in the South). The United Kingdom took a painfully long time to enfranchise all adult men, and even longer to enfranchise adult women. French women voted for the first time in national elections on April 29, 1945.

[9] Rawls viewed the Wars of Religion of the fifteenth and sixteenth centuries as the pivotal, negative, catalysts for modern, liberal democracy (see Rawls 1999b (1987), 424). The most influential rejection of the value of democratic political agency in modernity relative to its primacy in ancient Athens has been Benjamin Constant's "The Liberty of the Ancients Compared With That of the/Moderns" (Constant 1988 (1819), 307–28).

Because of this fear, moderns from Hobbes to the Federalists regarded "democracy" as sufficiently enacted with the *consent* of the people and did not require political participation, even as the citizenry composed a minority of the adult population and has no direct control over legislation, because of worry about the political extension of demotic power or resignation to the relative political passivity of adults. They assumed that the status quo reflects a consensus and that established institutions adequately amalgamated interests.[10] But each citizen of a *demos* deserves to be counted politically as one, regardless of their class position, and encouraged to exercise political power with regard to ongoing social and practical issues. Besides, the counterpart to *action* in politics is not agreement or consent but *inaction* or tacit consent, when that agreement ought not to be presupposed.

This study does not presuppose the goodness of democracy, precisely because action lies at its center. Accompanying any action in the mind of the actor is its near-term or long-range consequences and significance. Practical reason might be right in deliberate thought, or *logos*, but it surely is not automatically reliable in practice, or *ergon*. Moreover, there is the question of what is to be done *with* the action. Conflict lies at the heart of political actions on behalf of freedom and equality, and no choice occurs without loss. As a result, my focus on political agency as a locus for democratic ethics identifies contested, fragile, impermanent links between democracy and goodness. They hover on the horizon of citizens' actions that reflect and affect political power. Highlighting activity for democracy does not require political activism for all citizens as a way of life – which anyway is impossible and practically undesirable. Rather, it makes active citizenship central to democracy as a practice, instead of the radically imperfect identification of the consent of the citizenry, of the ruled by the rulers, that has characterized liberal political thought from Hobbes to Habermas.

"Action" simply makes evident one's intellectual convictions in a context where they *may* be seen and judged by others. *Action* highlights the importance of history for democracy because it presupposes a contextualized dynamic of thought-affecting deeds. As such, it is a variable combination

---

[10] Whether or not Robert Dahl had that worry (although he did refer to "populistic democracy" as the "unlimited power of majorities"), he identified the expression of interests in an open and competitive electoral process as sufficient for democracy and defined the latter in terms of empirical criteria rather than political ethics. He also claimed that political passivity was a norm of modernity and that the political activity of ancient Athens reflected a "bias." For various published statements on these subjects by Dahl, who championed democracy and political equality in his own way, see Dahl (1956, 35; 1961, 276–81, 311–25; 2008 (1998), 38). For critiques of overemphasized authority stemming from "consensus," see Foucault, "Politics and Ethics: An Interview" (1984, 379) and Ranciere (2010, 188–9).

of *logos* and *ergon* (not as in thoughtless or impulsive movement that disrupts – as in "propaganda by the deed" or fetishism of the act).[11] The couplet of *logos* and *ergon* does not offer a critical benchmark, insofar as each houses dynamic elements. *Logos* marks the articulate expression of ideas, thoughts, emotions, and words that stem from a variety of sources. Its power comports with free agency. *Ergon*, as the point of an effective deed or practice, marks the beginning of consequences that are taken up by a variety of actors for myriad purposes – unless they are predesigned to fit a determined form, as is the case with particular, practical arts and crafts whose boundaries politics and ethics never respect. The assertion of Plato's Socrates in the *Republic* (472e–473a) that *logos* always transcends its effect in action affirms the (relative) power of philosophy over existence – even as the dialogue also signifies its limits in the face of the ability of hard power to shape, and frustrate, ethics. Action is the medium through which *logos* and *ergon* interact and, in the uptake of the meaning and significance of actions, split apart.[12] These interactions, however, are hardly random or entirely contingent. The gravity of institutions and persons channels them.

Participatory action by citizens as the mainstay of a democratic political order in which the people really exercise authoritative power has been recognized from the Greeks to Montesquieu, Rousseau, the Federalists, Marx, Mill, and Arendt.[13] Much as the inherently anti-historical character of technology, capitalism, and force dominates the present, history is produced every day. It is up to us to appreciate its value, as Orwell knew.[14]

---

[11] Although using these Greek terms disrupts seamless English prose, I do so in place of the usual binary of "theory" and "practice." The former typically reads as didactic or ethereal while the latter reads as a galloping horse that resists the power of deliberate thought. *Logos* entails not only conceptual thought but speech that informs action; while *ergon* implies the effect of a deliberate action or expenditure of energy. For how *logos/ergon* more suitably describes democratic action, see Euben (1977, 28–56 (notes 239–46), 33–5).

[12] In Arendt's terms, speech (a critical capacity) is crucial to the practice of politics as action that counts as a beginning and effort to shape an indeterminate future. Arendt (1958) defines "action" in three ways in *The Human Condition*: (1) the composition of life, including the *vita activa* and *vita contemplativa*; (2) the elements of the *vita activa*, in contrast to the *vita contemplativa*; and (3) the element of the *vita activa* that involves self-presentation to others and by nature marks beginnings in the world, in contrast to "labor," and "work." My definition is neither derived from nor leads to Arendt's trifold catalogue of those activities which reveal "the human condition."

[13] The linkage between individuality and politics occurs in the stories of personal lives and *history*. Again, Arendt: "… the reason why each human life tells its story and why history ultimately becomes the storybook of mankind … is that both are the outcome of action." While this statement is useful to my argument, it may imply that my argument views action solely through the lens of stories or narrative structure. It does not, although the deeds most relevant to politics and history are enacted by individuals who believe they are creating stories for themselves and others.

[14] See Orwell (1938, 1939).

Although "action" does not have a Greek equivalent, its etymological roots in Latin *agere* (past participle = *actus*) extend to the Greek *agein* (which was related to *agon*, a contest in games or an assembly).[15] Acts produced by actions are things done.[16] The roots of action in agency certainly tie its meaning to the dispositions and agency of individuals. But the agency of the *demos* is not simply a colligation of practical interventions of individual agents. Action, as part of reality and democracy therefore, has a kind of collective or coordinating (if not public and purposeful) feature.[17] If it does not, then whatever collective action is authorized in a society that is called democratic stems from the state, civil society, or individuals acting in relatively apolitical contexts, not from a *demos*.

Given this meaning and value of democracy, its full portrait needs supplementation by a political ethics that practically and essentially defines what is done with demotic power, wherever it can or could be exercised. One *either* radically questions the ethical sufficiency of the *demos*, thereby questioning the moral legitimacy of democratic activity, *or* assigns ethical virtue to the inherently fallible character of political actions undertaken by a human collectivity. Grabbing *neither* horn is the better choice for articulating a politically beneficial account of democracy and any corollary ethics. Unless one presumes the ability of intellectuals to articulate the basic features of what the *demos* ought to do or to have done, our necessary (not sufficient) bearings for that judgment best derive from accounts of how democratic collectivities in historical time have generated democratic ethics in politics, in terms that are best understood as relationships between democracy and goodness.[18]

"Goodness" denotes a positive version of ethics that involves the exercise of power – whether it is a good knife or a good person. In Attic Greek,

---

[15] See "action" in the *Oxford English Dictionary* (hereafter, *OED*); the Latin etymological origin of "action," namely, *actio*, in the Greek *ago*, noted in the *Oxford Latin Dictionary*, 2nd ed. (Oxford: Oxford University Press, 2012), and the more forward-looking senses of "*ago*" in Attic Greek listed in *A Greek–English Lexicon* (Oxford: Clarendon Press, 1968). See Connolly (2013).

[16] *Nota bene*: the verb "to do" stems from the Greek *drao*, from which comes "drama." Another name for them in Greek is that of "deeds" (cf. *erga*, which refers to expended energy or work). In all cases it is associated with deliberate, conscious engagement with the world, to further the cause and purpose (unless involuntary) of its agent. See above n. 9.

[17] Bruce Haddock makes this point in a different context in his article, "Contingency and Judgement in History of Political Philosophy: A Phenomenological Approach." In Floyd and Stears (2011, 71), n. 10.

[18] Before discussing the role of "goodness" in relation to democracy, it's worth recalling that "ethics" may be good or bad – unlike (Kantian) "morality" (although when defined by Aristotle and taken up in English 1,700 years later "ethics" referred to an art and science of morals understood as socially sanctioned practices). See "ethics" in the *Oxford English Dictionary*. In Attic Greek – which lacked a direct antecedent of "morality" – "ethics" referred to socially sanctioned habits of action.

"good" – *agathos* – is an adjective describing a practical, praiseworthy action. The nominative version was *arete*, typically translated as virtue or excellence.[19] The sense of purposive, excellent activity embedded in the notion of "goodness" relates to both democratic ethics and demotic activity. Plato positioned it at the top of the divided line, where it graced justice. But Plato was too confident (although he was not very confident) about its intelligible relationship to and authority for justice. Setting our sights lower, its use here refers to the beneficial prospects of the power of individuals in deliberately and practically determining goals that advance democratic citizenship in collective life.[20] "Is it a 'good' policy for the people?" is always the more pertinent political question than whether or not it's a moral or even ethical policy, because it implies concern about the outcome. But "goodness" has an ethical aroma to it, and if it's only used in technical ways – as in the "good" knife – it loses political resonance. I emphasize "goodness" as an umbrella term for aspirations for excellent performance and social justice in different walks of life – from interpersonal relationships to those in the family, civil society, associational, and officially political life.

This conception of goodness differs from Hobbesian to Schumpeterian, to Rawlsian usages that undergird liberal conceptions of democracy. Apart from his hypothetical conceptions of natural right, Hobbes identified notions of good and bad, vice and virtue, as dependent on sovereign authority, even if they strike one as emanating from civil society. Schumpeter de-authorized any agent-dependent conception of the political good or the common good because it had to reflect a commonly agreed upon set of apodictic political perceptions and pre-sumptively beneficial programs of action. Rawls allied his conception of goodness with utilitarianism and "comprehensive moral doctrines." Each of these seemed designed to marginalize the relevance of everyday notions of goodness from democratic politics, to be substituted by some

---

[19] For a modern, pragmatic, and non-moralistic rendition of "good" (nonetheless influenced by Plato's Socrates arguments overcoming Thrasymachus in *The Republic*, Bk. I), note the following: "Good consists in the meaning that is experienced to belong to an activity when conflict and entanglement in various incompatible impulses and habits terminate in a unified orderly release in action" (see Dewey 1957 (1922), 196).

[20] This book deploys "goodness" as an umbrella term for different kinds of ethics that effect and affect political power, broadly understood. How it is similar to and different from the Greek words *arete* (typically translated as virtue or excellence – even, at times, goodness – and *agathos* (the adjectival form of *arete*) that Plato made into a noun with his articulation of "*to agathon*" in his *Republic*) will be discussed in Chapter 2.

superordinate conception of political right interpreted and enforced by an enlightened political class over and against the many.[21]

The notion of goodness admits interconnections between personal and political life by drawing discourses of goodness from history rather than philosophical categories. It preserves the connection of ethics to action, thereby preventing presupposed notions of collective justice from constraining the terms of justifiable democratic action. Here, "goodness" has more aspirational than apodictic characteristics, in order to be useful in comparing competitive forms of social action that always will generate some degree of social conflict but can foster cooperation. (Democrats are not communitarians.) The usage of "goodness" as an enlightening horizon of democratic activity may apply in different degrees to different social activities – from the personal to the social, economic, cultural, or political. At every instance – when discussing the maintenance of individual health, the skill and beauty of a pianist, the social benefits of profit and nonprofit organizations, and the official opportunities for voting on issues and officials – political goodness may or may not be involved. It depends on the degree to which the performance meaningfully effects or affects social conflict.

By sinking the roots of democratic ethics in human activity, I do not presuppose a *theory* of the good or human nature. First, in every regime that is plausibly called "democratic" there are meaningful traces of democracy in the literal sense, and I want to maintain a connection between democracy and actual citizens or would-be citizens who act (even if by inaction) to shape the world in preferred, relatively ethical directions (even if by omission).[22] Second, I am not taking *any* ideas that may count as part of a putatively universal set of democratic ideas (liberty, equality, autonomy, rule of law, etc.) *and then* arguing about how these supposedly normative notions may look if historicized. This project does not regard ideas as self-contained concepts, activities that originate in a God, or markers of a predetermined destiny. In this light, the notion of goodness in democratic ethics does not function as either a noumenal idea, Aristotelian end, moral concept for our times, or measure of practical success. Rather, it functions as a conceptual and practical horizon for conjunctures of ethics and power. For they sustain

---

[21] Hobbes (1991 (1651), Chs. 6, 8, 17); Schumpeter (1950 (1942), 250–6); Rawls (1971, 446–51); Rawls (1999b (1985), 411–12); and Rawls (1999b (1987), 480–1).

[22] Raymond Geuss has noted the inseparability of ethical and practical features of democracy (see Geuss 2001, 112–13).

democratic life and enable society to be an adaptive whole.[23] These rough stipulations and guidelines for what follows do not reject analyses of goodness that have principally conceptual *or* instrumentally practical dimensions, but they suggest that if they take pride of place the result will not directly foster democratic action. For such action requires ethics and power (in varying relationships), and the combination of the two produces a paradoxical sense of goodness for democratic ethics, politics and, more generally, collective life. But this also doesn't reduce ideas to sociological formations of power or superstructures contingent on a first-order base. Rather, they are conceptual usages that arguably connect to a society's democratic self-understanding, identify such worlds in historical locations, argue for the best way of interpreting ethical justifications for democratic practices in those contexts, and then evaluate these interpretations as kinds of democratic legitimation. In our political world where "democracy" is a term for *both* supporting extant governments *and* radical criticism of those governments and their social underpinnings, the result of these parameters enables the ensuing discussion of democratic ethics to connect to actual and possible democracies.

Here I should reiterate two assumptions about democracy that inform my argument. Both call for understanding democracy in relation to historical and ethical phenomena. *First*, democracy emerges and is promoted by psychological motivations, ethical discourses, and institutional currents that are not wholly democratic. Even if one, like Marx in 1843, inverts the traditional relationship of political constitution and democracy, identifying the legitimacy of the former only as an expression of the latter, that very argument draws on preexisting discourses and power.[24] The meaning of democracy and any ethics associated with it always attends to its outside, its future as well as its present. This is why, from the standpoint of democracy, the most important sources of learning what one ought to do primarily stem from what has been done – more historical than philosophical (despite its analytical and critical value). Altogether, democracy is not *self-legitimating* (in *ergon*), which then calls for historicist contextualization. The *second* is more analytical and ethical

---

[23] Over twenty-five years ago, two fine collections of articles dealt with the political salience of goodness. One was edited by Douglass et al. (1990); the other was edited by Rosenblum (1991). Both started with academic conceptions of liberalism and mostly reference the work of John Rawls's theory of justice as fairness as their point of departure. Neither focused on democracy.

[24] Compare Marx's configurations of democracy in *Contribution to the Critique of Hegel's Philosophy of Right* (1843), *The German Ideology* (1845), *The Communist Manifesto* (1848), *The Civil War in France* (1871), and *Critique of the Gotha Programme* (1875), parts or all of which may be found in Robert C. Tucker, ed., *The Marx-Engels Reader*, 2nd ed. (New York: W. W. Norton, 1978), 19–21, 160–1, 490–1, 631–3, 530–1, 536–40.

than historical; it asserts that no democracy is entirely *self-justifying* (in *logos*) – for, as mentioned previously, it always is a work in historical progress. Democracies seek to sustain themselves and endorse the basic values of their citizens. But unless the citizenry is perfectly just, they act toward a future horizon in order to make their democracy good or better than it is at present.

Both of these features of democracy mean that it does not automatically signify "goodness" even as its citizens (rightfully) believe they are entitled to act as political agents on behalf of the political order to make it better.[25] The relationship between democracy and goodness is partly secured by dedication to the standard definition of democracy as a social array of free and equal citizens. But whatever these ideas are taken to mean, freedom and equality do not automatically yield just political action. Whether equal freedom stems from a noble lie, mythic state of nature, or (some kind of) God, democrats always must ask when they think and act: liberty to do what? equality with respect to what?[26] Accepting these two qualifications for understanding democracy does not undermine democracy's promise; on the contrary, it helps to understand it because every democracy is socially embedded, politically related to traditions, institutions, practices, rights, mores, and ideas that are not *per se* democratic.[27]

The constraints of historical dependency and ethical justification work as follows. First, to explain the actual or hypothetical choices available to a democratic agent or an agent who seeks to become democratic, one must presume that every such political agent is hypothetically or naturally free and equal in *logos* (words, reasoned account relevant to deliberate action) and able to act on that *logos*, even as we know (and Plato and Aristotle knew) they are probably unable to fulfill completely the desire associated with their *logos* in *ergon* (deed, act, function). The intellectual merits of democracy are importantly mythic, but the leap

---

[25] Rousseau was, alas, right when he said in his discussion of democracy as a form of government in *The Social Contract* (III.iv) that democracy is for gods, not men, given the imperfections of human beings and their limited capacities to both identify the general will and administer it effectively and ethically.

[26] This point echoes Aristotle's, in the *Politics*, III.9. For Aristotle, justice was an inherently practical and relational concept. Here, he is probably distancing his political theory from Plato's, similar to his debunking of a purely theoretical (by which he understands a Platonic) conception of the good (*to agathon*) in the *Nicomachean Ethics* (I.vi.)

[27] Ian Shapiro approaches the subject of democratic ethics from a kindred but significantly different point view (analytical, conceptualist, and, ultimately, more realist than historicist) when he refers to democracy as a "semicontextual ideal" (5), "subordinate foundational good" (18, 21–4), and "conditioning good ... subordinate to the activities whose pursuit it regulates (48)" (see Shapiro 1999, 5, 18, 21–4, 48).

of faith fueled by a belief in the equal freedom of citizens beats alternative cornerstones, and this is the only one that inheres in every kind of
democratic ethics. Democracy cannot survive if commitment to it as a
society of free, equal, and politically active citizens (to different degrees)
is treated simply as a matter of choice of wants to pursue or ideals to
follow. Its citizens must like, respect, and revere their public forums if
democracy is to thrive.

But let us be more direct: why is history and historicizing so important
for understanding democracy and goodness? After all, they might produce standpoints that lie outside the landscape of political democracy
and nourish its opponents' arguments. But we need to appreciate where
we are now. We live in an age that pressures us to think incessantly about
the present and future, to keep up with the innovations of capitalist technologies, to forget the past, and prejudicially to discourage historicist
thinking because of the shadows of the political horrors of the twentieth
century or its legacies of racism, sexism, colonial imperialism, gender
bias, etc. The effect encourages ahistorical, analytical theorizing about
politics from liberal or poststructuralist, moralist, positivist, and realist
perspectives.[28] Futurist imaginaries tend to have an ideological valence,
while historicist inquiry tends to promote more useful, critical thought. To
historicize, therefore, provides the most useful sources for understanding
democracy as a dynamic confluence of power and ethics, in terms of the
history of human action.[29] It does not choose "agency" over "structure"
per se, as neither is reified, and the historicism of this approach presupposes innumerable structures of power that inform and delimit political
agency. But even if there is no science or *techne* of history, and while
my argument insists on the centrality of history for articulating the
demos and its ethics, one needs to delimit plausible trajectories of
democracy and goodness. Democratic ethics should be conceptually

---

[28] I do not treat the illuminating, critical work of poststructuralist political thinkers, because
their perspective avoids making responsible political action for a collectivity part of their
interpretive perspective. Moreover, poststructuralism as such devalues democracy insofar as it focuses on decomposing ethical horizons for an active public.

[29] As indicated in the book's Introduction, "power" and "ethics" are not mutually exclusive. "Power" generally comes in two forms – coercive and dynamic. As the latter, a
force for actualizing potential, it flows into "ethics" as sanctioned dispositions to act.
Ethics uniquely comes into play for human action in the train of thought that moves
from deliberation and decision, drawing on social cues and individual interests. In this
mode, ethical considerations reflect observations about the force of power in the world
as obstacles or impediments to action, as well as opportunities for self-development that
individuals in their right minds seek to take advantage of by choice. This picture of the
drama of human action much more nearly reflects "reality" than any characterization
that severs "power" and "ethics" as independent factors in the world. At the same time,
collapsing the two, I argue, leads to determinism or moralism.

historicized – that is, grounded in a critical appreciation of historical currents that background democratic political action in the present, defying reduction to ideologies, idiosyncratic discourses, normative rendition of concepts, or the ambit of one-dimensional realism.

When each of us acts, as a citizen in a state that reasonably can be viewed as neither fascist nor dictatorial, we do so from a social (not a natural) standpoint that reflects a temporal, practical dynamic. As a result, we act as political beings and historical animals. Reality for us that does not derive from the physical forces of nature (and even that has political elements) is political – constituted by an array of discourses, institutions, and ethical vocabularies that have histories and cannot be reduced to individual actions and so reflect an exercise of power. There is no specific, naturally communal, character to any of these, but they possess a *shared* reality that cannot be ignored lest *stasis* determines the character of social life, making that life a state of war. (See Syria, Haiti, Libya, Congo, *inter alia*.) But how do such conceptions avoid becoming sedimented in moralistic ideas or authoritarian practices? And if that is prevented, is the historical "reality" coherent enough to provide a focus for critical political thought?[30]

This is where it's worth recollecting the constituents of political activity that sustain a collectivity, as understood, for example, by Thucydides' Pericles speaking as a mentor for Athenian democracy in a time of war with the Spartans. *Political* activity in a democracy is never stable, as either a *logos* or an *ergon*. Its instability constitutes its nature and allows it to succeed. But that success also depends on joint action undertaken by a collection of (relatively) free and (relatively) equal citizens.[31] And they must rely on some common *ethos* to point their action in a constructive direction. The instability of politics in a democracy provides the landscape for its character, but it primarily functions as a force that engages and changes a collective context; as such, it is not simply a calculation of the benefits of obedience or disobedience – except in those extreme situations in which one has virtually no ties to an extant community to which one voluntarily contributes (e.g., prisoners of war or inmates of a concentration camp; refugees fleeing what is, for them, a hopeless society). Democracy is *healthy or viable* to the extent that its citizens flock to

---

[30] To say that there are myriad realities and potential political formations which may result from contestation (i.e., "agonistic realism") is to gut the practical value of a realistic political outlook. That may be the point, but the result has nothing to do with realism (see Floyd and Stears 2011, 201–5).

[31] To be sure, freedom and equality are no more "things" than "democracy" or "politics." Their meaning requires an appreciation of their social use and historical context. But one cannot do without them in thinking about the basic engine of democracy.

assemblies or polls and *sick or corrupt* if it reacts to racism and economic desperation for vast swaths of the citizenry primarily with distorting prejudice, misleading rhetoric, petulant anger, or passive despair.

The task for historicizing democratic ethics is how to identify these collective elements without demeaning their centrality for democratic action that promotes goodness and itself, without reifying either as a constellation of power or a code of ethics. The key to doing so is never to view *logoi* or *erga* as stable sets but comprehending them first and foremost as part of a practical dynamic that has myriad sources – that is, as actions dependent on power and the formation of ethics. This will be insufficient for a devout Marxist, and unsatisfactory for those seeking scientific theories of history or those who trust in rational deliberation as the basis of democratic justice. But it enhances political judgment with democratic ethics. To say so does not deny the potential value of ahistorical or transcendental political theory, the significance of ideology, or historical or critical accounts of ethics *per se*. My claim is that the aforementioned critical discourses work better as supplements to, instead of first-order authors of, democratic ethics – that is, so long as one believes that democracy offers the best anchor for political action. But how *do* various approaches to democratic ethics devalue democracy?

1.2   Alternative Approaches to Democratic Ethics: Liberalism, Moralism, Realism

The thrust of my argument seeks to demonstrate the centrality of *activity* and *action* as both the main constituent of history and the pivotal support for democracy, even as the latter also enacts ethical justifications in politics. This results in part from the fact that actual democracies always will be incomplete as practices of power and ethics. These limitations are not good, however, and they are worsened by prevailing lenses for the current study of politics in Western societies – namely, analytical liberalism, moralism, and realism. While critiques of each abound, I want to point out their limitations as assets to democratic life – especially in relation to my historicist approach.

The first approach is most prominently and significantly reflected in the political theory of John Rawls and the work it has spawned. Of course, "liberalism" is not reducible to "Rawls." "Liberalism" is an amorphous entity, more so than democracy because it inherently lacks any theory of power. In the wake of the Allies' victory in World War II, it provided the political terms (rights, rule of law, etc.) for discussing reasonable accommodations of economic and ideological conflict. Rawls's conceptual parameters for his theory of justice derive from his triangulation of

Benthamite utilitarianism and Kantian deontology. But he also identified the principal political problems addressed by his work as stemming
from the corrosive effect of conflicting, comprehensive world-views evidenced in the religious wars of the sixteenth and seventeenth centuries,
while its consensual base stems from his intuitions about the moral geog-
raphy of American political life.[32] Nonetheless, his conceptualist or hypothetical approach features prominently in his theory of justice or political
liberalism for single nation-states and his international theory of a law
of peoples that accords with American foreign policy. None of his arguments, however, provide direct support for democracy as understood
here, as power for the people that would be exercised on behalf of goodness. His work highlights reasonable consent, rather than citizenship, as
the justifiable core of his political theory.

Rawls's hypothetical consent or institutional regulations regard
demotic activity as secondary and particularistic, rather than primary
and constitutive, of a good society. His point of departure is the basic
soundness of the status quo without registering or calculating (albeit
admitting to and being concerned about) its injustices.[33] Like most liberals, Rawlsians regard democracy as radically in need of salvation from
itself. In *A Theory of Justice*, a penchant for "political activity" is incidental to a just society, because any further endorsement generates a divisive
"comprehensive moral doctrine." But one could say that this has defined
the rules of engagement and easily wins because of that. Alternatively,
one could regard his theory of justice as a kind of comprehensive doctrine insofar as it justifies collective authority in the hypothetical consensus of "reasonable pluralism" *over* the political consequences it
might generate and offers mostly hypothetical hope that his *pluribus* will
generate *unum*. Rawls presupposes a "basic structure of society," later
referred to as "the fact of reasonable pluralism," as the background for
his political and philosophical arguments.[34] The content of these concepts has been drained of social conflicts; racial tensions; systematic
economic exploitation; sexism of one sort or another, ecological degradation, or political apathy. That is not to say that Rawls does not recognize that these exist or deplore them. He believes that his theory is the
best answer to Thrasymachean rule by "the stronger." It's just that he
believes that his principles of justice provide the best way of addressing
them without addressing them! Similarly, in *The Law of Peoples*, Rawls

---

[32] Rawls (1999b (1987), 424).
[33] Note, for example, the greater social and political equality Rawls's theory would promote if a country satisfied his conditions for a fair distribution of primary goods.
[34] Rawls (1971, 7ff.; 1999 (1987), 425).

presupposes a fundamental social unity within the individual societies that he takes as members of a "society of peoples" which upholds "the law of peoples." The "fact" that actual societies evolved from centuries of war, conquest, and conflict counts mostly as practical details to be regulated by his "realistic utopia."[35]

By themselves, invocations of rational deliberation only marginally engage serious political issues. Unless one thinks that democratic politics are sufficiently conducted in committees or courtrooms, reasonableness and hypothetical history are inadequate starting points. *Principles* of justice will be useful features of argument, but they will not reach the democratic actors whose actions are to be enlightened. And unless one thinks that philosophers simply can employ political rhetoricians to translate their theories into practice, this problem is a critically democratic one. A gaping chasm separates Rawls's principles of justice from the actual political world. One might bemoan the chasm's existence, so as to regard it as an academic political theorist's inevitable fate in doing political theory in our post-Edenic world. Or, we could see it as a projection of contingently valuable theoretical assumptions that are themselves subject to critique. But if we see it as either, we find that Rawlsian theory always will be running to catch up with the conflicts that harm democracy *because* it subordinates the significance of history and demotic action in conceptualizing principles of social justice. Rawls's hypothetical political agents who sit behind one (if national) or two (if international) veils of ignorance do not have to grapple with the noisome qualities of politics.[36] They only engage in politics if one asserts a reasonable, moral authority that is simultaneously separate from from also the basis of democratic politics. It is illusory to isolate such doctrines as arbitrary choices of individuals that can be managed by impartial spectators generating restrictive rules for their political reach from an original position or, to use the language of Jurgen Habermas, from an "ideal speech situation."[37]

This inadequacy in Rawlsian liberalism fueled two (or three) kinds of theoretical rebukes – one of which stemmed from Aristotle but drew on moralist, more than naturalist, critiques of democratic politics, taking to task the distance between Rawls's two principles of justice, his constructive, rationalist *logos* and the need for morals and ethics to buttress

---

[35] Rawls (1999a, 11–25, *sc.* 17, 124–5).
[36] The situation is not much different in his portrait of international justice as a product of a "realistic utopia." For a useful collection of articles on Rawls's *The Law of Peoples*, see Martin and Reidy (2005).
[37] See Rawls (1971, Secs. 60–3, 395–416). See Wallach (1987) and Geuss (2008).

political life. This argument made a big impact through the arguments of Alasdair MacIntyre and Michael Sandel and the subsequent interest in "virtue ethics" as well as "virtue politics," along with a theoretical lineage stemming from the work of Leo Strauss that situates philosophical truth as the legislator for the dirty work of politics.[38] These moralists, or the practical moralists sometimes labeled as communitarians or Aristotelian republicans (e.g., Sandel) fault Rawlsian liberalism for its presumptive standpoint of ethical neutrality and "reasonable" *logos*. But they typically disguise their own moral and political convictions and preferences for certain traditions of thought. Another set of critics (best exemplified by Raymond Geuss), exasperated by both liberalism and moralism, have argued that Rawls's attempt to engage practical, political life (*ergon*) displays an unrealistic – and hence politically harmful – point of theoretical departure, which moralists mostly invest with liberal rationality and an implicit, ethical bias. (One could identify poststructuralist criticism as another strand, but poststructuralists abjure a coherent posture toward politics or democracy because of an unwillingness to address questions of political responsibility. A harsh view of poststructuralist politics would be moralism in bad faith.) I discuss moralism and realism below – in relation not to Rawls but to democratic ethics.

In his 1981 book, *After Virtue: A Study in Moral Theory*, Alasdair MacIntyre took issue with Rawls for failing to acknowledge the constitutive role of moral judgment and virtue in articulating notions of social rationality and justice. Despite my own critical accounts of MacIntyre's political theory, my democratic criticism of Rawls agrees with MacIntyre's, in that Rawls's overlapping consensus cannot stand on its own independently of crucial moral, ethical, and practical or political judgments.[39] That said, the alternatives offered initially by MacIntyre and Sandel remain equally disengaged from democratic ethics by adopting transpolitical standpoints of "tradition" or "community." Neither MacIntyre nor Sandel intentionally endorse conservatism as a political doctrine, but each is skeptical about the political agency of the *demos* as a basic constituent of practical ethics.[40] As such, their works effectively function as cousins to conservative political thought which from

---

[38] For a good collection of representative articles of this genre, see Crisp and Slote (1997).
[39] See Wallach (1983, 1987, esp. 582–90, 603–5, 2016). Cf. Wolin, "Fugitive Democracy," in Benhabib (1996), 31–45 and Geuss (2008, 70–3, 80–94).
[40] In *After Virtue*, MacIntyre dismisses political ethics as a *fata morgana*. Sandel (1996 (1982)) endorses a kind of republicanism that has no clear place for, or endorsement of, specifically democratic politics.

the beginning has been suspicious of democratic change.[41] While doubting that social rationality, methodologically conceived, can take root as a political philosophy, conservatives conceptualize their own hierarchies that enforce truth vs. falsity and justice vs. injustice without apparent regard for the vagaries of history and power that make possible not only political but philosophical life. These strands of conservative political thought prefer Aristotle to Kant as their ancestral theorist, and so do not embrace the rule-governed Kantian moral principles that feed liberalism; however, their distance from social and political practices, and the constitutive character of ethics as a social practice that (especially for Aristotle) had an ineluctably political dimension, justifies the categorization of their conservative position as moralistic. This moralism stems from views of politics and practicality as issuing from an ultimately apolitical but hierarchical ethical posture that precedes the drama of action – whether that hierarchy manifests particular visions of tradition or community.[42] From the standpoint of democratic ethics designed to promote the compatibility of democracy and goodness, the problems with these moralisms is that they fail to account for the practicalities of political reality, of how it reflects the activity or passivity of citizens. "Virtue ethics" may claim to address human experience more fulsomely than liberal rationalities that bracket it, but they remain dedicated to beliefs in moral and practicable ends of life that are to be persuasive without regard to power or *political* practicality.[43] As a result, for those who do not presuppose the truth of their interpretive or historical theories, one easily might grab the other potential weakness of liberalism, namely its inability to generate productive political strategies that ensure the well-being of the *demos*. In the discursive trends of political theory, the critical perspective on liberalism has moved from varieties of virtue moralism to political "realism."

[41] This has characterized the aristocratic opposition to increasing political power for the Athenian *demos*; English anxieties that delegitimizing the authority of the Crown would threaten private property; Burke's homage to the fine drapery of inherited norms of the Church and aristocratic privilege as a bulwark that could prevent the incendiary actions of French revolutionaries taking hold in the British Isles; and Leo Strauss's anxiety that the absence of philosophical authority rooted in singular interpretations of ancient and medieval philosophy would lead to democratic crowds steering Western ships of state into the rocks.

[42] Self-identified radical democrats cannot also assume kindred postures of self-righteousness by unilaterally assigning a practice of justice to particular configurations of politics or class. But in the current political climate, that kind of non-conservative moralism only exhibits practical salience in religiously motivated, rather than secular and political, critiques of extant governments.

[43] See n. 38, *supra*. Ryan K. Balot has offered noteworthy accounts of "virtue politics" in ancient Athens; they tend to focus on the dispositions of citizens more than their roles in the power politics of the *polis* (see Balot 2001, 2014).

"Realism" in political thought has a long and storied ancestry, beginning perhaps with snippets of Thucydides' account of the Peloponnesian War; ironically reborn for the modern nation-state in the nominalist philosophy of Thomas Hobbes; captured and retooled by International Relations theorists in the wake of World War I (e.g., by E. H. Carr) and World War II (e.g., Kenneth Waltz), and experiencing another surge of interest in the wake of the end of the Cold War.[44] Because of the clarity and acuity of Geuss's realist critique of liberalism, I shall focus on his contributions to the renewal of political realism.[45] Geuss illustrates his "realist" approach to politics mostly in contrast to conceptualist, idealist, or moralist approaches that take for granted what they should seek to explain. For him, "action" and "power" are front and center for any useful understanding of politics. More specifically, he recommends that we take as our point of departure for political understanding actual motives and the pressures of circumstance on action rather than the architecture of beliefs.[46] He certainly does not ignore the roles of beliefs, ethics, morality, etc., in discourses of legitimation, or that such discourses practically influence and comprise the actuality of political life.[47] That said, Geuss is skeptical about democracy's inherent virtues (as well as those of other political perspectives), and his realism does not necessarily contribute to democratic ethics. But if democratic ethics are not unrealistic, this claim deserves an explanation.

Realistic political theories are not inherently democratic and do not attend to how the actions of citizens express a distinctive kind of associative activity, one that is nonetheless bound up in social relations and the exercise of power. Geuss is surely right to criticize the "ethics-first" approach to political thought, but if one takes for one's point of

---

[44] See Carr 1951 (1939). Early realists in the study of international relations, such as Carr and Hans Morgenthau, had much more subtle views of the workings of international politics than later neo-realists who sought to build theoretical systems of realist intuitions (see Waltz 1959).

[45] Geuss (2008). Also worth mentioning here are the articles and book by Ian Shapiro (2005 (1992), 2010, 2016). Shapiro's work does not offer a clear specimen of a realist approach to political theory, however, because he acknowledges that his realism does not produce a theoretical outlook on society (2005, 50) and is subject to "normative" considerations such as opposition to domination (see Shapiro 2003, 2016). Shapiro allows that no definition of domination can be precise, but he articulates its sphere of semantic influence most recently in the following way (from Shapiro 2016), as "... the avoidable and illegitimate exercise of power that compromises people's basic interests" (5, cf. 20–4). But each of the terms of this definition, when used, reflects ethical as well as practical considerations. Realists need to account for such considerations in their own intellectual perspective, rather than externalize them, at least if politics is constitutively influenced by ethical considerations – which Shapiro acknowledges.

[46] Geuss (2008, 59).

[47] Geuss (2008, 1–9, 97, 99–100).

immediate departure in political thinking a power- or action-first approach that does not fully acknowledge the relational character of individual and political action, then one does not fully appreciate the "realities" of political action. For realists, the political actuality engaged by the individual political actor appears mostly as an external phenomenon that happens to, or is produced by, the individual. But in this perspective, the ethical role in political action does not receive its due. For example, an under-appreciated factor explaining the rapid collapse of the governments of Warsaw Pact states after the withdrawal of support from the Red Army is that Soviet power was designed to inhibit power that sprang from *practical relations* among citizens in the countries it controlled. When the dominant force of the Red Army disappeared, the citizens showed their lack of ethical support for their governments as legitimate regimes. Although the media makes too much of them, the ethical dimensions of political discourse are not mere distractions. Voting stems from economic self-interest *and* ethical identification.[48]

The problem with Geuss's perspective, ironically, stems from an incompletely realistic view of politics that also reflects its distance from democratic ethics. He begins his book by championing Hobbes's realism without acknowledging its connection to Hobbes's radical individualism.[49] If politics takes place within (or against) a collective context, then that collective dimension includes a kind of coordinated equality among its members that informs whatever further equality or inequality they promote. But it is the commonality of human nature, a kind of "real" equality (however minimal), which makes possible political coherence. Geuss acknowledges that human action is dedicated to security, in the Hobbesian vein, *and* that it indicates constructive attempts at coordinated action. But Hobbes only accepts such action as abdication. Similarly, while correctly identifying the characteristics of politics as a *techne*, Geuss does not acknowledge the extent to which the *collective* context of action for politics necessarily has its own distinctive character as a cooperative, albeit contingent, *techne*, that may display virtuosity (but not like that of solo violinists or Olympic athletes).[50] The very possibility of politics or peaceful social relations disappears amid real raw individualism in social life or civil war, in which *logoi* (words, arguments, accounts), *erga*, and the correlations between the two do not have any

---

[48] This offers one obvious explanation for why certain voters do not vote in their own class interest when favoring one or another candidate for public office.

[49] Geuss (2008, 21–3, 49–50). This feature of his work dovetails with the Hobbesian assumptions of Williams (2005, 3–4, Cf. 12).

[50] See Geuss (2008) on politics as a *techne*, 15, 97. For the character of *techne* and a political *techne* in Plato's dialogues, see Wallach (2001).

common significance or practical meaning (except insofar as they are inverted).[51] There, the power of any kind of political discourse is futile.

This attempt to differentiate schematically the historicist perspective deployed here from prevailing political discourses also can be put in brief, schematic terms. My focus on democratic ethics as a feature of political action and critical discourse departs from current treatments of democratic ethics as semantic or analytical concepts; virtue ethics; a superstructure of one kind or another (Marxist or Nietzschean traditions); left democratists, who often harbor notions of political virtue but do not want to codify them; political conflict initially understood in terms of linguistic discourses (i.e., theoretical arguments that transpose Foucauldian or Skinnerian critical analyses into political theories); a political reality as lower-level practical concern of ideal political theory (the Straussian tradition), or simply as a deed of discourse (e.g., as often registered by journalists or bloggers).[52] In short, one may well theorize about democratic values, rights, or virtues, or the "values" of freedom, equality, virtue, equal opportunity, dignity, or justice. Doing so may improve the thought and action of citizens. But a historicist understanding of democratic ethics finds such claims insufficient by not fully acknowledging how social arrangements and ethical dispositions constitute actions and their consequences.

This different road does not simply diverge from the others. It promotes a historicist understanding of democratic ethics and practical possibilities.[53] The only way such an understanding can arise is by attending to historical, actual, or virtually real circumstances in which democratic action has been or could have been displayed, in relation to an actual or potential democratic society of the time – in which profits scooped up by the few, wage rates for the many, climate change and environmental pollution, political deception, wars, America's global involvements steered without guidance by its public; invidious discrimination, and more, play major roles. Attending to these conditions for identifying and interpreting

---

[51] Raw civil discord (*stasis*) was a conceptual pivot of his theoretical argument about politics and history in his book. Its extreme, paradigmatic form appears in Thucydides' account of the civil war in Corcyra in his *The War of the Peloponnesians and the Athenians* (III.81–4, Cf. Loraux 2009, 261–92).

[52] For statements by Skinner and Foucault that each is offering analyses of the past and present that do not indicate a full political theory, see Skinner 2002 (1969), 57–89 and Foucault's last statements from the early 1980s, in Rabinow (1984, 335–6, 375–6, 379–80). In the mid-twentieth century, Germanic critical theory explained the ethics of politics as a function of the disintegration of the left amid Western capitalism (see Geuss 2004, 103–38).

[53] The two most prominent theorists of democratic action who recognize its constitutively historical components are Dewey (1946 (1927)) and Wolin (2016). My account does not share the scientific optimism of Dewey or Wolin's silence on the ethical limits of democracy.

democratic ethics is historicist because the only way to understand what is going on in these arenas is, at a minimum, to know how they have come from dynamics of power. In terms of intellectual approaches, this mode of historicizing does not pose a conflict between Thucydides and Plato, the historian and the theorist, but draws on the contribution of each to ethical and political understanding through their accounts of the sources and remedies for civil discord (*stasis*) – destructive rather than constructive politics.[54]

1.3   Other Historicisms

The significance of historical reasoning (or, as Nietzsche put it, historical philosophizing) as a constituent of coherent ethical thought is a relatively recent source of ethical anxiety.[55] One might recall that Moses (in the Hebrew Bible) argued with God about the importance of not killing off the human race a second time (the first being the Great Flood). It would not be right, Moses intoned, to have the human race stem simply from him and not acknowledge the historicity of the Jewish people and the leadership of their patriarchs.[56] Aristotle pointedly refers to history in the formulation of his account of *ho anthropos* as a *zoon politikon* (not in the particularistic vein that led him to subordinate its philosophical value to the more universalistic pretensions of poetry).[57] No-one regards Moses or Aristotle as radical ethical relativists, let alone nihilists (surely because they have other arguments to counter the charges). Yet prominent twentieth-century theorists leveled this charge at historicism – particularly in terms of its authorial voices in the nineteenth century who made it a source for philosophy and political theory, whether in a rationalist (Hegelian, Marxist) or anti-rationalist (Nietzschean) mode – without having to offer to justify historically or philosophically the value of doing so.[58] But in the wake of World War I and the rise of fascism and Nazism, political theorists pegged historicism as a threat to favorably

---

[54] Thucydidean and Platonic thinking have been viewed as antagonistic – usually at Plato's expense. But if one understands Plato's dialogues as engaging the politics and philosophy of his time on a new intellectual plane, the two become less antagonistic than they are typically portrayed. For the centrality of *stasis* to Plato's dialogical account of justice, see Wallach (2001).

[55] Friedrich Nietzsche (1986 (1886), 1.2); for Nietzsche's dedication to historical reasoning, properly understood, as an enabling agent of "life," see Nietzsche (1997 (1874), 57–123).

[56] *Exodus*, 32:9–14.

[57] *Politics*, Bk. I. Cf. Aristotle's *Poetics*, Ch. 9, 1451b.

[58] Not surprisingly, those who theorize about history (e.g., from Hegel to Popper) generally are not well-steeped in history itself – Marx and Weber being notable exceptions.

regarded rational, ethical inquiry (Popper, Strauss), a virus that would attack its users and destroy their ethical compasses. In this light, I need to specify my use of historicism – for it differs from the meaning it has been assigned by historicism's critics.

Historicism in the human sciences highlights the centrality of human action in and across particular places and times as the principal consideration of human understanding. As such, it is anti-theological and anti-teleological; it belies claims to human destiny derived from the hands of God, history, traditions, or reason – unless they factor in the motivations of human activity.[59] Historicists recognize the constitutive connection between deliberation and action, *logos* and *ergon*, but emphasize the primacy of the latter in setting the stage for the exercise of the former in the world. In this sense, Thucydides' epitaph to this chapter complements historicism. Whereas Rawls seeks common ground for his political theorizing in liberal reasonableness, historicists look for prominent ground for political understanding in the common effects of action. A historicist perspective is presupposed by Thucydides in his account of the war between the Peloponnesians and the Athenians, along with his account of Pericles' eulogy to Athenian democracy in his "Funeral Oration" of 431 BC. His interest in writing his account of the war stemmed from the need to explain "the greatest disturbance" (*kinesis*) in the history of the Hellenes, and the central agents in producing these actions were the Athenians and Pericles, their leader from 441 to 429.[60] In this regard, it concerned how the exercise of (principally political) power indelibly recast the landscape of the Hellenic world, shaping political prospects for the indeterminate future. Thucydides' Pericles in his Funeral Oration (we have no other account) argued for the complementarity of *logos* and *ergon* as the primary, beneficial constituent of political action for the

[59] In making this claim, I diverge from Dilthey's notion of historicity – which he aligns with the progress of "the human spirit" and world history. See Dilthey (2002, 160–78, 274–5). Dilthey does not employ the term "historicism," but he does articulate the notion of "historicity" (*Geschichtlichkeit*). For a notion of history that is inhospitable to historicism but offers a lucid way of disentangling history from storytelling, see Hobbes, *Leviathan*, I.9: "The register of 'knowledge of fact' is called 'history,' whereof there be two sorts: one called 'natural history,' which is the history of such facts or effects of Nature as have no dependence on man's 'will,' such as are the histories of 'metals,' 'plants,' 'animals,' 'regions,' and the like. The other is 'civil history,' which is the history of the voluntary actions of men in commonwealths."

[60] Although Thucydides distinguished (I.21) what he did from the *logoi* of chroniclers (e.g., Herodotus) and poets (e.g., dramatists), he, as an Athenian in exile, still admired the virtues of his *polis* even as he also condemned its leaders and citizens for its failures, such that the Peloponnesian War was an Athenian tragedy. In this sense, his work complemented the tragedies of Aeschylus, Sophocles, and Euripides, even it was not written *as* a tragedy (see Cornford 1971 (1907)).

Athenians and their democratic *politeia* – a phenomenon that affirmed the perpetually interdependent relationship between reasoned speech and human deeds.[61] The *logos/ergon* couplet was a continuing template in Thucydides' history.[62]

Contemporary historicists draw inspiration from the work of R. G. Collingwood, who undermined the moral philosophy and epistemology of so-called "realists" who took for granted the nature of reality as presented by one's intuitions and did not believe that the act of thinking affected one's understanding of the world. For Collingwood, the world could not be known by way of propositions but via questions or problems arising in the world to which the thinker and actor is called on to offer answers or solutions. In reaction to his "realist" opponents, Collingwood tended to overemphasize the role of intention as an explanation of a historical phenomenon and underestimate how understanding the *consequences* of an action may augment one's understanding of the action – if not what the agent thought s/he was doing. But Collingwood's important perspective dissolved seemingly impermeable divides between history and philosophy or theory and practical action.[63]

Because activity is a dynamic process – stemming from thought that is conditioned by the world – the primacy of historicism for human understanding overrides not only the sovereignty of reason or self-contained moral beliefs but also the significance of the dead hands of empiricism or data as basic elements of social reality and truth. (Which is not to say that statistical information is not useful for historical understanding or that the Rodney King video had truth before it was digitally disembodied.) The intellectual activity of historicizing, however, distinguishes itself from social scientific research, analogical reasoning, or pick-and-choose (for Collingwood, "cut-and-paste") deployments of history by correlating and subordinating the significance of this knowledge to spatio-temporal locations, the historical dynamic that generated them, and what is done in them – without presupposing that discrete genealogies

---

[61] Thucydides (2013, I.1; II. 34–46, at 36–7, 40). Toward the end of the Funeral Oration, as Pericles waxes eloquently about the Athenians' destiny as imperialists, he leaves this complementarity behind.

[62] For the most trenchant, albeit overly triumphant, account of this relationship in the first two books of Thucydides' *History*, see Parry (1981 (1957)).

[63] See Collingwood (1939, esp. 29–43, 58, 61–70, 100, 106, 114, 147, 150). To accept this part of Collingwood does not require one to accept his more dubious claims about the "incapsulation" of the past in the present (98, 100, 106, 113, 141) or his idealist understanding of "political history" as the "history of political thought" (110, 127–8). It is nonetheless interesting that he identified his political allegiances as "democratic" (153ff.). For a fair-minded account of Collingwood's approach to historical understanding, see Gardiner (1996, 109–20).

are sufficient for critical understanding.[64] For example, historicists are more likely to address the phenomena of racism and inequality in terms of the history of slavery and economic exploitation than from analyzing the rejection of moral beliefs in human equality, psychological projections of "the Other," experiences of subjectification, or an inspirational speech from the past that addresses these concerns.[65]

Historicism begin from *erga*, however much they reflect moral or practical perspectives, in order to produce a common referent for political criticism. As such, it directly contrasts from the Rawlsian method of starting from a commonly accepted *logos* that matches hypothetical assumptions about society and history. Such relational thinking does not sanction a closed universe of radical, ethical relativism, even as it denies the sovereignty of the "universe" of reason. Radical relativism implicitly validates whatever ethical order dominates a social locale, and assumes that it forecloses critical thought outside its boundaries, while the notion of historicism or historicity I employ does not do so. Indeed, one of its ethical justifications is its ability to enable its users to use their critical faculties more perspicuously, thereby working against discursive or practical closures or tyrannies of all sorts.[66] This enables historicism to be, picking up a Nietzschean theme, "untimely."[67] Historicists take close note of what actually happens, as dauntingly difficult and elusive that task may be, in order to close off practically and intellectually fruitless lines of inquiry and, instead, direct one toward the ongoing activities of political actuality.[68] Historicists pay homage to the role of power in history, not to allow it to determine ethical judgment but to recognize its conditioning role in shaping the opportunities that face agents deciding what to do. Insofar as practical action involves a choice among alternatives, history narrows the range of these alternatives but also produces

[64] For a useful set of criticisms of faulty efforts to use historical analogies for policy-making or of policy-making harmed by the absence of historicist thinking, see Neustadt and May (1986).

[65] Cf. Lane, in Floyd and Stears (2011, 128–50). Historicists and "realists" take their object of study to be the world of action, not the world of academic thought about the world of action (*contra* 146–50).

[66] See Floyd and Stears (2011), particularly the essays by Kelly and Floyd.

[67] See Nietzsche: "For I do not know what meaning classical studies could have for our time if they were not untimely – that is to say, acting counter to our time and thereby acting on our time and, let us hope, for the benefit of a time to come" (Nietzsche 1997 (1876)). The indeterminate promise of such untimeliness does not make historicism ethically reassuring. It is a condition for the possibility of democratic ethics; not the essence of such ethics.

[68] For a good accounts of the value of history for political understanding, see Geuss (2008, 13–15, 68–70) and Dunn (1996, 11–38). For differences between historicism against nihilist relativism, see Skinner (1989, 255–8).

possible avenues for freedom. But this does not foreclose the importance of roads not taken, if not in the present then in time to come. At this stage in American history and political reality, for example, governmentally guaranteed medical care is not a practical, political option, even as it certainly is practically feasible. But it may become practicable in the near future, under an innocuous slogan and in the wake of failed alternatives. Gay marriage was a fanciful idea twenty years ago, but it currently is legally guaranteed in the United States. Aristotle correctly noted that political choice and deliberation concern that which is in our power to change; what that involves can change dramatically because of war, environmental disasters, and economic depressions.[69]

Historicism also has its own histories that can helpfully historicize *my* account. There have been two principal discourses of historicism – the first was Germanic; the second has been British or American. The Germanic began with Hegel, who inserted the course of history into his rationalist philosophy, thus making history's reality seem both rational and progressive.[70] They produced philosophical or practical historicisms. Marx's historicism shared Hegel's sense that history belonged to a relatively determined and progressive reality, but for him its rationality only stemmed from its particular irrationality as a history of class struggle that would have a happy ending. According to the *Communist Manifesto*, its rationality and reality would arrive via proletarian revolutions led by a selfless party that would end history as class struggle, as it had been known until then.

Nietzsche could not abide the historicisms of either Hegel or Marx. For him, both were infected by kinds of rationalism that disguised the power and conflict that drove social life. In particular, he could not tolerate Hegel's Kantian roots, which only take hold in the noumenal realm – a world of disembodied ideas, signified by the religion of a resurrected Christ. And he could not abide Marx, because of the latter's belief in, and endorsement of, the virtues of collective, proletarian agency. So Nietzsche broke with the classical historicism of German philosophy and political theory. But he hardly spurned historical interests, particularly human events constituted by Christian ethics or Kantian rationalism. He argued that they are better understood by clarifying their character as products of endless conflicts and struggles for power – an approach that has come to

---

[69] Aristotle, *Nicomachean Ethics*, III.3. In this regard, a historicist outlook possesses more links to Aristotelians (about whose arguments I tend to be skeptical) than to the "ideologues" who gave rise to the notion of "ideology" in the nineteenth century as a "science of ideas" (see Lichtheim 1967 (1965); Wallach 1992).

[70] See Beiser (2011) and Reill (1975). On nineteenth- and twentieth-century political theorists in relation to historicism, see Ferry (1990). Cf. Keedus (2015).

be called genealogy, history for life rather than antiquarian or monumental history, history without a rational narrative or practical arc.[71]

Max Weber's theory of history also lacked any intuitively rational arc. He believed in the power of historical reality, but disengaged it from any Hegelian or Marxist, logistic or practical, moving train. He hoped that well-informed political leaders, imbued with an ethical posture but attuned to the landscape of consequences on which they were likely to tread, could harness the modern *demos* and construct better political orders – although he was dubious about endowing the modern *demos* with authority.[72]

Foucault drew heavily on Marx, Nietzsche, Weber, and Husserlian phenomenology to produce his own kind of historicism against the state – a Franco-German historicism – one that identified the ways in which power permeated discourses of social and political rationality. But he also sought to disengage these from any overarching narrative and referred to his histories as accounts of discourse that belonged to a "history of the present."[73]

These historicisms lend themselves to relativist critiques, although each thinker would reject them, because their histories rely on the absence or presence of contingent historical arcs.

Across the Channel, historicism took on a much different cast. One might (glibly) say that it sprang from the head of the British empire. The so-called "Whig conception of history" did not have a rationalist frame in the Germanic mode but rather a self-congratulatory frame. Butterfield, Carr, and Collingwood, however, still valued the constitutive role of history for political knowledge. Indeed, Collingwood's emphasis on looking at archeological facts or philosophical discourse in terms of questions or problems to which they provided the answers or solutions was the first major assault on British analytical philosophy as a philosophy of social rationality. It, along with J. L. Austin's speech-act theory, encouraged Quentin Skinner's interest in identifying what political thinkers were actually *doing* with what they were *saying*.[74] Skinner's point was principally lodged at interpreters of historical political theorists who paid no or

---

[71] For these Nietzschean categories of history, see Nietzsche (1997 (1876), 57–124). Genealogy is a kind of historicism, with genealogists varying in their degree of respect and regard for history. The best source for Nietzsche's approach to a genealogical understanding of "morality" is, need it be said, *Zur Genealogie der Moral*.

[72] See Weber (1968, Vol. 3, Pt. 2, Ch. X, secs. 1–2, 8a–b). For a more positive but still skeptical view of Weber on democracy, see his wartime and post-war writings, in Weber *Political Writings* (1994, 219–24, 309–69).

[73] Foucault in Rabinow (1984, 178) [from *Discipline and Punish*].

[74] See Skinner (1989 (1969), 29–67, 231–88). Also note Tully (1989, 7–25).

little attention to the intentions of the authors of historical texts. Insofar as the texts were hugely influential, their intended meaning deserved greater respect, Skinner argued, not only in order to understand their texts as acts but also to respect their authors as actors. Unfortunately, Skinner's historicism, like Foucault's, has been badly understood when taken to preclude complementary or supplementary historical accounts of the writer, her text, and their contexts. That is, neither Foucault nor Skinner offered comprehensive political theories and did not seek to dominate theoretical or political perspectives that contracted their claims. Neither saw his work as a *method* of inquiry into the political world full-stop or a full-blown political theory of power and right. Each wanted his readers to think fundamentally for themselves.[75]

Anti-historicist political theories took hold in Britain and America in the wake of World War II and purveyed misleading conceptions of historicism. The British strand derived from the work of Karl Popper, in *The Poverty of Historicism*, a work initially crafted in the mid-1930s but not published until 1945 and not widely disseminated until 1957. Popper conflated a theoretically grounded Germanic historicism with his own devotion to the authority of covering-law hypotheses for validating empirical investigation – which, in turn, only could be proved or disproved by systematically collected facts – to yield a view of historicism as unjustifiable determinism. This stuffed historicism into a positivist mindset that understood reality to be comprised of "facts," thereby producing a self-serving and distorted confrontation between putatively clear-headed positivism and ideologically driven historicism.[76] Interestingly, Popper also championed the use of a method of falsification for validating useful political thought. This second-order method enabled Popper in *The Open Society and Its Enemies* (1945) to produce hugely influential but now generally regarded as wrong-headed interpretations of Plato as a totalitarian and Marx as a historical determinist. Popper's rejection of criticism that used evidence from beneath the surface of immediate experience or promoted an ethics of justice, effectively deprived Anglo-American, liberal, political theory of the authority of two of its most fertile sources for political criticism.

In the United States, the meaning of historicism was also distorted but not by positivism. Rather, this effect stemmed from an idiosyncratic philosophy of history that rejected history as a constitutive source of political truth. Historicism, argued Leo Strauss, allowed the effective use

---

[75] Skinner (1989 (1969)) and Foucault (1980 (1977), 109–33). *Contra* Foucault as a political theorist, see Wolin (2016, 283–99).
[76] Popper (1957). Cf. Keuth (2005).

of power in the world to constitute moral and political knowledge by either diminishing the authority of ethics or subordinating its merits to narrations of history that cramped ethical freedom and subordinated the value of truth for politics. Strauss believed historicism produced a slippery slope that would land its sliders into the darkness of radical relativism and nihilism, destroy the authority of morality, and place obstacles in the way of any abiding understanding of human truths about living in the world.[77] As a result, garden-variety accounts of historicism became squeezed by a politically conservative positivism and a politically elitist idealism, leaving its generative potential for critical political thought untapped. The critiques of "historicism" purveyed by Popperian liberals and Straussian anti-liberals marginalized historical inquiry as a constituent of critical political and democratic thought.[78]

The anti-historicist trend gained energy from the genealogical or neo-Nietzschean turn in political thought, fueled by the radically historicist work of Michel Foucault.[79] Neo-Nietzscheans neglected to note that Foucault denied that he was offering a full-blown political theory and that his histories of the present, from antiquity to human rights, were designed to pinpoint features of the world and its past – not *ipso facto* deny the value of other theories, histories, or approaches.[80] They downgraded historical context for understanding politics – holding that one could mix and match genealogies that disclosed the conflicted roots of all norms in order to disclose the possibilities of our political imaginary.[81] By contrast, historicist inquiry directs our attention to the quandaries of human action, which constitute any democratic ethics, and interprets historical dynamics with intellectual and political judgment.[82]

The very different attempts of Marx, Nietzsche, Weber, Wolin, and Skinner to integrate history and political theory eschewed the establishment of second-order epistemologies as methodological frames for first-order political judgments. My approach utilizes their contributions to historicist inquiry by highlighting the importance of human action

---

[77] Strauss (1959 (1949), 56–77).

[78] This was resisted, however, in Sheldon Wolin's interpretation of Western political theory (Wolin 1960/2004).

[79] Both Strauss and Foucault, obviously from different standpoints, are suspicious of consent and consensus (see Strauss 1953, 141; Foucault in Rabinow 1984, 378–80).

[80] See Foucault in Rabinow (1984, 73–5, 383–86).

[81] See Wallach (1997, 886–93).

[82] Geuss (2008, 68–9) values historical inquiry over abstract refutations, for it addresses how human beings use their freedom to change the contours of their world. The satisfaction that comes from refuting historical authors as "wrong" is particularly futile and is corrected by trying one's best to find out what the authors were doing intellectually and practically.

and its consequences in shaping human thought, while regarding such action and thought as necessary but indeterminate contributions to the construction of the political world. It relies on no particular trajectory of humanity or narrative arc of events, and valorizes no claim or person as sacrosanct, but it also dignifies the necessity of critical discourse of public life because of its necessity in constituting meaningfully shared experiences and realities. Whether or not one agrees with Aristotle's judgment of Pericles ("and men like him") as exemplars of practical reason, one should understand his claim as neither relativist nor hagiographic.[83] One may seek to uncover and clarify the motivations of power and ethics for democracy without reifying that search into a quest for a train that will take you where you must go.

The only other kind of interpretive approach I want to discuss that helpfully informs current conceptions of democracy via history is primarily linguistic or discursive, illustrated quite differently in the works of Michel Foucault and Quentin Skinner.[84] I discuss these historians and theorists for illustrative purposes alone. Neither presumes that his intellectual productivity grounds a full-scale political theory – each spurns that venture – but both make the linguistic turn in quintessentially political ways that do not directly sustain democratic conceptions of ethics. Foucault notably demonstrates the ways in which discourses are themselves kinds of power that shape social life and individual subjectivity. The worlds of discourse, truth, reason, ethics are saturated with power. While Foucault affirms that there can be a kind of "outside" to power insofar as its sustenance depends upon freedom to challenge its current configurations, this activity only can assume the form of resistance.[85] The only political activity Foucault endorses engages the capillaries of power that inform social life and reflect the postmodern performance of sovereign power over life (i.e., the capillaries of biopolitics). It is an ethics of resistance that is but instrumentally related to democracy. Perhaps that is all that we can hope for: democratic instrumentalism informed by savvy ethics. But one cannot know; whatever possibilities exist for democratic life today are not necessarily nourished by Foucauldian politics; they may or not promote democracy. If realistic possibilities exist for a

---

[83] Aristotle, *Nicomachean Ethics*, VI.5, cf. II.6.
[84] I say differently insofar as the former ignores and the latter highlights the importance of intentionality to understanding political discourse. This comparison was first and notably performed by James Tully in his introduction to *Meaning and Context* (Tully, 1988, 7–25). For Foucault's dismissal of concern about the identity of the author, let alone her intentions, see "What Is An Author?" in Rabinow (1984, 120).
[85] Foucault, "Truth and Power," in Rabinow (1984, 51-75).

more democratic society, Foucauldian politics cannot point out where or how they may exist.

Skinner's linguistic approach is more amenable to democratic ethics, because intentional political discourse constitutes democratic citizenship. But his insistence on closing the discursive context, even as he recognizes its causal connections to power and political community, tends to identify discourse as active interventions in ideological contexts – when it's not only that. It does not in itself direct our attention to how those interventions might be more democratic. Skinner recognizes the myriad historical sources for discourse, but, without supplementation, the gravitational pull of his work shifts attention away from the connections which illocutionary and perlocutionary acts have to causal forces or prospects for recasting power in political community.[86]

A historical approach to understanding and promoting democracy best identifies the conditions of power in relation to which the *demos* must act. In this regard, Wolin's work is instructive. Like Wolin, I understand democracy more in terms of power and history than ethics and philosophy. But my historicist perspective on democratic ethics departs from his. His Wittgensteinian treatment of "the political" in *Politics and Vision* yields insightful interpretations, but their cogency as part of a whole is deliberately left unwoven – partly because his theory is about interpreting texts, authors, and events concerning "the political" – not an Ur-text that defines it. Perhaps one does not need a "whole." But do these interpretations perform as much intellectual and political work as contributions of history to theory might? It's unfair to ask an author to write a book s/he specifically did not set out to write, but one can be a constructive critic. *Politics and Vision* may not have the tools to keep its insights from being disintegrated by specialists in intellectual history or philosophy. In addition, that book glancingly treats "democracy" – not surprisingly since Wolin wrote about "the political" as a way of saving political theory from dismissive, empiricist political scientists and analytical philosophers – which left it open to his own later work that focuses mostly on the present. So the question of democracy in history remained unaddressed. His later political theory of democracy avoids ethics or goodness except as part of democracy. Perhaps Wolin wanted to make sure his vision of democracy did not display moralism or theoretical scientism. I stay away from both while addressing goodness as a *complement* to democracy, not as one of its inherent features. Wolin does not address that subject directly.

---

[86] Shapiro on Skinner in Shapiro (1982) and Skinner's response in Tully (1988, 236–7, 250, 255–7, 265ff., 277).

The historicism of this book conveys judgments about discourses of democracy and goodness in time. They do not require *authority* from heaven or reason. The evidence, interpretations, and arguments that inform them come from us, which challenges us as thinkers to do our best with what we have at our disposal. This opens up arguments to charges of relativism. But such arguments do not foreclose argumentative contention. Still such arguments are not dispositive. The past evoked by historicist inquiry has doorways to the present by retaining the past's unique, distant but relevant, relation to the present. A historicist democratic ethics at least should be a useful addition and corrective to other strands of historicism. It will be more useful than theories that depend on stipulated propositions or historical arcs that constrain democratic action – at least a useful addition. This definition of "historicize" is somewhat unusual, insofar as "historicism" has been associated with a kind of determinism, ethical relativism, or radical contextualism whose roots in the past preclude its utility as an intellectual guide that encourages ethical and critical political thought in the present. The basis for my usage stems from its original usage by Herodotus, who believed that he had provided a "history" of the Greeks and the Persians, one that explained hostilities between them by inquiring into matters of note that happened or seem to have happened.[87] To good effect, his inquiries made connections between one's own standpoint and another that is "outside" it.

1.4   Historicity and Democratic Ethics

How can historicist thinking facilitate understanding *democracy* in particular, since historicism has no inherent affinity for democracy? What belongs to the domain of history is not really everything that has happened in the past; it is that which has happened that finds its way into the storytelling of contemporary accounts of the past (which limits the degree to which it is, wholly, past). History always goes for the big story, even as what counts as a big story certainly changes with the times. Ethics, by contrast, do not have to belong to a big story. As every member of any religiously ordained clergy will tell you, it's the little things that count; the actions one takes every minute of every day, the significance of which may not be known to others (but certainly are recorded by the designated Almighty). But they also factor politically, as discursive tools of legitimation that cannot be reduced to a singular account of "reality." Hence, ethical domains often range across historical periods, even if their meaning is constituted by and perhaps instrumentally

[87] See Herodotus, *Histories*, Preface; II.19, 113, 118; VII.96.

derived from historical forces. This enables ethical questions to extend over and through the particularities of historical events or trends, the manifestations of power. While ethics surely carries less immediate power than force, I do not position them in a lexical order. For example, the impact of the Occupy Wall Street movement that began on September 17, 2011, had little direct influence on public policy, but it arguably introduced (finally – the arguments had been soundly made for fifteen years) "economic inequality" as a major focus of public discourse that also fostered the Presidential candidacy of Bernie Sanders in 2016.[88] That said, *democracy* is primarily a historical formation and configuration of practical relationships. "Democracy" has been used to describe various regimes and ways of life at various points in human history. In these contexts, democratic ethics count as those conceptual standards that seek to uphold or promote the goodness of a democratic order. Here, democratic ethics count as a *logos* for the *ergon* of democracy, even as they constitute its *ergon*. Ethics do not occupy a smaller domain than democracy – one cannot capture their efficacy in physical terms anyway – but they cannot be identical to it; they must contribute to it; at least if they are not merely to cheerlead the dominant exercise of political power in a would-be democratic society. What differentiates democratic ethics from ethics *simpliciter* is that they directly concern the well-being of the collectivity as such – not just individuals in their private lives, even as private lives often have public dimensions that contribute to the well-being of the collectivity. To be sure, questions of individual or social character *may* have democratic dimensions; after all, thoroughgoing hypocrites are not likely to provide a consistent public posture for the *demos*. Yet relating democracy and social ethics in mostly analytical terms – e.g., in the matters of equal opportunity or migration – constrains our understanding of how meaningful ethical concepts that directly concern democracy are shaped by historical trends and horizons of power.

These qualifications make sure that the following account is historically embedded but not dependent on accepting long-term historical trends as necessary events. Nor does what follows hinge on the preliminary definition of democracy as essentially about action offered at the outset of the essay. It differs from conventional views about democracy, which are ultimately rooted in notions of individual rights and institutional power, such as the American definition of its own republic (or democracy) "deriving its just powers from the consent of the governed."[89]

---

[88] For one of the first, sound accounts of the growth of economic inequality in the United States and other Western states since the 1970s, see Wolff (2002).

[89] *Declaration of Independence of the United States of America* (1776).

I emphasize understanding democracy in terms of action on practical grounds. If the *demos* is relatively inactive in practically shaping the politics of a society that calls itself democratic, then it makes no sense to say that such a *demos* has significant political *kratos*. Rousseau notably claimed in *The Social Contract* that a society in which the people do not flock to political assemblies bears the marks of corruption. That criterion also might serve to differentiate societies that are or are not democratic. "Realists" such as Joseph Schumpeter dismiss the relevance of Rousseau for modern democratic theory because one only can imagine the unified expression of a general will as the effect of coercive domination, but one can attend to political concerns realistically without being a Schumpeterian realist who ethically validates competition as the gateway to political virtue. If one wants to urge political thinkers to recognize the unreal prospects of direct democracy in contemporary times, it is also true that the "liberal" in liberal democracy, the "constitutional" in constitutional democracy, and the "capitalist" in capitalist democracy are all sustained by human activities and ethical regulations they sanction – which may or may not promote democracy. To understand democratic ethics, which is first and foremost to historicize them, is to emphasize the importance of the train of powerful action in public worlds as the multifarious foundations for democracy. I have already argued for why rational or liberal consensualists (e.g., Rawls) or dissensualists (or poststructuralists) cannot contribute directly to democratic ethics – although they may do so under the shade of unarticulated ethical (or unethical) beliefs. But I have not yet, however, elucidated two issues for democratic ethics. The first takes up my previous comment that "realist" perspectives have a limited capacity for contributing to our understanding or practice of democratic ethics. The second concerns a perennial, question for democratic politics, namely, the importance of ethical character in defining the nature of power and political conflicts, problems, or questions that call for democratic solutions, answers, and settlements.

The first tends to consider action in materialist or individualist veins. Military firepower and corporate wealth or capital are amassed in measurable quantities, enhanced to one degree or another by the technological tools that enable them to be to put to use. These are pushed or pulled in singular directions by individuals or institutional authorities, typically to push or pull others around. The resulting actions are certainly real and call for focused attention, but they also do not exhaust the dimensions of political reality or power. It surely is a good idea to amass as much firepower as possible if a political entity is to go to war with an enemy. This served the Union Army in the American Civil War and Allies in World War II very well. It also convinced German military planners to invade

France and not to worry about public reaction to its violation of its treaty of neutrality with Belgium.[90] But despite the protestations of then Secretary of State Kissinger, no amount of firepower that would not have wholly decimated the landscapes of Vietnam or Iraq could have secured an American "victory" in those countries. (More attention to the history of those lands, occluded by preoccupations with "communism," "oil," one's father, or the lust for domination could have mitigated these tragedies. Which isn't to deny the importance of Cleopatra's nose or James Comey's intervention in the 2016 election as tipping points for defeat.) Observations of the real phenomena "on the ground" in those countries were radically insufficient and faulty as guides for political action, even as calculations of phenomenal power hold important insights about how power can be used and how immediately consequential that use will be. Crucial to the understanding of political landscapes, as the Athenians found out much too late after they invaded Sicily, is knowing the extent to which the agents of massive power can put it to effective use in political environments. That requires knowledge of a political agent's ethical disposition for calculating consequences for exercising collective power, as Thucydides interpreted the Athenians' acquisition of power and its defeat in Sicily.

This kind of utility can be understood ultimately in terms of justice, as Socrates believed it must in responding to Thrasymachus in Plato's *Republic*. But less grandiloquently, one could simply take note of the extent to which cooperation continues to drive the use of that power – a concern of Plato's Socrates but also recognized by Thucydides in assessing the power of ancient Greek citizen-states, Machiavelli, in assessing the power of Italian city-states, or Hobbes, in assessing (and generating) the power of modern states. Despite her truncated interpretation of political power, Hannah Arendt referred to *real* power as "in-between" political actors.[91] This may encourage mysterious political thinking, but she also is highlighting the capacity of cooperation and coordination among political actors in a society. After all, as it once was written, "A house divided against itself cannot stand."[92] Although realists such as Geuss are not ethical individualists, their realist perspective, composed as it is by ethical beliefs and motivations, is not likely to grasp as

---

[90] See Tuchman (1962, Ch. 2).

[91] Arendt (1958, 199–205); cf. Arendt (1972 (1970), 112–13). Also note Arendt's emphasis on the etymological root of "interest" as *inter* + *est*. While Arendt certainly understood the pressures on political actors, her interest in reviving politics as an ethical human activity in the wake of totalitarianisms and World War II seems to have led her to deny without justification consideration of consequences as a constituent of political action.

[92] *Matthew*, 12:25; *Mark*, 3:25.

perspicuously as it might the collective sinews of political power.[93] This lack stems from the insufficient appreciation of *ethical* dimensions of *logoi* – understood historically – that constitute *erga* (and vice versa).[94]

This identification of actual problems, what to do about them, and how to understand them leads to the final broad issue for justifying the merits of historicizing democratic ethics. In defining the relevant features of democratic ethics, the elements of character and structure, ethics and power, inevitably come to the fore – but not as they are counterposed in the pairing of David Brooks and Paul Krugman on Op-Ed pages of *The New York Times*.[95] For the division may be heuristically useful, but it's disingenuous as an account of political actuality. Politics is never a matter of ethics *or* power. Matters of character are certainly matters of virtue and ethics, but their makeup for particular persons dramatically depends on the practical obstacles they must confront and the power they have to overcome them. The fact that folks from Manhattan would be much happier about raising gasoline taxes than folks from rural Texas has much less to do with their moral character or ideology than it does with the force of their circumstances. Similarly, recent literature on terrorism has shown that those who engage in that activity (against state power) do not typically come from desperate economic circumstances as much as socially alienated ones in which their ethical compasses have broken apart (or have been shattered). Terrorists engaged in hate crimes or attacking established states typically are responding to *anomie* or psychological disorientation and seek out fellow terrorists or like-minded persons for emotional support. Their cause may have historical roots, but they mostly are not fighting against poverty or injustice as members of a political order.[96]

---

[93] Geuss's conception of power acknowledges the nature of power as both the ability to do (of an individual or group) and to get others to do what one wants – in ways varying from changing the atmospherics of belief to coercion. See Geuss (2008, 27–8, 50–4); cf. Geuss (1981).

[94] Need it be said, such understanding is hard to come by, especially if one attributes significant political insight to arguments by Marx, Freud, or Foucault that expose our inadequate understanding of every statement about political reality.

[95] The differences between these two authors have become less political and more methodological in the past few years, as the conservative Brooks as humanistic sociologist has radically scorned Donald Trump and the liberal economic pragmatist Krugman has dismissed Bernie Sanders' neo-New Deal platform and single-payer healthcare as simplistic. *The New York Times* has positioned the two in indirect dialogue on its Op-Ed pages for more than a decade.

[96] The recent literature on terrorism, of course, is voluminous. But my statements are widely accepted as explaining necessary, not sufficient, conditions for terrorist actions. For supporting scholarship, see Smelser (2007), Krueger (2007), Stein (2010), Atran (2010), and Miller (2013).

The conjunction of deliberate ethical–political choice up against the pressure of imposing institutional power generates the circumstances of political action. As a result, the assessment of a political problem in relation to the primacy of ethics or power (given that ethics is a kind of power and power a kind of ethics) depends less on its theoretical analysis than on the interpreter's assessment of responsibility for the problem (no matter how large) and its solution (no matter how much time it requires to be accomplished or how deep it must reach), ethically and historically understood. This perspective does not embrace a "Hail-Mary" approach to hitting the target. Instead, it emphasizes attention to the dynamics of power, wherever they occur, and the justifications that motivate its political acceptance. Is the problem of inequality due to contingent imperfections in the economic market or systematic domination by capitalist and political elites over our social structures? Of course, the answer to this question will never be answered satisfactorily for everyone, but it can be researched. And this is where historicizing fosters understanding of democratic ethics. Therefore, the following explores and examines conflicts between democracy and various instances of "goodness," which offers the best intuitive marker for a successful combination of power, ethics, and political judgment. I attend especially to the historical periods in which they emerged as markers for complementing democracy and goodness – whether or not that combination could be said to have been practically successful.

Practical, demographical information and statistics about income and wealth distribution *inter alia* as well as conceptual analysis surely help in carrying out this task, but I have embedded them in spatio-temporal dimensions. For unless the analysis is historicized, conclusions about democratic activity may just as well misinform as inform political understanding. Snapshots of inequality and turning points in collective life do not help in explaining trends and illuminating ways to change them, for we don't know whether power of one kind or another will change their character in one direction or another. Interpretations of "freedom," "equality," "virtue," "the rule of law," or "justice," have little political significance unless one knows about what "freedom" entitles one to do (hang-up on a solicitor or invade Iraq); the relevant measure for equality (opportunity to eat at McDonald's or Le Cirque), or what kind of law is ruling (driven by force or consensus). Thus, every instance of democratic ethics manifests particular conjunctions of power and ethics and determines relevant horizons of democratic ethics. In turn, whenever a particular vision of democracy becomes glued to particular ethical convictions, both democracy and practical ethics suffer. On the other hand, whenever democracies lack a constructive ethical moment, democratic activity suffers and ethical activity becomes anti-democratic. Ethical guidelines and political power should be neither collapsed nor separated; ideally, they should nourish each other in an ongoing dynamic that legitimates each.

Politics depends on a narrative construction of the past and present for the sake of a future, even as the boundaries between and among these temporal categories are surely porous.[97] But its significance mostly yields in action. Think of the *Declaration of Independence* after 1789 (relatively weak, until its rehabilitation by Abraham Lincoln) or the presidential candidacy, election, and terms in office of Franklin D. Roosevelt (relatively strong). The power of political action may be paltry in the face of tsunamis, various cancers, or a deep heritage of individualism or disregard for history, but whatever power it has becomes real and known once it has been enacted.[98] Even then it will obviously be contested. As there never is a last word in politics, it always requires ethical justification, no matter how disingenuous that may be, to garner support across the differences among individual citizens. That is how citizens find common ground and dissenting minorities or authoritative majorities become effective. This "common ground," forged in history, not theory, is particularly important for *democratic* political action. A continuing issue for radical democrats is whether or not that common ground can be located on the political turf where citizens tread. Indeed, that is why democracy as a *practice* is relatively conservative, while democracy as an *idea* and *ideal* is remarkably radical.

The ideas I have singled out to exemplify a historicist account of democratic ethics occupy singular roles in the periods that undergo analysis. Together they make up much of the ethical and practical universe that informs democratic action. Thus, if we are to understand the ethics of democracy in terms of political action *rather than* philosophical ideals, theoretical commitments, or the circumnavigation of the public realm by way of Rawlsian "political liberalism," we should look at those standards of goodness or political virtue that historically provided standards of ethics and power in sectors of society that legitimated democracies – and particularly when they were politically salient. The rationale is not to validate traditions or to embrace Whiggery; rather, it is to generate the parameters for practical, democratic action in light of a critically formulated notion of goodness.

---

[97] For an illuminating and sensible portrayal of the mixtures of these in the American historical imagination, see Kammen (1991).

[98] For the combination if individualism and anti-historicism in the American imaginary, see Hartz (1955). Cf. Marx (2000 (1964)).

Contemporary political conceptions of virtue, morality, and character, for example, deserve comparison to the historical locales where their components were initially developed – in accord with the maxim of Plato's Socrates that the beginning is the greatest part of every work (*ergou*).[99] As a result, each chapter begins from a present political springboard, circles back to the historical sources of the relevant idea of goodness for a democratic society, and then returns to the present. (I think Thucydides, despite his different historical position and intellectual outlook, would approve; thus, the epitaph.) This has led me to focus on five constellations of democratic ethics in the five following chapters that serve as standards of goodness for different collectivities known as democracies: virtue, representation, equal opportunity, legitimacy, and human rights. Each illustrates a kind of political goodness that emerges at distinct historical periods in which democracies reach for new ethical sanctions to foster their well-being. Notably, they still belong to democratic ethics and provide the focuses for the five substantive chapters of this book. Briefly, I invest the discussion of these concepts and discourses as kinds of goodness that complement democracy in the following way.

The evolving political context of ancient Athens, where its political character was also personal and often counterposed to democracy (*sc.* Socratic ethics and democratic power), was often sanctioned by virtue (*arete*). Its character as a virtue for the few rather than the many ironically functioned as an ambiguous horizon for the democratic citizenry as a whole. The institutional value of "representation" should be seen in terms of its emergence as a relatively oligarchical synecdoche for the institutions of modern, liberal democracies, insofar as the very idea of "representation" is little more than a *fata morgana* that induces trust in having a few public officials act for the many. Our fidelity to "equal opportunity" deserves to be read in terms of its significant role in sanctioning virtuous activity in the civil society and economic realms of capitalist democracy in the nineteenth century, as well as legitimizing norms of both equality and inequality. "Legitimacy" ought to be read against its new prominence for identifying national boundaries and acceptable governments in particular nations and the "international community" in the twentieth and twenty-first century, when it links democratic sanctions to the power of states that are *ipso facto* inimical to democratic activity. "Human rights" needs to be seen less in terms of vague references to its antecedents in monotheistic religions but to its secular invocations in the late eighteenth-century revolutions of particular nation-states, its spectacular display in the United

---

[99] Plato, *Republic*, 377a.

Nations' 1948 *Universal Declaration of Human Rights*, and its paradoxical proliferation in speech but not actualization in deed (for the most part) post-1989.[100] In this way, we may best begin to understand the political stakes of linguistic conventions of "values" and personality; how money and economic power shape the conduct of democratic elections; how equal opportunity and human rights forever fall short as political goals; and how "legitimacy" exudes an ethical standard in speech but is primarily the product of actual political contests. Historicizing democratic ethics does not explain what these political ethics are, but it improves our horizons for understanding what they can be. It enlarges our capacities as democratic, ethical political agents. Historicity not only reveals how ethics are political; it shows their democratic potential. One might suggest that this virtual truism has become obsolete, but I would argue that it is particularly important today – not primarily for politicization, since that can be done without attention to historicity – but so as to deconstruct the historical and philosophical artificiality of dichotomies such as theory/practice; ancients/moderns; left/right that have been used to interpret democracy since the Renaissance.

Various sources can serve to make this point. One may readily turn to Machiavelli, who – though hardly a democrat – sought to energize and enlarge republican action over and against the domination of the Medicis in Florence and the violent wrangling among Italian city-states in the face of the burgeoning powers of Spain and France.[101] I take my first cue from Machiavelli, who wanted his readers to appreciate what human beings had *done*, rather than simply what they had *said*, because historical events provide more reliable parameters – not determinants – for understanding the range of possibility in political action.[102] Need it be said, Machiavelli did not make this point in order to reify or deify the past. He very self-consciously wanted to break from the past and from tradition.

---

[100] Part of the difficulty of identifying these discursive terms as markers of democratic ethics is their relative incoherence if viewed primarily from a practical point of view. "Virtue" pertains to a collective standard that reflects the judgments of particular actors and is held up by ladders that often neither reach their declared height nor take root in their putative ground. "Representation" *ipso facto* declares what it cannot deliver, the representation of a sack of individuals in a whole bag that the potatoes do not make or see. "Equal opportunity" avers that one can equally coordinate the inherently unequal and individual character of opportunities. "Human rights" simultaneously speaks to the generically transpolitical and the constraints of particular political communities. But these problematic features of terms in democratic ethics, if not political ethics more generally, merely replicate at the conceptual level the mixture of part and whole, deeds and words, that anchors coherent political activity.

[101] Cf. McCormick (2011).

[102] See Machiavelli, *The Prince*, Chs. VI, XV; *The Discourses*, Bk. I, Introduction; Bk. II, Introduction.

But in order for him to be successful in doing so, he needed to know what he was up against. Understanding "what one is up against" is of course contested terrain. That terrain reflects deep currents of power, stemming from hypothetical but plausible projections of human nature or from the means and relations of production, or from the inevitable forces of myriad dominations in social life. But these constraints on human possibility are also conditions of political possibility and may be transformed. In the past and in the present, they were inflected by ethical purpose. To be sure, we need political theory to explain them, but we also need to look in the right places for guidance. The argument here is that the drama of history is the first place to turn.

In light of this Machiavellian invocation, what about history and democratic ethics today? Democratic societies that take citizenship seriously call for the widespread exercise of power by the *demos*, broadly conceived, as the ideal limit of authoritative collective action. These days, however, democracy is more a concept than a practice. It is a concept used either by reigning authorities to justify their anti-democratic reign over the citizenry or by academic democrats who believe in democratic power but do not have not many more adherents than the plutocratic 1 percent they (rightfully) criticize. The problem is how to empower the disempowered and how to legitimize their claims to power. To answer these questions about political agency for the *demos*, one is much more likely to succeed by drawing on historical moments of action than hypothetical elements of thought. This is because democracy is more about action than about thought, even if deliberate thought ought to direct it as a rule. Citizens cannot express solidarity mostly in imaginations. Their commonality and potential for democratic activity takes place in the forum, on the streets, in the presses, amid legislative activity – for the sake of common worlds. Of course, a democratic or social contract society may become corrupt, in which case both the thoughts and the actions of citizens systematically private interests more than the public good.[103] Or, there simply may be a need for down-time after an intense period of public involvement.[104] But in these circumstances, philosophical solutions to our conditions have even weaker anchors in our experience and thereby become even more unreliable.

Historicized ethics is a necessary aid for democratic action, but it cannot direct it. What it can do is empower the political agency of human

---

[103] See Brown (2015), who gives us hope by invoking "democracy" as both the injured target of, and weapon against, neoliberalism.

[104] See Albert O. Hirschman, *Shifting Involvements: Private Interest and Public Action* (Princeton: Princeton University Press, 1982).

beings for that action. Without that power, democratic actors play interesting roles; they don't exercise lasting power – either inside or outside the beltway. As for contemporary circumstances, we can recall two trenchant analyses of contemporary totalitarianisms – the totalitarianism identified by Arendt and the inverted totalitarianism identified by Sheldon Wolin.[105] Both totalitarianisms seek to have citizens forget their past, to lose touch with their traditions, to focus on their feelings and consumptive needs, to become passive rather than active, to think rather than act. In a democracy, action, not thought, constitutes the public realm, even as it ought to be preceded by deliberation; and for that action to shape knowledgeably and ethically a democratic order, democratic ethics requires a perspective on the present and future that centrally recognizes the legacies of the past. These days, with political boundaries so porous (migration; the internet) and problems so vast and hard to determine with specificity (global warming), the meaning of democracy as the power of a political people is hard to grasp, if not evanescent. Yet we are better able to deal with our problems if more people understand them and act together to address them. Directly assessing the nature and prospects of democracy remains the best way of ascertaining the political form of collective power that advantages most human beings. *How* that power is enhanced and exercised *best* is the central concern of democratic ethics, and for them to be understood well and extensively practiced, they need to be historicized.

[105] See Arendt (1951) and Wolin (2008).

2 Democracy and Virtue in Ancient Athens

2.1   Introduction

Democracy and virtue have long connoted opposing political projects –
with the former indicating freedom and equality and the latter emphasizing excellent performance, typically expressed by a few rather than the
many (and often the few that are materially well-endowed).[1] These terms
have maintained a tense compatibility, in ancient or modern democracy,
as both had to accommodate claims of the few over the many – such as
the vulnerable power of aristocrats, the rising power of capitalists, and the
staying power of cultural elites. Thucydides' Pericles sought to smooth
over these divisions in his Funeral Oration, rhetorically integrating virtue
and democracy. Montesquieu combined them at a theoretical, not practical, level, and Rousseau associated them in a powerful but ungainly way.
Liberal political theories, however, do not address the tension between
the appeal of virtue or excellence and the requirements of liberal political
equality (despite the huge market for those who can afford the training to
acquire superior skills and test scores that best those of their peers). As a
result, recent scholarship has ignored this essential feature of a successful democratic society, leaving it to sloganeering in public schools and
community colleges that hail equality and excellence.[2] The gap between
the ancients and the moderns when it comes to matters of ethics is overdrawn. An illuminating sign of their relations of similarity and difference
is the notion of character.

The word "character" etymologically stems from the Greek *charakter*,
which refers, according to the *Oxford English Dictionary*, to "an instrument
for marking or graving, impress, distinctive mark, distinctive nature." It is
a signifier – potentially of things but mostly of language and persons. In
sixteenth-century England, Shakespeare used it to identify facial features
that displayed a certain moral quality. In seventeenth-century England,

---

[1] Portions of this chapter appeared in Wallach (2011).
[2] For a critical analysis of some works that have not done so, see Wallach (2000).

it could be used to identify – again according to the *OED* – the "sum of the moral and mental qualities which distinguish an individual or a race, viewed as a homogeneous whole; the individuality impressed by nature and habit on man or nation, mental or moral constitution," as well as invented personages in novels or plays. Except for the era between the seventeenth and early twentieth centuries, when nations were given homogeneous personalities – often with the purpose of either degradation or elevation – it referred to the posture of an individual, tending toward her or his "moral" features – at least more so than the morally neutral term "personality." While it still may refer to the "character" of a nation, the notion of a national character today is generally pluralized in the form of "characteristics" – unless one wants to make a rhetorical point, as in American "exceptionalism" or "America First," English "eccentricity," or an Italian or French sense of "beauty."

In the United States since the 1990s, however, the notion of character has been used more politically, mostly by conservatives (or those on "the Right"), to emphasize the "moral" dimensions of personhood, over and above an individual's practical circumstances, as the primary factor in determining their life chances. One is "responsible" for one's life, even for one's parents it would seem. Circumstances into which one is born – such as wealth, well-educated parents, or a well-heeled neighborhood – appear to be matters of choice, and the power to shape one's life circumstances is primarily placed within the domain of personal judgment. The defrocked neo-conservative William J. Bennett emphasized the notion of personal virtue in the 1990s; and the notion of character was emphasized more recently by the moderately conservative writer and *New York Times* columnist David Brooks, in his book *The Road to Character*, which offers historical, philosophical, and cultural anecdotes and homilies about which "virtues" (résumé/utilitarian vs. eulogy/valuable-for-life virtues) are good for you – without addressing how the economic constraints of capitalism have altered the meaning and possibility of character for many.[3] In contrast to such moralisms that focus on remedies for the self without attending to the inequalities of power in society,

---

[3] A pundit on the meaning of virtue and the virtues, even for children, and Secretary of Education, he was later convicted on gambling charges – which we really shouldn't scorn given how much money is raised by states from gambling venues that gobble up the inadequate resources of low-income individuals. Brooks (2015) observes social corollaries to personal characteristics but makes no reference to the political identity of individuals or how their version of it (engaged or disengaged, upper-class or lower-class, white or colored, male or female, etc.) may affect the meaning and attraction of the behaviors he blames or praises. For a more economically attuned discussion of character, see Sennett (1998).

critics from the left too often disregard questions of responsibility, in line with a Marxist tradition that primarily regards ethics as epiphenomenal to human endeavor. Although conservatives have monopolized discourse about character, issues of character still warrant attention for democratic ethics. For citizens have choices to make; it's a matter of properly understanding their parameters.

Assessments of the parameters of choice are viewed in relation to political responsibility or the common good. Major media mostly focus on ordinary individuals as victims of crime or "natural" disasters, not as potential political agents. This view may be changing in the United States and Europe, as disingenuous, chauvinistic populists evoke anger in citizens already harboring resentment – all of which points to the need for understanding a personal–political axis of alienation from public experiences in societies that are supposed to be democratic. In addition, the ongoing damage to the character of American soldiers fighting in endless wars has now been identified as a socio-political harm, the long-lasting "moral injury" that soldiers often experience after having performed actions that normally they would not perform because they are "wrong."[4]

Politics, always marked by a dynamic of power and ethics, can be a tool of citizens to refashion and improve the world. But this discourse is so fulsomely colored by self-serving, partisan conflicts, crime drama (real or fictional), celebrities, and disasters of one kind or another that the very mention of the word induces cynicism more than activism. Public analysts too often focus on the technical rather than the substantive, in order to maintain their funding. Social science relies on the synchronicity of abstract data rather than historical dramas that span generations. When electronic media try to convey political meaning with a personal touch, the effect is anecdotal or vague – leaving its general significance up for grabs. Thus, notions of ethics and its perfection understood as the conduct of virtue in ways that engage the dynamic of politics remain relatively uncharted – because they are consigned to non- or anti-democratic mediums, such as private religion (which, when made an instrument of politics, tends to be exclusionary, as in anti-Muslim rhetoric, or violent,

---

[4] This term tends to apply to actions that go beyond the legitimation of standard-killing-at-a-distance warfare. For elaboration of the term, see the work of Jonathan Shay and Brett Litz, cited by Wood (2016) in his account of the non-medical damage to the characters of American soldiers who have fought in Vietnam, Somalia, Afghanistan, and Iraq as "moral injury." It results from both the harsh circumstances of these wars and their fitful support by the wars' authors and supporters. Shay (1994, 180–1, 2002, 162–3) notes that such injury also damages the capacity for participatory, democratic citizenship and development of our natural desire for politically being in community.

as in the tactics of some anti-abortion activists), or strategic manipulations of politicians.

The factors affecting public or private involvement may be cyclical, and politics is certainly exhausting, but they are more likely to result from simultaneously, publicly experienced traumas (wars, revolutions, national economic crises, and cultural or political upheavals – such as those brought on by the end of the quiescent fifties, the growth of the civil rights movement, the emergence of adolescent baby-boomers, and the economic demand for, and moral claims of, the women's movement).[5] The contemporary academy does not make up for the deficit. Few studies focus on the dynamic of ethics and power as an inherent problem in politics. Scholarly studies often isolate analyses of this relationship into separate domains, conforming to the dictates of the scholar's disciplines, while journalistic efforts provide accounts necessarily based on relatively short time-frames and limited intellectual perspectives (although I obviously am indebted to both).[6]

The connection of power and ethics is less strained in accounts of the political and democratic literature and institutions of ancient Greece, because the *polis*, its exemplary mode of collective existence, so naturally connected the two. As Thucydides knew, Aristotle announced, and Hannah Arendt valorized, the *polis* was a community of (male) citizens that depended on political activity; their social stature and collective well-being depending on intelligent, regular (not incessant) political participation. Thus, there was understood to be a political art (*techne*) of virtue (*arete*) and a virtue in the political art that produced a kind of goodness. In democratic Athens, this practice was understood to be accessible to democratic citizens. Still, the relationship between democracy and virtue that marks the origins of democracy in ancient Greece displays both compatibility and conflict – from the heroic culture of Homer to the democratic adaptation of Solon's political reforms in the fifth and fourth century BCE. Because political *virtue* that pertains to democracy cannot derive directly from religious sources (even as they provide much nourishment), the effective relationship between democracy and virtue – literally, *demokratia* and *arete* – can shed useful perspectives on contemporary political discourse, at least since Weber's landmark and tragic 1919 lecture to German students about the modern (particularly German)

---

[5] Hirschman (1982).

[6] Journalistic accounts appear in the work of neo-conservative public intellectuals, such as William Kristol, or moderate conservatives, such as David Brooks, as well as the work of popularizing academics more sympathetic to the Democratic Party (see, e.g., Westen 2007).

crisis of political responsibility, *Politik als Beruf*. Various Athenian renditions of *arete* illuminate contemporary ethics because they transcend current categories of morality and ideology or link ethics and power.

The paradoxical feature of democratic ethics was one reason why partisans of Athenian democracy did not produce a self-standing ethics or theory of democracy, preferring instead to make use of conventional understandings and rhetorical argumentation. Given the ethics and practical authority lodged in the *demos*, as well as its political emergence in Athens via opposition to the power of oligarchs and aristocrats, anything that radically reworked the extant ethics and traditions of the *demos* seemed patently anti-democratic.[7] And yet, it is hard to claim that the close connection between Athenian *demokratia* and *arete* did not have its costs – namely in *hubris* (arrogance), which (at least as expressed by Alcibiades and his supporters, if not the imperial posture developed by Pericles) surely contributed to Athens' defeat at the hands of the Peloponnesians. At the very least, the Spartans' victory over the Athenians and the subsequent trial, conviction, and execution of Socrates, surely damaged Athenian society, its economy, and its self-confidence, leaving major questions about its ethical and political orders that Plato and Aristotle subsequently (if not sufficiently) answered in their trenchant but ever-puzzling ways. A useful account of democratic ethics should articulate a kind of coordinated relationship between democracy and virtue, one that is lodged wholly in neither the virtue of the *demos* nor the truthfulness of an *ethics*, so as to account for how democracies can sustain their capacities as societies of free and equal citizens and achieve political goodness as best they can in the face of the obstacles presented by power and the future. As such, it must address the psychologies and characters of citizens – how their practical, political actions achieve collective outcomes.

Nonetheless, secondary views of Greek virtue (*arete*) have mostly stemmed from philosophically analytical, philological, or principally ethical perspectives, often inflected by Kant (e.g., Adkins'), if not Christian (or anti-Christian, in the case of Nietzsche) criticism.[8] As a result, we have not adequately understood ancient Greek ethics in relation to the intensely political and, at times, democratic context in which *arete* assumed such significance for ancient Greeks. We also miss how the

---

[7] See Jones (1957) and Ober (1989). Athenian tragedy and comedy offered radical criticism of Athenian ethics, but they did not indicate any path that would extricate them from their predicament – other than greater self-knowledge (necessary but not sufficient) (see Euben 1989).

[8] See French et al. (1988) and Paul et al. (1988).

ancient Greeks understood the political dimension of "character," typically emphasized in political discourse by "conservatives" on the right, as well as the ethical dimension of politics, too often underestimated by "liberals" on the left. This chapter highlights the political character of *arete* in ancient Greek thought, particularly in Athenian democracy.[9] It illustrates the interdependence of power and ethics in the political thought of ancient Greece (more particularly, Athenian democracy) and evaluates the relationship between democracy and *arete* by proponents and critics of their complementarity. The aim is not to offer a paradigmatic contrast to contemporary political ethics but to illustrate how the first major democratic political order existed as a "community of citizens" by intertwining ethics, power, and demotic politics.

The result both debunks and emphasizes the significance of ancient Greek relationships of democracy and virtue for us. For over 200 years, ancient Greece and Athenian democracy have been touchstones for newly crafted political theory or newly envisioned political practices. In the late eighteenth and nineteenth centuries, the American constitutionalists read Athenian democracy as the black sheep of political forms; Benjamin Constant projected onto it his theoretical and political ambivalence about modernity, and John Stuart Mill linked his purified vision of liberal democracy to Athens. In the twentieth century, Ernest Barker found in ancient Athens his lodestone for reforming imperial Britain; Leo Strauss found in it a benchmark for recasting Western civilization, and Hannah Arendt found inspiration there for imagining a revitalized politics in post-World War II Western societies. More historically oriented theorists have seen in the Athenians' "direct" democracy few institutional roots for remodeling modern, "representative" democracy, while others see positive and salutary connections between ancient democracy and contemporary democratic life.[10]

All of these writers rooted their political theories and conceptions of political ethics in ancient Athens, even as they wrote in and for their own eras. Each demonstrates the fertile soil provided by ancient Greek texts and institutions for innovative intellectual constructions. I do not wish here to gainsay such contributions to scholarship in the history of ideas or institutions; however, I do not regard the Athenians' legacy in terms

---

[9] *Arete* is untranslated for the sake of clarity. There are differences between *arete* and many common notions of virtue, the significance of which becomes clear in other chapters of this book. Here, it is worth noting that, unlike the English "virtue," derived from the Latin noun *vir*, i.e., "manliness," *arete* has no etymological connection to masculinity. Instead, it is etymologically related to the verb *aresko*, source of the superlative noun *aristos*, "the best."

[10] See Finley (1985 (1978)), Ober (1989), and Hansen (1990, 2005).

of self-contained, relatively trans-historical arguments about either political theory or political practice, political ethics or political institutions.
The *polis* provided a home for distinctive relationships of power and ethics whose irreducibly practical roots keep them at least at arm's length
from us. And yet, our (indeterminate) human commonalities allow the
facticity of their historical existence to reach beyond their time – even to
the twenty-first century, when the contours of any particular people (or
demos), the character of power (or *kratos*), and the nature or authority
of virtue (or socially sanctioned excellence) are so elusive because of,
e.g., the proliferation of usages and diminished regard for conventionally
authoritative boundaries.

For political theory, the pivotal issue for understanding *arete* in relation to ancient Greek politics and, subsequently, Athenian democracy, is
the extent to which it carries irreducibly authoritarian, elitist, moralistic,
or class- or gender-based features. Did social or political understandings
of *arete* always promote the stature of aristocracy, if not aristocrats in particular, at the expense of democracy and democratic values in social life?
Did *arete* denote modes of behavior unique to, or predominantly manifested in, the behavior of men as a dominant gender? If the answer to
each is clearly "yes," then later, theoretical or practical conceptions of the
relationship of democracy to virtue will invariably exhibit antagonistic
features. And, indeed, this is the answer given by notable classical scholars and political theorists.[11] Democrats are seen either to oppose virtue
and democracy or to maintain the ready compatibility of the two. But
the answer to both questions, in fact, is "no." Democracy and democrats
challenged aristocratic claims that the wealthy and powerful or, conceivably, tyrannical rulers, were exclusive exemplars of *arete*. The *demos*
sought to emulate *arete* to the extent that they could, although this would
have been difficult: their daily lives did not exhibit publicly noteworthy
excellence or heroism and even their contributions as sailors (*nautai*)
did not entail the achievement of *arete*.[12] Modestly, the *demos* named
the political order in which they were ascendant, a *demos-kratia*, where
they did not automatically exercise power as an *arche*, or dominant rule
(*contra* "monarchy," "timarchy," and "oligarchy"; *pace* the ideal order of
aristo-kratia postulated by Plato and Aristotle).[13] But according to Pericles
and Protagoras, at least, the activity of the *demos* could exhibit *arete*. During
the heyday of imperial Athens, *demokratia* and *arete* exhibited a practical complementary that was supported mostly in ethical conventions

---

[11] See Loraux (1986 (1981)), wherein she connects democracy, *arete*, and empire.
[12] See Raaflaub (1994, 139).
[13] See Mosse (2013, 260).

and political ideals. In late fifth- and fourth-century Athens, Socrates, Plato, and Aristotle pounced on the Athenians' democratic politics as faulty and lacking in virtue, although their criticisms often were conflated with critiques of the limits of political life *tout court*.

To put the matter starkly, proponents of Athenian *demokratia* identified their political order as virtuous, a collective embodiment of *arete* – understood as a standard of practical and ethical excellence.[14] Freedom, equality, and virtue complemented one another. However, Plato and Aristotle – the principal theorists of the ancient *polis* – disassociated *demokratia* and *arete*. They continued to link democracy with the principles of freedom and equality, but they defined democracy as a structure of power that did not directly sustain *arete*. As a result, its operation was not sufficient to effect adequate ethical guidelines for the conduct of power. Their disassociation of democracy and *arete*, of political freedom and equality, on the one hand, and virtue, on the other, subsequently informed much Western political thought. Indeed, the relationship between democracy and virtue remains problematic, and this creates a continuing legitimation crisis for democracy that seems more troublesome than it actually is. These criticisms misunderstand the complex relationship of *demokratia* to *arete* – particularly the nature of demotic claims to *arete* and the principal political achievements of the *demos* in challenging aristocratic claims that they are the unique agents of *arete* – as well as the democratic tenor of ancient Greek conceptions of "the political" as a dimension of ethical and social life. The account offered here of the ancient Greek relationship of democracy and virtue in political thought in history and philosophy illustrates the contingency of their relationship and demonstrates that both can flourish when they maintain distinct but complementary conceptual and practical identities.

2.2   "The Political" in Ancient Greece and *Arete*

What has come to be commonly translated as "virtue" (*arete*) temporally preceded in ancient Greece both a fully developed political realm and democracy. To be sure, if we regard "the political" or "political activity" or

---

[14] Hereafter, *arete* will be translated as "virtue," although the difference between conventional connotations of "virtue" and ancient Greek conceptions of *arete* often present obstacles to a full appreciation of the argument presented here. For *arete* is the nominative for "goodness" and also connotes "excellence." A similar disconnect occurs between modern conceptions of "democracy" and ancient Greek conceptions of *demokratia*, the interpretive issues of which I address at beginning of Chapter 3. Nonetheless, I shall use here the English words "democracy" and "virtue" as stand-ins for the Greek words *demokratia* and *arete*.

"political institutions" simply as forms of life that demonstrate bounded contestation for power and authority, the Homeric poems surely exhibited "the political."[15] This is the view taken by some recent scholars, over and against the previously dominant perspective that views "the political" emerging two to three generations after the Homeric era, when constitutional government took shape in Sparta and Athens.[16] Although the differences in these two perspectives partly stem from how "political" is defined – does it require a functioning *polis* or can it simply exhibit activity that anticipates or illustrates collective conflict that later would be called political? – the meaning of this question also depends on the extent to which one finds the major conflicts in both Homeric poems occurring not simply between heroes or elites – e.g., Agamemnon and Achilles, Achilles and Hector, or Odysseus' heroism and life's obstacles, including the suitors who are devouring his livelihood and threatening Penelope – but between classes, including the *demos*, such that the poems could be seen as critiques of aristocratic domination on behalf of a common good.

Both sides of the debate have merit. In the *Iliad*, "Homer" recognizes the limits of both Agamemnon and Achilles, and the intervention by Thersites in Book II against Odysseus' attempts to prevent the Athenians from losing heart for any more fighting and going home is given enough credit by the poet to suggest that a genuine dynamic between leaders and led certainly existed. Yet Thersites was roundly beaten by Odysseus for challenging his authority, without anyone coming to his defense, and most of the poems include the *demos* or *laoi* as background figures that do not substantively shape the epic narratives. In *Works and Days*, written contemporaneously with or not much later than the Homeric poems but in the different milieu of Boeotia, Hesiod condemned the rapacious behavior of "gift-devouring kings" for damaging the commons.[17] But, again, the character of that collective life was relatively amorphous. Hesiod's writings may have been popular or daring, but they do not seem to have had a following that posed practical threats to the powerful authorities in his society.[18]

---

[15] Historically speaking, I understand the Homeric poems as epic poetry written down in the eighth century BC that seamlessly combine accounts of contemporaneous Greek life with those of a sometimes mythical, Mycenaean past that preceded it by at least 400 years.

[16] See Raaflaub (2013a). Cf. Hammer (2002). They are disputing the view of Finley (1978 (1965)). Cf. Cartledge (2000, 17–22).

[17] Hesiod, *Works and Days*, 38–9, etc.

[18] See, e.g., Tandy and Neale (1996, 1–38).

In the quasi-political context of the Homeric and Hesiodic poems, however, *arete* exhibited political features that, *mutatis mutandis*, continued to mark it until the end of the classical era. Starting in the archaic or "heroic" era, *arete* denoted a particular sort of excellence for living things, manufactured tools, persons, and social relationships. Homer's and Hesiod's iterations of *arete* signified various forms of merit or excellence. They could applied to horses or humans; men or women; military or non-military achievement; individuals, groups, or collectivities; competitive or cooperative behavior; upper-class and ordinary individuals.[19] In every case, the excellence inhered in a distinguished performance that implied a social or informally political, superb, *active* display of an agent's character; it could not derive from suffering.[20] Nor could the achievements of *arete* be "bad" (*kakon*); indeed, they were understood as "good" (*agathos*, in a pre-Platonic sense) and often opposed or were contrasted to "bad" actions.[21] As such, their excellence exhibited a comparative, ranked judgment of meritorious action. Our sources for that judgment in this era were certainly "Homer's" and Hesiod's works, but as such the judgments implicitly reflected their interpretations of potentially shared values. Each placed himself both above and inside practical life – over and against, as well as potentially with, the one or few and the many. Gregory Nagy has argued that the central theme of early Greek poetry was heroism, which personified *arete*.[22] But *arete* was also more than heroism, since it was used not only to describe but also to criticize "heroes" or "heroic" behavior. The superiority that an individual's *arete* denoted was disputable – and hence partly politically determined.[23]

The meaning of *arete* was extensive and authoritative, enabling it to announce a socio-political banner of distinction. But its boundaries and references were indeterminate. *Arete* was particularly associated with the excellence of an individual *or* group's character – a disposition that signified a major aspect of that entity's identity. But an entity's virtue was more than a role or practice; it also exhibited the development of its potential to do good in the world, sometimes through the exercise of

---

[19] See Homer's *Iliad*: VIII.35; IX.442–3, XI.90–1, 761–2; XIII.237–8, 275–7; XIV.118; XV.641–3; XX.242–3, 411; XXII.268–9; XXIII.276, 374, 571, 578. In Homer's *Odyssey*, see II.205–7 (and XVIII.251); IV.629 (and XXI.187); IV.725, 815; VIII.237–9; XII.211–12; XIV.212, 402; XVII.322–3; XVIII.133, 205, 251–3; XIX.114; XXII.244; XXIV.193–7, 515. The contrast between "competitive" and "cooperative" values was famously coined by Adkins (1960). For a summary of criticism by classicists, see Rowe (1983). For a philosophical as well as historical critique, see Williams (1985, 1993).

[20] See *Odyssey*: VIII.329; XIII.45–6; Hesiod, *Works and Days*, 289–97, 313.

[21] Cf. Nietzsche's *Zur Genealogie der Moral*, Pt. 1.

[22] See Nagy (1999).

[23] MacIntyre (1981, 271–4). Cf. Wallach (1983, 2016a).

practical reason. *Arete* did not develop as part of a "tradition."[24] Nor was virtue a function of being "weak" or "strong," although it was associated with the prowess and eminence of those at the top of the social order. Greek literature regularly criticized its putative agents as falling below social expectations. From Homer to the fourth century, *arete* was most notably used to criticize social and political actors who were not using their power or wealth for the common good *or* to hypothetically identify standards for those who did. Thus, *arete* expressed functional and ethical, descriptive and evaluative, meanings. This range of denotations of *arete* cuts against the grain of many schematic contrasts between conceptual (functional or ethical) or temporal (archaic or classical) or "moral" ("competitive" vs. "cooperative") types of virtue. It distinguishes it from many contemporary notions of virtue that emphasize *either* a functional *or* an ethical connotation and a political meaning that connotes coercion. Because of its prevalent and authoritative use in Greek epics and lyric, *arete* may have seemed to belong to the natural firmament of the human world. But it also was susceptible to cultivation, acquisition, disputation, and education – though exactly how so was surely contested and not expressly known. It typically reflected a combination of what ancient Greeks referred to as *phusis* and *nomos* – nature and convention or law (which includes what we might call nurture, culture, unwritten laws, and sanctioned social constructions, as well as written law).[25] Uniting its meanings, however, was its inherently active nature. *Arete* was ultimately and always a matter of action and achievement – not merely thought, attitude, or ascribed disposition. As such, *arete* always appeared as effective action, even if at times only in the reputational sense.

Actions that displayed *arete* also were embodied in discourse (*logos*). *Arete* connected *logos* and *ergon* in the minds of its hearers and readers. Although it served as a socially sanctioned discursive standard, *arete* was presumed to effect deeds or action (*ergon*), even as it maintained a distinctive distance from them. In any event, *arete* manifested a kind of "power."[26] Power was necessary but not sufficient for the existence of *arete*. Power in the archaic age was typically associated with elite forms of life, but the

---

[24] Hannah Arendt noted the absence of a notion of "tradition" in ancient Greek discourse (see Arendt 1968; also see Euben 1990; Finkelberg 2002).

[25] See Adkins (1960) for the categories and contrasts between "competitive" and "cooperative" or "quiet" virtues (Cf. Long 1970, with subsequent response by Adkins 1971). For a critique of the way Adkins's Kantianism inflected his history of Greek ethics, see Williams (1985, 1993, 81–4).

[26] The English word "power," like "virtue," is rooted in Latin, rather than Greek – the Latin verb *posse*, which *The Random House Dictionary of the English Language* renders as "to be able" or "have power." For more on "power," see Section 2.3.

concept of *arete* did not immediately express or endorse specifically elitist values (the traditional reading of Homeric poems and archaic values).[27] Yet literary deployments of *arete* do not manifest an inherent opposition between ethics or ethical behavior and the exercise of power; they signify the best imaginable displays of power; that is, they presumptively illustrate power as the potential for actualizing virtue without domination, and operate as an ethical horizon for human activity.[28] Moreover, they are not coterminous with various kinds of socially effective power. *Arete* may be defeated – by "bad" things or people, fate, or Zeus – and comports with an ethical judgment of excellence.[29] *Arete* maps – but not neatly – onto the socio-political values, ideals, and life of the archaic era.

The explicitly or implicitly political dimensions of *arete* become much clearer in the seventh century, during the class conflict that led to the establishment by Solon of an Athenian *politeia* ("constitution"), and his composition of poetic political theory. From the eighth to the fifth centuries, textual accounts of *arete* do not so much depart from archaic understandings as they extend or enlarge upon them because of their new social context – that of a political community, or *polis*, most notably incarnated in Sparta and Athens.[30] Solon's poems offer the clearest evidence of the character of the new political realm. It provided discursive public space, institutional procedures, and laws that were agreed by Athenian citizens to apply to rich and poor alike – in other words, political contestation among individuals from different classes and clans. For Solon, public disputation contributed to political well-being, because it brought into

---

[27] See Donlan (1999 (1980)). For the view that *arete* originally and essentially denotes an aristocratic value associated with wealth, good birth, and manliness, see Jaeger (1939–45). For a more complex analysis of *arete*, embedded in an account of "Greek man" in archaic Greek poetry, see Frankel (1975 (1951), 532–3).

[28] Understanding the political dimensions of *arete*, indeed, requires an appreciation of Greek notions of power. These, too, have to be contextually defined. References to power for ancient Greeks had horizontal and relational, as well as vertical and dominant attributes – i.e., features of "communal" or "associational power" as well as "power over." In fact, the Greek equivalents of our concept of power had three dimensions. One was *dunamis* – which, depending on its practical context and authorial use, may be properly translated as potentiality, ability, or capacity. The second was *kratos* – power used as force or "power over." The third was the most elusive: it was understood as "political" and arose from cooperative practices. See Liddell, Scott, and Jones, *Greek–English Lexicon* (Oxford: The Clarendon Press, 1968). Notably, when Aeschylus characterizes the brutally forceful and violent exercise of power (in *Prometheus Bound*), he personifies power as both *kratos* and *bia*. Both Plato and Aristotle linked power and capacity via the word, *dunamis*. In the late fifth century, Thucydides noted that it was distinctively linked to the collective, purposeful energy generated by "political" life.

[29] *Arete* is not equivalent to abstract standards of ethics, morality, or virtue, especially because of its kindred relationship to the cardinal virtues of life, namely, "self-restraint" (*sophrosyne*), "courage" (*andreia*), "wisdom" (*sophia*), and "justice" (*dikaiosyne*).

[30] See Lloyd-Jones (1971, 44–51) and Gentili (1988 (1985), 63, 71, 130–6).

the light of the commons the strategies of ambitious individuals and groups. He asserted the primacy of a public realm that treated rich and poor alike with (what he regarded as) equal justice; viewed wealth as a gift from the gods rather than evidence of human worth – something that was more likely to be a source of *hybris* than *arete*; sympathized with the plight of the *demos*; and recognized both the essential links between ethics and power and the imperfections of that connection.[31] Solon rendered *arete* as goodness – it was the nominative form of *agathos* – and used it to criticize the use of power by any and all classes but particularly those who had the most power. For they had the greatest obligation to use it well and were most prone to exercise it badly – dominating others while flattering themselves as exemplars of *arete*.[32]

The proclivity of early Greek writers to use *arete* as a critical standard for, and potentially against, aristocratic behavior (conventionally understood) is strikingly apparent in the poetry of the Megarian poet, Theognis.[33] He lived a generation or two after Solon, when his *polis* was experiencing much political turmoil, almost continual *stasis* as the Megarian aristocracy experienced antagonistic opposition. Theognis frequently noted how difficult it was to cultivate, educate or produce *arete*. He also observed that one could err in the pursuit of *arete* and seek it obsessively or instrumentally. Along with wealth, *arete* was subject to the Delphic saying, "Nothing too much" (*meden agan*).[34] Although democratic politics was not a factor in this era, Theognis seemed to pity the Megarian *demos* for having been treated as pawns in the political conflict among the upper classes for control of his city.[35] Most important for our purposes was his linkage of *arete* to *dikaiosune* (justice) – which he, anticipating Plato in the *Republic*, believed included all of *arete*.[36] For Theognis, achieving *arete* was remarkable and unusual, likely to be attained by only

---

[31] See Frs. 3, 4, 5, 9, and 15, collected in *Elegy and Iambus with the Anacreonta, Part 1*, J. M. Edmonds, ed. (London, 1931) (see Fisher 1982; Vlastos 1995 (1946)).

[32] See recent scholarship on Solon: Almeida (2003), Irwin (2005), Lewis (2006), Blok and Lardinous (2006), and Noussia-Fantuzzi (2010). On how Solon's reforms made democratic citizenship possible, see Manville (1990).

[33] He was notably and unfairly cited by Plato as an exemplar of poetic inconsistency and conventionally regarded as a house poet for the aristocracy. See Plato, *Meno*, 95cff. Theognis's views on this subject are quite complex, accurately reflecting the nature of the subject. See 33–6, 305–38, 429–38, 465–6. He notes the uncontrollable role of fortune or luck (*tyche*). For Aristotle's reference to Theognis, see *Nicomachean Ethics*, 1179b4. For readings of Theognis as an aristocratic poet, rather than as a poet who lived in an aristocracy under political stress, see Campbell (1967).

[34] Theognis, 129–30, 133–42, 315–18.

[35] See Theognis, 43–52 and essays by Cobb-Stevens, Nagy, and Edmunds in Figueira and Nagy (1985).

[36] Theognis, 145–8.

a few. But this was not a judgment about class, favoring the wealthy over the demos; it was an illustration of *arete* as a critical standard that was unlikely to be met by many – whether rich or poor. It belonged more to discourse, *logos*, than to any group of partisans in a *polis* who actually shaped its practices in *ergon*. Indeed, *arete* acquired its contested character because various social groups regularly asserted that their power, their practical prerogatives, their *erga*, necessarily expressed *arete* – when only the gods (creatures, after all, of *logos* rather than *ergon*) reliably achieved their intentions.[37] Nonetheless, when living in aristocratic societies, poets often praised those actions that were most likely to benefit their society, and such activities – like bravery in battle – were typically associated with aristocratic behavior, as the *demos* did not fight in land battles. This feature appeared in the work of Tyrtaeus, an Athenian who became a Spartan.[38] But by the sixth century, this trait was no longer obviously aristocratic, for military combat was mostly conducted by individuals fighting as part of a *"phalanx"* of similarly situated soldiers. This social formation evoked social praise for what has been called a relatively "strong" notion of equality that fostered democratic ethics.[39]

Arete had a *political* dimension from its outset, of an unusual sort.[40] For Homer, Hesiod, Solon, and Theognis, *arete* evaluated practices of social life, and criticized or praised special human achievements that pertained to ethical standards for the whole society. Understanding "virtue" as a feature of an exemplary social practice that its agent was supposed to but might not manifest – because of misfortune, injustice, limited power, or the gods – associated it with the contingent success of social activity in their communities. Simply because powerful social and political action emanated from the upper classes, *arete* was associated with them – for good or ill – but it was not theirs alone to exemplify or fail to manifest. Power and ethics constituted early conceptions of *arete*. In turn, it affirmed a common good, signified a performative activity that had a noteworthy social purpose, and was supposed to be but might not be successfully realized by its agent. In this regard, the Greek notion of *arete* depended on histocrical and material conditions as well as discursive traditions. *Arete* denoted a contestable assertion about the appropriate relationship between *logos* and *ergon* in human action. It signaled a political ideal that political actors and poetic observers sought to claim as their own.

[37] Theognis, 133–42.
[38] Tyrtaeus, Fr. 10, 11.
[39] See Morris (1996).
[40] See Finkelberg (1998).

2.3   The Political and Democratic Challenge to *Arete*

After Solon's attempt to establish a political constitution that encompassed and accommodated both rich and poor citizens under law rather than domineering rule, oligarchs rebelled against these restraints. Later, the Peisistratids unconstitutionally took power in the city, ruling as tyrants for three generations. Their political program did not always support aristocrats at the expense of the *demos*, for they used the new stature of the *polis* as a key to their power – the effect of which at times empowered the *demos* as well as the wealthy. Nonetheless, their rule became so oppressive by the end of the sixth century that a reputable Athenian clan, the Alcmaeonids led by Kleisthenes, rose up and threw off their yoke. In so doing, Kleisthenes sought to prevent other rich families and the power of wealth more generally from dominating the Athenian *polis*. He restructured the makeup of Athenian tribes in a way that limited the ability of any one tribe to create a power base of its own, transformed *demes* – previously understood simply as rural districts – into residential homes and places of political registration for all Athenians, and replaced the Solonian Council of 400, which favored the rich, into a Council of 500 citizens drawn by sortition from all of Athens.[41] These radical changes simultaneously empowered the *polis* in relation to traditionally dominant social groups and made the Athenian *polis* the world's first democracy. The Athenian *politeia*, which became a relatively stable political order in full flower during the fifth and fourth centuries, was known to be democratic. "The political" and "the democratic" displayed an elective affinity, anticipating the first literary references to *demokratia* and *politeia* in the mid–late fifth century.[42] In addition, democracy came to be regarded as a catalyst of community (*koinonia*), because it put citizens on an equal footing, and continued to be regarded as such throughout the classical era.[43]

What led the Athenians to choose democracy as their preferred political order over and over again until the mid-fifth century? And what did they think they were choosing? These questions have been asked and

---

[41] Herodotus, *Histories*, V.72–8; Aristotle, *The Athenian Constitution*, xx–xxii. On the Kleisthenic revolution, see Leveque and Vidal-Naquet (1992 (1964)).

[42] See Herodotus, VI.43, 9.34; Thucydides, VI.104. *Politeia* initially connoted the exercise of citizenship, a quintessentially democratic activity that was outlawed or severely limited in non-democratic societies.

[43] See Aristotle's statement in the *Politics*, which associated the main features of a democratic *politeia* with political vitality (VII.8: 1228a35–36). For an aged but valuable and brief account of the rise of Athenian democracy, which does not regard it as the *telos* of the *polis*, see Forrest (1966).

answered but not from the perspective provided here.[44] It is undeniable that Kleisthenes, from the Alcmaeonid clan, assumed power with the help of the *demos* and expelled the Spartans and Spartan sympathizers (Kleomenes and Isagoras) who had tried to fill the power vacuum left by the end of Peisistratid rule in 511.[45] Following upon the previous rule of disliked tyrants, he nonetheless was something of a *tyrannos* as well, for the Solonian constitution that the previous tyrants had disregarded lay in abeyance – and an unconstitutional political leader was not necessarily deemed irrational or anti-democratic at the time.[46] But he did not want the government to revolve around him; instead, he wanted to democratize the bases of political power. He presided over the redivision of the Athenian *polis* into ten tribes – not four – and *demes*, made up of *trittyes* (sections) from the coast, highlands, and mountains. This generated a genealogically mixed population for every *deme*, thereby diminishing the power of particular families. From these *demes* and sections, individuals were chosen by lot to serve in a new Council of 500. The Assembly allowed all citizens to attend, but how powerful it was in the early post-Kleisthenic era is hard to know. It clearly became more powerful during the Persian Wars. While the aristocratic general Miltiades led the Athenians in their fight with Spartans against the Persians, winning the battle of Marathon in 490, the *demos*, aided by Aristides and Themistocles, pushed to shift power in their direction, ostracizing friends of the previous tyrants. Themistocles was particularly notable, as he was responsible for sanctioning the major military decisions after Marathon – including the decision to build the navy and to ask the Athenians to abandon their homes for Salamis in 479–480 as a strategic maneuver against the Persian invaders (so successful that it ended the Persian Wars).[47] In addition, as the oarsmen of the Athenian navy were property-less, ordinary citizens, the stature of the *demos* naturally grew after Salamis, enabling it to make a political claim for more power and *arete*, having provided extraordinary help to Athens, without the armor that property-owning hoplites used to fight.

After the end of the Persian Wars, the Assembly continued to follow the advice of Themistocles not to reduce their army and return to normal, as the Spartans chose to do, but to build walls that both protected the Athenians and gave the Spartans reason to worry that the Athenians

---

[44] See Forrest (1966), Meier (1990 (1980)), and Raaflaub et al. (2005).
[45] *The Athenian Constitution* (Aristotelian), XX–XXI (see Ober 1996 (1993), 32–52).
[46] Andrewes (1956).
[47] *The Athenian Constitution*, XXII.

were no longer unquestioned allies.[48] It also was during this time that the Athenians began to acquire a slew of tribute-paying allies that formed the Delian League and Athenian Empire.[49] When the Treasury of the Delian League moved to Athens in 454, after twenty-three years on Delos, and the Athenians tried many citizens of subject city-states in Athens, not only Sparta but also Athenian allies had reason to worry about its growing power. Pericles seemed to have promoted this move, and he had been able to push aside the other major contender for political power at the time, the oligarchic sympathizer Cimon. With Pericles' ally Ephialtes, the democratic faction gained power after the ostracism of Cimon. Pericles consolidated his rule in the 450s, after the decision in 462 to remove aristocratic privileges in the makeup and conduct of the Areopagus (the highest court in Athens, which held the power and authority to adjudicate homicide charges, even as it was still composed only of ex-archons who belonged to the city's highest classes). (This event surely influenced Aeschylus' tragic trilogy, the *Oresteia*, produced in 458.) In 451, Pericles changed the laws of citizenship, limiting that honor only to individuals with two Athenian parents.

In the wake of Kleisthenes' reforms, the power of the *demos* steadily grew – initially as a result of its newfound political agency and later in the growing power of the Assembly and the diminished power of the Areopagus. In addition, the strength of the Assembly in relation to the Council was still uncertain, and this provided room for a democratic deficit in the politics of the Athenians.[50] The Athenian democracy now became associated with the word *demokratia*, coined for the first time (as far as we know) by Herodotus in his *Histories*, probably read aloud and composed and published, we think, between 450 and 430.[51] A political order had become associated with the power of the

---

[48] Thucydides, I.90–93.

[49] The emergence of the Athenian empire was overdetermined by: overpopulation; the desire to maintain military strength against another Persian attack; the need to protect trade routes that facilitated the transportation of grain to Athenians; chauvinism and anti-Spartan sentiments, etc. (see Finley, 1978). For a general view of the impact of the Athenian empire on its subject states, based on the view that Thucydides was overly critical (owing to the personal harm to which he was subjected by Cleon), see Ste. Croix (1953/4).

[50] See Raaflaub et al. (2005) and Ste. Croix (2004).

[51] VI.43. This usage, however, did not refer to Athens but to a hypothetical suggestion by Otanes of a possible, new political direction for Persia and the institution of democracy in Ionian cities. Herodotus's *Histories* are well-known in the history of democratic thought for offering the first general characterization of democracy as a form of political rule (III.80, 82 – without using the word *demokratia* but rather "equality before the law" (*isonomia*) – in contrast to oligarchy and monarchy (III.83). For a date of publication, see Cartledge (2013).

demos, even as all known as demotic surely did not think alike. Athens, with this new democracy, became known as the land of political freedom and free speech, while ostracism was used to exile individuals who were seen as threats to political stability, and the *demos* became known as the ascendant political group in the city. Although the *demos* comprised the many and *arete* was typically associated with rare excellence, the *demos* could claim political credit for themselves, if not *arete*, because they had fortified the city – in their naval service, unswerving loyalty, and political acumen in approving leaders who formed policies that staved off the Persians and the Spartans. This also made possible the growth of the Athenian empire. But while there may have been an elective affinity between the growing power of the Athenian *demos* and the growth of the Athenian empire, the *demos* was not solely responsible for its acquisition – the benefits of which spread throughout the *polis* and stemmed from an astute attention to the power vacuum left by the Spartans' conservatism more than any specifically demotic motivation.[52] These conditions did not apply to other, lesser, *poleis* that became democracies in the fifth century and, perhaps, earlier.[53]

This claim would have been disputed by some aristocratic Athenians, but there had been a slow but steady democratic transformation of the Athenian *polis*. About this development, the following can be confidently stated. First, it reflected acts of power – which, *per se*, were not acts of *arête*. Second, the aim of the Athenian democrats' exercise of power was in particular to challenge and restrain unjustified, domineering power by either tyrannical cliques or numerically small classes of wealthy and powerful citizens. They succeeded where Solon's constitutional reforms had failed. In this respect, democratic power was the key to enhancing political power, which derived its unique authority from regulating the affairs of all classes and diminishing the disproportionate power of the upper classes. Third, the power of the *demos* was, from our perspective, relatively unusual, because its challenge to the aristocratic purchase on *arete* was more the work of a class than the work of individuals. The proletariat that Marx dreamed of as a coherent, political force that would overthrow the egoistic bourgeoisie had its symbolic incarnation in the Athenian *demos*. Of course, it was a symbolic and exclusive synecdoche – certainly not the vanguard of humanity. Many members of the *demos* owned

---

[52] For the potential of *arete* to refer to "the many," see the Aristotelian *Athenian Constitution*, XXXVI.2. Also see the discussion of Protagoras' speech in Plato's *Protagoras*. For the interactions between the political empowerment of the Athenian *demos* and the growth of the Athenian empire, see Raaflaub (1998, 1994, 323–50).

[53] See Robinson (1997, 2011).

property – though not much and not necessarily; many owned slaves, and the *demos* did not include the women who raised them and cared for their homes. Moreover, Pericles urged and achieved passage of a law in 451–450 that conferred citizenship only to Athenians who could prove (via the citizenship rolls) two Athenian parents.[54] But the *demos* was a class that gained status in Athens as a group, a group that achieved this status through its individual participation in the official and unofficial politics of the city. The *demos* did not acquire its power or authority *because* of the political subordination of women and slaves. No political movement in Athens at the time promoted women's rights or the emancipation of slaves – although the unequal and unfair treatment of both groups was clearly recognized in publicly performed tragedies and comedies. The only slave revolt of the era occurred when the Helots rebelled against their Spartan masters.

When the *demos* acted like a group (not a "crowd") that was potentially threatened by aristocrats (or oligarchs) in the wings, it could be regarded as "the many" in relation to "the few." Because this was a purely practical distinction, the ability of the *demos* to claim *arete* for themselves could be easily challenged. After all, the *arete* of the *demos* stemmed not from their being small farmers, slave owners, craftsmen, or laborers; it came from their being active citizens, from being political. But to identify their economic station and its immediate translation into political power as the source of democratic *arete* depends on a mistaken view of *arete* – one to which the *demos* as much as aristocrats or oligarchs might be susceptible – namely, claiming *arete* as a natural product of practical agency. To be sure, the practical agency of the *demos* as a *political* entity arguably brought *arete* to the Athenian *polis* – at least relative to monarchical or oligarchic societies – and dignity to the *demos*. But the distinctive *arete* of the *demos* stemmed from its role in empowering all full citizens with the capacity to participate politically in shaping the life of the city. It was the quality of the Athenian citizens as political actors, their collective ability to practice politics as a *techne* that constituted the *logos* of their *arete*.[55] How they acted politically in *ergon*, however, was not necessarily virtuous.

---

[54] For clarification of the motives for this law, see Patterson (1981) and de Ste. Croix (2004, 233–53). As the Athenians' power in the Greek world grew, they restricted citizenship – contrary to the Romans, who extended (and diluted) the privileges of citizenship as they enlarged their empire.

[55] That is, according to the Corinthians in their speech urging the Spartans to take up arms against the activist Athenians and Pericles in his Funeral Oration, where he sought to meld that *techne* of politics and the power (*dunamis*) of Athens with a vision of collective *arete*. See Thucydides, I.71; II.37.1; II.40.4; II.41.

As the Athenian *demos* and its leaders became infatuated with their *polis*'s imperial power, greater wealth, and more extensive domination of other Greek *poleis*, it became the leader in *ergon*. But whether or not that success in *ergon* also demonstrated success in the *logos* of *arete* became dubious – such that Pericles, at least in his speeches recorded by Thucydides, had to remind citizens not only that he exemplified *arete* but so did their domestic and international way of life – especially once it began to suffer losses in a war for which he was partly responsible. This was understandable, for, after all, the practical character of the Athenian democracy mandated that they believe that demotic politics and leadership automatically manifested political *arete* and political *techne*. These were distinctive virtues and arts that could only be sustained in a politically active democracy. Yet the practical success of democratic Athens as an empire (tragically or ironically) undermined its political capacity to exhibit *arete* – not because the *demos* had become corrupt but because of its susceptibility to mistaking its political *arete* and political *techne* as facts of their political agency rather than as a critical *logos* that potentially complemented their *ergon*. This limitation became painfully clear as it was unable to manage the responsibilities of both democratic life and imperial power during the war against the Peloponnesians. One might say that the Athenians' self-understanding before and during the Peloponnesian War as a *polis* that *automatically* embodied and expressed *arete* lay behind their most misguided political and military judgments. Indeed, the tortured outcomes of that war, including two oligarchic coups and the loss of its empire at war's end in 404, produced the greatest challenge to the political *arete* and *techne* of Athenian democracy.[56]

The uniquely great Thucydides, who combined the historian's concern for understanding what actually happened and the theorist's concern with its significance, indicated in his account of the Peloponnesian War where such gaps existed in the conduct of Athenian democracy. His commentary was constituted by but critical of extant political understandings, illustrating much of what later became known as political theory.[57] In his account of the war, well-known to Plato though never referenced by him, Thucydides recognized the major constituents of power – capital (or resources), technology (or naval skills), and social concord (i.e., the ability to accept difference and act effectively without producing *stasis*) – and how only the intelligent, ethical achievement of all of these would enable

---

[56] The classic location for the interconnection of *arete, politike techne,* and democratic practice occurs in Plato's recreation of Protagoras' bond to the Athenian democratic *ethos*. (Protagoras was an adviser of Pericles'.) See Plato, *Protagoras*, 319a–328c.

[57] See Balot (2017). Also see Raaflaub (2013) and Hawthorn (2012, 212–28).

a political order to fend off the slings and arrows of external enemies, internal foes, and the unpredictability of human life. The Athenians could not manage this task, such that their power and legacy of *arete* at the beginning of the war did not enable them to win the war.[58] Despite their relatively rapid recovery and relatively generous amnesty, well-noted by their critics, the defeat led to a generation of democratic and political self-criticism among the Athenians – notably Socrates and Plato.

2.4 *Demokratia* and *Arete* as Complements in Athenian Critical Discourse

The Athenians lost the Peloponnesian War, but that was not a foregone conclusion. At the beginning of the war, toward the end of Pericles' political ascendancy (444–429), the Athenians seemed able to manage both democracy and empire – the fruits of which they used for public buildings on the Acropolis and grain for their citizens. Not surprisingly, therefore, their innovative political order of *demokratia* apparently was seen as a beacon of ethical and political excellence, which Pericles eulogized, according to Thucydides' account, in his funeral oration at the outset of the Athenians' war with the Peloponnesians. In that speech, he lauded the *arete* of both the Athenians as a citizenry and their good judgment in selecting capable leaders (such as himself). Since the citizen's activities in fifth-century, democratic Athens entailed significant, authoritative, practical politics, *arete* could be deployed to describe political *and* democratic activities. *Arete* could be seen as an individual or group's "natural" trait, a matter of *phusis*, which an individual or group possessed as long as it acted freely, but also a matter of *nomos*, enabling it to be acquired or lost or diminished by experience, law, or policy. Whether or not an individual truly warranted the epithet could be subject to dispute, but it was understood nonetheless – at least by Thucydides – to harbor ethical and political significance.[59] After the war had begun, the tragedian Euripides in his *Suppliants* still found reason to characterize democracy as a model of virtuous self-governance where domination was minimal. Indeed, the association of their own political freedom with imperial rule linked Athenian conceptions of freedom with a dynamic conception of power. Freedom was freedom to act politically (for good or ill) – a notion

---

[58] At least according to Thucydides' Pericles: I.141–144; II.36.1; II.37.1; II.40.4.
[59] Note his references to Nicias and Antiphon, as well as Pericles, as men of *arete*. See Thucydides, VII.86.5; VIII.68.1.

that does not fit within the contemporary frames of negative, positive, and republican freedom.[60]

Figuring out the precise relationship among these constituents of virtue particularly interested fifth-century sophists – the first professional educators (whose dependence on Athenian largesse cautioned them against challenging Athenian cultural norms) and philosophical citizens who freely devoted their lives to educating the citizens of Athens according to a new form of *logos*. For the sophist Protagoras (c. 490–420 BCE), an adviser to Pericles and co-founder of the Greek colony of Thurii in the 440s) – at least according to Plato – *arete* required practice (*melete*) and teaching (*didakton*), as well as a suitable nature (*phusis*), in the kind of proportions that (as Theognis suggested) suggested only *tyche* (chance, fate, luck) could insure.[61] This was the Protagoras known for the maxim, "Man is the measure of all done things [*pragmata*] – of things that are, that they are; of things that are not, that they are not." The ambiguous dimension of this statement – justifying, on the one hand, "man's" ability to identify critically standards of evaluation for all human affairs but, on the other, allowing the power of extant human judgments to determine epistemic or moral standards – reflected the ambiguous ethical climate of democratic Athens, where Protagoras made most of his money.

The other effort to conceptualize a complementarity between *demokratia* and *arete* (apart from their asserted, gestural, complementary relationship in various plays) appears famously in Plato's *Protagoras*, where Plato imagines a conversation between Socrates and the famous Sophist about his ability to reliably teach political *techne*, political *arete*, or *arete* itself to citizens. While the subject of the teachability of *arete* also occupies Socrates in Plato's *Meno* (in which Plato referred to Theognis' poetry, as noted above), *Protagoras* more fully engages the relationship between *arete* and Athenian democracy. In that dialogue, staged just prior to the outbreak of the Peloponnesian War (but probably written in the late 390s or early 380s, forty years later), Plato has Protagoras present a justification for the democratic practices of Athenian politics as distinctive, sensible, and valuable that also would justify the need for his services as a teacher of the political art, political virtue, and, indeed, virtue itself, able to make men into good and practically influential citizens. Protagoras takes as his point of departure Socrates' observation that Athenians in the Assembly defer to experts but when it comes to matters

---

[60] See the discussion of Euripides and other democratic sympathizers in fifth-century Athens by Raaflaub (1989).

[61] See Protagoras, D-K. 3, and Plato's theoretically analytical, relatively late dialogue, *Theaetetus*, 152a; cf. 152b, 171e–172b.

of general, public concern, defer to no-one and believe that everyone has something meaningful to contribute – if they don't, they are chastised as moral and political misfits, not just criticized for lacking knowledge. What role might there be for a teacher of political *techne*, political *arete*, or *arete* itself in this context? Protagoras' response initially invokes a mythic account of a distinctive genealogy of political *techne* and its association with justice. Unlike other *technai*, which are distributed severally, so that only a few can practice each one, the political *techne* was sent by Zeus via Hermes to all, with the expectation, on the one hand, that all would have it but, on the other, that if anyone did not practice it he could be banished or killed. Thus, the Athenian *demos* as a whole possessed the political art and political virtue, at least to a moderate degree, leaving Protagoras as a Sophist to perfect their understanding and practice in his teachings.

Drawing on more common observations, Protagoras notes how educational matters for citizenship are not cultivated like ordinary *technai* but acquired osmotically in the relationships of citizens between one another – presumably in official political locales, as well as in the agora or elsewhere. Inevitably, however, they also require supplementation by sophistic education (positively) or official punishment (negatively). How are we to understand this supplementary activity provided by Sophists such as Protagoras? How does it relate to democratic norms, sustained by the many? At the same time, how does it reflect recognition and transmission of virtue, an achievement typically reserved for only a few – not the many?

Under the control of Plato, at least, Protagoras has no good answer to these and other probing questions Socrates puts to him, but he might have kept himself from being cornered – just as Theognis conceivably might have – if he hadn't been directed by Plato. That said, Socrates' questions were good ones – not only those that concerned the relationship between the virtues and virtue as a whole but also those that sought a practicable basis for the virtue Protagoras presumed to teach (which dealt with the relationship between pleasure, the *demos*, and *arete*). Protagoras' success as a teacher depended on phenomena over which he had no epistemic or ethical control – such as the fundamental political interests and concerns of citizens, not to mention the severity of the problems they faced as a collectivity. Theognis (or Machiavelli) would have referred to these as the stuff of *tyche*, but we know that *tyche* typically refers simply to the limits of our knowledge and human nature – neither of which are sensibly determined in an *a priori* fashion (unless one wants to rely on religious doctrine). And Plato's Socrates in the *Gorgias*, a dialogue staged after the Peloponnesian War had begun, suggests that any teaching of Protagoras to paying pupils would fail – given the structural predicament in which they had been put by the previously accepted policies of Athenian generals. As a combination of power and ethics, *arete* can be achieved only if both are properly shaped – if the structure of power is conducive to the acquisition of virtue and if the proper educational tools are used to develop it (a Theognidean perspective).

As we have seen in its historically earlier iterations, *arete* involved two dimensions – power and ethics. The power-dimension of *arete* most directly stemmed from how it could be demonstrated by an individual, species, or collectivity to effect change in the world, as in the case of a capacity (*dunamis*) or skill (*techne*); its ethical dimension derived from the extent to which it warranted qualitative judgments of excellence.[62] The exercise of *arete* did not preclude the *experience* of political power or personal pleasure, but these could not be its rationale or *telos*. As a result, a democratic exercise of *arete* could be associated with the good life for the individual and the *polis* in the Athenians' democratic *politeia*; it could be discursively interwoven by political leaders such as Pericles, Sophists such as Protagoras, and political theorists or philosophers, such as Plato and Aristotle. But this complementarity was fragile and unstable: understanding one's political power as an exhibition of *arete* could lead to overreaching by leaders and citizens. Yet the dissolution of the bonds between demotic life, politics, and *arete* also generated misplaced ambitions for theory.

To recapitulate: the ancient Greek concept of *arete* combined practical, ethical, and political dimensions; in relation to democracy, it uniquely included the quality of excellence, an activity typically demonstrated by the few rather than the many but now also putatively achieved by the many for the political community as a whole. This political dimension of *arete* was always contestable in democratic Athens. The complementarity of *arete* and *demokratia* was theoretically and practically conceivable – through the power of a politically interested and active *demos* guided by the *logos* of (political) *arete*. But this political manifestation of *arete* in democracy would be a particularly volatile phenomenon, since no special material or ethical status – such as that of a king, honored aristocrat, or wealthy oligarch who could be regarded as extraordinary rather than ordinary – accrued to the *demos* of a democracy, unless the democracy

---

[62] Contemporary theorists who like to draw on Aristotle for a conception of agent-centered "virtue-ethics" to argue against rule-governed Kantian or utilitarian ethics are often analytically astute. However, they distort the history of philosophy because they downplay the political and power dimensions of ancient Greek virtue. For a sampling of this genre, see Frank et al. (1988), Paul et al. (1988), and Balot (2009).

arrogantly asserted that it exhibited virtue and power through the mere exercise of freedom and equality.

2.5   *Arete* as a Challenge to *Demokratia*

When Athenian democracy was operating as a relatively stable political order in the fifth century, even oligarchic critics granted a kind of skill to its exercise of political power. When they did so – that is, when "Pseudo-Xenophon" or "the Old Oligarch" did so – they nonetheless were unwilling to ascribe *arete* to its conduct. This writer employed an ideological treatment of *arete*, ascribing *arete* to a feature of the activities of the oligarchic elite – "the hoplites, the high-born, and the useful" – while noting that the *demos* cared more about freedom in its political discussions than it did about displays of, e.g., *arete*, *sophia*, political insight or the potential effects of their absence, i.e., bad government.[63] In other words, the aristocratic elite displayed *faux-arete* in relation to the implicit *arete* of the *demos*. The "Old Oligarch" was impressed by the ability of the *demos* to protect its interests in a rational way and its concomitant ability to forestall corruption in Athenian political life.[64] Moreover, he noted and applauded the contributions of the Athenian oarsmen to Athenian power and overall political success, and he also found in them unusual displays of political courage, as well as an interest in public life that effectively empowered the *polis*. Unlike the wealthier, they – again anticipating Marx – had little to lose but their chains.[65] This ideological use of *arete* did not seriously challenge the merits of the *demos* as the ascendant power in their political order. The *demos* had *kratos*, and they used it sensibly to protect their interests. While the Old Oligarch surely preferred rule by the few, he had no reason to suggest they would do better. The fact that the Old Oligarch's commentary on the Constitution of the Athenians would have left no scrapes on the Athenian *demos'* claim to deserve their political prominence came from his inability to demonstrate any political matter in which the *demos'* lack of gentility or higher education worsened their political judgment.

The most significant initial use of virtue as a tool for challenging the virtue of democracy and the *demos* came from Socrates, an Athenian citizen who had no partisan affiliations, invented the vocation of philosophical–political gadfly, and at times was their ally. The seriousness of Socrates' challenge to the politics of the *demos* and the merits

---

[63] See Xenophon the Orator, in *The Constitution of the Athenians*, I.2; cf. I.4, 8–9, II.19.
[64] Ps-Xenophon, *The Constitution of the Athenians*, II.19–20.
[65] Ps-Xenophon, *The Constitution of the Athenians*, II.14–16.

of democracy stemmed from how he moved back and forth between challenging the *demos* because of their inadequate political work and criticizing their potential as a primary agent of the Athenian constitution – relatively reliable evidence for which comes from Plato's *Apology of Socrates*, in which Plato molds Socrates' defense at his trial into his own philosophical language. In Socrates' argument with Meletus, the accuser seemingly responsible for the charge that Socrates corrupted Athenian youth, depriving them of *arete*, he employed the well-known analogy of the horse-trainer who uniquely had the *techne* to train horses. Socrates had previously led Meletus to say that virtually all Athenians – Assemblymen, Councilmembers, Jurors, poets and playwrights, as well as the general public – enhanced the virtue of the citizens by their vocations; that is, *all* – or "the many" – were teachers of virtue. But in the analogy of horse-training, only the few horse-trainers could properly train the horses. In the context of the preceding discussion, this suggests not only that few could be skilled in *arete* – as Theognis claimed – but also that the many who were charged with the task of enabling the *polis* to achieve *arete* were unable to do so.

Plato's Socrates did not argue this point explicitly, but it appeared implicitly in the context of his argument. This was not surprising. After all, the Athenian jurors had been asked to affix practical content to the legal idea of the virtue of piety, and Socrates was charged with lacking what he needed – not only did he lack the virtue of piety but he positively deprived the young of virtue by corrupting them. *Arete* was being contested in court, and political rhetoric and prejudice as well as argument and clear thinking would decide the outcome. But, again, Socrates had not cited personal practices that would have endeared him to a democratic jury of a politically participatory constitution. He condemned out of hand the discourse of the Assembly and Jury as inclined to attend to emotional, illogical appeals, rather than the voice of reason – and referred to that as a justification for his absence from conventional politics. If he had made it a common practice of his own, he would have had either to compromise his virtue or to lose his life. Since he also claimed to have dedicated his life to *arete* by speaking to his fellow citizens or others one by one, he implicitly opposed his pursuit of *arete* with the political and democratic institutions of Athenian society. Even when he agreed to accept his duty to serve on the Council, he found himself in the minority – arguing vainly for a legally correct position that Athenians ignored but later, too late for the victims of their rash judgment, wished they had adopted. By asserting (if he actually did) that one should not listen to "the many" if one was to think ethically and knowledgeably on his own behalf, Socrates conflated the phenomena of specialized *technai* and *aretai* with general, human, and political *technai* and *aretai*. He employed the critical standard of *arete* as *logos* to challenge democratic practice. Overall, he testified that *arete* and the workings of Athenian democracy were mostly incompatible.

This was not to say that they were wholly incompatible either, of course. The life he led as a philosophical–political gadfly was only possible in Athens, and his refusal to accept an offer to escape his death penalty on the basis of his devotion to the Athenian way of life – especially its opportunities for free political speech and procedurally protected legal defenses – made Athens the only *polis* with the only (and democratic) *politeia* that he would tolerate. Nonetheless, by not specifically endorsing its democratic politics, he broke the connection between his *arete* and democratic practice. Socratic *arete* could now be imagined to be compatible with, to be fulfilled by, other constitutions. Indeed, *arete* itself now tended to be associated more with character traits than social practices, even though the Greek tradition recognized the practical prerequisites for *arete*. The use of *arete* as a basis for political criticism became practically more dubious; instead, it became an idea and ideal that naturally would seem to be accessible to and achievable by the few rather than the many. Because "the many" were typically associated in the public mind with demotic action, the effect was to undercut the ethical complements to and supports for democracy. The matter was not (as used to be thought) the elite's withdrawal from Athenian democracy, paralleling a supposed decline in Athenian culture.[66] The Athenian *politeia* worked well in the fourth century. Its new payment of citizens to attend the Assembly, along with its new restrictions on the immediate political power of decisions by the Assembly, arguably improved the operation of Athenian institutions. But the door had been opened for the naturalization of the *logos* of *arete*, so that it became again, as it had been contingently in pre-democratic times, associated with the *ergon* of aristocratic activity.

Although not intentionally, it would seem that Aristophanes' interest in lampooning the pretentious and powerful, from Cleon to the *demos* as a whole, fostered stereotypical and unpalatable visions of the *demos*, in which they were collapsed into single characters – who acted monolithically – and chastised for having tyrannical tendencies. Previously, the Corinthians had referred to prewar Athens as a *polis tyrannos*; after the war had begun, Athenian leaders referred to the burden of the empire as a *tyrannos*, but after Cleon's sabotage of a peace treaty with the Spartans in 424, the *demos* itself, the major power in a war-torn city

[66] This is an underlying theme of Jaeger (1939–45).

became caricatured as a *tyrannos*.[67] In the following year, he similarly caricatured Socrates in the *Clouds*, which surely did Socrates no good. In any case, such one-dimensional portraits of the *demos* and Socrates, funny as they may have been, surely performed reductive functions in social discourse. After all, even Plato acknowledged the diversity of democracy. The *demos*, along with its leaders and intellectual critics, had begun to seem feckless, even as the war had not been lost. Once the war had been lost, the Thirty wreaked havoc for nine months, the Athenians struggled back to expel the oligarchic hegemony of the Spartans, and Socrates had been found guilty and condemned to death by a majority of a jury of 501 peers, the political order could well have seemed ragged, in need of more repairs than could be produced by reforming and republishing its laws. According to the *Seventh Letter*, this was the case for Plato, who initially did not know where to turn.[68]

For Plato, the only sure alternative was an aristocracy, a purely theoretical construct (in the *Republic*, *contra* the "natural" aristocracy promoted by Callicles in the *Gorgias*), even as he believed in the necessary connection between *arete* and a *politike techne*, initially associated with democratic politics, and *arete* as a potential feature of virtually anyone's character or soul. In the *Gorgias*, Plato's Socrates ultimately dealt with the problematic connection between power and ethics in Athenian life by allowing the relatively apolitical Socrates to assert that he alone could practice the political *techne*. The only way this could be true was if the political context in which that art was effectively recognized was no longer that of democratic Athens – indeed, not that of any existing political regime. In the *Republic*, Plato's Socrates could "refute" Thrasymachus' Callicles-like argument, which made power the determinant of virtue (rather than, *pace* Callicles, the virtue of the willful, domineering individual), only by imagining a theoretical world in which each would be given his or her due. In this theoretical world, *arete* did not exercise any coercive force; indeed, its omnipresence dissolved the need for power as domination.[69] But in that world where soul and state seemed to complement one another, the balance was as fragile as the relationship between

---

[67] Thucydides, I.122.3, 124.3; II.63.2; III.37.2; Aristophanes, *Knights*, 1111–20, 1329–30 (see Kallet 2002; cf. Mhire and Frost 2014).
[68] Plato, *Seventh Letter*, 324b–325c. As the letter seems plausibly consistent with Plato's dialogues and external evidence about Plato's life, whether or not Plato was the actual author does not crucially affect readings of biographical features of the letter.
[69] This is a hallmark of *kallipolis* – at least as a counterpoint to extant society – in Plato's *Republic*. See, e.g., the end of Socrates' discussion with Thrasymachus in Plato, *Republic* I, the agreement between rulers and ruled in Book IV; the non coercive turning of citizens toward philosophy in the cave allegory in Bk. VII, etc.

democracy and *arete* in fifth-century Athens. It only could survive by its leaders knowing how to tell lies without living them, promoting cooperative virtue among the citizen-underlings, and allowing sex for themselves only at mathematically prescribed times.

Plato's Socrates sought to answer Thrasymachus by demonstrating how justice and virtue could be aligned in a proper constitutional order of the soul (*psyche*) and state (*polis*). One could accept its rationality but only because of its rhetorical force. Plato's Socrates in the *Republic* severed whatever connection the historical Socrates' life maintained between virtue and democracy when the former asserted in Book VIII of the *Republic* that a stylized democracy of injustice knew nothing of virtue and practically paid it no attention – tolerating philosophical contemplation but knowing nothing about how its freedom and equality could sustain political virtue. This radically ahistorical vision of the core features of democracy indicated that its citizens had no disposition toward political participation, the appreciation of which had been necessary for the functioning of Athenian democracy. Indeed, Plato's Socrates inverts the historical *arete* of democracy as an anti-tyrannical force when he associates a democratic regime with the absence of critical control, providing fertile soil for making demagogic leadership persuasive and allowing tyranny to emerge.[70] In Plato's later political works, namely, the *Statesman* and *Laws* – which presuppose the *Republic* as the ideal critical standard – democracy gets better play but never as a complement to *arete*.[71]

Aristotle transformed the Platonic tension between democracy and *arete* by providing metaphysical grounds and empirical judgments for separating *arete* and *demokratia*. Despite Aristotle's claim that connected an ethic of citizenship to human nature and provisionally endorsed the practical value of democratic deliberation, his theoretical perspective not only froze the opposition between *arete* and democracy; it also fused and degraded

---

[70] As Athenian playwrights had noted, the collapse of democratic discourse into unanimous acclamation makes the *demos* act tyrannically. But, again, this is a warning about democracy becoming dysfunctional – not a statement about the norms of Athenian democracy.

[71] The stylized character of Plato's rendition of democracy in Book VIII of the *Republic* is too often ignored. For Plato has deliberately stripped democracy of those social traditions and extra-political mores that, at least in Athens, had been crucial to making democracy possible. The connection between democracy and the political was so fraught in Athenian society and for Plato, that he only was able to disentangle them in critical discourse by grounding the latter in hypothetical philosophy and denying the former any practicable historical context (see Wallach 2001). Christopher Bobonich makes heroic efforts to show the change of Plato's philosophical and political views between the *Republic* and his later political dialogues – at the expense of minimizing the significance of the different problems Plato addresses in these dialogues on the claims that appear in them (see Bobonich 2002).

their relationship. Democratic principles are compromised if they defer to the authority of *arete*, and *arete* loses its deserved political power when it is fully adapted to the framework of a democratic political order. Although dependent on social and political practices for cultivation, *arete* became more firmly rooted in unchangeable nature and its associated social and practical hierarchies – which allowed Aristotle's political theory to be more readily appropriated by conservative political theorists, not something he necessarily would have wanted. The Aristotelian opposition between *demokratia* and *arete* generated a conceptual trope regarding their relationship that lasted for nearly 2,000 years – until Montesquieu theoretically united them in mid-eighteenth-century France and, soon after, American and French political theorists and practitioners found means to link them under the banner of republicanism and mechanisms of political representation.[72] The question for us is how Aristotle opposed *demokratia* and *arete* while offering critical sources for their accommodation – foreclosing their previous (unstable) complementarity in sophistic thought and democratic practice, and naturalizing the theoretical tension found in Plato's dialogues. How Aristotle's political thought produces these seemingly contradictory perspectives on the relationship between *demokratia* and *arete* deserves careful consideration, not only because of his penetrating, critical observations of political life but also because of the recent interest in Aristotelian political theory as a foundation for theorizing democratic potential and human rights.

The conventional reading of Aristotle casts him as a philosophical conservative who critically assesses extant traditions, overlaying them with a view of nature and purpose that allow one to be skeptical of both the ethical authority of Kantian rationality and the political authority of the status quo.[73] More recently, the pendulum has swung in the opposite direction, viewing Aristotle as a democratic critic of conventional practices. My historicist reading does not take sides in this debate but rather cuts against the grain of recent readings of Aristotle that use Aristotelian political thought as a critical foundation for theorizing democratic potential today.[74] Recent interpreters of Aristotle find within his

---

[72] How this was done will be indicated in Chapter 3.

[73] For a radically conservative reading of Aristotle, see Strauss (1964); for a more traditional, conservative reading, see MacIntyre (1981).

[74] Recent political philosophers and theorists have downplayed Aristotle's conservatism with great scholarly acumen and to good use, but efforts to find within Aristotle's thought a productive endorsement of democracy or complementarity between *demokratia* and *arete* have been managed by either ignoring core features of Aristotle's thought or selectively viewing it. See, e.g., the various works of Habermas, Nussbaum, Ober, and Frank cited in the bibliography.

political theory sources for an accommodation of democracy and virtue or a new global ethic for human rights.

Jill Frank, a political theorist and interpreter of classical texts, finds in Aristotle's conception of *arete* a potentially smooth fit with democracy.[75] Josiah Ober, an intellectual historian of ancient Greece and democratic theorist, finds in Aristotle's conception of democracy a deeper source for democratic ethics than typically provided in the discourse of rights. He sees a notion of virtuous politics embedded *within* Aristotle's conception of democracy.[76] From their different perspectives, each locates in Aristotle's notion of capacity a source for contemporary theorizing about democracy and human equality. Frank and Ober join Martha Nussbaum, who turned to Aristotle to replace (in varying ways and to varying degrees) the liberal, protectionist discourse of rights with a discourse of development more amenable to the political issues of non-Western societies.[77] But all three underestimate the manner in which Aristotle's political theory elides conflicts about the practical extent and political potential within the Athenian *polis* and its democracy. Moreover, as we have seen, his political theory transcends those conflicts only by limiting the opportunities for complementing democracy and *arete*. This silence about how Aristotle's political thought dampens deep-seated political conflict can be heard in the work of Ober and Frank, who have invoked him as an anchor for innovative democratic theory. Both, like Nussbaum, do not fully address the radical opposition in Aristotle's political theory between *demokratia* and *arete*. What Plato identified as a radical tension in theory and practice Aristotle established as a conceptual, categorical difference that also elided or rhetorically reduced the significance of various ethical and political conflicts.

The gap in philosophical outlook between Plato and Aristotle was enormous (although neither was a dizzy idealist or hard-nosed realist). Whether this gap was produced by their different historical and biographical backgrounds, political psychologies, or the latter's need to develop a unique philosophical identity, Aristotle took pains to distance himself from Plato – rooting his political theory in "observation," in what he "saw," rather than in (*pace* Plato) what he theoretically and logically established as a counterweight to perceived injustices of convention. These factors made possible a harsh, if not simplistic and misleading, account of Plato's ethical and political thought; Aristotle found no substance in Plato's conception of the good (in the *Nicomachean Ethics*) and offered literally mistaken readings (in the *Politics*) of Platonic

---

[75] See Frank (2005, esp. 1–16, 38–53).
[76] See Ober (1989, 1998, 2005, 2007, 2008).
[77] See Wallach (1992).

discussions of the community of property in the *Republic*.[78] But Aristotle's own subtle and often persuasive arguments deserve attention in their own right – especially because of their dynamic understanding of the relationship between ethics and power. These become clear if we, first, recall his formal conception of (ethical) *arete*; note its role in his conceptualization of the political realm in general and citizenship in particular; and, finally, explain how he deploys this political conception when accounting for the nature and operation of democracy.

Aristotle explicitly and famously defines "ethical" *arete* – the notion of *arete* that pertains to practical notions of right and wrong (rather than purely intellectual *aretai*) – in Book II of the *Nicomachean Ethics*. He engages in definition in ways abjured by Platonic dialogue. (For example, an *ergon*, for Plato, always connects to a *logos*, whereas Aristotle detaches each from the other.[79]) Ethical *arete* has six features, having and expressing all of which is extremely demanding. It is (1) a disposition (*hexis*); (2) involving rational choice (*prohairesis*); (3) oriented toward a mean (*ho meson*); (4) a mean relative to "us"; (5) in accord with a rational principle (*logos*); (6) as discerned by a man of practical wisdom (*ho phronimos* – who quintessentially embodies intellectual virtue).[80] As such, ethical *arete* – hereafter *arete simpliciter* (because it is used exclusively in the *Politics*) – is a formal characteristic that has an indeterminate relationship to democracy; its political embodiment is not here set, but a gap between *demokratia* and *arete* emerges in his subsequent account of the political realm in Book I of the *Politics*.

At the very beginning of Book I, Aristotle tells us that "we see" (*horomen*) that the *polis* is the highest, natural association, guided by a *telos*. It is self-sufficient and the most highly developed association, one that enables human beings to develop their fullest potential as political animals intended to associate with each other, in part as equals, endowed with the capacity for speech and judgment about ethical and political phenomena.[81] A *polis* enables human beings to develop their distinctive *arete* and establish a mutually dependent relationship between "political" and "ethical" life. *Arete* is natural to human beings, but it is developed to varying degrees by each sort, depending on their physical endowments, conventional circumstances for its cultivation, and an individual's own choices.[82] The highest version of that *arete* is the statesman's art of political deliberation. Yet his

---

[78] Aristotle, *Nicomachean Ethics*, I.5–6; *Politics*, II.1–5.

[79] Cf. Angier (2012, 2016).

[80] *NE*, II.6: 1106b36–1107a2.

[81] *Pol.*, I.1, *passim* (e.g., 1252b32–1253a10).

[82] See *Pol.*, I, *passim* and the implicit choices offered by his commentary about and advice for the stabilization of political regimes in Bk. VI.

possession and exercise of *arete* does not guarantee happiness. Indeed, good statesmen may be unhappy and ultimately unsuccessful, because fulfilling their *arete* depends on contingent circumstances and external goods whose presence often depends on fate and chance (*tyche*).[83] (In fact, its conventional expression can be abused as an instrument for becoming wealthy – which recalls Glaucon and Adeimantus's concerns in Book II of Plato's *Republic*.[84]) Nonetheless, *arete* marks the best exemplar of human, social practice. It is achieved only through the best practices (*technai*), and providing it with adequate power in the *polis* assures its minimal justice.[85]

Still, *what arete* practically comprises remains undefined – except negatively, in relation to imperfections in the natural world and its complementary social structure. But Aristotle does substantially define nature (*phusis*). It exhibits an inherently hierarchical dimension that relates ruling and ruled in associational, harmonious relationships. Thus, various social conditions and characteristics – such as mastery, slavery, gendered relationships, economic roles, and potentialities for intellectual or educational development – are defined as natural.[86] Major ethical virtues (such as self-control or moderation – *sophrosune*) that have singular definitions are nonetheless expressed differently by individuals in different roles, to different degrees. Altogether, these manifest hierarchical relationships of ruling and being ruled – fixing the rotational relationship of ruling and being ruled that (according to Aristotle) crucially informs the practice of citizenship and the political operation of democracy.[87] Aristotle's conception of nature in society enables him to stipulate the exclusion of most human beings in a *polis* – women, "slaves," craftsmen (*demiourgoi*), manual laborers (*banausoi*), children – from the political realm. They do not deserve to be full citizens, and not all citizens deserve to be rulers. For they must have the *arete* of *phronesis*, an intellectual virtue available only to a few whose exercise is most important for promoting the best possible conditions of ethical and political life.[88]

The fact that Aristotle accepts the aforementioned hierarchies as "natural" is, he admits, contestable – and justifiably so. Some slaves are mistakenly regarded as such; they are slaves by convention, not nature. Presumably the same mistake could apply to judgments about

---

[83] It is in their common recognition of the role of *tyche* in political life, arguably more than a common "republicanism," that links Aristotle and Machiavelli.

[84] *Pol.*, 1258a13–15.

[85] *Pol.*, 1258b37–40.

[86] *Pol.*, I.1: 1253a35–40, 1254a31–32; I.12–13, *passim*; III.4: 1277a35–1277b7, 20–5.

[87] *Pol.*, I.2–5: 1252b32–1253a10, 1253a35–40, 1254a31–32.

[88] *NE*, VI. 1144a7–31; *Pol.*, III.5.

women – although he doesn't suggest that. Nor does Aristotle entertain the possibility of class mobility – between rich and poor or workers and "freemen." He identifies the cause for disagreements about, or unhappiness with, the social status of individuals as results of some mistakenly believing that which *truly* exists stems from *bia*, "power-as-force," rather than *arete* and *dikaiosune*. Following this mistaken view enables them to debunk practical and ethical norms of society (much as Thrasymachus argued in Book I of the *Republic*.)[89] Aristotle wants the reader to believe in the power of *arete*, not *bia*, but each one, he says, has some truth.[90] That "truth" allows Aristotle to infuse the relatively blank, conceptual category of *arete* with relatively conservative political dimensions.

This aspect of his political thought clearly emerges in Books III and IV, where he defines and discusses citizenship in relation to political or constitutional orders – ultimately and explicitly contrasting "*demokratia*" and "*arete*."[91] One basis for the opposition is the tension between the *arete* of "the good man" and that of "the good citizen." Aristotle notes that there is a special *arete* to every *techne* performed by various citizens. These possess varying degrees of value, but in a single *politeia* each must also demonstrate an *arete* of membership that facilitates political community.[92] Ideally, the good man is a good citizen, for the exercise of *arete* and practical politics cohere via *phronesis*, but they practically manifest a distinct tension, caused by the relative injustice of every extant constitution and the hierarchically differentiated roles of individuals and citizens.[93] Because the *arete* of the good citizen depends on the political order (*politeia*) in which he lives and since Aristotle, like Plato, finds all extant regimes faulty, there always will be a tension between the *arete* of the good man and the good citizen. But Aristotle also associates *arete* with a discrete identity and practical role *within* existing, unjust, political orders. After all, *arete* is socially as well as individually determined; it derives its features from the political and sociological "whole" of which its performance forms a "part."[94] This makes his conceptualization of *arete* as a political term inherently problematic.

Arete in a *polis* may illustrate that innocuous term, civic virtue. But since few are fully capable of performing it, the social and political dependence of *arete* creates an underside to Aristotle's views of the relationship between ruler and ruled as naturally harmonious, exhibiting

---

[89] *Pol.*, 1309b22–24.
[90] *Pol.*, I.5: 1255a14–24.
[91] *Pol.*, IV.7: 1293b17–18.
[92] *Pol.*, IV.4: 1291b2–8.
[93] *Pol.*, III.4, *passim*; 1277b26.
[94] *Pol.*, I.13: 1260a31–36, 1260b9–21; III.9: 1280b5–6, 1281a3–8; cf. V.9: 1309b10–14.

a just and proportional relationship. Since that relationship is defined hierarchically, Aristotle's most virtuous man of practical wisdom or civic virtue "naturally" facilitates a good and better relationship – even in an unjust society. Given Aristotle's deference to the power and structure of conventional practices and beliefs, the *arete* of the good, Aristotelian citizen acquires a fundamentally conservative, if not reactionary, role as he seeks to establish or reestablish proportionality in the unjust societies that typify organized life on earth. He may have the right to rebel and use violence for the sake of *arete*, but one might wonder how he chooses his political direction and comrades-in-arms.[95] This will be tricky, unless the man is perfect, for even virtuous human beings are prone to error, and who is to say that the politics of the man of virtue adheres to the genuine *logos* of virtue and promotes the common good, rather than promotes his own power and damages the political community?

Like Plato, Aristotle names the political order that fully honors *arete* an "aristocracy," a union of power and virtue that enables "the best" to rule. But he gives this term substantive content that evinces extant, social relations. Aristotle's aristocracy builds upon the material pillars of good birth and wealth. Moreover, a superlative man of *arete* should act as a king, and a superlative society of men of *arete* should be ruled as a kingship.[96] In theory, discourse, or *logos*, virtue exhibits practical perfection. As such, virtue should be able to exercise power without inhibition. Indeed, it is non coercive, and produces no conflict. But, unlike Plato, Aristotle relies upon, rather than reconstructs, the practical elements that enable *arete* to do its good work. Aristotle surely recognizes the conflict and unjust inequality that inheres in every practical, political society governed by a powerful class not steered by virtue, but he does not acknowledge how the politics of Aristotelian virtue produces no regrettable political conflict, even as the changes would produce new distributions of power.[97] This failure to recognize the potentially harmful and self-serving practical side of the *logos* of virtue rightly generates skepticism about the extent to which an "aristocracy" is the best society or a society that favors the power and authority of those who have inherited lofty positions in a hierarchical society. This is particularly odd, given that Aristotle follows upon the Greek tradition that defines *arete* as a human achievement, attained only with hard work and easily lost.

---

[95] *Pol.*, V.1: 1301a40; V.2, 7, 9.

[96] *Pol.*, III.17: 1288a8–20; IV.2: 1289a30–33; IV.11.

[97] This is not to say that Aristotle did not recognize the existence of political conflict. On the contrary, his analyses of *stasis* in Book V of the *Politics* remain some of the most trenchant in the history of Western political theory – well-recognized by Yack (1993).

Despite the blank, classless, non-ideological definition Aristotle gives to *arete*, it practically takes on the features of a radically hierarchical exercise of power that supposedly lacks any coercive force. In this regard, Aristotle regards "law" like virtue: although the latter is better than the former, the imperfect nature of man sanctions "law" as a rule of reason.[98] While Aristotle is not an ideologue who conflates power and virtue or, more particularly, presupposes the expression of *arete* by those who are rich or well-born, the critical conception of *arete* he articulates in the *Nicomachean Ethics* categorically possesses anti-democratic features in the *Politics*. This interpretive outcome reflects the practical, empirical roots of Aristotle's political theory, relative to Plato's, as well as his diminished belief in the transformative power of a philosophically informed politics; it reflects the different historical constellation of his time and his different personal investment in Athenian politics (at least, relative to Plato's). These factors enable Aristotle's works to exhibit both critical distance and practical plausibility, compared to Plato's. For example, his analysis of the sources of political conflict notes tellingly the politically troublesome character of oligarchies, relative to democracies, because the latter favor middle-class moderation.[99]

Aristotle's political theory sanctions apodictic oppositions between democracy and *arete* that have undermined democracy and conservatized the discourse of virtue for millennia. Still, one may wonder, how does the politics of Aristotelian *arete* work to the particular disadvantage of a democratic political order? The answer is less evident than it might seem, given Aristotle's attribution of natural hierarchies to the entirety of the society. The activity of citizenship is shared equally by all full members of the political community; as such, it theoretically most fully develops in a democracy because it has the greatest scope of political activities available to all citizens.[100] Moreover, what about the oft-lauded sections of Book III, Chapter 11, the source for what has been anachronistically called "the doctrine of the wisdom of the multitude"?[101]

This chapter offers three justifications for the practical value of having more citizens of lesser virtue contribute to political deliberations and decision-making than fewer citizens of greater virtue. One cites to the improved character of a pot-luck meal over one contrived by a single

[98] *Pol.*, III.16: 1287a17–b8.
[99] *Pol.*, IV.1: 1289a5–7; IV.3: 1290a8–11. IV.11; IV.12; V.1; VII.14: 1333b27–29.
[100] *Pol.*, III.1: 1277a26–28, 1277b13–16; III.7: 1279a9–10, 33–b3; III.13: 1283a38–40, 1283b39–1284a3; VII.8:1328a34–36, 1328b31–32.
[101] See Waldron (1995). Cf. Lane (2013) and Bobonich (2015).

great chef; the second notes the greater value of the judgment of one who uses an instrument over that of one who makes it – analogizing the "user" to political institutions receiving advice from experts or statesmen consulting (but not obeying) citizens; a third endorses the virtue of collective, democratic institutions (Assembly, Council, and Courts), which perform admirably even as their members display uneven skill and virtue.[102]

While these passages seem to endorse democratic practice, Aristotle's perceptions of human capacity, as previously noted, exclude most human beings from formal, political life. Most lack the capacity for fully developed *arete*. One might excuse Aristotle for being a "child of his time" who reflects commonly held social judgments through his political language, but his observations do not allow for structural change. That phenomenon results from the natural and empirical grounding for his teleological perspective. None of the excluded groups can change their nature (although they may be more or less virtuous – unlike members of the classes in Plato's *kallipolis*, whose nature emerges over time). Aristotelian virtue tends to perfect what is, not what ought to be.[103]

As mentioned previously, Aristotle notes that the only specific political activity that unites the *arete* of the good man and good citizen is that of being a good ruler – a man who exhibits simultaneously the ethical and political virtue of practical wisdom. Democracies do not promote rule by a man of practical wisdom. The practice of virtue ultimately involves justice (*dikaiosune*), and justice appears as proportionate and hierarchical rather than arithmetical – equality. This places the virtue of justice and justice as a virtue in tension with democracy, which more fully respects numerical or arithmetic equality.[104] Indeed, a democracy moderated by no other political phenomenon easily becomes tyrannically monarchical – although, as in Book VIII of Plato's *Republic*, this consolidation of power of the many into one results from the machinations of demagogues.[105] For Aristotle, democracy – like any practical, political form – condenses power on behalf of a group that does not immediately promote the common good. As such, it, like other political forms (as in Plato's *Republic*), operates in tension with virtue – which by definition promotes the common good.

---

[102] *Pol.*, III.11: (1) 1281a42–1281b9; (2) 1282a17–23; (3) 1282a25–1282a41.
[103] Hegel knew what he was doing by finding inspiration in Aristotle for his view that "the real is rational, and the rational is real." G. W. F. Hegel, *The Philosophy of Right*, Preface.
[104] *Pol.*, IV.12; V.1.
[105] Plato, *Republic*, VIII.564a, 565d–566d; Aristotle, *Pol.*, IV.4: 1292a10–20.

Aristotle's perspectives bolster a categorical opposition between democracy and *arete*, and they gain substance from his view that democracy as a political order lacks an ethical compass. A democracy favors liberty and equality, and while these together promote self-government, neither (as such) recognizes *arete*.[106] Here, Aristotle follows Plato's Socrates in Book VIII of the *Republic*, but the context is more realistic. As a result, all democratic forms Aristotle empirically identifies reflect serious ethical and political imperfection, and the degree of imperfection increases if a democracy is left to its own devices – it can readily become monarchical and tyrannical or despotic.[107] Conversely, the democracy tends more toward political virtue to the extent that the *demos* have less direct influence over the exercise of political power.[108] Aristotle's practical dynamic of power and ethics freezes the potential for changing major practical relationships and individual life-chances within his hierarchical view of the natural world. Fixed, natural hierarchies endow his political theory with teleological coherence, but they constrain the power he gives individuals or the *demos* to actualize their potential.

In his work on *politike*, Aristotle acknowledged the virtue of the political structure of democratic Athens but found its substantive use by ordinary citizens fundamentally flawed. How he arrived at this view involved not only his understanding of the naturally political nature of man, but his apodictic views of the naturally hierarchical character of all associations that are not strictly political. To be sure, no democracy functions in a fully free and egalitarian social environment. Nonetheless, Aristotle's natural hierarchies reduce flexibility in our views of unofficial political relationships and tend to buttress conventional authority. Whether these judgments stemmed from the dominant ethical atmosphere of his time, his effort to criticize Plato in a naturalist direction, his prejudices, or some combination of all three cannot be easily determined. But the judgment of practical wisdom must inform the good practice of *politike*, and Aristotle surely believed that it informed his own views of the best, practicable, and commonly practiced political phenomena. Yet the manner in which he identified and sought to reconcile the egalitarian and inegalitarian features of life in a *polis* balanced perception and criticism in ways that more often than not led him to advocate political change in non-democratic directions. If we disagree with his

---

[106] *Pol.*, IV.4: 1291b32–38; IV.8; V.1, V.9: 1310a28–34; VI.2: 1317a40–b17, 1317b38–1318a10.

[107] *Pol.*, IV.2: 1292a8–20.

[108] Correlatively, *arete* finds greater practical recognition in aristocracies than democracies, and the former are more likely to favor the rich and well-born, even though they do not directly reflect their power. *Pol.*, IV.8: 1283b21, 1294a10.

understanding of desirable political change, then we also must take note of their sources in his more fundamental perspectives on human beings, social life, and politics.

Aristotle's greatest contribution was to validate the practice of politics as an ethical practice, one which formally was actualized in the practice of shared, political deliberation. That defined the public contours of his unity of power and virtue. But how he understood the relationship between his perceptions of natural capacity and politics, and their relationship to democracy, remains a puzzle as much as an inspiration. Aristotle was both a critic and apologist for the extant distribution of power and virtue. He united these vocations in *politike*, the practice of which diffused conflicts between power and virtue. But his confidence in the process by which that power might be diffused was overdrawn. We need to be clearer than Athenian democrats and philosophers were about the challenges to defining and overcoming the sources of injustice in the distribution and exercise of power and virtue – especially if we would do so on behalf of a contemporary democratic society. But for us, engaging these challenges clears away substantial brush.

2.6   *Demokratia* and *Arete*: On the Road to Separation

Although the ethical standard of *arete* was continually opposed as an exemplar or ideal for politics – and hence extra-political – we have seen how it always reflected political relations that informed its usage in critical discourse. In the pre-democratic, if not pre-political archaic societies of ancient Greece, *arete* featured paradigmatic norms that often seemed simply to represent conventional behavior. More often than not, we found that *arete* also served as a basis for politically criticizing such behavior. It was not an inherently class- or gender-based, authoritarian, or elitist term of linguistic or sociological art. And when Athens became a democracy, *arete* was employed to enhance the ethical aura of the art of active citizenship. This demonstrated the contingency of any fixed conceptual opposition between *demokratia* and *arete*. But the intensely public and discursive life of democratic Athens also created the means by which thinkers could artfully criticize faults in the exercise of power from the standpoint of justice without appreciating the potentially coercive nature of *arete* as a political practice.

Regarding the conventional political order of classical Athens as democratic led Socrates and Plato to identify inherent tensions or, in the case of Aristotle, categorical oppositions between *demokratia* and *arete*. In every case, *arete* assumed a political but not obviously ideological or authoritarian cast – even though the work of Greek philosophers could be used for such purposes if slanted, particularly outside the Athenians' democratic *polis*. Problems resulted more from how to use *arete* politically than from a particular concept or practice – for example, whether it was an exclusive possession of aristocrats or aristocratic activities such as horse-riding (the *demos* did not own horses) or could be associated with demotic activities (such as naval or political practices in democratic institutions). This instability existed prior to the fourth century, but it became more dangerous once the relationship between discourse and practice became embedded in theoretical frameworks that could be mapped over, if not against, extant democratic practices. This emphasizes the extent to which the meaning of *arete* conjoins *logos* and *ergon*, but is not reducible to any particular linkage between them. As that dynamic paradigmatically informs a democratic political order that honors the continual involvement of citizens deliberating and deciding their collective fate, the conceptualization and practice of both *demokratia* and *arete* are not only highly contingent but potentially complementary.

This was particularly the case during the emergence of monotheistic conceptions of "virtue," which presumed to hover above the practical life of citizens. In the cases of Judaism, Christianity, and Islam, the original intent of the religion was expansive and relatively inclusive. But that changed in each case, for different reasons and causes. And when it did, religious understandings of virtue assumed a more authoritarian cast that lacked any close connection with democracy. When Machiavelli articulated his conception of political *virtu*, he did so in reaction to the prevailing Christian conception of virtue rather than the ancient Greek understanding that was connected to democracy. Moreover, when Hobbes developed his notion of virtue that could be compatible with the state, he did so in opposition to the scholastic–Aristotelian and Christian meanings that defined virtue in his time.

When democracy was reconstructed to fit the needs of liberal republics of the United States, France, and the United Kingdom in the late eighteenth and nineteenth centuries, the promise of *arete* was filtered through monotheistic and religious conceptual lenses – transposed onto elected representatives, the promise of life in civil society, with a legitimate nation-state and visions of human rights offering new frameworks for its realization. But in each case, the relationship between democratic practice as a political reality and the horizon of goodness became particularly vexed, partly because practical perspectives clouded our appreciation of political virtue and goodness as active combinations of ethics and power, *logos* and *ergon*. This has led some recent political theorists critical of "reason" as an independent authority to criticize the political significance of notions of virtue or goodness in politics, regarding them as inherently anti-democratic. But this is because "virtue" was read through the moralistic lenses of monotheisms and parallel conceptions of rationalism rather than activist conceptions of reason, ethics, politics, and power, that marked ancient Greek life.[109] Even Aristotle recognized that unity in a *politeia* was not a matter of complete agreement but a relative harmony of political thought (*homonoia*), needed to maintain concord about the use of political power and avoid a society's descent into civil strife.[110] And while Greek religion obviously played an extremely important role in the political life of Athenian democracy – given Socrates' trial and execution for "impiety" – its status, given the absence of a separate, institutionalized religious authority or text for the *polis*, was wholly enmeshed in political ethics.[111]

Despite the ambiguity of the relationship between Athenian democracy and the republics of the early modern era, the representative national states of the nineteenth century, the legitimacy-oriented democracies of the twentieth and twenty-first centuries, not to mention the challenges to finding equivalents to *arete* in the political discourse of later collectivities, this chapter illustrates the beginnings of an evolving historical issue, namely how and why *demokratia* and *arete* – as exemplars of democracy and goodness – should not be understood as separate entities governed by the rules of power or ethics. They rightfully belong to the initial phenomena of democratic politics without exclusively belonging to that or any subsequent political era – such as "ancient" or "modern," "first" or "second" comings.[112]

While the power of religious groups looms large in political campaigns because of strategic convenience, European and American political orders belong to post-theistic eras in which the reigns of God or rationality are suspect, agnostics, atheists, or self-proclaimed pragmatists may invoke politically opaque, secular terms that carry a semi-religious aura (e.g., "difference," "pluralism," "diversity"). But that simply kicks down the road the ball of how a political order ought to act – unless the very idea of a collective political order reasonably and ethically justified has become obsolete, which leaves the field of politics open to domination by actors who regard the public in wholly instrumental terms – as various sorts of "markets" or profitable sheep. Rendering our modern political situation in this light does not make the problem of democracy and goodness in modernity more remediable. There remain major obstacles

---

[109] See Honig (1993). Cf. Rorty (1979).
[110] For Aristotle on *homonoia*, see his *Nicomachean Ethics*, IX.6.
[111] See Sourvinou-Inwood (1990) and Parker (1996).
[112] See Dunn (2005).

to their accommodation because it often seems implausible or obscure. Discourses of virtue in modernity attach to positive evaluations of personal conduct without the ancient social cachet supported by communal ballast and undominated by monotheistic authority. As a (partial) result, modern political theory has typically undervalued democratic politics and its ethical dimension. But this discussion of democracy and virtue in Athenian democracy has shown how contestable phenomena once engaged the promise over the other without radically personalizing the the political elements of character. In the chapters ahead, we shall see how different iterations of goodness engaged different kinds of democracy.

3 Representation as a Political Virtue and the Formation of Liberal Democracy

Nothing appears more surprising to those, who consider human affairs with a philosophical eye, than the easiness with which the many are governed by the few; and the implicit submission, with which men resign their own sentiments and passions to those of their rulers.

David Hume, "Of the First Principles of Government" (1741)[1]

3.1 Introduction

Hume's observation resonates loudly today in political orders that are called democracies. For "we" live in constitutionally authorized *representative* democracies, in which selected and elected public officials make the laws for the people.[2] That modern societies call themselves democratic is an artifact of linguistic convenience and political ideology. It also has led to serious political confusion. First, it is not as if there *ever* has been a large, developed, urban society where the *demos*, understood as the entire population of adult citizens, has been in a position to exercise authoritative political power. Even the Athenian *demos* – which exercised political sway in a mostly agrarian, relatively small-scale, but culturally advanced society – excluded more than half the adult population (women, slaves, metics). Second, American and European citizens in the twenty-first century's second decade are very unhappy with the legislative process and their representatives, with the former manifesting distrust of what emerges from the halls of Congress and the presidency and the latter evidencing distrust of the economy and politics of the European Union. Demotic interests typically receive short shrift, when they are supposed to be steering the ship. At the same time, the practical reason required of political judgment is foreign to most citizens. The problem is

---

[1] David Hume, *Political Essays*, in Knud Haakonssen, ed. (Cambridge: Cambridge University Press, 1994), Essay Three, 16.

[2] Unlike the subsequent sentence in Hume's essay, which says that "FORCE" is on the side of the many, one might better say that, today, *force* is on the side of the state, militarized security personnel, and large banks and corporations.

not merely the formal one of collective action, because the discontent has grown in recent times. The matter is not only the substantive power of the wealthy few to shape political campaigns designed to obtain support from the rest. Most believe that elections operate in ways that disproportionately favor the wealthy, but Americans also do not believe that stricter campaign finance controls will fully fix the problem.[3] The problems of democracy cannot be fixed as one might a refrigerator or faucet. Our crisis stems partly from not fully comprehending the uneasy alliance today between representation and democracy.[4] Democracy's feet do not fit comfortably into the shoes of representation.

The ambiguous meaning of "representation," along with its shadowy substitution of the authority of the many to rule by the few, makes much room for shenanigans. First, "representation" means both a transmission belt of political desires from both the top down *and* the bottom up. Second, its historical emergence complemented the political establishment of individual rights – with the latter being a good thing, as a protection against tyranny but an uncertainty as an agent of the public good.[5] Third, given the reduction of citizens' voices to legislative votes and the secretive nature of the lobbying that occurs after the votes have been cast, the character of the correspondence between the Representer and the Represented is just as opaque as the meaning of the "natural" right and virtue of individuals to judge persons and policies of their political order.[6] Finally, representation *can* improve democracy. Because representatives stand at a distance from a *demos* whose action inevitably dominates and excludes, their position allows them to look out for imperfections in the exercise of demotic power and to protect the citizenry against mobs and

---

[3] See Lessig (2011, 151–9, 166–70) and Karlan (2014, 144, 236, n. 10).

[4] For a recent account, which puts representation and democracy at loggerheads, see Pitkin (2004, 335–42). For an historical and analytical account that relates formal structures of representative government and democracy, see Manin (1997, 236–8). For a more recent, analytical, and less historical interrogation of the relationship of representation and democracy, see Shapiro (2009) – especially Ferejohn and Rosenbluth. For historical accounts of the corruption of democracy through campaign laws and the official conduct of representatives, see Issacharoff (2011, 119–34) and Teachout (2014).

[5] On how the assertion of rights by individuals makes negotiations for coordinated political action very difficult, see Dunn (1988, 21–38).

[6] Compare Bentham's view of the nonsensical meaning of rights and, in particular, natural rights, to those expressed in the 1791 Declaration of the Rights of Man and Citizen sanctioned by the new French Republic. Bentham (2002, 330). Bentham also was loathe to use the term "representative" to refer to legislators; instead, he referred to them as "deputies." Constituents in a modern democracy, for Bentham, were encouraged to express their own political views to their deputies, but deputies had no formal obligation to listen to them – which meant a kind of democratized Hobbesian view of representation (see Bentham 1983, IV.A2 (26); V.2.A3/note (30), VI.1.A6 (43)).

gangs. In this case, modern political representatives ironically may play a Socratic role, representing the unconventional or downtrodden.

From this perspective of democracy, representation can help or hurt democracy, even if representation cannot be democratic since it cannot replicate the *demos*. But the phenomenon of representation reflects an emotional roller-coaster – great hopes during an election campaign; great disappointment from the work of governments in office. This problem stems in part from the fact that representative government and the *demos* potentially operate at cross-purposes.[7] The office of a representative results from elections, which elevate a set of political rulers above the ruled in order to make the laws. In office, they make compromises to get legislative business done. Representatives may feel proud of what they accomplished, because they made the decisions that led to the compromise. But citizens can't take pride in legislative work, and they mostly suffer the consequences required by the compromise. That doesn't mean representatives always will be scorned; as mentioned above, their office enables them to undertake political initiatives not viable during an election campaign or to protect minorities whose needs may have been neglected. That said, the necessary activity of legislative compromise takes place above the heads and behind the backs of the people. As such, it contradicts the Athenian and Aristotelian understanding of democracies as political orders that depend on the deliberative and decisive power of citizens (i.e., the *demos*) acting with authoritative power. Citizens of the Athenian democracy were said to rule and be ruled in turn, but in every case their power required the political presence and deliberative action of citizens.[8]

Political "representation" nonetheless is the vehicle that enabled the reintroduction of "democracy" into the modern, practical political vernacular. The resulting liberal democracy does not directly descend from the ancient Athenian democracy. Between these eras virtually nothing existed that approached "democracy" as an actual or named political form, and when it again became a focus of politics and theory, it was wedded to representation – so that what we call a democracy is, in fact, a distinctive kind of democracy, a "representative democracy." While elections and popular pressure surely have political impact, the actions of representatives are the primary, official mechanism for translating democratic citizenship into political power. We rely on the representative

---

[7] See Manin (1997), 1 and *passim*. Manin's articulation of "principles" of representative government is insightful but limited as an account of the relationship between representation and democracy in political reality.

[8] Aristotle, *Politics*, III.1, 4; VI.2.

process to promote political goodness in a democratic society. But when one imagines the idea of "representation" these days, its association with ethics or goodness does not spring to mind. It's an impersonal process, after, all – a mechanical method by which one entity stands for or re-presents another, politically required by the need to channel the judgments of millions of citizens into the legally authoritative hands of a small number of public officials, or even the sentiments of thousands into the leadership of single persons.

It's not as if the major problems that inform the drama of representative democracy today, therefore, did not exist in Athens. But they clearly emerged later, when representation became the official vehicle for the transposition of the people as an author to the people as an enabler. The major political task in the early modern era was establishing new kinds of government and sanctioning new sources of legitimation. Because representation hypothetically elevated the voices of the people, it could be said to resemble the way in which *arete* had set a hypothetical standard for elevating whatever *arete* to which the Athenian *demos* could lay claim. At a much greater distance and with many more curtains between the acts of the Representatives and the aspirations of the Represented than in a direct democracy, the *activity* of representation – starting with campaigns, continuing through elections, enacted in office – nonetheless was presented (often disingenuously) as a neutral filter, practically and ethically, for the judgments of the citizenry. As such, it offered an office and platform for leaders. Because political representation was the main practical vehicle for expressing public virtue, and despite the potential of representation to collapse dialogue between the Represented and Representers into domination from above or mere empowerment from below, the introduction of representation as a mode of political legitimation practically embodied an ethic of politics, intended to complement democracy with a new kind of goodness.[9]

The political ambivalence of representation did not make it representation a neutral tool. For representation is more than a technical practice of transposing power from the citizenry to their "representatives." Representatives never were intended to receive and enact "mandates" from citizens. The activity of representation is invested with special ethical characteristics that are designed not only to maintain a complementary relationship between the citizenry and public officials

---

[9] Montesquieu directly associated "virtue" with "democracy," referring to the former as the animating principle of the latter. But he defined virtue as "love of country" rather than a political practice; he did not contemplate a democracy for France. See his *The Spirit of the Laws* (1748), Bk. 2, Chs. 1–2; Bk. 3, Ch. 3.

but also *are supposed* – unless the activity is merely an ideological cover for private interests in civil society – to filter and improve the political judgments of the many, potentially expressing a modern kind of political *arete* (for its components depend more on institutional mechanisms than personal achievement). Since democratic citizens are formally regarded as basically virtuous in their political judgments – thus, the jury system – then that quality also should inhere in representatives as well. At one remove from the political authority of democratic citizens, the function of representatives still involves ethics and power. But the relationship is, as previously noted, decidedly unhappy. Some of the reasons are structural as well as political, inherent in the activity of representation itself.

Representation is never entirely a direct reflection of the judgment of citizens – an impossibility in any event, given how representatives are singular while the represented comprise an enormous multitude – and its role as a vehicle of political legitimation requires that representatives, via elections and other communicative means, maintain a respectable connection with citizens. We regularly suspend disbelief in order to count on them being better than ordinary citizens. We do so not because we are sure that elected officials do better than individuals who would be selected by lot but (arguably) because the election bestows an aura of legitimacy that lottery selections cannot claim. Yet we also know that our views will not be transcribed and uniquely channeled with those of others into the mental box of the representative who is supposed to divine the merit of what the Represented think. Representation, initially by candidates for public office and subsequently by electoral winners endowed with political power, is a montage – in fact a selective, unequal interpretation – of the judgment of citizens. But it also is the case that different practices of representation reflect and promote different meanings of "the public" for office-holders, affecting to what extent, and how, the views of the former influence what the latter do in their own official capacities. These differences comprise the range of ethical practices that inflect the power of representation and make various institutional experiments difficult to translate into new representational models.

As the activity of citizenship depends on the ethics and power of citizens, whatever meaning is associated with representation depends on the political condition of its referent, the people or the Represented; every conception of representation depends on a corollary, ethical and practical conception of the people. Political concepts are never self-contained atoms. It is because their meaning depends on their use and uptake, which in turn involves other conceptual referents, that historicism drives our discussion. So when we analyze the meaning of representation for democracy we also presuppose indeterminate but real answers to generic questions about what the people want or need. These days, answers typically appear in the form of polling data that offer fungible answers to questions of who makes up a political collectivity apart from a bundle of individuals. But are data the equivalent of *vox populi*? Once we get beyond a direct democracy, who are the people? How can we really assess their dispositions toward political representation and their representatives? Radical democrats tend to envision a hypothetical *demos* as automatically virtuous. Conservative critics of democracy assume that the *demos* is *not* virtuous, even as they typically believe that actualizing a particular moral and/or epistemological concept or institutional arrangement can make democracy (not the *demos*) as virtuous as it can be. Liberals are skeptical of democratic power and seek its rational control by institutions and meritorious elites.

Our concern is with how democracy was redeployed from its Athenian origins to its role in a modern republican state – that is, how did representation become accepted as a political virtue and practical stand-in for democracy, something that could ally democracy and goodness? Does the initial incarnation of representation as a political virtue in early modern liberal democracies resonate with contemporary complaints about political representation? To answer these questions, we need to understand the historical dynamic that formed representation as a complement of ethics and power. Doing so not only can foster more democratic political campaigns for public office and diminish the pressures that lobbyists place on office-holders but also make representation a political virtue that complements, rather than simply opposes, democracy – a feature of democratic ethics that may connect democracy and goodness.

I address this lacuna by analyzing the historical introduction of representation as the primary synecdoche for demotic activity that would complement ethics and power.[10] By making sense of representation as the principal vehicle for inventing modern, liberal democracy, I clarify the problematic way in which representation emerged as a distinctively new political practice and virtue that might serve as an agent of democracy – that is, a catalyst of active citizenship available to and desired by the many, not just the few – but which typically did not. In so doing we can ask, *what* did representation *do* to democracy – at least to democracy as it was originally understood by the ancient Athenians? *How* did representation at the time of its political inception as a complement

---

[10] Notably, "democracy" was grafted onto "representation" in the early modern era – not the other way around. The practical virtue of representation as a link between the people and their government via some sort of consent emerged in the Middle Ages and preceded any notion of democracy as a semantically legitimate political form.

to republican governments perform the relatively magical act of representing, practically and ethically improving (or not), the political judgment of the *demos*? *To what extent was* it an ingenious adaptation *or* was it political legerdemain? *Can* answers to these questions enable us to understand better and begin to remove the obstacles to current dilemmas of generating democratic representation, when it operates in a politically open society that accepts myriad inequalities as natural facts rather than fungible political constructions?

These are large questions that warrant book-length answers, but the particular historical and theoretical dimensions I have identified can be usefully explained in a book chapter. I shall address them by, first, recalling the introduction of representation as a synecdoche for translating popular authority into political power; second, reviewing the practical and conceptual context that led to the incarnation of representation; third, interpreting principal justifications of representation as a means for enacting public virtue amid the liberal revolutions and their aftermaths, noting how the new liberal ethic sanctioned by Kantians and utilitarians consolidated political rights for some but excluded those of others, requiring a century or more of workers' protests, women's protests, the American Civil War, and another century of struggles by racial, ethnic, and sexual/gender minorities to equalize the rights of citizens; and, finally, analyzing past and present relationships between the ethics and practices of political representation, on the one hand, and, on the other, demotic power and judgment.

3.2 Historical Tributaries of Representation as a Political Virtue

There's no point at this late date to buttress Madison's effort to identify American society as republican rather than democratic. These days, despite the extension of individual civic rights to categories of adults who lacked them – in Athenian democracy, the Roman Republic, Renaissance Florence, and early modern republics – it is difficult to state with a straight face that a contemporary equivalent (insofar as one can say there is one) of the Athenian *demos* wields the levers of political power.[11] Representation presents a practical and ethical filter for how citizens politically matter today, and it effects a qualitative and quantitative reduction in the power of citizens, insofar as (selected and) elected public officials make laws, not citizens. Citizens are at least one step removed

---

[11] See Manin (1997, 8–93).

from the official exercise of political power – even as they endow law-makers with a vague ethical and practical posture for their conduct of politics. But the distance separating contemporary citizens from the practical conduct of political power does not mean that they are powerless or that their ethics do not shape political discourse. The power of citizens is mostly effected via information and slanted views they absorb from media as well as their direct contributions of time and money to public agitation and voting. But the question remains, how did republics governed by representatives come to be called democracies, and what does representation *do* as an ethical practice and form of political power?

"Representation" actually is not a Greek word, and "representative democracy" does not have deep roots in the original democracy of the Athenians. Representation as we understand it did not exist practically or theoretically in the politics and culture of Athenian democracy, for no citizen exercised more power than another except through the lottery and one-year rotations in office. Moreover, the Assembly (supreme legislative body) allotted one and only one vote to every citizen who appeared to listen to and decide upon public policy. Certain politicians exercised extraordinary influence in shaping the opinions of the *demos* – examples include Themistocles, Pericles, Nicias, and Alcibiades. But the power of these politicians (who, in these cases, had been elected to one-year terms as generals) grew from their political skills, wealth, and stature (or, potentially, their *arete*). But it was measured by the degree to which the *demos* accepted their political judgments.[12] They had no more official power than a shy, retiring shoemaker. Moreover, the *demos* checked public officials who served in the name of the *demos*. Their reputation was vetted before they could assume their public position (*dokimasia*), and they were subject to scrutiny for their conduct in office once they stepped down from limited terms of service (*euthuniai*). In addition, a law declared that citizens who proposed decrees or laws that (by majority vote) contravened existing laws would be guilty of a crime (*graphe paranomon*). These filters for the exercise of political power reflected a sense that a power or majorities cannot rule without scrutiny. Apart from

---

[12] Not long after Pericles, who regarded himself as an agent of *arete*, gave his famous funeral oration, he was fined. See Thucydides, II.37 and II.59–65.

the lethargic Spartan regime, the Athenians' democratic *politieia* was the most stable government in ancient Greece.[13]

There is a Greek term that is sometimes (mistakenly) translated as representation: *mimesis*. It's worth noting what is lost in this translation. Representation involved an effort of x to "re-present" y when y was absent. The gerund and noun of representation imply that it can effectively reproduce that which is represented. *Mimesis* did not do that. First, it always involved a faded, second-, or third-best mimicry of that which was represented. Plato's Socrates famously criticized theatrical and pictorial representations in Books III and IX of the *Republic*, because, in their disorganized, uneducated forms practiced in Athens, they failed to produce a virtuous or excellent representation of that real thing to which they referred. Imitators were impostors of one kind or another, that is, if they hadn't been educated in Platonic virtue. Second, the mimetic process was not temporal. There was no delegation from the represented to the representative, no intervening time or space. *Mimesis* was an artistic process that was enjoyed or criticized, depending on whether or not you believed in demotic or philosophical standards of judgment.[14]

Roman institutions, which arose independently of the Greeks', are the more important source for our institutions – with their elections, senators, executives, and the absence of direct political power in the hands of the enfranchised citizenry.[15] Our sense of democracy arises out of the English, American, and French revolutions of the seventeenth and eighteenth centuries that invented what were called republics and now may be understood better as liberal democracies – that is, democracies that rely on the constitutional authorization of individual rights to protect citizens from state power and that operate through designating representatives, through regular elections, to make policies and laws on their behalf. "Democracy" disappeared from political vocabularies until the

---

[13] This "fact" rebuts the critiques of Athens from its conquest by the Macedonians until the nineteenth century (see Roberts 1994).

[14] See Plato, *Republic*, III.392d–398b; IX.597b–603c.

[15] Western political institutions stem from Rome, and Rome developed its own republican institutions along with their preternaturally imperial reach on their own, not by way of imitating the democratic institutions of the Athenians. Roman philosophy tells a different story, with Athenian philosophical academies serving as a proving ground for learning philosophical skills (e.g., for Cicero). On the *sui generis* character of Roman political institutions, see Lintott (1999). For the relative irrelevance of Greek political institutions for Rome, compared to Greek philosophy and culture, see Mousourakis (2003, 39, 119–20, 168–9).

mid-seventeenth and eighteenth centuries in England, the United States, and France, where it hovered on the horizons of their liberal revolutions.[16]

"Democracy" changed from a political descriptor of a particular constellation of power to a metaphor if not myth. This was not only due to acknowledging the practical realities of larger societies but also to changes in the ethical and practical habits of citizens. To be sure, there were democratic tendencies in the Italian city-states and republics, but they were not named as such.[17] Meanwhile, *arete* did not have offspring that shared its public and political valence. As Christianity replaced ancient polytheisms as the source of social legitimation, *virtue* mostly became practically associated with private, not public, life (unless expressed in hortatory political rhetoric). After all, it was supposedly realized in true love, not power and status – even if it was not.[18]

Soon after Christianity had replaced ancient religions as the template for sanctioning social ethics, the (Catholic) Church became notably regarded as the "representative" of God on earth, and "representation" became code for representing the divine to the laity. Representation moved from the top down.

"Representation" stems from the Latin verb, *repraesantare*, literally, "to present again." A present action is reconstructed in the future, by an image or an actor, in practice or simply in the mind. Thus, representation conjures a temporal phenomenon of deferral that creates a gap that is covered by semantics, not an actual bridge. And these semantics only allow contingent participation and power for the *demos*. Machiavelli did not use the term to describe the vexed relationship between the Prince, on the one hand, and the nobles and ordinary citizens, on the other.[19] Only in the seventeenth century did "representation" begin to signify movement from the lower to the higher realms of social and political authority.[20] But whether it transposes the top to the bottom of the hierarchy of power or the bottom to the top, "representation" requires the

---

[16] The word "democracy" still appeared in intellectual treatises, e.g., those of Aquinas, but mostly as part of a series of named political orders derived from Aristotelian categories, the Hebrews, or the Romans – not as a practical, political idea (see Aquinas 2002, 9–13, 54, 136).

[17] See McCormick (2011, 7).

[18] See Francis Hutcheson, *An Inquiry into the Original of Our Ideas of Beauty and Virtue*, revised ed., Wolfgang Leidhold, ed. (Indianapolis: Liberty Fund, 2008 [1726]). Cf. Adam Smith, *The Theory of Moral Sentiments*, Knut Haakonsen, ed. (Cambridge: Cambridge University Press, 2002 [1759–90]), in which Smith tends to discuss "virtue" in isolation from the practicalities of social life – left to *An Inquiry into the Nature and Causes of the Wealth of Nations* (1776–89).

[19] See Skinner (2002 (1972), 13–14).

[20] On these kinds of representation, see Ullmann (1975).

suspension of disbelief. Just as the views of the *demos* or *populus* could not be transmitted without remainder to representatives, so, too, the task of representatives as individuals who in fact re-presented their constituents was impossible. There was no way they could unify the views of their disparate constituents, whether seriously divided or not, without making significant changes in the content of their constituents' views. "Representation" was a creative act, not a mere "re-presentation" of the views of electors. There was a double-lack, in terms of the activity of the *demos* or *populus* and the activity of the representatives, no matter what theory legitimated their particular role. Nonetheless, "representation" connoted the re-presentation of the people – *if* the representatives functioned as fiduciaries of the people.

Nowadays, we understand representation as a kind of interpretation – intended to be faithful to the original even as it occurs subsequently to it (which limits its fidelity). The activity of representation *aims* to be faithful to the original but necessarily cannot duplicate the original. This facilitated the initial, aesthetic understanding of representation and religious art as representation, generating images of an object or entity that was more substantively real.[21] When used during the era of its independently *political* introduction which *related* citizens to "their" representatives, it complemented modern ideas of physical nature and Christian views of the nature of human beings as God's creatures.

The gap created by the temporal dimension of representation reappears in modern ideas of human nature endowed with freedom, reason, and equality associated with liberalism but which, in the Augustinian tradition, has been *corrupted* "after the fall." These conceptions obviated the need to rely on antiquity's secular judgments of virtue, excellence, or goodness. In contrast to "antiquity," "modernity" adopted the standpoint of the individual, from whom relatively *populus*-based regimes relied on their *consent*. But the political need for representation – because of "the fall," population growth, and, of greatest importance, the invention of the Hobbesian state – produced a gap between the Representers and the Represented that could be used to corrupt the Representers, traducing their activities as agents able to promote the public good. Athenians regarded their democracy as worthy because they understood the *kratos* of the *demos* informed by a sufficient modicum of *arete*. Major critics of Athenian democracy, such as Plato and Aristotle, doubted the

---

[21] To be sure, however, aesthetic representations often performed political functions (see Kantorowicz, 1957). For early, aesthetic uses of representation in ordinary language, see the *OED*. For a theoretical account of political representation as an aesthetic, see Ankersmit (2002).

extent to which the *demos* possessed sufficient *arete* to make *demokratia* just. With representation, the problem shifted. The citizenry was not expected to be knowledgeable about politics or able to conduct it virtuously. Instead, it was endowed with a human nature that was ill-suited (Hobbes) or divinely suited (Locke) to make political judgments without political experience. Its judgments were directly or indirectly transferred via consensual legitimation or elections. Indeed, representation is a corollary to the invention of the state via social contract theory. But those judgments applied to less than half of the adult population in the late eighteenth and early nineteenth centuries – given the political exclusion of women, the existence of slavery in the United States, and property qualifications for voting in the United Kingdom and France – not exponentially better than was the case in Athenian democracy.

Because political representation in a fully democratic or practical sense was a myth, political representatives never could be transmission belts for the voices of the people. In the main, they were intended by the advocates of the predominant practices of representation to be *better* than a multitude of politically active citizens. In this respect, the demotic political *arete* of the Athenians was historically transposed to the activities of the *representatives* of the people – not the people themselves. Since this transposition did not include formally or radically exclusive qualifications for the representatives, the assumption was that an impersonal, practical procedure and its practical effects would produce an ethical politics of representatives who would benefit the country as a whole. Via elections, representation presumably enacted judgments potentially lodged in a mute vote that, by virtue of the authority of the representative majority, signified expressly or tacitly the *consent* of the people, entrusting legislatures to act properly on behalf of the citizenry. The resulting deliberations and decisions of elected representatives were intended to manifest political virtue – unless the representatives betrayed the trust of the people.

If not from antiquity, where did "representation" come from as a *political* idea, practice, and virtue, so that it could legitimate the liberal democracies of modernity? The theoretical constructions of the great social contract thinkers – Hobbes, Locke, Hume, Rousseau, Madison, and Kant, supplemented by Montesquieu, the English utilitarians, and others – justified the practical, political ethics of representation. Starting in the seventeenth century and continuing through the mid-nineteenth century, their political language of rights, consent, interest, utility, and happiness – none of which requires political action – became means for legitimating the newfound power of the modern state. It sanctioned individual rights but consigned the practice of democratic power to the margins of political life.[22] Moreover, whatever *demos* was empowered was initially (as mentioned before) a fraction of the population – particularly in Great Britain in the early nineteenth century, where, even after the Reform Bill of 1832, only 6 to 7 percent of adults voted – because of qualifications based on wealth, sex/gender, and the idiosyncrasies of Parliamentary power.[23] While representation was regarded as a practical means for re-presenting Englishmen in colonial legislatures, thus bearing a democratic potential, this changed once the American Constitution took hold and nineteenth-century states began to wield imposing power. In the works of Publius (responding to the Articles of Confederation) and Kant (responding to the French Revolution), representation entailed a corollary (not necessarily absolute) diminution of democratic power.[24] Although this was not true for Bentham, whose conception of representative democracy was simply designed to defang the British aristocracy, it was true later in the nineteenth century in the work of J. S. Mill, who worried that the Reform Act would unduly empower the lower classes, enabling them to become a dominant majority in the House of Commons. A counterpoint to demotic power, electoral representation was supposed to make democracy virtuous, even *better* than it was in antiquity; it provided an institutional means for vetting the virtue of the *demos* without formally elevating the virtue of a few over the power of the many, as Aristotle thought it would.[25] Thus, it marked progress – even as the result of elections obviously elevated representatives to rule over the citizens they served, the few over the many.

The practical, political function of representation came into its own after the Reformation had taken hold in northern Europe and the Treaty of Westphalia (1648) had subordinated religious prerogatives to states. Its practical function stemmed from the need to connect leaders and led, rulers and ruled, in societies that were geographically and numerically much larger than the ancient Greek *polis*. But it also was invoked to serve an ethical function, legitimating the power of the state over the people

---

[22] These theorists differ dramatically about what counts as acceptably democratic in a legitimate political order, but that is not my concern here. However, it is worth noting how the late twentieth-century political philosopher John Rawls regards the practice of political participation as an optional choice, not a constitutive element of articulating his basic principles of justice.

[23] Reid (1989, 52).

[24] Kant regarded the actual exercise of democratic power as "despotic." See Kant, "On the Common Saying: 'This May be True in Theory, but it does not Apply in Practice,'" in Reiss (1991 (1792), 101).

[25] Aristotle saw elections as oligarchic, in *Politics*, IV.9: 1294b 31–33, IV.15: 1300b1–4. The oligarchical character of elections is noted with varying degrees of remorse by Hobbes, Locke, Rousseau, Madison, and Kant (in accord with their different theoretical perspectives).

whom it supposedly represents. This was not an ethical function that interfered with religious ethics; rather, it complemented religious ethics *if* that they sanctioned the dominant forces in the political order. This was a big *if*, for there were many possibilities of conflict or collusion between "church" and "state."

In the thirteenth century, Aquinas redefined Aristotle's definition of the human as political to the human as social; human character was to be uplifted and fulfilled by the Church and its handmaid, the government.[26] But with the Church having been demoted in England to an arm of a nascent State, one was left with the body of a relatively apolitical population or citizenry and the government. Theories emerged articulating criteria for a "legitimate" government that would honor the people.[27] But there no longer was discussion of the citizens themselves ruling, as in antiquity; the issue becomes the obligations rulers have to their people, and how to understand the nature and protection of these obligations through their Representatives, officers of the state.

The meaning of representation in the early modern era as a re-presentation of the absent occurred in new kinds of aesthetics that saw certain paintings as more or less successful attempts to replicate the real – to be "realistic."[28] And its newness eventually became appropriated in the political realm, generating hopes for a new virtue of *political* representation that produced practical interrelations between the represented and the representative – but no attempt at a realistic reproduction of the agency of the former in that of the latter. In addition, in a fascinating linguistic development, the word "vertue" morphed from being exclusively an indication of meritorious ethical character into an approximation of the real *and* a genuine link between Parliament and the people.[29] This occurred at the time in England when kings were sorely interested in reducing the power of the Church, consigning its moral weight primarily to the private realm, leaving the public realm to the sovereign's decisions about the proper use of power. Eventually this theoretical bifurcation of individual ethics to the private realm and its powerful use to constrain practical behavior in the public realm infused social contract theory,

---

[26] Aquinas (2002, 4).
[27] The most widely circulated, radical version of evaluating the relationship between the people and their rulers, offering guidelines for determining when a leader became tyrannical and deserved to be removed from office, see *Vindiciae, Contra Tyrranos*, trans. & ed. (Cambridge: Cambridge University Press, 1994 [1579]). The author used the word "representation" only once, without particular emphasis.
[28] See Franciscus Junius, *The Painting of the Ancients* [1638], in Skinner (2005, 161).
[29] See references to Henry Parker's *Observations upon some of his Majesties late Answers and Expresses*, 1642, 11.

which variously distributed political power between the represented and the representatives, allowing the boundary to shift as a result of politics.

The idea of social contract theory as a new means for empowering the citizenry as an authority that constrained rulers was, initially at least, hardly a strike for democracy. It validated the sovereign's right to rule because of its/his ability to protect citizens as endangered, isolated individuals – not as agents of legitimate political power, as they were in Athenian democracy.[30]

Moreover, unless one believed in the state of nature as a historical reality and the stories of human beings leaving it in order to authorize a state to be actually *true*, the attempt in social contract theory to have rulers legitimate their power and sovereignty by means of the people is *also* little more than a charade, if not hoax – a projection by proponents of new state-forms of the kind of citizens that would legitimate them. In fact, it was *representation* that served as the practical vehicle for validating social contract theory in the late seventeenth and eighteenth centuries, but attention to the representation was outdone by the weight of the terms consent, covenant, and contract – possibly because "the people" and their consent was mostly sought as a device of legitimation, not their representation. As is now common knowledge, "democracy" was a derogatory political term until the late eighteenth and nineteenth century.[31]

Democracy only gained currency in public discourse by the *demos* accepting its *lack* of directly political *kratos* in exchange for its indirect power of the vote, which legitimated the power of their "representatives" to rule over them. But the historical conditions of the time – such as the corruption of aristocratic and imperial rule; the waxing power of secular reason in relation to the declining authority of centralized religious control, and the early era of capitalism as the engine of economic life – made the general public the most plausible and politically relevant basis for legitimating political rule. An increasingly liberal though unpolitical people accepted its voice in the body of representation. This broad historical context provides the practical addressee for the arguments or claims of representation as a complement to democracy at the dawn of modern, constitutional republics. Whether or not it fits the bill is the question.

For there was a sizable gap between the meaning and actuality of representation. To be sure, there were gaps in ancient democracy as well as modern democracy. We have discussed the ancient gaps. And when democracy today is understood by its semantic meaning, as rule by the

---

[30] For the seeds of such theories, see Henry Parker, *Observations* [1642], cited in Skinner (2005, 156–65). Cf. Skinner (2002 (1972), 296–307).

[31] See Hanson (1985) and Roberts (1994).

demos, it is a myth or metaphor that citizens accept and deny or reject. But just as importantly, "representation" was – and is – *also* a myth or metaphor – above and beyond the distortions wrought by the deployment of wealth to manipulate voters' opinions (which are not always blandished as irresponsibly as they are in the United States). It may or may not produce misleading actions by "representatives" in the name of the "*demos*" – or, more literally, the *populus* (even though a *populus* never possessed the political power of the Athenian *demos*).[32]

If this fiduciary responsibility had teeth, it chewed the previous meaning of representation. At least in the Christian adaptation of the Latin, representation meant representing God and the Church *to* and *for* the people, without any inherent respect for popular authority.[33] However slightly, Hobbes's theoretical transposition of the feckless power of individuals to the protective power of the Sovereign included the allotment of natural rights – even if only the Sovereign had the practical authority to protect them. While Hobbes crushed democratic claims to political authority, he established, as he intended to do (see the Preface to *Leviathan*), a secure framework for accommodating the claims of both Regal and Parliamentary power. In this agreement, the ethical justification for political rule lay in the conceptualization of the human nature of the ruled and in lodging the practical entitlement to legitimate power in the Sovereign. Thus did social contract theory transpose the "goodness" of the citizenry to their government. Exactly what the fiduciary responsibility consisted of, to what extent power and preference should lie with the rulers or the ruled – not to mention what occurred in the growing realm of civil society (which included the ethical, social, and economic activities of the citizenry) or questions about the qualifications of citizenship – became the principal items of contention in theories of representation as the practical means for the invention of modern democracy in the liberal political orders of England, the United States, and France.

By way of social contract theory and its attendant theories and practices of representation, modern democracy was depleted of its ancient power in exchange for an ethical endowment of natural rights, becoming a shadowy imitation (practically necessary as that might have seemed to be) of what it once was. A new dynamic appeared, with the People allotted certain basic rights, the State identified as their protector, and the vehicle of representation – engineered from above or below – supposed to match

---

[32] Notably, there never has been a term that denotes a political regime of, by, and for the *populus* – only a political disposition, i.e., populism.

[33] Clarke (1936, 293).

the interests of the people and the actions of their government (incarnated as the Legislative, Executive, or Judiciary). Of course, whether the match was a good one depended on your point of view, but the activity of electoral representation supposedly enacted a resemblance that perfected that relationship, whether it was understood to operate by means of a mandate (rarely) or the Member of Parliament's independent judgment (tethered by elections of one kind or another).[34] While representative government was supposed to cure the ills of ancient democracies, the distance between the Representer and the Represented, the practical dissipation and targeted enticement of individual judgment, made possible the state's assumption of the virtue of the people. The state wielded power over the people, diversifying rather than restricting the problems of demagoguery in ancient democracy that modern republics were supposed to correct.

The representative dimension of the new liberal political orders designed to protect individual rights appeared as the best mechanism for actualizing popular rule or sovereignty – indeed, democracy. As a result, it is more beneficial to assess the meaning and value of "rights" as historical and political practices, rather than conceptual forms (especially as counterpoints to "virtue"). In this respect, the discourse of rights reflected a new, official mode of combining ethics and power for political conduct. But the formally equal treatment of citizens belied a relatively arbitrary element, for the involvement of the citizenry in shaping the conduct of their representatives was left to elite-influenced election procedures, qualifications, and voluntary participation. Still, representation became the mythical means of transposing the authorizing power of the people to the new authorities in government. After all, representatives had more time and money to perfect their virtue and skill in conducting their work and were not supposed to be corrupted by the power that attended their offices. They were supposed to be better guardians and agents of public virtue than ordinary citizens in the new as representation became institutionalized in the new states of Europe and America.

3.3   Establishments of Representation as a Political Virtue

As a means for authorizing the modern state with the legitimacy of the people, the activity of representation resulting from the English, American, and French revolutions was served as an ongoing means to address civil discord (or *stasis*) and promote peace and justice. Representation had become a practical necessity for large states that sought to ground their

---

[34] For the classic view of the latter, see Edmund Burke's speech before the electors of Bristol, partly reprinted in Kramnick (1999, 155–7).

legitimacy in popular consent. But the representatives also must be regarded as virtuous agents of the citizenry. Moreover, as the articulation of the presumed nature and role of these representatives reflected attempts to marginalize the *right* of various, national, aristocracies to political rule, the authority of the new representatives in some way needed to carry the previous sanction of the aristocracy as those "best" able to rule. Representatives should deserve their title on the basis not only of property and genealogy but also as a (rhetorical) warrant to rule virtuously on behalf of the whole citizenry and their servants. This was done in different but kindred ways in Western Europe and the United States.

3.3.1   England

During the English Civil War, small farmers, craftsmen, laborers, and rank-and-file soldiers and leaders in the New Model Army argued for their place in the newly forming Commonwealth of England, seeking respect for their *consent* to authorize legitimate political action. In 1642, Henry Parker provided a theoretical justification for having the state re-present the People as a corporate body, but his argument principally advocated the rights of Parliament over and against the King.[35] Partisans of democratic change supported the Parliamentary faction in the early years of the Civil War, but five years later, Colonel Rainsborough, as spokesman for the democratic New Model Army, addressed and opposed the Parliamentary Army in his enduring words recorded during the Putney Debates of 1647, when he said (to no immediately practical, political effect):

… the poorest he that is in England has a life to live as the greatest he; and therefore truly, sir [General Ireton], I think it's clear that every man that is to live under a government ought first by his own consent to put himself under that government, and I do think that the poorest man in England is not at all bound in a strict sense to that government that he has not had a voice to put himself under.[36]

Although the germs of Hobbes's theory of sovereignty and representation certainly antedated the English Civil War, his own political theory as published in *Leviathan* (1651) – his first work to discuss the idea of

---

[35] Henry Parker, *Observations upon some of his Majesties Late Answers and Expresses*, July 1642. Interestingly, in his effort to highlight the right of the Parliament versus the King, he notes that the "multitude" may be more or less disregarded because it "hath onely a representative influence" (9). See http://eebo.chadwyck.com/search/fulltext

[36] For signs of early democratic support for Parliament and Parliament's subsequent disdain for democracy and, in particular, the politicized populace as a "many-headed monster" (see Hill 1975, 181–204). Rainsborough's words can be readily found in Sharp (1998, 103).

representation – provided a theory of political institutions and a political ethic that would limit the effective agency of ordinary Englishmen and those Parliamentary representatives who imagined themselves as democratic agents (the only "democratical gentlemen" who warranted his concern) on the conduct of government.[37] Hobbes emphasized that the moral philosophy he articulated in *Leviathan* (Chapter 15) provided a much-needed "science of Vertue and Vice, a theory of political management in which the people managed could only be trusted if their allegiance was based on the near oxymoron of rational fear."[38] The Hobbesian Sovereign immediately acts as a government that is legitimated by the people whom it represents – indeed, it also may be called their "representative," thereby linking the idea and practice of representation with a popular legitimation of modern states. At the same time, it unquestionably controls them, rejecting any practical limitation on its power or authority by the actions or opinions of citizens.[39] The "representative" Sovereign is, therefore, "higher" than the people. The function of the Representative's superiority to the Represented connects its practical, ethical, and political role to that of the role of "virtue" in ancient Greece as that guidepost for a higher kind of practice which authorizes the implicitly virtuous (i.e., ethically skilled) practice by an individual or group (*pace* Hobbes, *qua* monarchy, aristocracy, or democracy) to exercise power over the less virtuous, putatively without domination (though mistakes will be made). However, unlike the power–virtue relationship in Athenian democracy, Hobbes held that the *lack* of reliable "virtue" among the citizenry or class leaders made it necessary to allow the Sovereign to declare the meanings of virtue and vice and to link their political authority to the power of a superior State (and subordinate Church). This, along with his theory of representation, makes Hobbes the major theorist of the modern state.[40]

Hobbes's argument in *Leviathan* for the legitimate sovereignty of the early modern state provides the theoretical baseline for the opposition between representation and democracy as political practices. For Hobbes justifies a sovereign who has the inherent ability to dominate *all* political partisans that question his prerogatives and power – in Hobbes's day, the

---

[37] Hobbes (1991, 26–31; cf. 4–5, 68–9, 144).
[38] See Skinner (1996, 316–26).
[39] Notably, the book that launched the recent discussion among political theorists about representation, Hanna Pitkin's *The Concept of Representation*, initiates its substantive argument work with a discussion of "the problem of Thomas Hobbes." For a more recent, overarching, and historical treatment by Pitkin of "representation," see Pitkin (1989, 132–54). More recent treatments of political representation also begin with considerations of Hobbes (see Shapiro 2009; Vieira and Runciman 2008).
[40] See Guarini (1990, 22–3, 30–1).

democratic remnants of the Levellers outside of Parliament, "democrati-cal" Members of Parliament itself, along with the thinking of Monarchists and Republicans.[41] While the authorization of the Sovereign's power comes from the individuals who choose to leave the state of nature that is a state of war and achieve personal and collective security, once that stability is achieved, the sovereign's dominance becomes legitimate as a form of power and virtue through his stipulated theory of representa-tion. Thus, in *Leviathan*, Chapter 16, Hobbes famously wrote:

> A multitude of men, are made *One* person, when they are by one man, or one Person, Represented; so that it be done with the consent of every one of that Multitude in particular. For it is the *Unity* of the Representer, not the *Unity* of the Represented, that maketh the Person *One*. And it is the Representer that beareth the Person, and but one Person: And *Unity*, cannot otherwise be understood in Multitude.

Despite, and because of, the willful, if not sinful, character of man, there simply is no modern equivalent of the *demos* to which political attention should be paid. Hobbes designed his Sovereign as a political represent-ative who embodied the people and public virtue in a time when virtue had become primarily a term of relative deficiency shaped by the neces-sarily imperfect, principally private virtue of Christians and a good many from lower classes were poised to grasp (in aspiration if not in actuality) political power. Once peace had been achieved among warring parties, his theory of representation, as much or more than his theory of sovereign authorization, rendered the voices of political subjects virtually mute.

If one accepts that there can be modern equivalents of a *demos* – itself a stretch given the absence of an equivalent political role for the ancient *demos* amid its Athenian democratic *politeia* in modern times – its signifier would have to be able to have a major hand in determining the exercise of legitimate political power. Hobbes's conception of representa-tion excludes that possibility. Only the Representer – i.e., the Sovereign, Leviathan – exercises the power of the Represented – i.e., the people – lest anarchy or uselessly disruptive squabbles ensue. The Sovereign's subjects are not entitled to restrict his actions in any collective form. As individuals they can run and hide, but they are not entitled to oppose his rule. They have less power than the citizen-subjects of Plato's philosopher-guardians in *kallipolis*. Platonic Socrates' lowest class had the capacity for sound judgment (*sophrosune*), and that enabled them to determine who was a proper philosopher-guardian worthy of room and board. Hobbes could

---

[41] Need it be said, I am claiming that this issue is more settled than it actually is. For a pro-ductive debate on the relationship between Hobbesian sovereignty and representation, on the one hand, and democracy, on the other, see the articles by Tuck and Hoekstra in Brett et al. (2006), 171–98 and 191–218, respectively.

be seen as a democrat, too, as the covenant that legitimates the Sovereign is made possible by the agreement of the People to have the Sovereign *protect* their lives, but the People are deprived of direct, political agency.[42] And Hobbes opposed Parliamentary attempts to transmit popular (e.g., Presbyterian) interests and indirectly scoffed at Rainsborough's attempt to urge General Ireton at Putney to heed the wishes of every Englishman. To be sure, *how* this consent was to be channeled was radically unclear. But Rainsborough's words distinctly proclaimed the requirement that everyone was entitled to a *voice* that is effectively *heard*. Empowering that *voice* threatened the owners of real property, for only they, according to General Ireton, had a "permanent, fixed interest" in the kingdom and they were the only ones would should stand as "representers," a comment that was only remarkable for being so blunt.[43]

But *as* a theorist of representation, why should Hobbes be so indisposed to "democratical gentlemen," let alone ordinary Englishmen? He had no particular devotion to property or its preservation. For Hobbes, property needed regulation by the Sovereign lest it become a threat to his power; its owners were no more intrinsic benefactors to the realm than its subjects. The key to understanding the Hobbesian theory of representation, as with subsequent justifications during the time that liberal republicanism became enshrined as the synecdoche for modern democracy, is his distrust in the political judgment of ordinary persons. In *their* natural state, they generated a state of War that was "solitary, poore, nasty, brutish, and short," because they lacked any natural capacity for caring for or thinking about the well-being of their fellow subjects or the common interest of their social and political order. In addition to lacking any inherent quality of "vertue," they lacked the capacity of discerning it when presented to them by others as something that could be represented by elected or in some other sense politically representative individuals. For Hobbes, the determination of political virtue ultimately had to reside in a discerning Sovereign, that is, a virtuous agent of state power that can intimidate its subjects into (equal) subservience.[44] The evidence justifying every element of this proposition has been scanty from the beginning, but it also has remained fearfully persuasive as a

---

[42] Tuck pursues this argument in his discussion of Hobbes on democracy (above n. 20).
[43] In the Putney Debates, General Ireton is recorded as having said to Colonel Rainsborough: "it is not fit that the representees should choose as the representers – the persons who shall make the law in the kingdom – those who have not a permanent, fixed interest [i.e., be owners of real property] in the kingdom." See Sharp (1998, 116, cf. 104–5, 107–8, 113–14, 122–3).
[44] See Skinner (2005, 178–9).

necessary attribute of modern republics, the governments of which claim to provide practicable political virtue for the bulk of their citizens.

Representatives were supposed to be virtuous, in both ethical and practical senses, if they were to contribute constructively contribute to government. For Locke, this depended on fealty to 'the Members of Society whom the Representative represented, and the extent of the membership ought to be as wide as practically possible. Relative to Hobbes, Locke inverted the source of representation from the government to the people, in accord with his more positive view of human nature. But political power was mostly associated with the Legislative, acting (somehow) for the Majority, unless the Legislative or Executive violated the considered views of the Majority of Society – the calculation of which, given property qualifications for voting, would be hard to estimate.[45] Nonetheless, Locke does not point fingers at Parliament, and so must presume that its Members normally serve competently and virtuously in their offices, functioning as rational, practical agents of the electorate. But as Locke does not enter into a political debate about the proper qualifications for being a full, consenting member of society; seems to require ownership of land for proper membership in society; accepts slavery, as long as slaves do not revolt; gives the Executive plenty of room for unilateral action, and pushes only for mild Parliamentary reform, one might wonder how much more democratic is a Lockean Parliament than a Hobbesian one.[46] (After all, only 3 percent of the adult male population were entitled to cast votes for Members of Parliament in Locke's time, which meant that MPs invariably would act paternalistically toward the *demos*, not as their partners or agents.)

But, *contra* Hobbes's theoretical scheme, Locke's honors individual rights independently of governmental authority, and endows individuals with independent property rights as a matter of their nature, along with executive political power. They are in a position to influence their Representatives who, in turn, would be less tolerant of Executive Power than a Hobbesian Sovereign.[47] But from Locke forwards, representation

---

[45] See Locke, *Second Treatise of Government*, pars. 88, 140, 151, 157–8, 192, 213, 222 (Locke (1988 (1690))).

[46] See Skinner (2005).

[47] Nonetheless, this gap is particularly interesting, for Locke recognized that the ethical and moral content of private life would, in the context of politics, shape practical affairs. Locke distinguished private and public realms in order to promote toleration, but he noted in *A Letter Concerning Toleration* (1689) that asserting a fixed boundary between moral and political issues did not map onto legal divisions between private and public domains: "Good Life, in which consists not the least part of Religion and true Piety, concerns also the Civil Government: and in it lies the safety both of Mens Souls, and of the Commonwealth. Moral Actions belong therefore to the Jurisdiction both of the outward and inward Court; both of the Civil and Domestick Governor; I mean, both of the Magistrate and the Conscience." *A Letter Concerning Toleration*, in James H. Tully, ed. (Indianapolis: Hackett, 1983 [1690]), 46.

was always as much about taking account of the interests of property as transmuting the voices of the citizenry.[48] Because Locke's belief that the primary loyalty of citizens is to their property, the agency of Representation – and Parliament more generally at his time – would be mostly devoted to protecting the status quo from the arbitrary exercise of power as domination. The revolutionary potential of Locke's political theory of representation principally extends to societies whose governments have abandoned any representative function – either from the top down or from the bottom up.[49] Apart from its ineffective gesture toward extending Parliamentary opposition to more "Members of Society," Lockean representation in practice, if not in theory, remains subordinate to Hobbes's attachment of political representation to the sovereignty of the modern state.

Considerable irony, therefore, lay behind English attempts to incorporate the (male, white, propertied) citizenry into the basis of government and the state as a lever for dethroning the aristocracy as the social basis of government. Hobbes's initial, major step in this direction required the infantilization of human nature and the depoliticization of a state's subjects. With such citizens, a monarchical state or one dominated by executive power had good warrant to be emboldened. That remained the case with Locke's more salutary vision of human nature, as the "express consent" of politically autonomous citizens mostly occurred before "civil society" and government became established.

Four generations later, in the context of rebellious politics gaining traction across the Channel, Edmund Burke's conservatism spurned "rights" as a political ethic but associated representation with independent judgment by representatives on behalf of their constituents. The indeterminate power of the modern state led some political thinkers to draw on the traditions and heritage of established institutions in civil society (such as the Church and aristocratic culture) as the networks of humane political community. Edmund Burke did so by according these institutions a natural ability to "represent" and contribute to society "as a whole." "Ancient chivalry" was accompanied by "noble equality." In his rhetorical condemnation of the abstract principles guiding the French Revolution, Burke claimed that this unequal equality, "without force or opposition ... subdued the fierceness of pride and power [providing] all the pleasing illusions which power gentle and obedience liberal."[50] These,

---

[48] See Pole (1966) and Reid (1989).
[49] See James Tully's Introduction in Tully and Locke (1983 (1690), 1–16).
[50] From Burke's *Reflections on the Revolution in France* [1790], excerpted in Isaac Kramnick, ed. *The Portable Edmund Burke* (Penguin, 1999), 447.

as he said in a previously composed reverie, comprised the constituents of "natural society."[51] The fact that these institutions also ingrained inequality among different religions, classes, statuses, and genders did not bother him as long as the differences were autonomous, not products of imperial imposition, the hedonistic rich, or irrational prejudice. Burke proclaimed his theory of "virtual" representation in the following form, with Parliament offering a check on both the arbitrary power of the King and the willful passions of the people:

> Parliament is not a *congress* of ambassadors from different and hostile interests, which interests, which each interest must maintain, as an agent and advocate, against other agents and advocates; but Parliament is a *deliberative* assembly of *one* nation, with *one* interest, that of the whole – where not local purposes, not local prejudices, ought to guide, but the general good, resulting from the general reason of the whole. You choose a member, indeed; but when you have chosen him, he is not member of Bristol, but he is a member of *Parliament*.[52]

In other words, MP Burke's version of political virtue would have virtue "represent" the *demos* (limited as it was by property qualifications and the exclusion of women) independently, as Pitkin put it, by means of his own, superior political judgment that would, as much as he was able to work it, reflect his vision of "character" – a notion that consolidated virtue within the public personae of individuals.[53] Although it is important to recall Burke's rhetorical appeal, the conceptual position he articulated traded on traditional understandings of the central political and ethical authority of Parliamentary representatives over their constituents.[54] Representation did not move from the ground up.

As a synecdoche for democracy, the authority of elected representatives demonstrated a *de jure gap* as well as an informal, *de facto connection* between the *demos* or *populus* and directly effective political power – one might say, between the performativity of political rhetoric (*logos*) and political realities (*ergon*), between the claim to represent virtuously the interests of the people when most of the people had no say in determining the manner in which they exercised their power. Moreover, the early modern period experienced a growing ratio between the number of the represented and the representers. One can understand how Marx could have viewed the political emancipation of the liberal revolutions enabling

---

[51] See, for example, Edmund Burke, "A Vindication of Natural Society" [1756], in Kramnick (1999, 29–63).

[52] Edmund Burke, "Speech at Mr. Burke's Arrival in Bristol" [1774], in Kramnick (1999, 156). For this political tack as the practical perspective that lay behind "virtual representation," see Reid (1989).

[53] See "A Notebook of Edmund Burke," in Kramnick (1999, 14–23).

[54] See Pole (1993).

the propertied few to dominate the many even as the latter had gained new political status, legal rights, and moral dignity.[55]

Although the United Kingdom experienced no political revolution on the order of the violent upheavals in the United States and France, it did find itself pressured to incorporate the working classes more fully into its constitutional fabric. This began to occur with the Reform Act of 1832, which expanded the franchise to include one-fifth of the adult male population. But the conceptual seeds of the reformist agenda were planted much earlier, by social critiques of utilitarians such as Jeremy Bentham and James Mill, who generated new theories of representation from their philosophical and political outlooks. For them, the issue was how to incorporate ordinary British (male) subjects into the electorate, given that the extant property qualifications for voting and Parliamentary service disenfranchised the vast majority of British adults – most men and all women. This stemmed from the standpoints of radical (Bentham) or, later, modified (J. S. Mill) utilitarianism. While all were serious advocates of greater British democracy and more widespread political representation for adults (with J. S. Mill later arguing for women's suffrage), each offers a problematic understanding of the relationship of representation to democracy that reflects the vexed character of their political and ethical relationships.

Bentham was the more pathbreaking and radical figure, founder of the group that came to be called the "Philosophic Radicals."[56] Bentham stitched together unbending social and political criticism with Enlightenment philosophy that sanctioned the dignity and rationality of "all" human beings. Piercing the privileges of land-owning aristocrats and Britain's political elite, Bentham argued for the equal merit of every individual's experience of pleasure and pain. Taken altogether for political purposes, this amounted to "Utility, or the greatest happiness for the greatest number," constituted by a rational determination of the collected quanta of pleasure over pain. Bentham spelled out many of the social, political, and democratizing consequences of his views in two

---

[55] See Karl Marx, "On the Jewish Question," in Tucker (1978, 26–46).

[56] See Halevy (1972 (1928)). Rather anachronistically, Halevy refers to "Philosophical Radicalism" as "Utilitarianism [*viz.*] nothing but an attempt to apply the principles of Newton to the affairs of politics and of morals" (6; cf. 3, 14–5, 29–32). At 261–2, Halevy notes the introduction in 1819 of the phrase "Radical Reform" into the political vernacular, coinciding with the publication of *Bentham's Radical Reform Bill: with extracts from the reasons* (London: E. Wilson & Royal Exchange, 1819), which adamantly argued for universal male suffrage and the secret ballot, extending arguments made in his *Plan for Parliamentary Reform* (1817).

books published in 1776 and 1789, respectively.[57] But, apart from his noteworthy advocacy for extending the suffrage and the secret ballot, his most prominent treatments of representation came later, after his honorary award of French citizenship and disappointment with the British Parliament's rejection of his political reforms and never-adopted plan for a new kind of prison, the Panopticon. These were his *Radical Reform Bill* (1819) and the *Constitutional Code* (1830), both of which were composed after his disillusionment with the belief that rational demonstration would readily persuade persons of their true, utilitarian interests.[58] Bentham initially believed that as individuals learn (readily and mentally, he thought) to calculate their true interests, the result would naturally align their individual interests with the general or common interest as well as the greatest happiness. No politics or interaction between representatives and constituents were required.[59] But his political disillusionment led him to recognize how ingrained prejudice and the interests of the powerful would make rational recognition of the truth of his philosophy hard to come by.[60] And yet, this rather pessimistic realization also energized his belief in a kind of apolitical, representative democracy.

Bentham's dedication to the political representation of persons – thus pointing to representative democracy – paid little attention to any problems of representation that could not be solved by a rational application of the utilitarian calculus and a deft organization of political institutions and penal reform so as to encourage the right recognition of one's experiences of pleasure and pain and, hence, one's true interests. To be sure, while Bentham believed that active participation by the enfranchised was a necessity for modern politics to work, he did not sufficiently address the problems of representation noted previously in this chapter – namely, the gap between a summation of citizens' views and what a representative might consider them to be for the purposes of representative action, and the bias of the activity of political representation toward the power of representatives over and against demotic power. There was in truth, he argued, an identity of interests between the people and their representatives, and conflicts between the two could be resolved (hypothetically) by institutions designed to effectuate their alignment. This inattention to the powers that the economy and civil society made sure that the politics of the people did not disturb them indicated an undeveloped

---

[57] *A Fragment on Government* and *Introduction to the Principles of Morals and Legislation*, respectively.
[58] See Bentham (1983).
[59] See Bentham (1983, Section 11, Articles 4 and 6.1).
[60] See Rosen (1983, 5ff.) and Schofield (2006, 108), etc.

analysis of class or ideology. That said, one must note that Bentham was highly suspicious of those in power and sought to restrain their anti-democratic tendencies with the establishment of a Public Opinion Tribunal that would sanction unfit representatives and funnel the public's views to the press.[61]

Through his differentiation of pleasures and pains into "higher" and "lower" varieties (perhaps gutting the critical power of utilitarianism), as well as more complicated analysis of history as an agent of political realities and reform, John Stuart Mill's political theory of representation addressed these limitations of Bentham's philosophic radicalism. In addition, Mill, having learned from his contemporary Grote about previously unappreciated virtues of Athenian democracy and Greek political thought, more explicitly advocated the alliance of representation and democracy as a matter of political virtue. In his important work, *Considerations on Representative Government* – published two years after *On Liberty*, the same year as his essay, "Utilitarianism" (1861), and the same year he drafted "The Subjection of Women" (published in 1869) – Mill begins by identifying the organic and technical, progressive and conservative, approaches to the political problems of societies. He quickly turns to ancient Athens and its political thought, which had critically influenced his early intellectual development. In Mill's idealized but not entirely erroneous picture of Athenian democracy, its capacity to engender virtuous political activity stems from the open discussion of public issues in cultural, social, and powerfully political spaces. Yet Mill's "ideally best form of government [the Athenians'] will be found in some or other variety of the Representative System" (which contradicts the argument made previously in this chapter).[62]

Since Mill rejects the view that Athenian democracy was a representative system, how could the former provide the bedrock for his representative ideal? For him, its relevance was twofold. First, modern society needed to foster the public enunciation by citizens of different ethical and political perspectives – the kind of robust free speech he lauded in the first three sections of *On Liberty*. In *On Liberty*, Mill's concern was "the tyranny of the majority" exercised by the dull conformism of dominant ethical customs and the dangerous tools of Parliamentary majorities. Mill desperately sought to find ways to catalyze a culture of political debate, intelligence, and virtue. But in *Considerations*, his praise of Athenian democracy also was complemented by fear of how democracy would operate in contemporary Britain, which began to enfranchise

---

[61] See Rosen (1983, 19–40) and Schofield (2006, 259–63, 294–6).
[62] See Mill (1991 (1861), Chs. I–IV, quotation at the end of Ch. II).

workers in 1832, albeit barely, but slowly and steadily increased their voting rights during his time. Mill was well aware of how economic and social classes were prone merely to advocate their own, narrowly defined interests. Despite his presumptive belief in the inevitably civilizing power of Britain, if not the white West, Mill harbored no immediate trust in the virtue of Britain's ruling classes *or* working classes.

Since Mill had no faith in the political judgment or virtue of the working classes, one had to worry about what might happen if the working class (soon to be a majority of potential voters) became politically ascendant. Conceivably, the major intellectual, economic, cultural, and political elements of the British establishment would come under attack. Thus, the Representative System could not simply reflect and refine demotic judgment. Second, the effective pillars of representative government could not be built from the ground up; they would have to be parachuted in (from the top down). So, the *Demos* had to be "represented," as it was not prepared for the responsibilities and practice of government. In Mill's vision of modern democracy, the *Demos* engendered anxiety not trust.[63] Its potential political power would have to be transformed by political mechanisms into practical virtue. Mill's ironically top-down application of participatory democracy mimics his view of Great Britain as the benevolent imperial educator of India. He was dedicated to identifying a conception of political virtue that accommodated burgeoning democratic power without threatening the capitalist economy or imperial sweep of nineteenth-century Britain.[64]

Two vehicles could make up for the people's distorted and self-interested political predilections that, without tutelage, would result from demotically guided political rule. One was an electoral system that counterbalanced voting power that could compose, in Mill's view, a tyrannical majority. Forgetting the suspicion of institutional authority he demonstrated in *On Liberty*, Mill now seeks out a counter-majoritarian voting system that enables "independent opinion and will" to prevail in the political system. He settles on a provision that enables Oxbridge graduates and other members of "the liberal professions" capable of passing equivalent examinations to have more than one vote. They are more likely to work in high-status occupations whose members possess the requisite "mental superiority" for modern-day representative government.[65] In other words, a democratic Representative System offset by extra power allotted to a country's intellectual elite would provide the political virtue

---

[63] Mill (1991 (1861), 328–9).
[64] See Mehta (1999).
[65] Mill (1991 (1861), 335–8 (Ch. VIII)).

for democracy in modernity; it would reflect the proclivities of, one might say, the best and the brightest. Mill's other measure was conviction about the potentially close link between the active promotion of the common good and the governmental manifestation of overarching political intelligence – namely, a governmental bureaucracy managed by non-partisan, non-ideological but politically competent public servants.[66] They were to be the agents of Parliament and Country, personified, one hoped, in a virtuous Prime Minister. But this liberal hope deferred to the continuing power and authority of the economic and social ruling classes.

3.3.2   North America

Locke had no theory that justified democracy *per se*, given his association of rational and moral independence, acceptance of vastly unequal holdings of property, and toleration (at least) of slavery.[67] But his theory seemed to intend to energize the English "base,"[68] and across the Atlantic it certainly inspired Americans interested in expelling their British and establishing self-government. The Declaration of Independence composed by Thomas Jefferson, et al., incorporates Locke's language ("unalienable rights to life, liberty, and … happiness" [not property, until 1791]); justifies Lockean rebellion against governing rulers by the governed who suffer "a long traine of abuses"; and accepts the overall Lockean view that identifies government as legitimate only if it stands authorized by the consent of the governed.

In the colonies, during their early years as States, and under the authority of the Articles of Confederation, representation in America had a decidedly more democratic cast. American colonial legislatures and, later, Anti-Federalist rhetoric articulated the importance of close practical connections between representatives and their constituents. They did so in order to restrain British power over them as colonies and to prevent the emergence of a new elite in the new nation of the United States, one that might reconstruct a new version of the previous dominance of the United Kingdom over the American colonies. Colonial representation was not, for the most part, regarded as a specifically democratic form of representation (prior to the Ratification Debate in the United States) but simply as the

---

[66] See Thompson (1976, 54–90).
[67] Ian Shapiro's claim that Locke "has" a democratic theory fits uneasily with Locke's basic acceptance of Parliamentary rule over more than 95 percent of the people, the extant distribution of property, and a wide prerogative for an unelected Executive. See his "John Locke's Democratic Theory" in Shapiro (2003b, 309–40).
[68] See Ashcraft (1986).

legitimate, constitutional means of representing the people.[69] Nonetheless, it reflected the *ethos* of political equality that accompanied the revolutionary establishment of the United States. Unlike Great Britain, where the House of Commons *ipso facto* represented the British people, and politically incarnated all British subjects, the American colonies understood the function of most colonial legislators to remain in close contact with their constituents – women and slaves notably and obviously excluded – and to be faithful to their political beliefs.[70] Despite the much closer link in the British colonies of North America between political representatives and ordinary citizens, the growing population of the colonies during the eighteenth century decreased the proportion of representatives to the represented. But the population growth and an expanding economy also led to a greater array of individuals from more walks of life entering public office. Not long after the birth of the United States, Alexander Hamilton described the new nation as a "representative democracy."[71] The politics of representation during the period in which the new Constitution of the United States was being debated and ultimately ratified complemented the introduction of democracy as self-government. But institutional procedures for representation determined how the American people would accept or legitimate a new set of rulers to rule over them.[72]

Two lines of argument support this view – and don't require Rousseau's depressing recollection of human beings running headlong into chains by accepting political representation.[73] First, there is the practical difference between direct and indirect representation. The very idea that tens or hundreds of thousands of citizens could be "represented" in the views of a single representative is, as previously noted here and at the historical moments of political institutionalization, absurd. This is not simply

---

[69] See Reid (1989) on the dismissal of the significance of "democracy" in the colonies because of their reliance on democratic understandings of representation and constitutionality.

[70] See Pole (1966) and Reid (1989).

[71] For Hamilton's articulation of this phrase during the Revolutionary War, see *The Papers of Alexander Hamilton*, Vol. 1, p. 255 [1777]. Hamilton's reference to the new American state as a "representative democracy" either reflected political views he subsequently changed or was merely a rhetorical posture, given his later arguments in *The Federalist*. On Hamilton's political thought, see Wolin (1989, 82–99, 120–36). Wolin does not address the ethical significance for the American colonists of "constitutionalism."

[72] John Dunn refers to this era as the "second coming" of democracy, but, relative to Athenian democracy, it is marked by more civic rights and less political power. Whether both political orders are rightfully called "democracy" is debatable and a matter that Dunn does not discuss, as his interest in mostly in democracy as a linguistic term with various referents (see Dunn 2005).

[73] See Rousseau, *Discourse on the Nature and Origins of Inequality Among Men*, in Rousseau (1973 (1754), 99).

because much inevitably would be lost or just left behind in the transposition of demotic power to representative rule; after all, there could be a lottery, in which case the few would more likely be a cross-section of the many. Second, in the debates between the Federalists and the Anti-Federalists, representation was viewed as a kind of practical, political virtue – albeit conceived much differently by these opponents. Anti-Federalists wanted representatives to reflect or, at least, hew closely to the views of the Represented. Political representatives have rarely been exemplary, virtuous stand-ins for the *demos* – even if political theorists such as Madison and Burke (during the era when representation resurrected the idea of "democracy" as a legitimate form of government) regarded them as such and commendable political leaders emerged in large numbers during the era of the American Revolution and the early years of the republic.

Debates over representation in a new Constitution for American government, consequently, amounted to debates about its character as a political order. The previously demotic character of political representation was radically altered with the establishment of the Constitution of the United States as the law of the land.[74] The Federalists distrusted the political activities of ordinary citizens and scorned "democracy" as a form of government. To remedy its imputed incapacity to temper majority rule, Madison believed that the new Constitution would encourage leadership by a set of virtuous men who stanch the corruption that marked British colonial rule. They would have diverse constituencies that, in the manner of Adam Smith's invisible hand, would not only impede the formation of runaway majorities but also filter the passions of the people into a deliberate consideration of the good of the nation as a whole. Hamilton had a different view; he believed that federal representatives would tend to share the practical interests of the merchant class more than any other and that *they* served as stand-ins for the common good. Anti-Federalists remained highly suspicious of the transfer of power from the states to the national government. The distance between representatives and constituents would foster corruption. They believed that representation only would be genuine if the representatives resembled the citizens and reflected their views, spawned by the diverse walks

---

[74] The view that their opposition was overcome by their agreement about the need for "communication" between voters and representatives understates the seriousness of the disagreements between Federalists and Anti-Federalists. After all, the former scorned "democracy" and the latter regarded the former as the new nation's so-called "natural aristocracy" but feared it would become a "tyrannic aristocracy." See Madison, *Federalist*, No. 10 and "Letters of 'Brutus,'" in Ball (2003, 43, 457, 438). Also see the comments of George Mason and the "Federal Farmer," in Kammen (1986, 258, 278).

of life lived by the American people, an unlikely event if a small number of representatives in the federal government would wield a predominance of political power.[75]

The question of how political representation could serve the wishes and interests of "the people" exposed class conflict at the beginning of the republic and generated directly opposed conceptions of representation and virtue in the American debates over the ratification of the Constitution. The Anti-Federalists resisted the nationalization of political power and embraced an idea of representation that *was* democratic, as it was rooted in the diverse dispositions and practices of "the people."[76] They were neither individualists nor socialists, pro-government nor anti-government, pro-slavery nor anti-slavery. They worried that corruption would set in if the representatives spent most of their time away from their constituents. While most of the revered American Framers were obviously commendable political leaders, they opposed the authority of the pre-1787 constitutions of state governments, because they sanctioned a kind of "constitutionalism" (a practical equivalent to political virtue or legitimacy) that called for a continuous dialogue between representatives and their actual constituents. The Anti-Federalists believed that this would guarantee a kind of mutual understanding that would prevent the attributes of wealth, status, and talent from determining the character of the elected representatives – potentially becoming an aristocratic elite that could tyrannize their democratic electors.[77]

Madison held that "the republican principle" and the corollary principle of "representation" embodied in the Constitution would be able to cure the ills of "pure Democracy," which not only was unrealistic for a large society but "can admit of no cure for the mischiefs of faction."[78]

---

[75] See *The Federalist*, No. 10 (Madison), 44; No. 35 (Hamilton), 160; "Letters of 'Brutus,'" 458, all in Ball (2003). Of course, the proximity of representatives to their constituents does not itself sufficiently protect against corruption, as the activities of local and state governments in the United States have demonstrated through the years.

[76] For the *locus classicus* of this perspective articulated by Anti-Federalists, see "Letters from Brutus" (III, IV), in Ball (2003, 453–65). For the Anti-Federalist version of representative democracy, see Bailyn (1968 (1965), 80–3) and Bailyn (1967, 295–300). Cf. Pole (1966, esp. Pt. 2, Chs. 2, 4 and Pt. 3, Ch. 1) on the practices of political representation in the early days of Massachusetts and Pennsylvania as states.

[77] See Handlin (1966, 59–60, 75–6, 78–9, 98) and Reid (1989). For a British example of the woolly locution of representative democracy, see Mill (1991 (1861), Ch. 7).

[78] Madison, *The Federalist*, No. 10, in Ball (2003, 43). Madison contestably finds evidence for this claim in Athenian democracy. Interestingly, he also believed that "the principle of representation" was found in antiquity; its problem was its dependence on democratic agency. See Madison, *The Federalist*, No. 63, in Ball (2003, 309). I disputed the claim that political representation was practiced in antiquity earlier in this essay, and my position finds sanction in the judgments of Constant and Mill – theorists who also sought to differentiate ancient and modern polities.

Most remarkably, perhaps, Madison argued that the very fact of the distance of the Representatives from ordinary citizens would improve their political judgment, preventing it from being driven by demotic passions of the moment. He does not presume that the mere occupation of national office sanctions the Representatives as "enlightened statesmen," and yet he claims that they will be less likely to perform "the vicious arts" of politicians. Then, he optimistically links top-down representation, anti-democratic proclivities, and virtue at the end of *The Federalist*, No. 10:

Does this advantage [of the new Union over the Confederation of States] consist in the substitution of Representatives, whose enlightened views and virtuous sentiments render them superior to local prejudices and schemes of injustices? It will not be denied, the Representation of the Union will be most likely to possess these requisite endowments.[79]

Perhaps the most remarkable feature of Madison's paean to representative government as a corollary to popular sovereignty is his later insistence, in *The Federalist, No. 51,* that these same enlightened statesmen would need to have their virtuous political judgment restrained and channeled by countervailing tendencies generated by the checks and balances produced by the interconnected branches of the Federal government. So even if the Representatives are not as virtuous as they are made out to be, their faults will be compensated by a Federal state that regulates national affairs.[80] My point here is not to grace localism as itself naturally virtuous but to present more evidence that identifies the principal role of representation in this era as a practical and rhetorical tool for assuming the stance of a moral political practice in order to legitimate the power of ambitious new states. In theory a tool for inclusion and safeguard against corruption, in practice it sanctioned a conception of public and political virtue that not only complements the power of the state *over* democratic power rooted in civil society but also effectively discourages the participation of wide swaths of the electorate from politics except in times of emergency (if they know it when they see it) – all this when democracy was hailed in public discourse as the complement of representation.[81]

---

[79] Ball (2003, 46; cf. 40–5).
[80] While the Federalists took pleasure in enlisting Montesquieu in their defense, they did so only to sanction their construction of a three-branched federal government – which did *not* resemble Montesquieu's class-based mixed government (see Wood 1969). Nor did they note Montesquieu's conceptual point made in the first pages of *The Spirit of the Laws* [1748] that articulated "virtue" as the spring of democracy, and only democracy as a fully republican form of government (Pt. 1: Bk. 2, Ch. 2 and Bk. 3, Ch. 3). Montesquieu did not ever argue for representation as a feature of practical political virtue or good government; he sought an accommodation of the various orders of society.
[81] See Arendt (1963, 252–85).

Thus did the new American government obtain legitimacy from "We, the People" and represent its motley citizenry and degraded slaves in a new government. In 1816, Thomas Jefferson bemoaned the Constitution's effect on the nation and "republicanism," assigning the well-being of American society to "the spirit of the people."[82] And of course the Founders imagined this scheme without political parties acting as intermediaries between citizens and the state.

The debate about representation that surrounded the authorization of the Constitution of 1787 was pivotal; its resolution in favor of the Federalists launched a political order that would grow in land and wealth over the next century to become the world's most powerful state. Though it was obviously insufficient to surmount its previous authorization of slavery without a civil war, the new idea of political representation embraced by the Framers surely provided a constitutional order that entailed a thin kind of democracy.[83] That democratic veneer only would be thickened in the future by extra-representational efforts by groups of citizens who felt de facto, if not de jure, disenfranchised – whether they were slave-holders in the South, resentful white men across the country, or civil rights, anti-war, and anti-capitalist protesters.[84]

3.3.3   France

The major opposition to the Hobbesian view in theoretical terms came from the pen of Rousseau. Rousseau imagined the closest theoretical connections between democracy and representation, via his connection between the diversity of natural citizens and their political "representation" (he would not use that word) in the general will. And yet, Rousseau famously condemns both the English practice of representation as a

---

[82] Thomas Jefferson, "Letter to Samuel Kerchal," in Jefferson (1999 (210–17, at 212) "Where then is our republicanism to be found? Not in our constitution certainly, but merely in the spirit of the people. That would oblige even a despot to govern us republicanly. Owing to this spirit, and to nothing in the form of our constitution, all things have gone well."

[83] For discussions of the idea of "constitutional democracy" as ways of protecting society against the impetuosity of the demos, see Elster and Slagstad (1988), especially the essays by Stephen Holmes and Cass Sunstein (19–58, 195–240, 327–53).

[84] Nonetheless, states can be "laboratories of democracy," and scholars have recently extolled the virtues of state power without forsaking civil liberties for all. Of course, it depends on the nature of the politics in the states and the relative extent of demotic power in them. But it should be easier to supersede the power of elites in smaller contexts, as long as the latter do not function like legal gangs. For the original attribution, see Louis Brandeis, in New State Ice Co. v. Liebmann, 285 U.S. 262 (1932). For a more recent endorsement, see Freeman and Rogers, "The Promise of Progressive Federalism" (2007, 205–27).

means of legitimizing political enslavement, and democracy, because its conflation of legislative and executive power, in his theoretical framework, guarantees corruption. In the stead of both, he embraced the practices of the Roman republic as an ancestral model for reforming his native Geneva and other small-scale contemporary societies.[85] But insofar as he sanctions the authority of the general will, one could say that Rousseau endorses both democracy and representation. He endorses democracy, understood as the legislative activity of an empowered general will as constituting the sovereignty of the state, and representation, when he calls for the "representation" of the *natural* self as a *citizen* in order to create moral political unity out of natural diversity. Yet he does not countenance political representation as it had been understood in either England or North America, where the only "representation" of the general will occurs in government.

For Rousseau, such governmental actions tend to debilitate, rather than enhance, the general will, making the participatory construction of the general will a necessary counter-force in order to keep a state from becoming corrupt. In making this argument, Rousseau left vague the practical ramifications of his argument, though he generally lauded the institutions of the Roman Republic and, like Machiavelli, believed in the benefits of a civil religion.[86] But from his few, terse, strictly theoretical statements about the basic centrality of citizen-power, Rousseau required a politically informed and active citizenry to supervise and authorize the activities of whatever government acted in its name, and believed that this was more likely to be possible in smaller, rather than larger, political orders. Overall, he downplayed elections as tools of the people.[87]

As the French began the process of turning their country from a society made up of three estates to a nation of citizens, the question of representation surfaced with practical urgency. Emmanuel Joseph Sieyes notably addressed it in his essay, "What is the Third Estate?"[88] For him, the Third Estate (all non-dependent citizens, artisans and workers

---

[85] Rousseau, *The Social Contract*, III.15, IV.3, IV. 4; cf. I. 6–7, II.4. For Rousseau's abiding connection to, and concern for, Geneva, see Rosenblatt (1997). For his recommendations for reforming Corsica (1765) and Poland (1772), see Rousseau (1986, 275–330), and Rosenblatt (1997, 177–260).

[86] Rousseau, *The Social Contract*, IV.8. Cf. Machiavelli, *Discourses*, Bk. I, Chs. XI–XV. Rousseau's debt to Machiavelli for his discussion of virtue and corruption is widely accepted.

[87] For Rousseau, what the contemporary political theorist Bernard Manin has called the "anticipatory effects" of the exercise of electoral power have marginal, practical, political effects in shaping, as opposed to reacting to, the exercise of political power (see Manin 1997, 178ff).

[88] This essay has been recently retranslated into English, and appears in Sieyes (2003).

as well as property holders without titles) were "everything." Until now, they were "nothing," and they simply wanted to be "something."[89] During the turmoil of the early stages of the French Revolution, debates about "representation" concerned "orders" not persons. Sieyes argued that the Third Estate morally and legitimately included the first two orders, as long as they gave up their special political privileges. For him, the issue of representation was not one of transmitting the views of individual citizens but fairly constituting in a political system the unity of "the nation."[90] The nation tied every ethical and practical tether to transform the French state.[91] He surely believed that a new National Assembly would be composed of "representatives" selected by individual citizens, but his main argument was that both citizens and their representatives – adapting Rousseau's language – automatically would reflect "the common will," which itself embodies the views of "the majority."[92] Once in place, representatives were supposed to act independently on behalf of "the nation." (Like Rousseau, Sieyes scorned "democracy," because it was "impossible."[93]) Indeed, "the nation" becomes the ethical corollary to the powers of the new French state, whose agents instrumentalized and distorted Rousseau's and Sieyes's ideals of political legitimacy and moderate understanding of how practically to integrate the new French state with the *ancien regime*.[94]

Sieyes's theoretical hopes for making generic representation of the (male, property-holding) citizens as an amicable solution to France's political problems proved to be naive. Various attempts to modernize ancient ideas of quasi-democratic republicanism in the French Revolution (1789–94) were sabotaged by practical obstacles and political actions. The retrospectively inevitable revolution was marked by bloodshed and violence that shook up Europe. It was most obvious and deadly during the leadership of the Committee of Public Safety by Maximilian Robespierre (July 27, 1793–July 27, 1794).[95] But in terms of our question

---

[89] Sieyes (2003, 94).

[90] Ibid, 99.

[91] For a useful account of the role of the nation or "polity" in the practical measures taken in the first part of the French Revolution to unify a new state, see Fitzsimmons (1994).

[92] Sieyes (2003, 133–44).

[93] Arguing against aristocrats who might impugn his view, that the Third Estate was the representative of the nation, by calling it democratic, Sieyes states that "representatives are not democrats and that since a genuine democracy is impossible among a numerous people, it is mad either to believe in it or appear to fear it" (Sieyes 2003, 147, n. 33).

[94] See Rousseau (1997, 200–3) and Baker (1987, 469–92). An updated version appears in Baker (1990, 224–51, 252–305).

[95] That said, the elements that made an official Terror both possible and likely antedated Robespierre's unchecked legislative and executive power (see Gough 1998/2010). Cf. Baker (1994).

of representation as the ethical virtue that legitimated the invention of liberal democracy, the excesses of the Terror are an unsurprising result of the overlay of democracy by representation. As Keith Baker has noted, the tradition of "representation" under the old regime actually operated from the ground up and justified the distinctive character of French provinces and the diversity of social orders. Their "representation" practically supported aristocratic privilege against the attempts of Louis XVI to unify the French nation under the rule of law. When the Revolutionaries began to view themselves as embodiments of the general will, they needed to detach themselves from the nation's political diversity in order to manifest unity. Thus, *contra* the argument of Rousseau, the Revolution's supposed theoretical ancestor, "representative" bodies such as the National Assembly, the Committee of Public Safety, or Robespierre himself, now regarded *themselves* as the embodiment of the general will.[96] Apart from possible theoretical complements in opinions, that posture detached them from the *actual* sources of their legitimacy. Democratic representation from the newly formed political districts was soon replaced by representatives *of state power* sent to the new districts to convey the meaning and authority of the new political order. Representation amounted to Parisian ambassadors of the government traveling to the countryside to enlist supporters.[97]

The relatively short period of morally justified, despotic, and violent rule, now known as the Reign of Terror, has cast "a long shadow" over modern democracy, principally because Robespierre so loudly proclaimed that his unilateral exercise of state power against major segments of the French citizenry was the unity of virtue, terror, and democracy.[98] He sternly implored members of the National Convention to be democratic representatives of the Republic, the practice of which he understood as follows: "... intimidate by terror the enemies of liberty; and you will be right, as founders of the Republic. The revolution's government is despotism of liberty over tyranny."[99] Louis XIV's infamous statement, "L'état c'est moi," or its evolved form in the politics of Louis XVI, ironically acquired the cachet of representative democracy through the words of Robespierre and his executive arm.[100] Yet the mark of Robespierre's

---

[96]   See Baker (1987).
[97]   On the temporary character of representation "from below" (i.e., democratic representation), see Woloch (1994, 309–25). For the role of "representatives on mission" as agents of the Revolution sent to persuade Frenchmen in the countryside (e.g., the Vendee) of its virtues, see Gough (1998/2010, 41).
[98]   Dunn, *Democracy*, 119ff.
[99]   Robespierre, "The Principles of Political Morality," 115.
[100]   See Scurr (2006, 57).

rule was his imaginary representation of himself as the agent of the general will and French people. The French *demos* only acted episodically, and large segments of it were either excluded from political participation or deemed enemies of the nation (understood as the dominant representation of themselves). Indeed, no better evidence was there of Rousseau's warning about joining institutionally distant, nominally representative, legislative, and executive functions in "democracy" than Robespierre's presumption that one institution or one voice of the people could incarnate its reason and desires or govern in its name by executing its will by the work of the guillotine – deemed more modern and humane than the aristocratic means of flogging, hanging, or beheading by the sword.[101] In particular, it was principally when the public policy of the Revolution transcended the conventional boundaries of the sovereign state and legal equality, moving toward its emancipatory efforts to liberate France's neighboring regions and extend the responsibility of the state to economic welfare, that "democracy" became linked to the ideology of Robespierre and the French Republic.[102] For him, democracy was a trope, not a political activity that exemplified a political order.

The Athenians erred in their conduct of the Peloponnesian War hectored into the venture by narcissistic generals and their conviction of Socrates, whose reputation had been tarnished by a comic playwright and then degraded by angry politicians, but neither of these failings compares to Robespierre's embrace of terror and death as tools he wielded for the state of the French people and nation. The idea of himself as the people's representative, an individual who embodied democracy and virtue on behalf of (his vision of) equality, was perhaps made ideologically possible by his imagined consolidation of democracy and virtue, but practically it was actualized by a new, modern state that claimed its institutions to be virtuous representatives of French sovereignty.[103] In short, the Terror's travesty of revolutionary politics most exemplified

[101] Foucault has made the ancien regime's execution of Damiens, which he recalls in the opening pages of *Surveillir et Punir*, an iconic historical event.

[102] Robespierre initially opposed war against foreign enemies outside French borders but came to support it: a "defensive" war that nonetheless was launched preemptively by France after the decapitation of Louis XVI and was called "democratic." Despite never dressing like one of the *sans-culottes*, he regarded himself as a representative of France's "poor." Although the 1793 Declaration of the Rights of Man and Citizen was never officially adopted as the law of the land, Robespierre's ideas informed its egalitarian social and economic ideals, also understood as "democratic" (see Scurr 2006, 41, 47, 117–18, 211, 271–2).

[103] Urbinati notes that Robespierre dismissed Condorcet's recommendations for localized political and democratic representation as means for unifying France. She finds inspiration in this eighteenth-century French writer (1743–94) for a contemporary theory of "representative democracy" (see Urbinati 2006, 176–221).

what might happen when politicians can claim officially to be the agentic representatives of the people without any official political restraint from demotic agency itself. This indeed makes possible the conflation of democracy, virtue, and tyranny.

Robespierre's ideological brew imitated democracy as institutional and personal representation while self-righteously dignifying his political judgment as the manifestation of "vertue."[104] In a revolutionary political context, he managed to unite the French affection for qualification and distinction with the anti-aristocratic and humanitarian impulse of the Revolution.[105] Most problematically, he also distorted Rousseau by imagining himself as the Lawgiver, even as Rousseau stipulated that anyone able to exercise its powers has to come from *outside* the society that would acquire his principles – rather than from inside – and have divine-like qualities (*pace* Moses and Lycurgus).[106] But Robespierre imagined himself as the representation of republican and democratic virtue, which gave rise to mid-twentieth-century ideas of plebiscitary, extra-parliamentary, even "totalitarian democracy" that, according to its analysts writing in the wake of Fascism and Nazism, (dubiously) found common ground between Rousseau (the critical theorist of small-scale republics) and Robespierre (the dictatorial ruler of Revolutionary France).[107]

That said, Rousseau theoretically imagined the general will as the construction of individuals who subordinated their private interest to the public interest or common good, thus exemplifying "virtue." When it came to political practice, he envisioned various institutions that would filter the wishes of participating citizens up the pipeline to a few leaders – resulting in aristocratic governance.[108] Thus, Robespierre, "the Incorruptible," could imagine himself as the personification and "representation" of Rousseauian public virtue, the general will incarnate, even a secular Christ, as well as a dominating political figure.[109] He made "virtue" a criterion for both personal behavior and public policy, in a

---

[104] See Scurr (2006) for the now readily accessible written comments by Robespierre in letters as well as speeches by him and others viewing himself and the Revolution as embodiments of "*vertue*," noted below.

[105] See Scurr (2006, 24–6, 46–7, 117–19, 152).

[106] See the autobiographical passage quoted in Scurr (2006, 232).

[107] Note the influential post-war arguments of Talmon (1952), Schmitt (2006 (1922), and Schmitt (1996 (1932a)).

[108] Rosenblatt (1997); cf. Rousseau, *The Social Contract* (1973 (1754), IV. 4–5). Rousseau favored "aristocratic governance" at times in order to avoid the potential for corruption in democracy, a government that was most suitable "for gods, not men" (see Rousseau 1973 (1754), III.4–5).

[109] For validation of this unsurprising connection, especially given the French Revolution's evocation of the Roman Republic and the subsequent religious pretensions of its emperors, see Scurr (2006, 193, 245–8; 279; cf. 46, 50, 107, 194).

way that gave a decidedly Christian and authoritarian twist to the more social, practical, and ethical, as well as political, features of Athenian and Spartan *arete*.[110] The French nation was to be "a republic of *vertue*."[111] As elucidated by Robespierre, "vertue" *was* a representative activity that depended on no practical constraints. As the principal citizen and premier leader, he represented himself as a republican and democratic patriot – the criteria for which increasingly stemmed from Robespierre's political judgment about how to preserve the Revolution from enemies foreign and domestic, imagined or real.

Anachronistically combining Rousseau's theory with French revolutionary–republican practice has sometimes served as an alternative framework for democratic representation in liberal modernity. When Rousseau devised a theory of popular sovereignty that aimed to correct for the problems of ancient democracy, liberal social contract theory, and European political practice, he claimed that political representation only aimed at correcting the defects of modern society and ancient democracy; it was not supposed to deprive the *demos* of power, which the practice of representation normally did. As he put it, in representative government, the people only make contact with the popular will at electoral moments, after which they return to the condition of slaves.[112]

The contrasting ethical and political posture generated by French representation during and after the Revolution both reflects and departs from the Rousseauian vision of a proper social-contract society governed by the general will. For there can be no Assembly big enough to concatenate and reconcile the political views of citizens in modern states, while briefer rotations in office for legislators or executives (such as one year) would render ineffective the powers of either or both. Some sought to resolve the issue by establishing protections for individual rights (defined in terms of property, religious expression, privacy, and freedom of speech). But such rights legalize difference as much as commonality and, in any event, only exist at the mercy of a potentially intrusive state.

The emergence of French liberalism after the Revolution nonetheless sought a place for these rights as a way of stabilizing France in the aftermath of Napoleonic rule. Writing in the nineteenth century's second decade, Benjamin Constant tried to differentiate the Revolution's exemplary and regrettable features. But of course his problematic is different. Rather

---

[110] Rousseau notably praised Sparta for its civic virtue, but he often praised the ancients in general – including the Athenians – even as they also came in for criticism for having conflated legislative and executive politics.

[111] See Scurr (2006, 230, 329, 340–1).

[112] Rousseau (1762, III.15, cf. I.6–7, II.4).

than seeking rational and moral sources for the public legitimation of a monarch, Constant wanted to formulate principles for the new French republic that would accommodate the diverse factions and currents of his society that were not contained by the Bourbons and only might be accommodated by more modern political representatives. In his famous speech of 1819, "The Liberty of the Ancients Compared With That of the Moderns," Constant identifies representative government as *the* political safeguard of modern liberty.[113] Like Madison and, later on, J. S. Mill, he does not believe that the ancients knew political representation. But hats off to the moderns, said Constant, who praised political representation as a virtuous, modern invention. Although there were valuable features of ancient governments and societies, particularly the public spirit of the Athenians, they were most fearsome because of their capacity to enable tyranny – particularly that of a democratic majority or cultural prejudice. As a result, it (putatively) deprived (anachronistically) individuals of any prospects for modern freedom. The greater size of modern societies and the necessity for representative government, he says, provide room for the exercise of private, personally generated, commercially oriented conceptions and practices of liberty that receive protection from the state. Apart from a relatively gross treatment of what comprises "the ancients" and "the moderns," Constant notably laments at the end of his speech that the social incentives for the exercise of modern liberty do not provide the requisite sensibility that would promote the public interest. What began as a speech that condemns the revival of ancient republicanism by partisans of the French Revolution (e.g., Gabriel Bonnot de Mably) ends by pointing out the political inadequacies of modern liberty and political representation, which tend to get hijacked by private interests. And Constant offered no idea of how to incline representatives from different classes to attend to the common interest (e.g., during elections in which the well-to-do disproportionately vote).[114]

***

The formation of the American Constitution and the French Republic occur at a time when the power of capitalism has not yet become the major motor of social change. In the colonies and early United States, property either took the form of farms of various sizes overseen or worked by their owners, slaves, or relatively small craft and merchant operations. Banks were local businesses and barely able to sustain themselves under

---

[113] See Constant (1988 (1819), 309–28).
[114] See Constant's "Principles of Politics Applicable to All Representative Government," in Constant (1988 (1819), esp. 205–13).

the pressure of the Revolution. In France, aristocratic privileges still drove the economy, though the growing bourgeoisie surely empowered the Third Estate. It was therefore mostly *in the wake of* the efforts by various Americans (most notably, Alexander Hamilton) to increase the power of the American state and economy, the commercial growth that followed the French Revolution, and the pressures of British labor to gain the vote, that economic activity became a more *generally* powerful influence on the habits of citizens and a factor in determining the practical operation of political representation. In the nineteenth century, as European states evolved and Great Britain continued to wield its considerable national, naval, and imperial power, representation retained its character as a link between the state and the people but one that primarily served the economic interests of the state more than the individual or collective interests of the *demos*. But we first should note Immanuel Kant's philosophical sanction of representation, given its importance to Western liberalism in the mid–late twentieth century, starting with John Rawls's work and complemented by the Kantian turn of Jurgen Habermas.

Kant wrote his political philosophy just before and shortly after the French Revolution, during the unconstitutional monarchy of Frederick II – a distillation of French revolutionary principles without a revolution to carry them out.[115] His central philosophical treatise, the *Critique of Pure Reason* [1781/7], is not usually cited for its contribution to political thought, and rightly so, as it constitutes his conception of "theoretical" reason as opposed to the "practical reason" articulated in *The Metaphysics of Morals* [1797] and essays from the 1780s and 1790s, from "What is Enlightenment?" (1784) to, e.g., "Perpetual Peace" (1795).[116] Nonetheless, that work is filled with political language, and it offers an account of Platonic justice in terms of ideas that clearly establishes his connections to and differences from him.[117] Outstanding among these for our purposes here is Kant's discussion of "representation" (*Vorstellung*). For him, the fundamental idea of representation stems from its character as an "*a priori* determinant of an object." It operates prior to the synthetic apperception of an object or appearance. The capacity for representation *makes possible*

---

[115] Note Kant's laudatory reference to Frederick (King of Prussia 1740–86) as an agent of enlightenment, in "What Is Enlightenment?," in Kant (1991 (1784–95) 58).

[116] Kant's *Metaphysics of Right* [Recht] and *Metaphysics of Virtue* [Tugend] comprise the two parts of *The Metaphysics of Morals*. Excerpts from the former and many of his most relevant essays for political theory are usefully collected in Kant (1991). Kant's dates are 1724–1804, and it's worth noting that he began lecturing on his theory of right in 1767, after studying Rousseau and Natural Law, much before he began to develop the schematic for his critical philosophy (see Reiss's introduction to Kant 1991, 15).

[117] See Kant (1929/33 (1781/7), 309–14; cf. 630–44).

knowledgeable, empirical judgments of experience.[118] But such intellectual representation does not embrace the practical judgments of citizens.

Formalistic as Kant's philosophy is, with the mind dictating what counts as a moral or justifiable understanding of the actual world and extant law authorizing official institutions as the responsible parties for applying them (with citizens also having the rights of freedom of the pen). It practically operates as a top-down *political* (as opposed to *ethical*) philosophy. Thus, when he turns to more direct considerations of politics after the French Revolution, he emphasizes the primacy of a sense of duty to the moral law over any consideration of human motivations for happiness and regards democracy as a majoritarian equivalent of despotism. He favors "republicanism," which instantiates the moral law in legislation by *representatives*. Legislators make the law, and their laws are offered to citizens for their approval. But the legislators themselves are not selected by citizens. Their representative function stems, *sui generis*, from their virtuous exercise (one hopes) of practical reason, as "moral politicians" seeking virtuously to uplift and transform the conflicts of practical life into harmony – rather than as "political moralists" who instrumentalize the moral law for their personal, particular ends (with dire results). By contrast, if actual representatives tried to form a Rousseauian general will, Kant would say that it expressed the general will's antinomy, the "will of all."[119]

For Kant, representatives are "guardians" of the citizenry, not their agents or partners in political dialogue. Moreover, only citizens who own property or make a livelihood from a skill that produces exchangeable objects and are male qualify for the suffrage. As for the right relationship of morality to politics, as promoted by Representatives, it exists as *theoretically valid*, when they scrupulously obey the moral law in their role as politicians. But Kant leaves unspecified how practical agents of politics enact that theoretical ideal in a world of conflict. The unity of theory and practice, he hypothesizes, is stipulated by means of his philosophical outlook; he does not demonstrate its political utility. Indeed, his endorsement of the Latin phrase, "*fiat iustitia pereat mundus*," makes him a political thinker potentially more terrifying than the Hobbesian Leviathan whom, in this essay, he places in the cross hairs of his intellectual

---

[118] Kant (1929/33 (1781/7), 125–6).

[119] This interpretation of Kant surely would arouse dissent from Kant's sympathizers, from Ernst Cassirer to the present, if one regards Kant's moral laws as ideal targets rather than real but impossible principles that only can be practiced by means of extant practices that enforce the law. For Cassirer's Kantian Rousseau, see Cassirer (1963). For a recent, influential rehabilitation of Kant that moderates the practically authoritarian character of his political philosophy by highlighting the rational freedom of his moral philosophy, see Korsgaard (1996).

bow.[120] Even when he promotes the idea of "common sense" for aesthetic judgment, he reassures the reader that it is "a mere ideal norm" and does *not* derive from experience but as a condition of the possibility of experience, "a regulative principle" of a still higher reason.[121]

Not surprisingly, therefore, Kant does not specifically endorse *representative* government; instead, he values *republican* government as the government that both respects the rule of law and allows for the public expression of political opinion by citizens. *Representative* government is *the* institution of the moderns, for Benjamin Constant and John Stuart Mill, that plausibly and most beneficially accommodates democracy and virtue. But if subjected to critical analysis, the endorsement their arguments provide to this form of government does not achieve the accommodation they assert. In the works of both Constant and Mill that deal with political representation, its achievements rest more on the shoulders of hope than argument or historicity. In both cases, this results from intellectual stipulations that praise the virtues of representative government without identifying exactly how it will overcome the factious effects on political power generated by commercial interests and class prejudices. To be sure, there have been noteworthy efforts to specify representation for groups that are arguably under-represented in the American political system, but the indeterminate membership and contestable interests of such groups have made such arguments problematic – although gerrymandering in American electoral districts certainly eviscerates the equal representation of individuals.[122]

3.4   The Gap between Representation and Democratic Ethics

Representative democracy in modernity, in short, belies its pretensions to re-present politically the needs, desires, and interests of the *demos* or the people in any more than a procedural way. But elections in societies with coherent constitutions and civil societies continue to function as the tools by which political representatives gain their legitimacy. Establishing an electoral system by which competing parties generate candidates seeking the votes of the people, their consent to be legitimately governed, has

---

[120] See "Theory and Practice" and "Perpetual Peace" in Kant (1991, 85, 99–101, 116–26). Of late, Kant is read – e.g., by Rawls and Habermas – as a champion of liberal-democratic humanitarian liberalism. Also see Benhabib (2004, 2006).

[121] See Kant (2007 (1797), 70–1 [Part I – Critique of Aesthetic Judgment: First Section, Analytic of Aesthetic Judgment; First Book, Analytic of the Beautiful, par. 22]).

[122] See Young (2000, 81–153); cf. Guinier (1995).

become the signal of "democracy" for mainstream political scientists.[123] Given that the initial settlements of liberal republicanism that sanctioned representation as a political virtue excluded women, African-Americans, property-less workers (to varying degrees), politically active residents of the new political orders made obtaining "the right to vote" their rallying cry for political inclusion – ignoring the extent to which having such rights would not automatically enable them to wield effective political power.[124]

For "realists" or "elitist" theories of democracy (Schumpeter's is both simultaneously), that is the best one might expect.[125] After all, the *demos* in modernity never really ruled – except when it was invoked as a legislative "tyrannical majority."[126] This does not mean, however, that "virtue" has become an irrelevant or inherently dangerous term for understanding or improving representation in public life.[127] For the term retains its connections to "excellence," and such excellence can be ethical as well as technically practical. No democracy, no matter how thin, can do without a serious, ethical language of legitimation that draws on conceptions of personal and civic virtue.[128] *Not* doing so indicates an inability to appreciate the constituents of the political choices of ordinary citizens and a tendency to regard politics as a technical matter that can be mastered by experts who claim to know its realities. In fact, democratic theorists known as objective "realists" are anything but.[129]

Alternatively, one might follow Bernard Manin's account of the features of today's representative government as inevitable products of history that indicate we have as good as it gets – a "mixed" form of government that operates as an "audience democracy" which combines

---

[123] This is a central criterion for democracy according to Robert A. Dahl, who has been a paradigm for American political scientists thinking about democracy for forty years. See, most recently, *On Democracy*, 2nd ed. (New Haven: Yale University Press, 2008 [1998]).

[124] See Keyssar (2000/9) and Berman (2015).

[125] See Schumpeter (1950 (1942), 243–83).

[126] See Guinier (1995).

[127] For a lament about the decline of virtue in the era of the American revolution, especially in terms of pre-revolutionary "Christian, political, and moral" embodiments (the categories derive from Montesquieu's mid-eighteenth-century *The Spirit of the Laws*) or "Christian, republican, and moral conceptions," see Kloppenberg (2000 (1991), 696–700).

[128] Authors who bemoan the disappearance of "virtue" from political discourse tend to have a nostalgic affection for an imaginary, historical time or theoretical idea as well as a tendency to ignore the extent to which *every* notion of virtue relevant to politics possesses a practical dimension linked to potential and actual constructions of power.

[129] To associate "realism" with one's political theory is certainly a plus. But Schumpeter bowdlerizes the English language in referring to his theory as a realist theory of democracy. After all, he presumptively views the political attitudes of ordinary citizens, singly or collectively, as incoherent and those of leaders or cerebral analysts, as clear and focused. See Schumpeter (1950 [1942], 253–64, 269–73).

monarchical, aristocratic or oligarchic, and democratic elements, with the "democratic" element functioning as the electoral system, a kind of modernized version of Aristotle's "polity" and the *ancien regime*'s three orders.[130] But as was the case in pre-1789 France, the democratic element in Manin's model is the weakest. To be sure, it exercises retrospective and prospective power at the ballot box when it issues a "verdict" on its current or future representatives. But generally the damage already has been done by the previously elected politician – whether Lyndon Johnson's Vietnam or George W. Bush's Iraq. The problem with Manin's institutional analysis is that it deliberately refers to politics in theatrical terms, with politicians in the state and ordinary citizens in the audience. He offers little sense of who has produced the "play" or what takes place behind the scenes – for example, in the form of campaign financing, lobbying, or ideological filters that shape the relationship between citizens and their representatives before and after elections.[131] Representatives and the Represented have political content that shapes the nature of representative activity. If representative government is to maintain a genuinely democratic component, that requires democratic activity not only during campaigns but between elections, and *that* requires a palpable sense among the *demos* that their involvement makes a difference. It requires full, free, and egalitarian opportunity and desire for informed debate that counteracts the deficiency of the modern *demos* relative to their leaders in wealth, access to power, and psychological confidence.[132] For a democratic republic to work, most of its citizens must exhibit continual interests in politics. That cast of mind will be insufficient if it's mostly an optional choice – as Plato warned about and Rawls normalized.

My point is not to idolize popular judgment, which is bafflingly difficult to measure. Rather, it is to emphasize how, after the onset of representation as the procedural means for the institutionalization of democracy, "democracy" came to signify less a political order or political procedure than a field of political contestation – a contest, on the one hand, between the official operation of democracy as government by representatives acting on behalf of the ascendant powers of society and, on the other, the expression of citizens' agency by petition, demonstrations, civil disobedience, public discourse, and periodic elections. Democracy today is necessarily more defensive and oppositional than authoritative – even

---

[130] See Manin (1997, 223, 218–35 *passim*). Manin historically views it as a successor to the "party democracy" of the early twentieth century, which succeeded the "parliamentarism" of the eighteenth and nineteenth centuries.

[131] Manin's metaphor appears in *Principles of Representative Government*, 223.

[132] Manin (1997, 155, 160, 179, 192, 237).

as it responsibly must act as both the agency of citizens and the operation of institutions.[133] This means that it is associated with "populism," demotic activity which, in the dominant discourse, lacks a practical political purpose and easily is driven by unreflective anger. (See the anti-government rhetoric of demagogic politicians and resentful ordinary citizens.[134]) But something will fill the gap between the mechanisms of representation and the claims of democracy, and just because the demonstrators lack passes into the established circles of political discussion, that does not mean that they know (or don't know) what they're about. Nowadays, democratic activity mostly functions as a political challenge and corrective; it confronts (via public dissent) established politicians and their agents, to transform the political, cultural, and economic experiences of ordinary citizens into political power.

When the boundaries of states have become so porous to border-crossings by capital, communication, and migrations of refugees, the manner in which ethics and power shape the interactions between democracy, virtue, and representation is difficult to identify. The gap between representative government and democracy may not seem large, given the media's preoccupation with the rhetoric of political candidates and public officials who play the roles of tribunes of the people. But it is *between* elections and *amid* the currents of ordinary life that accommodations or tensions between the ethics and power of democratic citizens and their representatives take shape. More, myriad, and practical conduits of discourse must connect citizens, their representatives, and government for democracy and goodness to complement each other. If contemporary political representatives are to warrant the adjective "democratic" they

---

[133] The idea of "fugitive democracy" crafted by Sheldon Wolin may describe features of democracy's current condition, but it cannot function as an equivalent for democracy as a political ethic – for in that mode it must imagine itself as steering institutions as well as inciting opposition, lest it seem politically irresponsible. See Wolin's essay, "Fugitive Democracy," reprinted in Wolin (2016). Nonetheless, previous justifications of civil disobedience in the American political tradition have focused on opposition more than practicality – in ways that have fostered major practical change. See, e.g., Henry David Thoreau, "Civil Disobedience" (1849) and Martin Luther King, Jr., "Letter From Birmingham City Jail" (1963) in Bedau (1970). Also see Arendt, "On Civil Disobedience" (1970), in Arendt (1972 (1970)).

[134] In American politics, one might think of some of the Republican Party's Presidential candidates for the party's 2016 nomination, as well as the illegal occupation of federal land by armed Oregon ranchers who feel that federal ownership destroys their livelihood. See Kirk Johnson and Jack Healy, "Armed Group Vows to Continue Occupation at Oregon Refuge," *The New York Times*, January 3, 2016. For an interesting commentary, see Justin P. McBrayer, "This Land is Your Land, Or Is It?," *The New York Times*, January 5, 2016. Similar outcroppings of populist resentment against the downsides of globalization in Western societies include displaced anger against immigrants and reactionary patriotism in the United Kingdom, France, and possibly elsewhere in Europe.

must harness every opportunity to enhance conversations among diverse constituencies. Persistent efforts in this vein that yield palpable consequences for attendees will build their own momentum. While representation generates breathing space for the corrupting power of money and economic power in politics (which warrant greater regulation), it also allows for the neologism of Socratic leadership.

Many studies, some of which I have cited above, identify elite culprits in this constant political movement of a putatively democratic society into anti-democratic directions, but they do not explain the whole story of how the *logos* of democracy becomes, in the *ergon* of representation, anti-democracy. What kind of ethics empowers the anti-democratic directions of politics, especially at the national level? As we have seen, the gap between democracy and representative government is enormous. In strictly practical terms, this is inevitable given the size of contemporary societies. But the issue is less the gap in and of itself, less representation in and of itself, than how representation operates. How is it possible for the few elected by the many to act for the most part against the interests of the many? Part of the answer surely stems from the different political traditions in different societies and the trends in political power noted above. But we also need to pay attention to the ways in which political discourse, as the rhetoric of manipulating ideologies, aims to shape the political ethics of citizens and bridge the gap that makes the relationship between representation and democracy so tendentious.

Since the 1970s, the proportion of the United States' citizenry that falls within the economic middle class is said to have declined – from 61 to 50 percent.[135] With stagnant wages for the past four decades, its relative economic influence and prosperity has declined as well.[136] This has meant a disconnect between political rhetoric that favors the middle class and actual politics that undermines it. Not surprisingly, political polarization has increased, principally marked by a rightward movement in the Republican Party, fueled by latent racism against President Obama that energized the Tea Party, and the corporatism of Democratic National Committee leadership of the Clintons, which fostered the widespread

---

[135] For data documenting the erosion of the economic well-being of the middle class in the last four decades, see Pew Research Center: Social and Demographic Trends, "The American Middle Class is Losing Ground" (December 9, 2015).

[136] Pew Research Center, "For most workers, real wages have barely budged for decades" (October 9, 2014). But the pay of executives has skyrocketed. See Robert Reich, *Saving Capitalism: For the Many, Not the Few* (New York: Alfred A. Knopf, 2015), 97–132.

support for Senator Bernie Sanders.[137] No surprises here. With the election of Donald Trump and his brand of hateful, economic nationalism, along with its resonance in Europe, it is hard to tell what will eventuate. After all, Trump's winning margin depended on the votes of individuals whose interests his policies do not serve. These facts do not answer the question of why Americans have not been able to mend the fissures between their interests and the actions of their representatives. Among and beyond the myriad power dynamics we have addressed is the distortion of political discourse by the vehicles through which the interests of ordinary citizens are transmuted into political power (or apathy), namely, the tilted channeling of the *opportunities* for political discussion and deliberation among the many relative to the few, principally by the powers at the top and their interests in institutional stability (aka the Establishment), or the ability of wealthy demagogues to exploit the old canards of patriotism and economic resentment to "represent" the emotionally disenfranchised. In the next few years, there will be clashes between the dispossessed who have been enticed by the lure of economic nationalism and Democrats – who must democratize their connections to capitalism if they expect to draw on disaffected populists. How this plays out depends on too many unknown factors to predict with intelligent confidence.

Political rhetoric designed to reconcile citizens and their representatives plays a much more ambiguous role in the United States today than it was intended to, for example, in the monolithically ordered Leviathan state of Thomas Hobbes. In Hobbes's hypothetical state, order would stem from the ability of the Sovereign to define himself publicly as the source of peace, freedom, and order for his subjects in his role as their Representative. When representative government is understood as democracy, political responsibility for the exercise of power becomes more dispersed and difficult to identify. Moreover, in contrast to the industrial age, when profit stemmed primarily from the capitalist's use of the labor of industrial workers, most profits are made in finance, technology, and real estate, in ways hard to see. As a result, the political rhetoric that identifies and evaluates this process, in conjunction with the technological decentralization of communication, is hard to validate.[138] This makes it difficult for individual Americans to link

---

[137] For data on political polarization, see Pew Research Center: U.S. Politics and Policy, "Political Polarization in the American Public" (June 12, 2014). For changes taking place particularly in the Republican Party, see Hacker and Pierson (2005).

[138] This point resembles Foucault's studies of the dissemination of power in Europe and the United States away from the sovereign – especially since the nineteenth century.

their own economic and political experiences to those of others. Such a circumstance is beneficial if the preeminent political danger is from political cooperation fueled by the actions of ordinary citizens, which, in the form of the power of states thwarting national action, concerned the Federalists.

But one might question whether coordinated democratic activity currently threatens American well-being, especially given this familiar list of horribles: the disconnect between democracy and representation; the increasing difficulty of most Americans to hold their own amid the financial capitalism of the twenty-first century; a system of taxation tilted to benefit the fortunately rich; nearly unregulated access to weaponry by citizens with little to fear; a program of energy production and consumption that damages the ecology of the planet, and, apart from the serious play of social media, and corporately funded national media that often informs but also displays conflicts of interest as it broadcasts amid a hypothetically unregulated "marketplace of ideas."

Major sources of the problem lie in the invitations to political corruption resulting from political agendas that appeal to private, capitalist interests. Only if the sources and nature of their noxious effects are clearly felt and understood by all classes of citizens can democracy and representation become complementary sources of goodness.

The historical origins of political representation indicate that citizens must make special efforts to alter the processes that constitute political representation – the principal roads *to office*, the conduct of representatives *in office* – if the activities of representatives are to become better complements of democracy. But the task is even more daunting. For making representation a virtuous complement to democracy not only must address the ailments of corruption but the inclination and ability of citizens to hold their representatives accountable, providing plausible guides for their conduct. This requires greater political attention by citizens to politics and in the direction of common goods, so as to engender democratic resistance and reform.[139] If we understand the sources and continuing reality of the grating tension between representation and democracy, how it partially reflects: long-standing tensions inherent in political ethics and the practicalities of political power exacerbated by the attractions of digital technologies, the effects of global capitalism, the intermixing of

---

[139] Bruce Ackerman has offered an interesting idea that addresses the problem of inequality in campaign funding. He suggests that the federal government give every voting citizen $50 on a credit card that they could donate to the campaigns of their favored candidates or parties, as long as neither accepted funding from private sources. This would cost the Treasury some 10 billion dollars (see Wright and Rogers 2011, 372–3).

national ethnicities, and the "enhancement" of military weaponry and its extensive use in political conflicts, then we shall recognize the contours of political action in the political waters we navigate, so as to place us in a better position to alleviate this tension's inevitable turmoil.

We have found how the contemporary experience of the gap between representation and democracy has deep historical roots. Americans have often dealt with their political exasperation by seeking personal advancement and desiring that their efforts are sanctioned by fair social standards. The ethic of equality of opportunity has supported these efforts for some. But even as the circle of opportunity has formally widened, we shall see that this often useful complement to democracy also and always will harbor disappointment.[140]

---

[140] For a more optimistic view, see Dionne (2012).

4 Civil Rightness: A Virtuous Discipline for the Modern *Demos*

4.1 Introduction

Despite urgings from educators and politicians, and apart from periodic demonstrations, mass petitions and posts in the lands of virtual communication, elections for public officials provide the principal occasions in which contemporary adults perform their status as free and equal democratic citizens. But outside of these occasions, a phrase resonates throughout public life, particularly in the United States but also (albeit less prominently) in other economically developed, liberal-capitalist republics that regulates official conduct in social life. It is supposed to reconcile democracy and public standards of goodness, freedom, and equality in civil society, where most citizens spend most of their waking lives. That phrase is "equal opportunity," which emerged from the social transformations that gained steam after the liberal revolutions of the late eighteenth century.[1] It mixes practical and ethical standards that set guidelines for realizing that exceptional, ethereal, and often deceptively attractive individual ideal of happiness for each and all – even as no government sees *its* mission as promoting freedom, equality, and happiness for *all*. In the United States, this ideal has assumed a mythic form named "the American dream" – a socio-philosophical standard coined in the United States, as it was coming out of the Great Depression, to describe a practicable goal of personal happiness, the attainment of which is a kind of virtue, supposedly available to all and so widely desired that it is more attainable than love, fueling the perpetual search for success. One might view it as a modern capitalist economist's city of God on earth.[2] The first recorded iteration of the American Dream follows:

---

[1] Pole (1993 (1978), 150–7).
[2] This chapter is marked by a preponderance of references to American history and political experience. While the result is, I trust, good for my argument, it is a function of my limited knowledge more than the potential reach of its claims. Citizens of many other countries surely will find, *mutatis mutandis*, comparable experiences in their own politics and history.

The dream is a vision of a better, deeper, richer life for every individual, regardless of the position in society which he or she may occupy by the accident of birth. It has been a dream of a chance to rise in the economic scale, but quite as much, or more that, of a chance to develop our capacities to the full, unhampered by unjust restrictions of caste or custom. With this has gone the hope of bettering the physical conditions of living, of lessening the toil and daily anxieties of life.[3]

The American dream supposedly hangs like an apple from a tall tree that everyone (particularly those not born with silver spoons in their mouths) can climb with disciplined effort, without which it will remain beyond reach. The practical quest for the American dream rhetorically unites politically divided citizens in ethically sanctioned, practical ventures. Indeed, this dream marks the hopes of citizens in other American and European societies, to which immigrants and refugees travel for dramatic change in their lives, if not refuge. It even found its way into the 1916 Proclamation of Irish Independence.[4]

Formalized and institutionalized, "equal opportunity" is the law in most secular workplaces, from businesses to universities, and governmental organizations. The phrase draws on the Equal Protection Clause in the second sentence of Section 1 of the Fourteenth Amendment to the United States Constitution, ratified in 1868 and extended in the 1960s. It holds the promise of legal, if not social, fairness to citizens and persons residing on American soil.[5] As part of conventional law as well as common social ethics, it operates within the conventions of existing society and mostly negatively, as a form of non-discrimination that protects selected minorities and women who might otherwise not receive equal treatment under the law. One might think that it is a wholly recent invention, a remnant of the civil rights era and its associated, increasingly beleaguered programs for "affirmative action" for African-Americans, as well as, potentially, women, ethnic, racial, and sexual/gender minorities.

---

[3] The above quote was penned by James Truslow Adams in 1938 and quoted in Samuel (2012, 13).

[4] "The Irish Republic is entitled to, and hereby claims, the allegiance of every Irishman and Irishwoman. The Republic guarantees religious and civil liberty, equal rights and equal opportunities to all its citizens, and declares its resolve to pursue the happiness and prosperity of the whole nation and of all its parts, cherishing all of the children of the nation equally, and oblivious of the differences carefully fostered by an alien Government, which have divided a minority from the majority in the past."

[5] The section in which the clause appears reads fully as follows: "All *persons* born or naturalized in the United States, and subject to the jurisdiction thereof, are *citizens* of the United States and of the state wherein they reside. No state shall make or enforce any law which shall abridge the privileges or immunities of *citizens* of the United States; nor shall any state deprive any *person* of life, liberty, or property, without due process of law; nor deny to any *person* within its jurisdiction the equal protection of the laws."

But it is an informal injunction to good citizenship authorized by the American Declaration of Independence's "pursuit of happiness." As a collective ethic for the American state, it functions as a kind of statist ideology that smooths over cleavages of class, race, gender, ethnicity, and religion. As such, it has been referred to (not unreasonably) as America's equivalent of Plato's noble lie.[6] But in fact, the idea of equal opportunity is incoherent from the standpoint of citizens as agents – for opportunities are radically individual phenomena, literally doors opening out of the harbors of their selves, and as such cannot be equalized unless we literally became homogeneous.[7]

As a social standard, "equal opportunity" concerns processes – the selection of a few from the many. Inevitable irritants produced by the egalitarian starting point and elitist outcome are dissolved by the implicit assumption that a selection process governed by "equal opportunity" will be determined by (interpretations of) "merit," a fair and just measure of excellent performance. The notion of "equal opportunity," and its associated benchmark of "merit," have been important guideposts for democratic ethics in civil society and democratic politics since the nineteenth century and continue to serve in these capacities today. They provide nominal compasses for secular notions of "virtue," particularly in liberal, constitutional republics.[8] The historicism deployed here accounts for them in both the present and past, subjecting each to critical scrutiny. I argue that the notions of equal opportunity and merit – which I combine in an ethical standard that I call *civil rightness* – generate standards of goodness or virtue for practical conduct in civil society that have both democratic and anti-democratic effects.

"Civil rightness" links the fraternal twins of "equal opportunity" and "merit," with the former supposed to guarantee the social production of the latter. "Civil rightness," therefore, functions as a kind of secular religion that generates a rhetorical ether; it designates an operative (but disappointing for most) ideology, guide for social aspiration, and virtuous discipline for all working citizens. It actually regulates the conditions of social conduct and achievement, thereby producing a "virtuous discipline."[9] I am not so much interested in judging "civil rightness" as I am interpreting its conjunction with a family of civic ideals – *arete*, representation, legitimacy, and human rights – that function as ethical hori-

---

[6] See Andrew (1989, 577–95).
[7] See Fishkin (1983) and Dahrendorf (1979).
[8] See Wallach (1994, 319–40); cf. Wallach (2003, 219–41).
[9] I distinguish "civil rightness" from the rightfully maligned notion of "meritocracy," which enforces "merit" through a disciplinary, exclusive form of power.

zons which both enhance and inhibit democratic life, evincing important but elusive democratic ethics that associate democracy and goodness. I attend to how this and other political concepts are best understood in dynamic relation to political action and social structures more than self-contained moral or theoretical articulations and political views.[10]

Without encroaching on religious beliefs, equal opportunity sanctions prevailing, accepted, non-partisan notions of good behavior. But the notion of civil rightness was, and has been also understood as a deceptive and pejorative ideology. It always promises more than it delivers, for it presupposes contests in which most "lose" while a few "win," serving as a countervailing force to democracy understood as a political order where the many win, potentially at the expense of the few. In this regard, it refracts the idea of "competition," engagement in which one can promote competence, if not excellence, and possibly destroy cooperative social relations. No philosophical analysis of the concept of "equality of opportunity," or equality and opportunity, can ignore the manner in which equal opportunity constrains democracy, even as it is supposed to be its complement. It reflects the uneasy balance between the dominance of socio-economic inequalities amid formal, political equality enforced by representatives – a feature of social life that marks modern, liberal democracies.

Given their historical roots, equality of opportunity, merit, and "civil rightness" encode basic legal and ethical assumptions of *capitalism* (such as competition, monetized value, and rosters of winners and losers) and *democracy* (understood as liberty and equality under state law), although they could be socially meaningful in situations dominated by neither capitalism nor democracy. This raises the following questions for civil rightness as a bridge between democracy and goodness. Is the notion of civil rightness so radically compromised by the systems of justice in which it operates that it inhibits rather than promotes democracy?[11] Can notions of "civil rightness," "equal opportunity," and "merit" supersede R. H. Tawney's dour observation that it systematically betrays hopes by offering "equal opportunities to become unequal"?[12] In what follows, I sanction the enduring appeal of "civil rightness," despite its problematic character as a feature of democratic ethics, because of its historical roots in anti-aristocratic movements – as long as its pretensions are carefully

---

[10] I do not directly engage the views of liberal-minded, analytical political philosophers (such as John Rawls, Gerald Cohen, Richard Arneson, and James Fishkin) who parsed the notion of equal opportunity with ideas of "fairness."

[11] See Schaar (1981 (1967), 193–210).

[12] See Tawney (1931–51, 103).

circumscribed. The notion and discourse of civil rightness has more integrity than that of an ideological cover for "postmodern capitalism," "neoliberalism," or the *faux* democracy of "inverted totalitarianism."[13]

Three specific reasons bolster this claim. First, it has been used by various groups outside the club of first-class citizens to succeed in social life. Second, it reflects (albeit often in distorted ways) actual legal protections of equal treatment and political notions of equality that are deliberately embraced by the less as well as the more powerful. Indeed, there is as much resistance to civil rightness by the more powerful as there is self-deception with regard to its promise in the less powerful. Third, not only is there a rational, practical, utilitarian, and instrumental value to rhetorical concepts as means of progressive or reactionary politics. They also function in social discourse as part of political action – drawing on the ancient Greek insight that a constitutive and mutually beneficial link between *logos* and *ergon* crucially informs virtuous democratic politics.

Civil rightness may be used to buttress the status quo, but that is not its major feature. It defines the discourse that legitimates the rights and virtues of citizens in modern democracies, intending to accommodate democracy and political goodness in civil society – often a source of useful resistance to the politics of the state and the powerful as long as conceptions of "civil rightness" remain open to criticism, not serving as tools of enforcement by the policemen of conventions (a difficult requirement to meet).

To substantiate these points, I discuss civil rightness in relation to contexts of justice and injustice that shelter it. My aim is to clarify the political confusion in current Western political orders that stems from the overarching ethical standards of their civil societies.

4.2   Historical Origins and Conceptual Elements of Civil Rightness

Amid the bare facticity of the ordinary life of citizens and the operation of governments that depend on their consent; in the wake of the forced abdication of James II, along with the ascension of William and Mary to the English throne in 1688, and after the liberal–republican revolutions in the United States and France, a realm of civil society took shape that required a new political ethic that would serve both disciplinary and

---

[13] The term "postmodern capitalism" is mine, linking contemporary capitalism's (1) globalism, (2) focus on shaping and boosting consumer's desires, and (3) the shift of its gravitational center from manufacturing to finance.

emancipatory functions in societies that increasingly called themselves democratic. Born amid the eighteenth and early nineteenth centuries from the wombs of the English, American, and French revolutions, many citizens of this age – though hardly a majority with the exclusion of women, the marginal political status of property-less workers, and the enslavement or subordination of African-Americans – now possessed free and equal rights to actualize their individual lives in vastly unequal circumstances, in contrast to the legalized political and social limits placed upon them in colonial or aristocratic societies. Entrance into the realm of civil society became the desired political target for the disenfranchised seeking full citizenship (property-less workers, African-Americans, women), a somewhat sub-political realm for realizing democratic conditions of life. Yet it also was a locale where lapsed aristocrats and the remnants of aristocratic privilege asserted their power and new capitalists staked their claims. While the emancipation of millions of American and French adults from colonial and aristocratic tutelage in the wake of their revolutions sharply reduced religious and aristocratic sanctions as tools for promoting virtuous behavior in social life, aristocratic behavior and privileges did not lose salience in social and political life – particularly in Europe.[14] But its power had been reduced to varying degrees, and new social standards and sanctions slowly emerged to replace them. Tocqueville's accounts of the changing societies in the United States and France notably describe and theoretically analyze the significance of these transformations.[15] The resulting ethical matrix inherited notions of reputable behavior, and these shaped the ethical indeterminacy of newborn political ideas of freedom, equality, and moral autonomy (albeit radically compromised by inequalities of wealth, the subordination of women and ethnic minorities, and the enslavement of blacks in the United States who had been captured, enslaved, and transported from Africa in the 1600s).

As new political orders slowly emerged from efforts to remove the remnants of monarchical and aristocratical power in France (e.g., the "revolutions" of 1830 and 1848); to extend the suffrage in the United Kingdom (e.g., the Reform Acts of 1832, 1867, 1884–5), and to open up civil society to white American men (e.g., the Jacksonian notions of "equal protection under the law" and his call for the "equal representation" of citizens in government), the need arose for a political ethic that would informally constitute notions of goodness for *what* all citizens

---

[14] The idea of emancipation or moral tutelage of "others" was notably articulated by Kant (1991), in "What is Enlightenment?" (1784), 54–60.

[15] See Tocqueville (1969 (1835, 1840), Vol. 2, Pt. 4) and Tocqueville (1955 (1856)).

should do in their ordinary lives *with* their new political rights of liberty and equality, *without* direct regard to religious beliefs but accepting social and economic equalities.[16] In these new contexts, the idea and ideal of "equal opportunity" began to take hold as a legal standard and socio-cultural ideal – thus did "civil rightness" coordinate democracy and goodness amid the capitalistic and immigrant-population driven growth in nineteenth-century American society.

This evolving emancipation of the working man generated paradoxes, which produced one of the ongoing puzzles of political life in advanced capitalist democracies. How could a few be selected from the many for scarce positions in civil society and government without sabotaging democratic equality? What ethical standards comport with the political system of constitutional republics, the economic regime of capitalism, and the popular vision of democracy? We know useful explanations of this puzzle by Hume, Rousseau, Marx, John Stuart Mill, and Foucault. Moreover, Tocqueville, J. S. Mill, and, most notably, Nietzsche, differently dreaded the effects of practical elaborations of "liberty" and "equality" in the post-revolutionary era of modernity, for they saw instantiation of these concepts as likely to herald mediocrity as promote progress. Whatever their value, they and more popular correlates instantiated anew the old tension and conflict between *logos* and *ergon*, words and deeds, reason and actuality, that preoccupied ancient Greek and, later, Western political thinkers.

In the early nineteenth century, societies sanctioned this tension in a new political ethic for civil society. In the United States and France, and less formally so in the United Kingdom, governments presumptively allotted time and space for individuals to achieve the limits of their abilities – no longer fettered by colonial powers, aristocratic privileges, or religious identities – in what came generally to be called "civil society." John Locke had previously referred to "civil society" as

---

[16] From President Jackson's Veto of the Bank Bill (1832): "It is to be regretted that the rich and powerful too often bend the acts of government to their selfish purposes. Distinctions in society will always exist under every just government. Equality of talents, of education, or of wealth cannot be produced by human institutions. In the full enjoyment of the gifts of Heaven and the fruits of superior industry, economy, and virtue, every man is equally entitled to protection by law; but when the laws undertake to add to these natural and just advantages artificial distinctions, to grant titles, gratuities, and exclusive privileges, to make the rich richer and the potent more powerful, the humble members of society – the farmers, mechanics, and laborers – who have neither the time nor the means of securing like favors to themselves, have a right to complain of the injustice of their Government. There are no necessary evils in government. Its evils exist only in its abuses. If it would confine itself to *equal protection* (author's italics), and, as Heaven does its rains, shower its favors alike on the high and the low, the rich and the poor, it would be an unqualified blessing."

the entire gamut of officially rule-governed society overseen by government; it now referred to an area of life whose practices were seen (by Hegel and others) to be primarily rooted "between" the family and the state (even as both crucially affected its practices), a realm that was at once semi-private and semi-public. It also was uniquely Western, dependent on representative government, a capitalist engine of economic growth, and patriarchal family life.[17] This realm of civil society was officially non-political and ethically indeterminate, but personal conduct within it constituted their ethical lives and legitimated extant political orders. From the mid-nineteenth century to the 1990s, the United States welcomed millions of immigrants (while also excluding many on racial grounds) for the sake of economic productivity as well as its reputation as a haven for political refugees from the seventeenth century until 2016.[18]

Two phrases and two signposts characterized the appropriate functioning of civil rightness as the preferred term for signifying the legitimate accommodation of equality and inequality in nineteenth-century civil society: the Napoleonic guidepost used in 1799 for hiring non-aristocrats into his civil service – viz., the standard of "careers open to talents" (*La carrière ouverte aux talents*) – and the particularly American aspiration, elevated to eminence in the 1830s, of equal protection of the law to become successful in life (later rendered as "equality of opportunity").[19] "Careers open to talents" and "equality of opportunity" (or equal protection of the laws) became linchpins of an informal but widespread idea of civil rightness as counterpoints to the legacies of aristocratic and feudal society that nonetheless sanctioned the hierarchical power of some groups over

---

[17]   Its location at the intersection of the familial, economic/social, and political (in Hegelian terms) reflected its difference from the previous, direct association by social contract theorists of "civil society" with legitimate government.

[18]   This is not to deny or diminish the significance of the colonies or the United States as a (restricted) haven for refugees, from the seventeenth century to the present. As Wright and Rogers put it (with no temporal boundaries): "In fact, U.S. *citizenship* and *political control* are well bounded; but American *society* is not." Wright and Rogers (2011, 21) (authors' italics). President Trump has used his executive authority to subvert this truism and has been resisted by American courts.

[19]   Indeed, the clearest intellectual source for this phrase "equal opportunity" is a passage from Adam Smith's *Theory of the Moral Sentiments* (IV.1.8) that imaginatively narrates the fruitless attempt of "a poor man's son" to acquire power and riches that, in the end – according to Smith – are hardly worth the struggle. Andrew Jackson is known for holding out the equivalent prospect of equal opportunity for all citizens via "equal protection by law ... and government" against entrenched privilege, given the rights of entrepreneurial individualism amid the beckoning frontier. See his Veto of the Bank Bill (1832), in Mason (1965, 452).

others.[20] This civil society was blanketed by obstacles that could impede the display of an individual's virtues and talents but might not warrant regulations by government or the general will. It was hardly a state of nature of the variety imagined by Hobbes, Locke, Rousseau, imputed by Thomas Jefferson, or philosophically presupposed by Kant, and more recently John Rawls. Myriad roads, bridges, ditches, white-water rapids, and other historically (as well as naturally) produced obstacles invariably complicated one's journey in this realm. As alluded to above, the word "opportunity" derives from a French word that described a position in that opened to the sea, awaiting the shifting winds and waves that contingently determined what came one's way. Opportunities had no rhyme or reason; they often stemmed from chance, and how one did or could address them was left undetermined.[21] As such, each individual's experience of them was highly individualized and radically contingent. The very idea of opportunity, therefore, could range from a desperate chance to avert a black death to facing a world that supposedly bends to one's will.[22] Equalizing opportunity has a nice, rhetorical ring, but it is analytically incoherent as a situation for agency insofar as no opportunities are actually equal for a number of persons across the board. The phrase is a useful political code or ideology (neutrally understood) presented by society to its citizens that actually is absurd without an infinite number of qualifications.

The linguistic term to adjudicate differences among those competing amid conditions of "equal opportunity," to signal desert for the few who warranted the scarce positions in selective institutions, was "merit." "Merit" was a purportedly apolitical quality, a secular version of virtue that marked generally accepted criteria for the demonstration of personal worth in work, the arts, and professions. It became a notable social term in the seventeenth and eighteenth centuries, during the relatively pacific era of the early Enlightenment and pre-revolutionary Western societies. According to the *Oxford English Dictionary*, it derived from the Latin word, *meritum*, which referred to worth, desert, or warranted praise. The idea of "merit," therefore, predates "equality of opportunity" by hundreds of years, and was initially associated with institutional corollaries in

---

[20] For illustrations of the means by which utilitarian theories of political economy linked notions of marginal value, merit, and opportunity, see Halevy (1972 (1928)). The notion of "careers open to talents" found its way into Rawls's theory of justice as fairness as a reference point for the concept of "natural aristocracy" and, later, his concept of "liberal" equality of opportunity. Rawls (1971, 65, 72–5).

[21] For the origins and early uses of "opportunity," see the *OED*.

[22] Williams (1962) clearly identified the instability of the notions of both equality and equal opportunity, 110–31.

the realms of religion, education, and economic performance that reflect a notion of "desert" linked to divine or secular notions of individual worth and justice.[23] In the nineteenth century, it would cultivate more ground. Because of the purported dedication of the increasingly rationalized institutions to equal respect for those who would become part of them, "equality of opportunity" and "civil rightness" became understood as preconditions for the recognition and practice of "merit."[24] Given the virtual impossibility of administering "merit" in a wholly impartial and apolitical way, "merit," like "equal opportunity," is vague as an ethical standard and social myth that nonetheless has been politically useful as a benchmark for fair recognition of skill and virtue in civil society. It denotes conventionally accepted standards that combine ethical, performative ideals and powerful social practices.

The simultaneous connections of "equal opportunity" to social virtue, rule-governed capitalism, and modern democracy stemmed from the fact that institutionalization of "equality of opportunity" occurs amid a competitive context of power in which one or a few outdo many others – the losers – albeit on the basis of an open yet selective, putatively rational determination of "merit." Those who made it through the gauntlet of regulations that guaranteed equality of opportunity implicitly acquired the trait of "merit," the secularized, social, and practical equivalent for the now mostly ethical, private, and religious usage of "virtue."[25] In this vein, civil rightness disciplines the social expectations of the *demos*, creating conditions whereby they blame themselves as the losing "many" relative to the successful "few." As it primarily concerned social behavior and not private life, civil rightness was not explicitly an ethic of virtuous behavior. And yet, as free citizens no longer were legally destined for subservient drudgery, citizens came to be regarded as almost wholly responsible for the limits of their lives, subject to social judgments about their virtue, even though political decision-making by governments played crucial roles in shaping the nature of the opportunities made available to them and from which they made their presumptively free choices. "Equal opportunity" operated as an ideal standard designed to guarantee legitimate social freedom for individuals, meaningful to all – and thus a social virtue – despite the significant differences of tradition, custom,

---

[23] See the various definitions and entries for "merit" in the *OED*.

[24] As a new word that signaled the evidence of social virtue, "merit" was highlighted in the early eighteenth century by Anthony Ashley Cooper, third earl of Shaftesbury, in his work of 1699/1711 (Cooper 1699/1711).

[25] Nietzsche bemoaned the domination of the meaning of virtue in his day by rationalistic concepts and Christian doctrine that sanctioned the label of "equal rights," viewing it as a feeble replacement for its previous association with "great" action and achievement.

connections, and wealth (let alone genetic endowment) that limited the lives of individuals. The idea, concept, or principle of equal opportunity, linked to the discursive sanction of merit, offered a political ethos for nineteenth-century Americans that would resolve these tensions. *Qua* "civil rightness," it held out the promise that everyone more or less had the ability and would have the opportunity to open doors to success. The extent to which opportunity was equal was almost impossible to assess. Apart from the incoherence of its logic, the doors of opportunity had different degrees of difficulty at different stages of life – each of which depended on the circumstances of one's birth, parental upbringing, neighborhood, and the economic conditions of one's time and place.

While governments allowed the exercise of much greater economic and political freedom than before the liberal revolutions, freedom's shape and power assumed forms akin to those in earlier, aristocratic or colonial, times: special privileges were reserved for the rich; entire echelons of workers lived as their servants. Women in most cases still had to defer to men. Now, the governing powers were not the effects of social status as much as the constraints of market forces regulating the exchange of goods and services produced by the engines of capitalism and the constraints of an ever-larger political society.[26] Even as it legally mattered less and less what your biological and economic inheritance was, it still dramatically affected one's prospects at birth.[27] How could these freedoms manage to harmonize with the unequal life chances of citizens in a single political community, when the rebirth and formal extension of states' rights promised progress for all its members and greater inclusion for those not yet full participants? Athenian democrats were able to discuss these problems in the *agora* and address them to their satisfaction in the *ekklesia*. But what about in large-scale societies where freedom and equality played themselves out on the landscape of civil society, only mildly affected by their representative governments? An in-built tension marked the articulation of this new political ethic, placing the *demos* at odds with the conditions of political power. Indeed, as the term "democracy" began to be accepted as the nameplate for these societies, the power of the *demos* became identified at times with resistance to the status quo.[28]

---

[26] To be sure, sociologists like to emphasize the primacy of status or "social structure" over class (see, for example, Dahrendorf 1979, 40–95).

[27] This was true whether one lived in the United States, France, or the United Kingdom. After the Reform Act of 1832 in the United Kingdom, five out of six adult males still lacked the right to vote; and no adult females had the right to vote; in the United States, slavery still thrived, and nationalism in France marginalized ethnic minorities – while each of these countries (and all others) denied women the suffrage.

[28] See Hanson (1989, 68–89).

The "natural" liberalism and touted democracy of these societies was not enough to legitimate their political norms, for the discursive and practical realities of citizens' lives did not cohere and required reconciliation that the nostrums of freedom and formal political equality did not provide.[29] A new political ethic was needed to foster a collective belief and solidarity independent of the aristocratic privileges of status and estate, the ethnic bonds of national heritage, the divergent religious beliefs of citizens (especially in the United States where waves of immigrants had begun to land), and the unequal results of economic competition. Even with "equal rights," the question of what to *do* with one's liberty and quality always remained; no religion or ideology could answer this question. A political ethic would need to legitimate conventional conduct in civil society and complement representation as a political virtue that sanctioned the election of lawmakers in public realms. It would need to speak to historical experiences and engage motives for future action. The aim would be to square a circle: demonstrate the actual and potential worth, merit, or virtue of citizens who belong to a competitive, hierarchical, capitalist society *and* a nominally republican or democratic society.

This new ethic social goodness for the *demos* acting as republican citizens in capitalist society thus functioned as a kind of liberal *virtue* and social *discipline*, a guide for how to behave and succeed within the institutional constraints of a liberal, capitalist, representative democracy, a practical idea that seamlessly combined virtue and rights in relation to which one could identify abnormality and social vice.[30] At its inception, "civil rightness" functioned as a political ethic that promoted ideally equal and practically unequal standards of the new, nominally democratic (or republican) political order. As such, it reflected the paradoxical relationship of ethical norms and practical power that enacted and reenacted a gap between its own *logos* and *ergon* – akin to the manner in which the new form of political representation would be a synecdoche for democracy and virtue in modern, constitutional republics. The rhetoric of civil rightness asks one to imbibe the double-edged promise of liberal freedom in the democratized civil society – experiencing both emancipation from aristocratic shackles and practical oases (or mirages) of equal opportunity. When implicitly associated with equality, it becomes an ethical and political standard for regulating the interplay of citizens' activities toward a good end.

---

[29]   This was so, despite the liberal consensus (see Hartz 1955).

[30]   In 1835, Alexis de Tocqueville proclaimed (without elaboration), "The idea of rights is nothing but the conception of virtue applied to the world of politics" (see Tocqueville 1969 (1835, 1840), Vol. I, Pt. 2, Ch. 6, 237–8).

4.3   Historical Trajectories of Civil Rightness

The result of these Machiavellian ethical terms legitimating goals that presumably could serve everyone but actually could and would not be widely fulfilled had indeterminate results. In some cases, it fostered demotic victory and ethical validation; in others, practical defeat and disproof. Proclamations of freedom and equality in England, the United States, or France did not in themselves put food on the table. Of course, arithmetical equality in life situations was neither possible nor desired. But the rhetorical promises galvanized political hope, while the state's and capitalist authority initially enforced the justice of the strongest – which sometimes was necessary and proper, as in the case of a conflict waiting to break out since the formation of the United States' Constitution, namely, the American Civil War. Politics designed to democratize the political orders of France, the United Kingdom, and the United States that originated outside the official political order, however, met violent resistance from the state.[31] This meant that acceptable democracy implied primarily the relatively free and legally equal opportunity to sell one's labor wherever an employer would buy it, regardless of the personal characteristics of the worker or the outcome of serious attempts to find a happy home for one's talents. That is, the freedom and equal opportunity of civil rightness was experienced as a new "right" but a right whose substantive value was only experienced episodically by the average citizen competing amid unequal obstacles in civil society.

In this light, the notion of equality of opportunity and the historical situation in which it emerged gave its original incarnation an inherently individualistic, anti-hierarchical, rebellious, and dreamily democratic bent.[32] During the period in which the conceptual pillars of equal opportunity were established, Tocqueville referred to America as the land where "equality of conditions" was amazingly a "fact," not a political value or ideal.[33] And R. H. Tawney, reflecting on nineteenth-century America almost one hundred years after Tocqueville did, saw it as a veritable land of "natural equality" – prior to its becoming a land that facilitated

---

[31] Note the French uprisings of 1830, 1848, and 1871; the various British Reform Acts and the activism that spurred them; the Haymarket protests of 1886 and Ford Motor strikes of the 1930s, not to mention the ongoing civil rights movements in the United States.

[32] No ethical standard for social and public behavior has garnered as much support as a political ideal across the economic and social spectrums of modern societies as equality of opportunity – from the Jacksonian era of the 1830s to the 1970s of Milton Friedman and John Rawls, to the 1980s of Ronald Reagan, and the current era of the Great Recession and Barack Obama (see Schaar 1981 (1967), 193).

[33] Tocqueville (1969 (1835, 1840), Vol. 1, 1830), 9.

the concentration of "economic power."[34] As noted, equal opportunity promised, and promises, to accommodate the melange of equality and inequality that characterized life in civil society. How did the promise practically fare, especially given its attractive power for two hundred years? A number of scholars have analyzed the *concept* of equal opportunity, particularly in the last generation. For example, it performs a pivotal function in the political theory of John Rawls in *A Theory of Justice* (1971), particularly in his second principle of justice. However, Rawls does not analyze the inherent implications of the term itself, instead noting the ethical and political significance of various formulations governed by "pure procedural" rules – rendered as formal, fair, and democratic equality of opportunity.[35] Earlier and more recent scholars have noted its role in the emergence of capitalism as the primary structure of social authority in the nineteenth and twentieth centuries.[36] But no-one precisely analyzes how it constitutes a social ethic and how the prominence of that ethic has constituted the character of democratic life in liberal democracies from their inception to the present – which belongs to the task at hand here.[37] Attempts to accommodate democracy and goodness in the nineteenth century involved rights-based liberalism, utilitarian democracy, and the extension of the suffrage. But they did so without justifying how, in turn, they would sustain political democracy in social life.

How did this work? First, one should recall that before "opportunity" became part of political discourse in the nineteenth century, it was nourished by the soil of its complement elaborated in the eighteenth century, e.g., by Adam Smith, namely, "merit," for whom it meant the appropriate, sanctioned, approbation of socially useful actions and qualities that affect our sentiments.[38] The term stood on the shoulders of an emerging, relatively secular and apolitical, language of ethics that included determinate notions of "propriety," "beauty," and "virtue."[39] But "merit" did not become politically significant for democracy until the notion of

---

[34] See Tawney (1931–51). Cf. Marshall (1964 (1949), 71–134) and Pole (1993 (1978)).

[35] Rawls (1971, 60–90).

[36] Note the previously cited works by Polanyi, Tawney, Marshall, Young, and Pole, supplemented by more recent works – e.g., Hochschild (1995) and Goldsten (2014).

[37] When conceptual analysts do, they typically ignore the long-term historical dynamic that provides the context for their work. Noteworthy contributors to this literature are Williams (1962), Schaar (1981 (1967)), and Galston (1986, 89–107).

[38] See Adam Smith, *The Theory of the Moral Sentiments*, esp. II; III.iv; VI.iii. Ultimately, such sentiments flowed from the dispositions of our "heart," which marks Smith's Christian deism and differentiates his discussion of meritorious practices from the kindred, ancient Greek notion of a *techne* and its practical corollaries.

[39] See Hutcheson (2008 [1725]).

equalized, if not equal, opportunity emerged as the stipulated background upon which it could be measured or gauged. In any event, "merit" became the signifier for worthwhile distinction, justifying inequality, and would have to be reconciled with societies that increasingly presupposed a democratic or republican society as a whole and the legal treatment of citizens.

The major philosophical perspectives that grappled with this political conundrum when it crystallized in the nineteenth century stemmed from the work of Immanuel Kant and the British utilitarians (discussed in Chapter 3 in relation to political representation). How did Kant, on the one hand, and Bentham and John Stuart Mill (quantitative and qualitative utilitarians), on the other, justify the dichotomy of theoretical or moral and practical inequality – a dichotomy that needed to be rhetorically dissolved in order for their political orders to retain at least a patina of democratic legitimacy? Here, it is important to recall that Kantians and utilitarians were first and foremost critical theorists. As they developed philosophical systems to critique aristocratic regimes and philosophical theories, as well as to develop intellectual programs for their replacement, utilitarians and Kantians sought to ground social virtue on different foundations. Disgusted with the corruption of English government by influence-trading and aristocracy, Jeremy Bentham (1748–1832) argued that virtue and merit, though part of ordinary language, were rationally reducible to outcomes equivalent to the rational and social pursuit of pleasure or pain and ultimately aimed at utility, or the pursuit of happiness.[40] Bentham favored democracy as a much better political form than the aristocratic order of Great Britain. But his dedication to utility as the greatest happiness of the greatest number (an overall judgment of individualized calculations of maximized pleasure) erased any social role for the art of citizenship, finding better company in the capitalist ethic of production, distribution, exchange, and consumption.

Kant's republicanism championed critical reason and rational liberty, but it was effectively anti-democratic – and not just because he employed the ancient idea of democracy as popular rule. He wanted to understand ethics in relation to an individual's isolated, rational observance of the moral law amid the unique circumstances of individual lives. His idea of pure, practical reason that theoretically rooted liberal conceptions of liberty and equality stemmed from its ability to trump goals for political reconstruction born of extant motivations. Yet his theoretical liberalism practically assured the legitimacy of governmental power over and

---

[40] See Bentham (1996, Chs. I–IV).

against the individual or collective judgment of citizens – not so different from his deputized antagonist, Thomas Hobbes.[41] Publicity for political discourse: yes; democratic power, no.[42] One might infer that such philosophical frameworks have been more effective as partners for self-centered liberty and an ethic of consumption than for active citizenship.

But such language obscures the complexity of their arguments. For they articulated philosophical systems that promoted the satisfaction of desires and interests (Bentham) or rights (Kant), or some combination as politically legitimate bases for political liberty. Moreover, as previously mentioned the new states became nominally recognized as "democratic." In the wake of the secularization of the state in its modern form, political thinkers focused their attention on new terms of art that would serve as means for complementing the new forms of liberal–democratic government, burgeoning capitalistic economies, and moral virtue. Since republican or democratic states are not self-legitimating unless their citizens are unquestionably virtuous, secular, ethical and practical terms, discourses, and arguments arose that served to sanction the worth of adult citizens *and* the hierarchical differentiation of social structures and individual life-chances that complemented the new republican democracies.

These claims indirectly informed the political ideologies on both sides of the Atlantic. Andrew Jackson endorsed "the equal protection of the law" in order to dismantle concentrations of wealth and power. This ethic found widespread expression in the United States seen by Alexis de Tocqueville during his American visits of the 1830s.[43] In Massachusetts, Horace Mann's arguments in the 1830s and 1840s for extending public education also enacted conceptions of merit (as well as public support), both of which served to sanction "grading" *and* to socialize American Catholics into the Protestant mainstream and extend educational opportunities to all citizens.[44] Across the ocean, the "utility" of social work was morally validated by both critics who sought a philosophical reconstruction of moral and political ethics, such as the British utilitarians, or a critical rationalization of extant social conventions, such as Fourier and Saint-Simon.[45] For J. S. Mill, "competence" signified merit in

---

[41] See Kant, "On the Common Saying: 'This May Be True in Theory But It Does Not Apply in Practice,'" in Kant (1991, 61–92, esp. 73ff).

[42] See "Perpetual Peace: A Philosophical Sketch," in Kant (1991, 100–1, 125ff).

[43] See Tocqueville (1969 (1835, 1840), especially vol. 1.)

[44] For a good sampling of Horace Mann's Reports to the Massachusetts Board of Education, see Cremin (1957), particularly the Reports of 1846 and 1848 (59–78, 79–112). On Horace Mann and the introduction of public education in the United States, and its legacy, see Downs (1974); cf. Taylor (2010).

[45] See Wolin (2004/1960, 393–7).

the performance of socially sanctioned practices.[46] This idea correlated with his belief in education as the royal road to merit, reflected in his endorsement of plural voting for British subjects who attended Oxford or Cambridge.[47]

But these discursive ethics were misleading. A democratic view of individuals offered by utilitarians may have promoted individual welfare, but was often accompanied by the legitimation of new administrative apparatuses for social welfare, educational success, and governmental (including penal) reform that depersonalized and effectively disempowered a broad-based exercise of democratic citizenship. Particularly in the case of J. S. Mill, it also severed justifiable links in theory and practice between democracy and political goodness. And by protecting ethical diversity against the impersonal calculus of utilitarian administrators, the discourse of latter-day rights-based liberalism sanctioned individual pursuits of happiness and goodness in the civil society of liberal capitalism – over and often against the participatory exercise of democratic citizenship. The result opened conceptions of virtue, rightness, and merit to the play of capitalism and the authority of bureaucratic experts – rather than promoting democratic forms of legitimation that sanction political equality and the greater social good.[48]

In fact, only later, in the latter half of the nineteenth century, when capitalism more clearly structured the opportunities available in civil society and American chattel slavery had been abolished, did notions of civil rightness become linked to the idea of "equal opportunity."[49] The introduction of civil service exams to qualify for work in governmental agencies was designed to diminish the role of cronyism in staffing the federal government. It was the first instance of what later became the more political, Progressive ideal to establish single standards of public goodness that would diminish democratic and political contention in determining the slowly but steadily growing federal bureaucracy. The practices of law and medicine also began to become professionalized, limiting the role of commercial incentives as guideposts for the conduct of their work and elevating belief in "expertise" – a kind of logic shared by experts that, with the declining panache of "rationality," has been

---

[46] See Mill (1991 (1861)). Cf. Thompson (1976).

[47] See Mill (1991 (1861), Chs. VIII, X).

[48] One might recall here Max Weber's and, more recently, Alasdair MacIntyre's critiques of expertise. For the former, see *Politik als Beruf* (1919); for the latter, see MacIntyre (1981, 76–102).

[49] When the phrase "equal opportunity" or "equality of opportunity" was first used in public discourse is not certain, but it did not precede the end of the nineteenth century by much. The *OED* lists its first usage in 1891.

supplanted by the logically incoherent notion of best practices.[50] All of these efforts effected social sanctions for "merit" that operated *within* a convention of political legitimacy – because "merit" was a derivative, rather than principal, notion of social value.[51]

Although civil service exams had little impact on the general public in the United States, and no equivalent exams existed in the United Kingdom or France, they express the fact that opportunities cannot be practically equalized unless all individuals seeking scarce positions can be winnowed out by some acceptably fair and seemingly objective practice – whether that amounts to a standardized application or a standardized test. One's social freedom becomes practically realized through a process of supplication in which one accepts the authority of those who lead the institutions one is trying to join. One doesn't have to regard extant institutions as, in the terms of Edmund Burke, "the decent drapery of life" ultimately sanctioned by religion, to recognize that were all social decision-making to be entirely politicized, the door would be open for even more severe forms of domination.[52] Individuals cannot expect social organizations to adapt to their needs. The fact that a relatively large number of individuals could apply for such positions reflects what the American Progressive Herbert Croly notably labeled "the promise of American life." But its version of equality presupposed that a hypothetical equal starting point assigned to obviously unequal individuals unproblematically sanctions the unequal ways in which equal standards will be actualized – which may include inherited privileges of race, class, and religion.[53] Yet, its analytical tensions do not completely detract from its ethical, intellectual, or political potency. It was a genuinely new idea when it came on the scene of political rhetoric. For it did not simply update Aristotle's canonical two concepts of equality – proportional and geometrical (aligned with implicit notions of worth, merit, virtue, and desert, and more strictly egalitarian and arithmetical). Rather, it applied to the new realm of civil society that was marked by capitalism's requirement of profit, democracy's requirement of political equality, and the Christian (vs. the ancient) bifurcation of moral authority and politics.

---

[50] On how the professionalization of American medicine also reflected political interests and hierarchies, see Starr (1984). As for the nonsense of "best practices," the notion of a practice is localized while the idea of best is generic.

[51] See Schaar (1981 (1967)).

[52] Edmund Burke, *Reflections on the Revolution in France*, J. G. A. Pocock, ed. (Indianapolis: Hackett Publishing, 1987 [1790]), 67–80.

[53] The hallmark iteration of equal opportunity as the opportunity "to become unequal" is that of Tawney (1931–51), on "equality of opportunity," 100–11, at 102–3.

Equal opportunity, if actualized, presupposes a common starting point after which individuals would depart and go separate and unequal ways by virtue of their God-given talent and individual responsibility. The lives lived by citizens mostly would be seen as the "natural" results of various degrees of individual effort by free and equal citizens. This myth nonetheless has had enormous practical value and ethical meaning, promising that the future belongs to optimists and capitalists – not critical analysts or socialists, let alone critical pessimists. However, its mythical (i.e., theoretically transpolitical) character disguises the inherently political (i.e., contested) character of where and how one draws the line of equality in relationship to which differentiation is justified. That said, a question arises for "equal opportunity" that resembles Aristotle's question about equality ("equality with regard to what?"), namely, "opportunity for what?" The question has an accessible answer for us, when we trust individual citizens to make ethical decisions themselves, independently of any philosophical advice. But that answer is not complete, for the "opportunity" is actualized in a social context that has its own ethical gravity.[54] In addition, the manner in which that social context ratified the successful exercise of equal opportunity was radically shaped by judgments of "merit" – the ethical sanction that ratified the fair exercise of equal opportunity. That is why Aristotle, Schaar, and Rawls understood that equality, equality of opportunity, and merit or virtue only could be explained in terms of their conceptions of justice – and how such conceptions, in turn, constituted their conceptions of equal opportunity and merit. To recall, the point of equal rights and equality of opportunity was initially designed not to promote social equality but to allow an individual's talent to develop and merit to be recognized – to separate the wheat from the chaff. For while the collective myth is that we are born equal, the political ethic of post-aristocratic civil society seeks to establish a social hierarchy with achievement, not birth or inherited privileges (other than money), positioning individuals on a graded, social ladder.

The potentially invidious character of the connection between equal opportunity and merit from the standpoint of democracy involves the practical character of merit as a form of *ergon* that actually undermines the *logos* of equal opportunity (variously understood). This concern appeared in public discourse and scholarship, especially after World War II. The

---

[54] In 1967, Schaar wrote: "The facile formula of equal opportunity ... opens more and more energies toward the realization of a mass, bureaucratic, technological, privatized, materialistic, bored and thrill-seeking, consumption-oriented society – a society of well-fed, congenial, and sybaritic monkeys surrounded by gadgets and pleasure-toys" (see Schaar 1981 (1967)).

final, formal, decimation of the British aristocracy and the promise of new social opportunities for ordinary male citizens in the United Kingdom or the United States – whether because of the superior global position of the American economy and its largesse to Western countries potentially threatened by the Soviet Union or the professional prospects newly available to those qualified to acquire a college education in the United States because of the G. I. Bill – meant the entry of hundreds of thousands of new working citizens into new parts of society. And while this was going on, the disturbed condition of women now expected to return happily to home-life after contributing mightily to engineering materiel for the war and the chafing conditions of degradation and violence practiced toward African-Americans in the South under segregation produced a hothouse of rising expectations. How would the notionally democratic republics adapt, after a war that made possible demotic, social progress, without upending the social order? With difficulty. One way of modulating the tension was through exams that identified seemingly objective standards of merit that were not supposed to be class-based.

This tension, the outcome of the introduction of standards of equal opportunity into new walks of life along with doors to success opened by determinations of merit, was historically satirized and imagined in Michael Young's 1958 unique tale, *The Rise of the Meritocracy, 1870–2033*. Noting that aristocratic privilege no longer was sufficient to produce the kind of citizenry needed in post-war Britain, Young produced a narrative of how privilege was simultaneously eliminated and preserved in the educational system that emerged. This was possible through the administration of spurious but usefully single-gauged measures of merit, the principal one being "IQ + effort." This was not seen to be anti-democratic, as the same measure was applied to all. But the education in publicly funded schools widely differed and could not match the education provided by well-endowed private schools or well-to-do families attending the public schools.[55] As Young noted, Britain's Labour Party promoted the idea of equal opportunity in education and its utility for promoting merit. But, in Young's book, merit as a praiseworthy term acquired a bad odor when it became connected to the ancient Greek word for coercive power, *kratos*, in Young's term, "meritocracy." The problem was that "power" vitiates the supposedly impersonal and non coercive display of "merit." Its exercise could go wrong by the anticipatory privileging of either individuals or groups. Moreover, meritocracy implies that the few are entitled to power over the many by virtue

---

[55] At the time in Britain, what Americans call public schools were called private schools and private schools public schools – reflecting the public function practiced by the British elite in ruling the country.

of their "merit" – not only in walks of life that require technical training unavailable to the many but also in politics and the public realm.[56]

Injustices perpetrated by aristocratic oligarchies that were supposed to be overcome by the combination of equal opportunity and testing to assure that merit fairly separates the few from the many return to subvert the democratic character of the political orders that these rubrics supposedly enhanced. Young linked "meritocracy" to the social evaporation of a evanescent existence of a theoretically democratic understanding of merit.[57] In a sardonic footnote, he connected "democracy" and "equality of opportunity" as follows:

Today we frankly recognize that democracy can be no more than an aspiration, and have rule not so much by the people as the cleverest people; not an aristocracy of birth, not a plutocracy of wealth, but a true meritocracy of talent.[58]

In addition to noting how previously privileged families could game the tests in their favor through special preparation, Young lamented how this simplistic measure failed to recognize kinds of intelligence that are not subject to specialization and cannot be measured, many of which supported kinds of democratic and egalitarian intelligences. The book notes how the meritocracy eventually led to an uprising, fomented importantly by women, but not until the passion for measuring potential for merit had reached such a feverish pitch that lovers interested in producing families sought genetically pre-qualified mates – thus reinstating an aristocracy of birth.[59] The uprising stemmed from the recognition that no single measure of merit existed that remained true to the political and legal standard of giving every citizen "equality of opportunity."[60] "Merit"

---

[56] Michael Walzer famously imagined a plurality of "spheres of justice" within liberal society that would not allow hierarchies in one sphere to dominate equal citizenship in other spheres, thus reflecting the liberal ideal of social freedom marked by power but no politically intrusive domination (see Walzer 1983).

[57] Lani Guinier spells out a notion of "democratic merit," picking up on ideas articulated in the 1967 article of Schaar, in Guinier (2015, 27–43, 81–134).

[58] "The origin of this unpleasant term [meritocracy], like that of 'equality of opportunity,' is still obscure. It seems to have been first generally used in the sixties of the last [i.e., nineteenth] century in small-circulation journals attached to the Labour Party, and gained wide currency much later on" Young (1994 (1958), 11).

[59] That idea was not new (cf. Plato's *Republic*) and is not new now. But his book importantly deflated the view that "equal opportunity" would eliminate invidious inequalities.

[60] Young's calculation for "merit" was the product of IQ plus Effort ($I + E = M$; 84). One should note that in the mid-twentieth century, IQ possessed more credibility in the United Kingdom than in the United States – where the Scholastic Aptitude Test was invented partly to establish an educationally oriented equivalent of the IQ that guaranteed entrance of the truly meritorious to the elite private and public colleges and universities in the United States (e.g., the Ivy League and the University of California), institutions that (for the most part) were not inclined to increase the number of their students in proportion to the growth of the American population (see Lemann 1999, 5–6, 44, 48, 60, 122).

is a function of a society's determination of its needs, wants, and values along with what, and what inequalities it accepts, more than an objective criterion of qualitative excellence. After all, whether we are "unborn" or aging badly, we are supposed to possess recognizable, general merit that then is developed and used in various ways during our education, work, and retirement.

In the United States, a similar problem beset colleges and universities now open to vastly larger pools of applicants. The Scholastic Aptitude Test was publicly promoted as a measure of merit that overcame barriers rooted in privileged schooling, and hence was touted as "democratic." However, no single measure of merit will tell the whole story of a student's potential. Moreover, a commercial company produced this test. Despite the fact that the Educational Testing Service that produced (and produces) the test thoroughly vets its tests for fairness, its criteria for success or meritorious performance on their tests will be importantly shaped by the financial requirements of the institutions that administer them – i.e., that give "merit" "*kratos*." This point was validated by Nicholas Lemann's history of the Scholastic Aptitude Test in the United States – whose unique authority as a measure of general, intellectual aptitude has declined in the past generation (though not so the LSAT). It has become apparent that bright students from economically disadvantaged backgrounds or foreign countries do relatively poorly on the tests and that $1,000+ preparatory tests belie the test's promise to measure intellectual "aptitude" *tout court* (although it certainly does measure valuable intellectual qualities).

No single notion of "merit" should prevail without question in professional or political settings, because ability is not readily measured by a single stick. But it is not as if its meaning or use is easily escaped. It is more than an "instrumental value."[61] To be sure, problems arise when the concept of "merit" as a judgment of qualitative excellence is institutionally backed by the exercise of power by a clique or within an institutional framework – whether that is religious, educational, social, or economic. Evaluating contemporary decisions about "merit" takes into account what the judges (orchestral conductors; athletic team managers) need as much as what the judged (test-takers) have. But this is far less problematic in activities that are typically regarded as apolitical – such as orchestras and athletic teams – than colleges, which perform a general socio-political, as well as educational, function in society.[62] In this

---

[61] See Sen (2005, 5–16) and Section 4.4.

[62] Despite the racism in major league baseball, it desegregated before many other public institutions in the United States because team owners simply wanted to win and looked for talent, no matter what color it came in, in order to do so. This is not to say that ballet companies or athletic teams do not express sanctioned social values. But they do so in terms of their first-order social status more than their derivative judgments about the composition of members of their organizations.

sense, "fit" is a more appropriate term for justifying selective evaluations than merit, and is increasingly used in hiring decisions by highly selective institutions. But many institutions do not employ the less hierarchical judgment of "fit" because it lacks the consequences for self-esteem and a sense of elite achievement connoted by "merit."

Since Young's satirical jeremiad, "meritocracy" made an attempt at political rule in the United States during the ascendance of the Kennedy administration's "best and the brightest." Its product of the Vietnam War put that to rest.[63] The failure of the Reagan administration's economic policy of supply-side economics (acknowledged in the 1986 tax hike) and the neoliberal enthusiasm for deregulation from the Carter to the Bush II administrations – which associated "merit" with success in the capitalist marketplace – did not bury that ideological falsehood and contributed to the steady growth in economic inequality from the late 1970s and early 1980s. The substantiation of the long-acknowledged truism that extant economic wealth stems more heavily from inherited wealth (e.g., the financial sector) rather than achieved wealth (e.g., start-ups) belies the idea of equal opportunity in capitalist markets.[64] But this fact has not altered the ideological playing field on which political competition is conducted. Altogether contemporary attempts to accommodate democracy and merit, competence, or expertise as practical measures of goodness have not fared extremely well. More recently, however, researchers and scholars have tried to formulate more democratic ideas of merit, especially given the extent to which single-gauged measures of merit reliably produce unfair judgments.[65]

Pounding against the domination yielded when a one-dimensional idea of "merit" is used to discourage individual and group effort surely has *its* merits. But is it the case that we can do without it – any more than human beings can do without ideas of virtue or goodness? After all, even Nietzsche championed the criterion of "life" and judgments of "taste" while criticizing moralistic, Christian–Kantian ideas of *moralitat*, good vs. evil, etc. The question becomes whether there are respectable legitimating standards for achievement in civil society that both reward economically, professionally, and politically desirable effort and respond constructively to conditions of injustice that might distort who, at any one time, achieves virtuous rewards and meets justifiable standards of civic rightness. This question concerned liberal and communitarian proponents of "civic virtue" in the 1980s and 1990s, but none fully addressed

---

[63] Halberstam (1992 (1972)).
[64] Piketty (2014, Ch. 11).
[65] Jencks, "What Must Be Equal for Opportunity to be Equal?" (1984).

the manner in which the prospects and nature of civic virtue are often centrally constituted by social conditions of power, inequality, and injustice. These phenomena are ignored or marginalized, even though their central roles in affecting the lives of citizens cannot be denied, while notions of rights or community hardly solve the problem.

If there is no silver bullet for dealing with these issues but dealing with them is unavoidable, and imposed solutions also seem inadequate because of their bias toward either individualism or authoritarianism, the question of the relationship of civil rightness to democratic political ethics remains. What the range of evidence considered here indicates is that in addition to the above watchwords there are two other fundamental considerations – ones reflecting political versions of Scylla and Charybdis that have been raised before. The standard of equal treatment and equal protection of the laws for conduct in civil society would seem to serve as a basic constituent of democratic political ethics. Yet its virtue is double-edged. On the one hand, practical, institutionalized referents for equality reflect unjust (i.e., second- or third-best) settlements of political power. On the other, failure to determine standards conducive to widespread achievement by the *demos* often reinforces, if not promotes, unjustified inequalities and hierarchies of ethics and practice.

Constituents of civil rightness depend on related ideas of justice and contours of social power – thereby functioning practically as a common conception of the good within civil society. In this respect, they complement the manner in which representation acquired the aura of a virtue for modern democracy and how legitimacy and human rights subsequently acquired comparable auras for the nation-state and international politics. But how did these discourses of goodness function in their own terms, as terms of political ethics and practical solutions to conflicts of power? Answers to these questions should provide a more historically and politically informed understanding of the political discourses of rights, motives, and virtues that have been appropriated for contemporary theoretical debates. But there is no consensus among professional political thinkers and ordinary citizens about civil rightness (in *logos*) and what are endorsed as necessary means for its actualization (in *ergon*), with the tolerable gap between *logos* and *ergon* larger for "conservatives" than "liberals." The former derive the gap from individual effort or its lack, minimalizing the roles of capitalism and traditions, while the latter emphasize socio-economic conditions, condemning the sanctioned powers of wealth, racial and/or sexual/gender prejudice, and government as the major sources of widespread and unjust inequalities. Both groups, however, embrace "equal opportunity" and "merit" as standards and tools of legitimating performance and inequality; they judge individual actions according to how single persons play the cards they are dealt and regard as apolitical their "natural" talents or familial background.

4.4   Civil Rightness in Post-War American Judicial Decisions

While growing inequality belied the equality of republican citizenship from 1890 to 1930, no basic changes in the ethic of civil rightness occurred. The idea of a "second bill of rights" in Roosevelt's 1944 State of the Union speech died with him, and his strategic attack on America's economic barons collapsed when the United States entered World War II and emerged hugely victorious.[66] But the critical discourse (*logos*) about equal opportunity as an ideal more than a reality (*ergon*) began to reflect African-Americans', and subsequently the nation's, increasing concerns about racial inequality – fueled by a civil rights movement that became particularly forceful in the late 1940s, 1950s, and early–mid 1960s. While activism in the streets and laws passed in legislative chambers forged avenues of change, the United States Supreme Court determined their purview in the nation as a whole, setting the stage for much academic and public debate about equal opportunity and merit. Equal opportunity also acquired significantly new economic meaning in the context of President Johnson's "unconditional war on poverty" – and his dedication to civil rights, particularly "affirmative action" programs for African-Americans designed to remove the shackles that hampered *their* opportunities relative to those of others at the starting line of competition for society's resources, and the civil rights laws of the 1960s.

These two political goals for equal opportunity gave it different features as elements of civil rightness. The first, economic conception of equal opportunity was championed in a limited way by liberal political theorists John Rawls and Ronald Dworkin. The second, social and group, conception was promoted by theorists of racial and cultural minorities and women. As we shall see, the former had potentially greater political impact, affecting society as a whole, but the latter gained more practical traction in the form of anti-discrimination laws sanctioned under the cover of the Fourteenth Amendment's guarantee of "equal protection of the laws" for all persons subject to it. In any event, a historicist approach suggests that we look at what was done on the political and constitutional ground since the efforts of the 1960s to transform society in the name of equality of opportunity. After the passage of the civil rights laws of the

---

[66] More precisely, it died in the United States; it lived on in the *Universal Declaration of Rights* (1948) and the *International Covenant on Social, Economic, and Cultural Rights*, which the United States has never ratified.

1960s, Congress and various American social movements tried to expand the notion of equal opportunity in directions that made American institutions and political conditions more egalitarian. Overall, these ventures have been marginally successful.

Efforts to define "institutional racism," for example, operate at one remove from the legal boundaries that currently justify or condemn social practices (which means they resist clear practical identification). The boundaries stem from the Supreme Court's general (not absolute) unwillingness to find that patterns of discrimination which lack a specifiable *intention* traceable to individuals that engage in unequal *treatment* run afoul of the Constitution.[67] This view was sanctioned in the Court's *Bakke* decision (which nonetheless promoted the ideal of "diversity," but not "quotas," as standards for admission to public institutions of higher education.)[68] Yet the directly educational benefits of diversity in the classroom to individuals – even though society as a whole clearly benefits – are increasingly subject to severe judicial scrutiny.[69] However the economic benefits to beneficiaries have been documented; their career performances are no less respectable than those of their classmates, and the general educational benefit derived from hearing different viewpoints has been a staple of public understandings of free speech from John Stuart Mill to the present.[70] The requirement of "intent" has not been the decisive norm for judging affirmative action programs in universities, since whatever policy adopted by the college or university was presumed to promote the public good. Moreover, the welter of goals guiding admissions decisions (the university's preferences for individuals starring in athletics, music, geographical diversity, and legacy) make it hard to identify intentional, invidious discrimination. Nonetheless, Justice Scalia reverted to the assumption that higher education is only about learning intellectual material in classes – ignoring the intellectual development, social skills, understanding of leadership, and the formation of career connections that

---

[67] The relatively open-ended view of racial discrimination, enunciated in *Griggs v. Duke Power*, 401 U.S. 24 (1971), has been restricted, initially in *Richmond v. J. A. Croson*, 488 U.S. 69 (1989), and more decisively in *Adarand Constructors v. Pena*, 515 U.S. 200 (1995).

[68] *Bakke v. Regents of the University of California*, 438 U.S. 265 (1978), Justice Powell writing for a plurality.

[69] See the case of *Fisher v. University of Texas at Austin*. A useful critical analysis of the Supreme Court's discussion of affirmation action in university admissions appears in an article by Siegel (2012).

[70] Mill (1991 (1861)), Meiklejohn (1913, 1920, 1948), Jaspers (1958, 67–9), and more recently, Bowen and Bok (ex-Presidents of Princeton and Harvard, respectively) (1998, 155–92, 218–55). Also note Yale President Richard Levin's collection of presidential addresses: Levin (2013, 35–81).

inform undergraduate, legal, and medical education assumptions – as he questioned the legal counsel of the University of Texas when the *Fisher* case was presented to the Supreme Court in December, 2015.[71] In 2014, an affirmative action program supposedly covered by the Fair Housing Act was adjudicated by the Supreme Court. Its advocates employed the "disparate impact" argument that does not automatically require intent to prove discrimination, and their position survived. The dissent of Judge Samuel Alito insisted that the absence of *intent* belied the presence of unequal *treatment*. For Alito, the issue was whether the discrimination that justified "affirmative action" could be traceable to an activity that used reason to authorize a specific form of (unequal) treatment.[72] The 5–4 divide in the Supreme Court reflected the "liberal–conservative" division alluded to in Section 4.1, with the "liberals" recognizing judicial significance in structural discrimination and "conservatives" attending primarily to individual responsibility for (invidious) discrimination.

Assuring "equal opportunity" under the equal protection clause of the Fourteenth Amendment therefore bears no generally accepted political weight, and the Court is continually peppered with suits that require determination of the extent of individual "intent" that exists in the discrimination and to what extent that warrants governmental compensation. Judicial sanctions for equal opportunity within formally desegregated settings, as long as the Court works within the tradition it has carved out (from *Brown* to *San Antonio*), only can be carried out incrementally, not structurally, in patchwork fashion. The *San Antonio* case, which carried by a significant majority and has not been modified since, indicates that, lacking a clear component of identifiable racial discrimination, a background of social and economic inequality will not warrant compensatory legal and political measures that do not pass the Court's "strict scrutiny" test – which tends to require proof of intent to discriminate – either against or in favor of a particular group.[73] This explains why "equal opportunity" can be rhetorically used by both conservative political

---

[71] Glossed and put in historical context by Linda Greenhouse, "The Supreme Court's Diversity Dilemma," *The New York Times* (December 24, 2015).

[72] See *Texas Department of Housing and Community Affairs, et al. v. Inclusive Communities Project, Inc., et al.* (Decided: June 25, 2015).

[73] *Brown v. Board of Education*, 347 U.S. 483 (1954) invalidated racial segregation in public schools. In *San Antonio Independent School Board v. Rodriguez*, 411 U.S. 1 (1973), the Supreme Court invalidated a challenge to disparities in educational funding correlated with ethnicity and residence. Justice Powell, who wrote the plurality opinion in *Bakke*, wrote the majority decision in this 6–3 case. This view made possible the informal segregation of public schools and was strengthened in the decision not to enable the Detroit public school district to include its suburbs in determining its tax base for educational funding. See *Milliken v. Bradley*, 418 U.S. 717 (1974).

groups, who champion individual rights, and left-liberal groups, who challenge structures of power as politically discriminatory.[74]

Part of the explanation for this change stems from the venue for addressing equal opportunity – namely, the courts, not the public realm or discourses of political ethics. In the courts, it is *de facto* and *de jure* easier to identify the *violation* of an extant norm than the *fulfillment* of an ideologically attractive one. But channeling political movements into the judicial process causes partial depoliticization. Schaar, Rawls, and others understood that any notion of equal opportunity presupposed a conception of justice, and noted how the corollary conception was generally (and wrongly) not addressed. The sad irony of the progress made by the *Brown* decision is that it elevated formal equal opportunity as the standard of educational equality and placed in the background the inter-war and pre-*Brown* decisions that had highlighted the importance of substantive legal equality before the law (while they accepted segregation).[75] The notion of equal opportunity not only became the only generally accepted public term *as* a conception of justice but was defined critically in relation to the legal status quo, often involving attempts to compensate for it at the margins with a redistribution of commodified resources (e.g., by Ronald Dworkin), the provenance of which is left to the vagaries of politics.[76] From the perspective of political ethics that would reconcile democracy and goodness, equal opportunity as anti-discrimination became a political value especially dear to minorities and women – but not embedded in the rights of political and democratic majorities. In the new political environment, equal opportunity ultimately became more associated with antidotes to "natural" discrimination (i.e., against individuals and/or those who possess relatively innate characteristics) rather than socio-economic discrimination, leaving the latter to the political battlefield. The result has been widespread resegregation of public schools, illustrating the limits of the courts as vehicles of major social change.[77]

The new link between equal opportunity and group rights tragically could not overcome the connection of equal opportunity to individual achievement signified by civil rightness. When President Johnson imagined that "affirmative action" could remove the shackles withholding *groups* (particularly African-Americans) from advancement, legal

---

[74] Note the Heritage Foundation and the Equal Opportunity in Education Project.
[75] See *Missouri ex re. Gaines v. Canada*, 305 U.S. 337 (1938) and *Sweatt v. Painter*, 339 U.S. 629 (1950).
[76] See Dworkin (2000, Chs. 1 and 2), first published in the early 1980s.
[77] For a scholarly history of this evolution, see Orfield and Eaton (2016).

difficulties arose in defining the "merit" of groups *per se*.[78] This is not surprising, given the basis of anti-discrimination lawsuits in the individualism of the Fourteenth Amendment. After all, "group rights" supposedly could not stand on the individualistic ground landscaped by equal opportunity as the popular equivalent of equal protection of the law for persons.[79] Not surprisingly, the amount of room allowed for affirmative actions programs as instruments of social equality or civil rightness has decreased.

This trend has been validated by the recent Supreme Court ruling of *Schuette v. Coalition to Defend Affirmative Action* (No. 12-682, 2014). This concerned a dispute over a Michigan ballot measure called Proposal 2, which voters passed in 2006 to bar the use of race-conscious college admissions by the state's public colleges. A divided federal appeals court struck down the ban in 2012, finding that it violated the US Constitution's equal protection clause. Nonetheless, the Supreme Court of the United States (SCOTUS) overruled the appeals court, arguing (again) that special protection of racial groups does not comport with the Equal Protection clause of the Fourteenth Amendment. In an important dissent Justice Sotomayor noted the roots of affirmative action as a response to slavery and race-conscious practices in college admissions that have prevented racial minorities from receiving the "equal protection" of the law. But that compensatory argument has been marginalized in the past twenty years by SCOTUS, evidencing the difficulty of generating a clear standard other than an individualistic, formally egalitarian, and supposedly apolitical interpretation of what constitutes "equal protection of the law." An interpretive banner once championed as a lever for political change via the Courts, "substantive equal protection," has all but disappeared from Constitutional interpretation.[80] In general, whether inequality stems from race or economic power, the Court has decided that it is a "political question" that it leaves to heavily lobbied and gerrymandered legislatures to decide.

The other effect of having equal opportunity increasingly signified as the rights of groups who suffer discrimination was the rise of the notion of pluralism as an inherently good political value, one that complemented

---

[78] When President Johnson introduced the idea of affirmative action in 1965, he understood it as guaranteeing equality of *opportunity* and equality of *result*, for individuals *and* groups – thereby conflating the lines of argument that later would divide supporters and opponents of affirmative action. See Lyndon B. Johnson, "Commencement Address at Howard University: 'To Fulfill These Rights,'" June 4, 1965, accessible online.

[79] Other avenues of litigation to fight invidious discrimination have been tried, via the "due process" clause of the Fifth Amendment. But the institutional moorings of that amendment have limited its political reach.

[80] Kenneth Karst notably argued for substantive equal protection in Karst (1989).

the critique of single-gauged conceptions of reason or ethical value in the political order. Despite the serious injustices suffered by the groups now protected against discrimination, the effective result of promoting pluralism was to make social criticism increasingly indebted to principles that favored individual rights and ultimately accommodated structural (particularly economic) inequalities. This has been particularly troublesome, given that family income, rather than educational level, has been shown to be the single best predictor of a child's eventual, economic success.[81] Moreover, even though endorsement of pluralism may expand the range of acceptable forms of social behavior beyond conventional practices, it begs the question of how plural entities are going to be organized into a collectivity, and slogans (such as *E pluribus Unum*) similarly duck the political question. The unanswered, disturbing question is how conditions of equal opportunity (however defined) actually yield assignations of "merit" for various individuals. This conundrum reflects enduring historical conflict in determining a *political*, as well as a *legal*, rationale for equal opportunity and civil rightness.

This relatively individualistic or apolitical dimension of civil rightness as constituted by equal opportunity is, ironically, extended by some of its most radical critics. Influential and avowedly democratic poststructuralists who fault liberals for their narrow-mindedness, often respond simply by expanding or pluralizing the domain of individual opportunity – even equal opportunity – without considering the political dimension of adopting such an ethical perspective, at least how it interacts with the construction of political order.[82] Moreover, the pluralizing tendency focuses more on liberating the accepted domain of lifestyles than on reconstructing the social and economic order that would need to sustain them. This liberal dimension of poststructuralism has provided a theoretical complement to the association of equal opportunity with group rights – a development of the civil rights laws of the 1960s. Rather than denoting an economic or social ideal, especially relevant for enabling individual talents to flourish in educational institutions, it became transmuted into a term of critique – lodged against legal and ideological discrimination against citizens based on their race, ethnicity, gender, or sexual orientation. Equal opportunity has become a default concept for right–left liberals, the value of which is presupposed absent discrimination – however that is defined wherever that line is drawn in the lives of individuals. Its relationship to democracy and justice remains however, remains indeterminate if not blurred. The Supreme Court

---

[81] For an early account of this phenomenon, see Glazer (1978, 33–76).
[82] See Connolly (1995).

since *Brown* has rejected socio-historical causes in their determinations of the meaning of equal opportunity and merit. For the American political system and its Constitutional interpreters, conditions for both the expression and judgment of practical virtue have retained their individualistic roots – thereby to address historical injustices or enhance demotic power.

4.5   Civil Rightness, Liberal Theory, and Democratic Virtue

Despite the dangers associated with linking civil rightness to sociological categories that have variable, if not vague, ties between democracy and goodness, the idea of civil rightness still contributes to democratic political ethics. For it functions as a critical and constructive standard for the general citizenry, even as it also operates as an ideological disguise for particular, unjustified, economic, social, and political hierarchies. Standing upon these two pillars, it operates as a "virtuous discipline for the modern *demos*." On the one hand, it effectively disciplines the *demos* to act in ways that conform to an economic and political system that does not necessarily have its interests at heart. On the other hand, it holds out the possibility of more opportunities for social betterment for more segments of the *demos*. (Even Foucault would acknowledge that not all disciplines are bad.[83]) Given the aristocratic and financial legal hierarchies civil rightness nominally replaces, this gives it democratic allure. But then what are we to make of it as a double-edged sword? How are we to think about critical standards of conduct in civil society in relation to democracy and, more generally, political goodness when that relationship is absent or insecure?

Two considerations inform an answer. First, it is not a matter of grabbing one horn of the dilemma. Computers operate according to binary structures, while choices about history, power, and principle do not. Human activity does not allow retrofitting; cutting and pasting, ignoring the unintended effects of deliberate choices. Second, no purely theoretical answer to the question is sufficient – because context is a constitutive, not secondary, feature of a political answer, even if it also is not determinative. But we can ascertain how a motivational standard of civil rightness might comport with democratic activity. This has been tried in

---

[83] Confusion about Foucault may have stemmed from the English translation of *Surveillir et Punir*. His interest in the constitutive importance of ethics for understanding human society appears in his turn toward the ancient Greeks in his later life in order to specify "technologies of the self" that lack the features of modern technologies and disciplines. It's odd, however, that his "ethics" focuses on "the self."

the liberal political philosophies of John Rawls and Amartya Sen, which I shall turn to here because of their familiarity, in the wake of our accounts of historical practices of civil rightness. To what extent do they contribute to civil rightness as an ethic that makes democracy and goodness more complementary than antagonistic? And where ought we to turn if their accounts come short – without falling down slippery slopes toward moralisms of the left, center, and right?

Rawlsian justice defines rationally stipulated, ethical standards that coordinate equalities and inequalities in social and political life. As such, they have contributed to academic, if not public, understandings of civil rightness. But the egalitarian dimensions of a principle that would redistribute resources in the name of equality of opportunity have found little practical traction. Is that due to misguided politics or inherent limitations in Rawls's theory? The elements that comprise the baseline of material distribution and the markers for redistribution are "primary goods" – commodified resources (e.g., basic nutrition, education, and housing) necessary for self-respect. They would enable citizens to actualize their moral and intellectual capacities and accept his principles of justice. Does its version of civil rightness accommodate democracy and goodness? After identifying the first principle of justice as equal liberties, Rawls specified its practical complement in the second principle as "democratic equality of opportunity" – that is, traditional, natural equality of opportunity (careers open to talents), supplemented by the efficiency criterion of formal equality of fair opportunity, further supplemented by "the difference principle," which only accepted social inequalities if they most benefitted the "least advantaged" members of society.[84]

While the practical guideposts for calculating what amounts to "advantage" were sociologically contested given Rawls's interest in correlating them with "efficiency" and "effectiveness," there was a communitarian feature of this principle. Rawls pooled the extant distribution of economic resources and privileges that exist at the start of one's life into one heap that then was subject to redistribution according to the principles of justice. Given that many Americans are born on third base and congratulate themselves for having "hit a triple," those struggling to get on base blame themselves for a poor batting average. His theory sanctioned higher taxes on "the more advantaged" that would be used on behalf of "the least advantaged." In addition, Rawls wanted to make sure that his theory of justice informed all parts of society, even (belatedly) life in

---

[84] See Rawls (1971, 65, 71–83). The upshot of the combination of fair equality of opportunity and the difference principle was, for Rawls, "democratic equality of opportunity." Also see Rawls (2001).

the household, condemning the inegalitarian dominance that appears in Young's "meritocratic society."[85] But what about the idea of merit? Does it have ethical value in a democratic society for justifying the differentiation of favors for a few and consolation prizes for the many? If so, how are we to understand the relationship between the idea (or *logos*) of merit or virtue (*arete*) and liberal democracy?

Rawls's theory relies on there being a persuasive fit between his principles of justice, social and political intuitions, and the redistributive and potentially democratic features of his difference principle. But his theory provided no motivation for the political sensibility that would enable his idea to work, having prevented those sources from analytically underpinning "the original position" and his principles of justice.[86] As a result, Rawls's theory did not question: the democratic legitimacy of capitalism; the interaction of his theory of justice with the ideologically individualist and anti-governmental prejudices that inform American politics; or the efficacy of "justice as fairness" or "political liberalism" as self-limiting theories of philosopher-guardianship. A successful connection between theory and practice was presupposed, without providing any notion of how that would occur. This enabled Rawls to sidestep political irritants that might undermine the viability of his philosophical theory.[87] The individualistically based first principles of his theory of justice and their commodified character as primary goods also prevented his theory from engaging political issues in which the constituents of equal opportunity and merit could not be localized in individual citizenship or socially accepted standards of performance. Hence, Rawls's theory cannot speak to issues of affirmative action or, say, the differential rates of political participation between rich and poor in American society, beyond what the legal discourse of the US Supreme Court has employed in its interpretation of the Equal Protection Clause of the Fourteenth Amendment. These matters invoke standards of civil rightness that inform democratic ethics, and his theory of justice cannot helpfully address the problems relating ethics to power involving equal opportunity raised in Section 4.3. For Rawls, active citizenship is a personal choice for a way of life, not a constituent of (a theory of) justice.

Amartya Sen touched on many of these issues when he faulted Rawls's theory for not facilitating enhanced human capabilities – surely a Rawlsian goal. Sen has argued since the 1980s that the rights-based character of Rawls's principles of justice and the commodified character of his primary

---

[85] Rawls (1971, 106–7).
[86] See Sandel (1996 (1982)).
[87] See Wallach (1987) and Geuss (2008).

goods are unlikely to attend fully to the social conditions of liberal justice that generally constitute the active lives of human beings. It is not enough to provide persons with "all-purpose means," the aim of primary goods. One must enable individuals to have the capacity to act in such a way as to develop their freedom to use such means.[88] Moreover, Sen's theory more directly and critically connects to practical life, for also possesses a critical dimension, for its distinctive set of analytical terms (capability, well-being, etc.) lend themselves more directly than Rawls's theory does to characterizing the actualities of conventional socio-political life.

In a related though distinguishable vein, Martha Nussbaum joined Sen to develop what is now known as "the capabilities approach." Like Rawls's theory, this approach is pitched ahistorically, but it attempts to engage more directly than Rawls's theory does with what makes a difference in the quality of individual lives.[89] If adopted, this approach to human well-being would result not only in a fairer distribution of resources as a matter of individual rights and social justice but also would more reliably enhance the ability of individuals to actualize their potential and live flourishing lives. This conception of capabilities synthesizes features of ethics as a disposition to act and power as dynamic potential. In this regard, it speaks to our concern with civil rightness and its relevance as a democratic ethic that might foster democratic virtue. As with the discussion of Rawls's theory, the following does not pretend to engage all of the major dimensions of Sen's theory – something that has been done by many others – but to address its relevance to democratic ethics in general and the standard of civil rightness in particular.

Sen's and Nussbaum's capability approaches stem not only from dissatisfaction with how notions of rights relate to practical lives but also form their efforts to ameliorate the limitations which millions, if not billions, of human beings suffer, preventing them from actualizing their potential for well-being – such as poor nutrition, lack of education, gender discrimination, poverty in general, and, most importantly, the freedom to develop themselves.[90] Sen often cites the difference between someone "like" Mahatma Gandhi who starves as a matter of choice and

---

[88] See Sen (1999). For citations of Sen's work on this subject since the 1980s, see the bibliographies and notes of the aforementioned book as well as Sen (2011) – in particular 436–7, n. 10, for a list of commentaries on Sen's theory that accept its basic parameters.

[89] See Nussbaum and Sen (1993). Sen clearly differentiates important features of his theory from Nussbaum's, which develops lists of capabilities, one which Sen would not want to prescribe but to keep open to shaping by available information (see Sen 2009, 232, n. 8).

[90] Note the work of Sen on famines and of both Sen and Nussbaum for WIDER, the World Institute for Development Economics Research of the United Nations University.

someone who is forced into that situation by circumstances beyond her control (even if those circumstances could have been controlled by a good government).[91] Inadequate capability marks the latter person but not the former, and liberal rights theory does not define the difference. Capability theory is therefore more "realistic" than Rawls's insofar as it seeks to address what constitutes the freedom to *act*. Drawing on Isaiah Berlin's analytical differentiation of types of freedom, Sen characterizes the capability approach as positive dedication to preserving negative freedoms.[92] Parsing out what this idea practically amounts to, however, is, first, maddeningly difficult and, second, politically evasive.

The ambiguity of what a "capability" amounts to appears as soon as one tries to define it. Both Sen and Nussbaum depend on Aristotle in their approaches – the latter more so than the former – but the connection between Aristotle and a "capabilities" approach requires unaccounted-for intellectual amendments on Aristotle's work.[93] The word "capability" is an English word derived from Latin and combines roots for capaciousness or roominess, on the one hand, and ability, talent, power, skill, or expertise, on the other. For both Sen and Nussbaum a capacity is innate to the individual and the species but its development is decidedly social. For Aristotle, the closest equivalent was the word *dunamis* – power as potential, rather than power as coercive force. The actualization of one's potential amounts to *energeia*, pure, unobstructed energy in the successful performance of a particular task. The tasks could be practical skills, such as carpentry or flute-playing, that, as such, lacked ethical dimensions; these were called *technai*. Or, they could be skills that signified a standard of goodness for citizens in the *polis* – such as the cardinal virtues (*aretai*) of self-control (*sophrosune*), courage (*andreia*), and intelligent wisdom (*sophia*), all of which constituted (and were constituted by) justice (*dikaiosune*). The latter were higher capabilities, for their "end was internal to the activities, in the way that good violin playing constitutes the music of a good violin concerto" kite-making (a *techne*) is for the sake of flying kites.

Sen and Nussbaum's notions of capability become manifest in generally valued human activities (political judgment, notable athletic achievement) that recall the activities associated with *aretai* by ancient Greeks.[94]

---

[91] See Sen (1999, 292).

[92] It is not unlike republican theorists' modification of negative freedom – no longer freedom from interference or constraint but freedom from domination. See Sen (1985, 130–48, at 136–7), and, for republican political theory, see *inter alia* Pettit (1997).

[93] For a more extensive critical account of the connections and disconnections between Aristotle and contemporary adaptations of Aristotle, see Wallach (1992).

[94] The latter might not be considered a virtue as we understand it, but Homer believed that athletic skill was a human virtue (*arete*) (see *Iliad* XX. 411–18).

For Aristotle, however, such actualization only could materialize in a *polis*, the ancient Greek city-state or citizen-state, where citizens directly exercise the authoritative powers of governance. Moreover, the activity of political deliberation cultivated by the *polis* fostered the development of not only the capacity (capability?) for speech but also moral and political language that enabled one to distinguish between goodness and badness, beauty and ugliness, justice and injustice.[95] That the *polis* not only developed but relied on exclusionary distinctions belonged to its unique identity.

When it comes to determining the meaning of capacities according to Sen and Nussbaum, one is led to ask, how widespread and "inherent" or "politically" sanctioned are these capacities? They are not fully developed at birth – and to that extent are not "natural." But Sen wants to differentiate capabilities from the measure of "achievements" because of the extent to which the latter may be sanctioned in an unjust manner. He wants to keep "capabilities" as a *logos* that is not dependent on a particular political arrangement or *ergon*. Sen's concern with action, however, is limited. In order to make the notion of capabilities more worldly, Sen sometimes departs from the naturalistic roots of the notion of capacities for the sake of the anodyne, managerial category of "functionings." (Such are the wages of the language of welfare economists.) But we know that *how* "functionings" are organized makes all the difference when assessing their value, and that is a political question. This is how the indeterminate character of capacities as natural or social in the Sen/Nussbaum perspective slides into the slippery realm of politics.

While Sen's interest in capabilities over rights as the principal elements of justice stems from his belief that the former provides a better perspective than the latter on what individuals are actually able to do, how they are able to act, his capabilities approach offers no constitutive link to *political action*, namely, the kind of action that expresses power and contributes authoritatively to the formation of an ethically sound, collective life that includes ideals, laws, conventions, and human potential. For Sen and Nussbaum, like Rawls, these political concerns are merely one among many capacities. It is certainly one whose development each favors, but the fact that its exercise will have determinate outcomes, shaping the life of the community in one direction rather than another, is for them a matter to be left to individuals within their political orders. Political participation is one of many capacities to be cultivated. Better to have active rather than passive citizens. But for Sen the value of political

---

[95] See Aristotle, *Politics*, I.2, 1253a8–18; cf. Plato, *Euthyphro*, 7c–d.

participation is secondary, not primary; incidental, not constitutive. Correlatively, capability as "potential" (*dunamis*, or power as dynamic potential) does not reveal how it might be actualized in a political order that is not perfectly harmonious. The social dimensions of Sen's capabilities only gain their "functionings" from an anti-political, unrealistic, conflict-free world, similar to the idealized original position of Rawls, one at odds with the communities of difference that mark democratic life.

The failure to recognize the political connections between human capacities and democracy keeps the capabilities approaches of Amartya Sen and Martha Nussbaum from straying far from their Rawlsian, welfare rights-based alternative and fostering a better understanding of how equal opportunity, merit, and civil rightness can complement democracy. They seem to forget that as soon as human beings become capable of ethical choice, they are acting and choosing on the basis of dispositions engineered by their genes and cultivated by their families among alternatives placed in front of them by a discordant world of differences and power. This point becomes apparent by focusing on the limited way in which Sen (not unlike Rawls) discusses the idea of merit. The most direct place in which Sen does so sidesteps many of the disquieting issues the unavoidable assignation of "merit" raises for democratic ethics – namely, its often worthy but also contingent elevation of the few over the many and its proclivity to ossify an ideal standard into a powerful, exclusionary practice.[96] He does not discuss extensively the socio-economic conditions for democratic participation in political life.

In discussing Sen on the issue of merit, we are more concerned with how it functions as an accepted democratic ethic. Sen rightly notes that "merit" has two analytical features. One is incentive-based, as a reward for certain kinds of effort. The second possesses an "action-propriety" sense, signifying the inherent value of a "meritorious" action.[97] He also rightly notes, however, that in the latter case the "inherent values" may be perverse – such as racism – and in the former case the incentives may not ignite worthy or desirable actions, as in the incentives of so-called "merit pay."[98] In the end, Sen reiterates what we have known, namely, the dependent character of judgments of merit on sanctioned notions of social justice. Distinctions of merit may be justified if they further justice,

---

[96] In Foucault's *Discipline and Punish*, "merit" indirectly appears as a standard for rehabilitation or education that, in fact, also operates as a force of surveillance and control over the bodies and souls of individuals.

[97] Sen, "Merit and Justice" (2005, 8).

[98] Sen (2005, 14), citing Bok (1993, 155–222).

but Sen's idea of justice depends on his capability perspective – which creates an unhelpful hermeneutic circle.

Sen believed that his capability approach is compatible with democracy, understood via "public reasoning" and proper "practice" or "functioning."[99] Leaving politics to public reasoning echoes the hopes of Rawls's deliberative democracy, but, like Rawls's theory, its emphasis depends on the use of rational faculties yielding genial consensus, evidencing no harsh political conflicts – which, again, begs the most important questions about justice that involve accommodating historically conditioned ethical differences about the use of power. But what about his account of democracy as a "practice"? Sen favors the idea of "participatory governance," an interesting combination of republican and democratic values, citizen participation and governmental rule (comparable to "representative democracy," cf. Chapter 3). Unfortunately (albeit understandably), he does not elaborate the meaning of this term in other modes than governmental accountability and freedom of the press. He has managed to sew together Aristotle and Kant in the atmosphere of theory, but coming back down to earth is a problem. Interestingly, Sen does not find a way for welding the capabilities approach in his political account of justice. For it offers no basis for *politically* distinguishing among the various capabilities a society could possibly promote, regarding political activity as a contingent rather than a constitutive feature of social life.[100] Although Sen associates the word capability with potency, and potency has its etymological roots in the Latin *potens*, the Roman equivalent of the Greek and Aristotelian notion of *dunamis*, his account of justice does not acknowledge the requirement that any theory of justice must imply a treatment of power and inequality. It must comport with a kind of politics, about which he is mostly silent.

While Sen composes his theory from Aristotle, Adam Smith, and Marx, he does not go the distance (as they did) and consider how human capabilities can be fulfilled in a *political society* in which citizens actively, demotically, and responsibly shape a society that makes the free development of meritorious capacities possible. This is the challenge for any notion of civil rightness, as it imports an idea of merit into specified realms of social competition and ethical cooperation. But such realms cannot be neatly isolated into distinctive "spheres of justice" or "*technai*." This means that political and participatory considerations, not to mention ideas and practices of justice, are constantly in play and need to be taken into account as potential constituents of common goodness in the

---

[99]   See Sen (2009, Chs. 15–16).
[100]   See, e.g., Esquith and Gifford (2010).

activities of social institutions, linking social ethics and political power.[101] The issue for civil rightness is less about defining equal opportunity and more about fostering more equal opportunities for individuals to demonstrate critically (not traditionally or merely authoritatively defined) merit in their respective fields of endeavor, in such a way that also encourages political participation. This is not because political participation always generates meritorious outcomes. We know when it hasn't, but we also know when it has, as it has with the activities of the current social movements – e.g., Black Lives Matter. If we hear the voices of more citizens, we are more likely to make decisions that benefit the political community. For citizens to want to speak out, they need to feel the worth of so doing.

The notion of "civil rightness" as a discourse of legitimacy for modern democracies must be grasped for what it is – a productive and potentially useful discourse for both democracy and justice that nonetheless harbors negative and ambiguous features. If we accept this, we can proceed with the task of critically evaluating its virtues and limitations as an agent of democracy and goodness. We should accept its ethical features in the past and present before conducting that work. If we do so, we shall be in a much better position to grasp the dimensions of discursive talismans of contemporary political discourse – namely, rights, virtue, democracy, and justice – than if we read them in isolation or dismiss them as codes for something other than they are, namely, terms of legitimation for modern societies that are only nominally democratic.

This argument reflects previous efforts to accommodate democracy and goodness. When the ancient Athenian democracy embraced the previously aristocratic standard of *arete* for itself, as a measure of the successful performance of its citizens and polity, it understood the need for such an accommodation even as it acknowledged the inevitable imperfection of any attempt to solder one. For it could sanction *neither* any colligation of the judgments of citizens, abjuring law for power, *nor* a philosophically stipulated norm that degrades the value of citizens' political judgments. When democracy emerged in the liberal revolutions as liberal democracy, civil society became the arena in which the *demos* might be able to shape the state. Today, in the midst of stagnating wages, the decline of upward economic mobility, and the daunting prospects of climate change, this means that the relationship between democracy and goodness must be defined by neither moralist nor realist arguments of one sort or another. We cannot

---

[101] In this vein, the need for democratically regulating energy industries and encouraging the promotion of public values in the admissions practices of schools, colleges, and universities is much more pressing than surveilling the hiring practices of night clubs, baseball teams, or symphony orchestras.

move forward by trying to apply utopian or dystopian visions of human character or climate change, or deny the history of race relations in North America, especially in the United States since its inception. Nor can we expect that facts without contexts, narratives, or ethical arcs will persuade those impervious to the generic inequalities produced by capitalism and exorbitant inequality or the entanglements involved by America's imperial, economic and military reach (which practically often redound to the benefit of many citizens). Addressing the phenomena of civil rightness in a democratically constructive way has to engage public discourse comprised from myriad sources that accommodate arguments (*logoi*) and works (*erga*) of public life, taking into account how they reflect the dynamic trajectories of American and, *mutatis mutandis*, those of other societies.

The need for a discourse of civil rightness as a particular accommodation of democracy and goodness will remain with us for the foreseeable future, unless civil society or the state becomes radically corrupted. We will seek to maintain spheres of life with the direct power of political institutions limited by the efforts of individuals and groups asserting their democratic rights and virtues in private workplaces, educational institutions, and public realms of speech and action. In this context, civil rightness will generate more democratic vitality than anti-democratic domination, enabling the virtuous discipline to contribute to the well-being of established citizens and immigrants. This challenge comprises a dimension of the ongoing dialogue of democracy and goodness. It supports the aim of neither reducing social desert to power, from above or below, nor regulating individual efforts by unnecessarily restrictive conceptions of merit. With this in mind, we should act deliberately when possible and hope that citizens' activities and capacities that foster sound judgment have not been so corrupted by history and ideology as to make constructive political action that fosters civil rightness impossible.

To promote both democracy and goodness, achieving civil rightness requires eternal vigilance. However, it remains an exceedingly difficult notion to define and apply, because our engagement with political life in civil society is so elusive in the era of the nation-state.

5 Democracy and Legitimacy: Popular Justification of States Amid Contemporary Globalization

5.1 Introduction

The term "legitimacy" became prominently used for judging states in the eighteenth century, but this chapter regards the relationship of democracy to the modern state from 1900 to the present. Having presented itself in the twentieth century as the protector of its citizens and often extending the suffrage to previously disenfranchised groups, the state as guardian of tens or hundreds of millions of persons needs to make plausible claims as a benevolent behemoth for the citizenry. But this state also has become heavily militarized, bureaucratized, and hitched at the hip to the socio-economic engine of capitalism. As such, it does not enhance the political agencies of ordinary citizens. More like Hobbes's Leviathan, it must restrict them. Still, "democracy" has become the accepted term for legitimating a myriad of modern states and political programs. This has made the relationship of *democracy*, as an agency of citizens, to the *state*, as the main means for regulating the lives of citizens, questionable if not oxymoronic. We need to ask frankly, can one complement democratic legitimacy and the modern state?

After all, it has become used recently to evaluate justifications of rule not only in states where civil wars cloud the question of whom or what citizens should obey but also in developed states where the behavior of rulers is so unseemly and unconventional as to question whether certain individuals deserve to occupy the official quarters in which they live. We shall look critically at how democratic practices and discourses of legitimacy in extant states both constitute and subvert constructive relationships between democracy and goodness.

In dealing with the nexus of democracy and the state for democratic ethics via legitimacy as a kind of goodness after this opening section, I shall discuss, in Section 5.2, the historical roots of democratic legitimacy in Rousseau and the notion of "popular sovereignty" as a (dubious) conceptual linkage of democracy and the state.[1] In Section 5.3, I address its treatment by Max Weber – the major theorist of modern discussions of legitimacy, in contrast to Rousseau's mostly critical and ethical conception – thereby installing the contrast between ethical and practical conceptions of legitimacy; Carl Schmitt's attempt to modernize the Rousseauian idea of "democratic legitimacy," and some comparable, more recent efforts to elaborate that phrase. Then, I shall turn, in Section 5.4, to attempts of post-war liberal democratic theorists to connect democracy and the state via procedural reason and relatively neutral ethical postures. In Section 5.5, I move from the world of critical *logos* to actual political conflicts of political legitimacy and democracy in *ergon* today, in order to account more practically for these conceptions as tools for allying democracy and goodness. The conclusion (Section 5.6) offers some remarks about legitimacy and democracy in the digital age.

Current discourses of legitimacy call for this historicist turn, as they do not account well for its contemporary usages. Realist definitions cannot readily explain ethical justifications in political discourse about the legitimacy of modern states, and, by hypothesizing complementary relationships between modern states, liberal theories do not adequately address their actual character. This problematic expresses anew the issues of this book.[2] The distance between actual democracy and contemporary societies encourages seesaw movements between resentful populism and domineering statism – neither of which accommodate democracy and goodness.

5.2   Historical Background

The *Oxford English Dictionary* notes the entry of the Latin *legitimer* ("legitimate") in the late fifteenth century and the introduction of its later English cognate (200 years later), "legitimacy," as the activity of declaring or rendering an action, event, or process *legal* – without there being a clear agency that determines what counts as legitimate. That is,

---

[1] J. G. Merquior rightly roots that phrase in Rousseau's work. See his *Rousseau and Weber: Two Studies in the Theory of Legitimacy* (London: Routledge & Kegan Paul, 1980), 57ff.

[2] J. L. Cohen has conceptualized a version of this as "the new legitimation problematic." See her *Globalization and Sovereignty: Rethinking Legality, Legitimacy, and Constitutionalism* (Cambridge: Cambridge University Press, 2012), 6. Also see her "Rethinking Human Rights, Democracy, and Sovereignty," *Political Theory*, Vol. 36, No. 4 (August 2008), 578–606.

the meaning of legitimacy includes a notion of rightness that is linked to but does not automatically accompany "law" – whose distance from "justice" is legion. Not surprisingly, then, the *OED* records the first uses of "legitimate" *and* "legitimacy" to designate a socially accepted line of inheritance in a *family*.[3] It particularly applied to aristocratic or royal families, as they had sufficient property and power to make inheritance a political issue. Given the connection between familial and political rule in Europe through the nineteenth century, the *OED*'s second, more political, meaning of legitimacy initially associates it with monarchy, endowing the raw power of a family's rule over a polity with the aura of legal right. In high-status families and constitutional monarchies, the meaning of legitimacy was determined by rulers, not subjects.[4] But these references only designate its early usages in English. "Legitimate" and "legitimacy" derive from Latin, and Cicero invoked the former. He used the term *legitimo* as a general sign of approval for a social practice.[5] Indeed, if one strays from bonds of literal usage, one could say that "legitimacy" had equivalent usages in ancient Greece, without being tied to formal legality. The notion of *arete* in ordinary discourse sanctioned certain practices and their associated beliefs as "good," while Aristotle's identification of natural, communal relationships – i.e., among citizens and between husband and wife, parent and child, master and slave – legitimated (in his mind) various relationships of *inequality*, whether between the citizens of one *polis* and another or between certain status-positions within a *polis*. He softened the edges of inequality by legitimizing unequal and potentially harmful relationships as elements of *natural* "community" (*koinonia*).[6] Democratic Athens did not *ipso facto* offer such legitimation. While its laws (*nomoi*) sanctioned these practices, its egalitarian politics did not. Democracy in the Greek *polis* was not, practically speaking, a rented room in the house of constitutionality. The difference between *politeia* and *demokratia* was blurred in

---

[3] See *OED*, 2nd ed., Vol. VIII, 811–12. Also see Article 6 of The Basic Law of the Federal Republic of Germany.

[4] Johannes Althusius (c. 1563–1638) contributed to the justification of political authority stemming from the people, as a way of legitimating the political power of Dutch and Swiss states. But his bow to popular political power was filtered by adherence of citizens and kings to natural and divine law, the interpretation of which was not left to individual citizens or the king. See *The Politics of Johannes Althusius*, an abridged translation by Frederick S. Carney of the third edition of *Politica Methodice Digesta* (Boston: Beacon Press, 1964), Ch. IX, 61–8.

[5] Cicero, at *De Officiis*, 3.107, refers to constraints on Regulus's behavior toward his enemy deriving from it being "*legitimo*." In *De Re Publica* 5.7, "*legitimis*" notes how a good and virtuous republic makes sure that children have a proper – i.e., "legitimate" – character.

[6] Aristotle, *Politics*, I.1–3. See Chapter 2.

I

the fifth century and mostly invented in the fourth-century political theories of Plato and Aristotle.[7]

The unstable relationship between constitutionality and democracy sets forth the issues of this chapter. For "legitimacy" typically and simultaneously performs two functions. First, it creates an ethical umbrella for practical rules of law that authorize rightful political power.[8] But, second, this equal, legal framework provided for the regulation *and acceptance* of different and unequal social, economic, and political positions of rich and poor (or "privileged" and "disprivileged" social strata).[9] The association of political virtue with legitimacy and law protected differences and softened hard realities of institutionalized inequalities. In any event, the more stark problematic of legitimacy for democracy began to emerge in the Middle Ages.[10]

This two fold phenomenon appears clearly in the two theoretical sources of modern usages of legitimacy. In the mid-eighteenth century, Rousseau's demand for a "legitimate" society rooted in morally righteous republican (or, for us, democratic) authority stood radically at odds with existing states and endorsed political equality among *male* citizens.[11] This ethical–political meaning, however, did not fully take hold in the new republican states launched by the liberal revolutions. Large, modern states rhetorically legitimated by the *popular will* in the American and French revolutions framed it as a political ideal rather than a critical model for actual democratic politics.[12] A new phrase became

---

[7] Notably, the first instance of the word *politeia* (now translated in English as polity, political order, or constitution) simply described democratic citizenship in contrast to life in a society ruled by one man.

[8] Regulation occurred through the *graphe paranomon*, which punished individuals who proposed "illegal" motions in the Athenian Assembly, even as what counted as "illegal" in fifth-century Athens was not written down. They also subjected magistrates to vetting procedures before they took up, and after they left, public offices (*dokimasia; euthuniai*; Chapter 2). Aristotle's observations of the working of Athenian democracy did not see any radical opposition between the rule of law and democracy – to the contrary, he saw law as a corrective – although he, like Plato, imagined a tendency in democracy to disrespect the authority of laws.

[9] See Solon, Fr. 5, in *Elegy and Iambus*, J. M. Edmonds, ed. (London: W. H. Heinemann & Sons, 1931 [Loeb Classical Library]). Solon's achievement was so great that, even though it retained unequal political power among economic classes, it could be reinvented as an ideal for fourth-century Athens, *qua* "Solonian Democracy."

[10] See Merquior (1980, 2).

[11] See his *The Social Contract: On the Principles of Political Right* (1762), esp. III.1–4. The "Legitimists" in early nineteenth-century France traded on pre-revolutionary acceptance of the *ancien regime* in choosing their name and claiming to be the heirs of the French crown.

[12] Rousseau is often championed as the theoretical source for modern theories of popular sovereignty. He associated sovereignty, legitimacy, and popular will, but they implied each other only when a general will was in operation. The general will was a critical concept, not a descriptive concept, and so inappropriate as an equivalent for the (oxymoronic) concept of popular sovereignty (see Fralin 1978, esp. 71–88).

salient: popular sovereignty, which had to be single, not plural. In arguing for the Constitution and against the Articles of Confederation the Federalists condemned "*imperium in imperio*," over and against the dual sovereignty enshrined in the Articles of Confederation.[13] But in seeking to authorize the new, federal Constitution, they never referred to it as grounded in popular sovereignty, although the Constitution's legally powerless Preamble begins with the memorable phrase, "We the People of the United States ... do ordain and establish this Constitution for the United States of America." In France, "the people" (mostly Parisian, revolutionary committees) became known as "the nation." In the twentieth century, politicians and theorists proclaimed the *legitimacy* of states on the European continent on the basis of their power to maintain the submission of their citizenry. Weber developed a realist, anti-Rousseauian account of legitimacy to account for the new set of political realities that marked social life regulated by large states.[14] Weber argued that legitimacy depends on acceptability, and contemporary republics rely on the their governments being acceptable to, if not affirmed by, the consent of the citizenry. In Anglo-American legal and political thought, the notion of "the rule of law" – roughly, "no man and no governmental office is above the law" – operated as a practical correlate of legitimacy to sanction a relatively independent judiciary and to provide institutional guidelines designed to regulate the actions of both rulers and ruled.[15]

[13] See *The Federalist*, No. 15. Notably, the phrase "popular sovereignty" achieved traction in American public discourse only as a rough justification of states' rights and their power to protect the institution of slavery from regulation by the federal government. Thus, Abraham Lincoln had to resort to the Declaration of Independence, rather than the Constitution, in order to buttress his arguments against Stephen Douglas during their contest for an Illinois Senate seat in 1858 – which, it's worth recalling, Lincoln lost. On the meaning of popular sovereignty in early America, see Morgan (1989) and Fritz (2008).

[14] Weber's famous tri fold ideal types of political legitimacy and domination were first published in his late essay, *Politik als Beruf* (1919). He grounded them in observed phenomena of agreed-upon inequality – bureaucratic-rational, charismatic, and traditional – and thereby implicitly sanctioned these practices as forms of *de facto* if not *de jure* domination. While he identified them as sociologically and historically real, one also could view them as different incarnations of religious practice: the exclusive methodical cult; the prophetic and priestly, and the doxological attachment to historical practices. It should be noted, however, that his view of legitimation stems from his interpretation of how the "*ethos*" of Calvinism legitimated capitalism, in 1904–5 (see Weber 1958a (1904), 27) (from Introduction, written in 1920). See n. 19 below. He also identified these ideal-types in his posthumously published treatise, Weber 1968 (composed during World War I), 215. The connection between the character of these types and religious practices appears from a brief study of his introduction to *The Social Psychology of the World's Religions*, reprinted in Weber (1958b, 267–301). Also see Scott (1990).

[15] According to the American Bar Association, "the rule of law" has roots in Article 39 of the Magna Carta (1215): (www.americanbar.org/content/dam/aba/migrated/publiced/features/Part1DialogueROL.authcheckdam.pdf). The scholarship on "the rule of law," is various and extensive.

Understood as the acceptance of the state's rulers or consent to be ruled by distant authorities and laws, "legitimacy" immediately reduces the scope of democracy as "rule by the *demos*," either in the ancient Greek sense or Rousseau's modernized, democratic–republican sense. For Rousseau only ascribed "legitimacy" to a society whose rules were regularly and actively authorized by its citizens. In fact, the political emancipation of modern peoples generated a crisis of political legitimacy that analytically pits the *demos* against the state. The state survives because it has an easier time of maintaining a unified practical front than the *demos*. Nonetheless, politicians in electoral campaigns entreat citizens to accept them as their governors, making the notion of "legitimacy" inescapably important for conceptualizing democratic ethics in contemporary public discourse. We live by conceptions of legitimacy that confusingly combine the definitions of Rousseau and Weber. Rousseau's idea of the political order authorized by a general, popular will survives. Weber's assertion that legitimacy depends on the facticity of acceptance by the ruled informs the way that governments seek the consent of their citizens (one way or another).[16] Weber's sense dominates, but Rousseau's sense lingers.

This state of affairs has created an impasse in political understanding. The use of the term "legitimacy" to sanction governmental power in political discourse is inescapable. For, given that contemporary, legitimate governments cannot claim to be genuinely democratic, it performs a critical role in the discourse of democratic political ethics. Yet combining "democracy" and "legitimacy" as a two-word noun, rather than a noun plus a qualifier makes no sense – which hasn't stopped the practice.[17] The idea of legitimacy may reflect democratic concern for complementary and productive links between ethics and power, by referring

---

[16] One way this difference between Rousseau and Weber is theoretically split is by averring the (practically impractical) ability to change continually and democratically the rule of law. Robert Cover formulated the equivalent idea of jurisgenerative law in Cover (1983–4). This also means that the Rousseauian and Weberian alternatives, as ideal-typical definitions, are unsatisfactory.

[17] See the fatefully, if not fatally, vague combination of moral and military authority for the exercise of power by major over minor states in the notion of "the responsibility to protect" (R2P). Note *The Responsibility to Protect: Report of the International Commission in Intervention and State Sovereignty* (Ottawa: International Development Research Centre, 2001) and the Resolution of the United Nations General Assembly, adopted at the United Nations World Summit, A/RES/60, pars. 138–40 (2005). The notion of "the responsibility to protect" appeared in President Obama's public justifications for condoning the bombing of Libya in 2011 as a means of protecting civilians and ending the rule of its president, Muhammar Gaddafi, and evolved out of the effort to rationalize NATO' military support of Kosovo's secession from Serbia in 1999 – which Russia used to justify its coerced secessions by Crimea and southeastern Ukraine from the "legitimate" Ukrainian government in Kiev.

simultaneously to the practical power of law and the sanction of ethical approval by citizens and governments. But it nominally covers regimes that are non-democratic, and therefore has the possibility of detracting critical force for evaluating regimes that are relatively non-democratic and using discourse to enable them to become more so. However, the *kratos* of the *demos* in constitutional democracies is ambiguous at best, and international human rights via international law, the other favored global political term of legitimation, also has indeterminate practical correlates because of the inconsistent modes of its interpretations and enforcement (sanctioned by the great powers).

In conventional political parlance, the meaning of legitimacy places *weaker* constraints or guideposts for a society than does democracy (*qua* legally authorized rule by leaders over citizens via the latter's consent produced by regular elections open to virtually all adult citizens) but *stronger* constraints than those that might accept dictatorial power as legitimate rule. Moreover, the association of legitimacy with "the rule of law" makes it a relatively conservative notion that enforces extant legal and ethical standards in the present rather than seeks their change in the future. But could legitimacy complement democratic ethics? How might it do so and make sense? To gain proper bearings for answering this question, we need to focus more fully on the major modern source of the meaning of legitimacy, principally the work of Max Weber but also Carl Schmitt and the crisis of early twentieth-century Germany.[18]

5.3   Legality, Legitimacy, German Political Realisms

By means of his interpretive conception of social realism, through which we can see objective reality from partial standpoints, Max Weber has provided the linchpins for modern conceptions of legitimacy. Even as the internet undermines widespread authority for any political term and the consumer and finance-driven, neo-liberal turn in capitalism belies Weber's elective affinity between the practices of early Protestantism and capitalism, his tripartite division of types of legitimacy into traditional, bureaucratic-rational, and charismatic resonate with our political life. But it is important to understand the practical seeds of his conception, what gave him the tools for articulating these ideal types, and what enabled them so readily, widely, and continuously, to take hold. Intellectual and political motivation for his views stem from the relatively newborn

---

[18] See Weber, "Politics as a Profession and Vocation" (*Politik als Beruf*), in Weber (1994, 311); cf. Weber (1968, 31–51, 212–16) and Schmitt 1996 (1932a), 2004 (1932b), 2006 (1922), 2008 (1928), 2014 (1921).

Machtstaat of Wilhelmine Germany, girded with unstable political institutions and outfitted with a political class unsuited to use them, all in a period of declining religious faith and unwieldy nationalist sentiments. One can easily go back further, to Bismarck's Germany.

In 1895, Max Weber gave his inaugural address as professor at the University of Freiburg. In it, he worried about Germany's lack of "political maturity" and its need to develop a political class that would know how to deal responsibly with its political challenges. One might say that Weber's later development (at the end of World War I) of the notion of "charismatic leadership" stemmed from his pessimism about such a class ever emerging in Germany given its cultural divisions and hapless understanding of parliamentary government.[19] Only after he understood how dismal were the prospects of political education within the German state did he identify the need for genuinely political leaders who could draw on the better parts of Germany's cultural ethics in fashioning a political course for Germany.[20] It is this Max Weber, a political theorist with a tragic vocation, who provides our point of departure for a detailed analysis of the relationship between legitimacy and democracy.

Weber defined legitimacy as a practical condition in which the status of rulers has been accepted by the ruled, where there is subjective acceptance (by citizens) of objective power (exercised by those in control of the use of violent force), where there are "inner justifications" (*inner Rechtertigungsgrunde*) of "external means" (*ausseren Mittel*) or "material resources" available for (legitimate) domination. While Weber referred to these as "grounds of legitimacy" (*Legitimitatgrunde*), one might say that he was referring to a *logos* of legitimacy to complement the *ergon* of political domination (*Herrschaft*).[21] In this realist definition, Weber does not question whether the acceptance is justified in any other terms than the degree of subjective adherence by the ruled to the authority of the rulers. For doing so would raise issues of substantive or ethical legitimacy that Weber sought to bracket for the purposes of his social scientific analysis, especially as it related to the modern "state" (*Staat*) as "that

---

[19] Weber came upon the notion of charismatic leadership before World War I, but at this point he understood it primarily in religious terms. Its political application came later, and only was published at the end of World War I.

[20] See Weber, "The Nation-State and Economic Policy," in Weber, *Political Writings* 1994, 1–28 at 20–21; "Suffrage and Democracy in Germany" and "Parliament and Government in Germany in a New Political Order," Weber (1994, 80–129, 130–271). For the opposition between a *Machtstaat* and democracy, see "Between Two Laws," in 1994, 75–76. This point was anticipated by Kalyvas (2008, 29).

[21] See Weber, "Politics as a Profession and Vocation" in Weber, *Political Writings* 1994, 309–69, at 310–11. Cf. Weber's unpublished treatise, *Economy and Society*, 1978, 31–51, 212–16.

human community [*menschliche Gemeinschaft*] which (successfully) lays claim to the *monopoly of legitimate [legitimer] physical violence [physicher Gewaltsamkeit]* [Weber's italics] within a certain territory."[22] As a term that sanctions the unilateral exercise of lawful authority, Weberian "legitimacy" mostly designates rightful power and domination (*Herrschaft*) of the state over its citizens.[23] If democracy is understood as direct rule by the *demos* (in accord, roughly, with responsibilities of democratic citizenship), Weberian legitimacy does not comport *per se* with democracy. It sanctions a mode of subordination that naturally results from his definition of politics as "independent *leadership* (*Leitung* – my italics for the English) in action."[24] Weber's political leader must assume "personal responsibility" for his actions in ways that transcend following orders or rules (as citizens mostly do). He should draw on the most important ideal-types of legitimate domination in modernity – charismatic and legal-rational.[25] These had become prominent with the expropriation of traditional means of legitimacy exercised by lords and aristocrats. Yet both devalue demotic agency and elevate the role of leaders and leadership over the masses in determining political legitimacy, resulting in Weber's identification and endorsement of "plebiscitary leadership" and "plebiscitary democracy."[26]

Weber took pains not to identify the associated forms of *legitimate* authority or domination with a particular ethical valence. Any kind of legitimacy could be just or unjust. This feature of his discussion of legitimacy reflects his view that the existence of ethics and politics appears only through subjective judgments of cultural relevance – not through any socially validated ethic. This view has many practical sources, including his intuitive devotion to Christianity as an ethic of ultimate ends that also subverted a practical ethic of political responsibility. Since he recognized that ethics played an intrinsic role in the conduct of politics – whether as an "ethics of responsibility" (*Verantwortungsethik*),

---

[22] Weber (1994, 310–11); cf. Weber (1978 54, 56, 65).
[23] Often ignored is how Weber defines the state and its legitimate power in terms of "human community," which evidences Weber's recognition that ethical cooperation within a state is a *sine qua non* for the legitimate power of a state.
[24] That might suggest, however, that the notion of democratic legitimacy is inherently an oxymoron. But that is not true. First, Weber offered another, less hierarchical definition of politics in *Politik als Beruf*, as "striving for a share of power (*Machtanteil*) or for influence on the distribution of power (*Machtverteilung*), whether between states or between groups of people contained within a single state" (Weber 1994, 311; cf. 316).
[25] See Weber (1994, 311–12, 330–1); Weber (1978, 215–16). Weber's dismissal of the significance of "traditional" forms of legitimacy may be too cursory.
[26] "Plebiscitary democracy – the most important type of *Fuhrerdemokratie* – is a variant of charismatic authority, which hides behind a legitimacy that is *formally* derived from the will of the governed." Weber (1978, 268; cf. 266–9).

inherently influenced by the necessary use of violence and the need to account for the consequences of one's actions, or an "ethics of inner conviction" (*Gesinnungethik*), or, preferably, a kind of political ethics (or ethical politics) that included both – he only could draw on religion and ethics indirectly and individualistically (thus, pluralistically) for his treatment of legitimacy, in ways that resemble the "elective affinity" between Protestantism and the ethic of capitalism.[27] Weber's individualist ethics are odd, given that the "inner" character of justifications of legitimacy inevitably would need socio-political footholds, but he was reluctant to specify conditions of ethical legitimacy. They simply had limited rational justifiability.[28] His refusal to ally any political ethics with theories of practical history, religious salvation, or national chauvinism that affected politics in his world suggested that his politics fit within a wider, secular constellation of thought than Luther's defiant and merely individual stand (to which he referred as necessary for political judgment in *Politik als Beruf*).

From Weber's standpoint in 1919, however, the future appeared as "a polar night of icy darkness and hardness" – hard for us to read now as it must have been painful for him to write then.[29] Be that as it may, his self-imposed constraints about dealing with ethical substance concerning political matters, not to mention his disregard for the potentially useful role an active *demos* might play in guiding political leadership (besides demagoguery), handicapped his effort to produce a comprehensive ethics of *political* legitimacy that complemented law and virtue in the Weimar Republic. It also generated the issue that concerns us. Since legitimation invariably is connected to a political ethic of some sort, how should we think about it in relation to political activity, specifically democratic citizenship?[30] Can we understand legitimacy in a way that comports with *democratic* political ethics and links the dispositions of citizens toward favoring and maintaining a good state? Weber does not directly answer these questions.

---

[27] I could play psychoanalyst and interpret Weber as trying to reconcile the objectivist character of his authoritarian father and his kindly religious mother in an individualist, Protestant vein – something that clearly bedeviled Weber himself – but I don't know how to play. See Marianne Weber, (1950 (1926), 17–63). For a recent, one-volume biography, see Radkau (2011, 7–24, 52–69).

[28] Weber (1994, 359–69). One might explain away the oddity by invoking Weber's neo-Kantianism, but that just kicks the ball down the road. The notion of "elective affinity" (*Wahlverwandtschaft*) appears throughout Weber's works.

[29] Weber (1994, 368).

[30] See Hare (1967). Hare's "lawful government" functions as an English equivalent for legitimate government.

Carl Schmitt did. Writing in and out of Weber's shadow in the 1920s as a Prussian Catholic (Westphalian, excommunicated), before he joined the Nazis in 1933, Schmitt produced his own theory of legitimacy rooted in his realist theory of political existentialism – emphasizing the authority of the deed and oriented toward the decisive role of the friend–enemy practical dynamic in politics.[31] Within this framework, he conceptualized a notion of "democratic legitimacy" (as did Habermas sixty years later, see below). To overcome the *stasis* of the friend–enemy conflict, which could occur within a state as well as between states, Schmitt's theory relied on discretionary, executive political power as the political act *par excellence*. For Schmitt, a political order depended on legitimacy; legitimacy depended on sovereignty, and sovereignty was defined by the exception – as determined by the political executive of a state. He managed to reconcile his theory of (legitimate) dictatorship with democracy by linking practical democracy to monistic political "identity." The *demos* now became one, not many.

Schmitt's linkage of democracy to identity as the conceptual foundation of "democratic legitimacy" is distinctive but also odd.[32] Democracy always has been associated with the agency of citizens, for better or worse, and that generates plurality. (However, "plurality," "pluralism," and "pluralization" are strange political concepts, since how the parts that make of the plurality substantively relate to each as powers is never specified – when *that* is always the crucial issue.) Such plurality caused Hobbes such anxiety that sovereignty only could arise if the *demos* foreswore its political agency and delegated it to a monarchical sovereign who monopolized political authority (unless there was a democratic sovereign whose "democratic gentlemen" in Parliament uncharacteristically would not confuse matters).[33] Schmitt, on the other hand, assumes that democratic political agency and legitimacy cohere under the notion of identity. Given the inherently pluralistic character of democratic agency, how does Schmitt produce a concept of democratic legitimacy that does not deprive the *demos* of effective political agency? This question raises an issue theorized in ancient Greece but transformed in the conditions of the modern state, namely, the relationship between "the political" and democracy.[34]

---

[31] This presupposes that Schmitt's political theology, at the end of the day, has marginal significance for political ethics.

[32] One might diminish the oddity and complicate his theory by taking his conceptualization of political theology as ethically meaningful. See Schmitt (2006 (1922)).

[33] See Thomas Hobbes, *Behemoth, or the Long Parliament*, 1668.

[34] On "the political" in relation to pre-World War II German political theorists, see Kelly (2003).

Schmitt articulated a theory of legitimacy for the modern, "democratic" state in *Constitutional Theory* (1928) and *Legality and Legitimacy* (1932), both written during (what turned out to be) the waning days of the Weimar Republic. He initiates his discussion of constitutional legitimacy by affirming its difference from mere legality via its adherence to *existence*, not *ethics*:

A constitution is legitimate not only as a factual condition. It is also recognized as a just order, when the power of the constitution-making power, on whose decision it rests, is acknowledged. The political decision reached regarding the type and form of state existence, which constitutes the substance of the constitution, is valid because the political unity whose constitution is at issue exists and because the subject of the constitution-making power can determine the type and form of this existence. The decision requires no justification via an ethical or juristic norm.[35]

For Schmitt, democracy naturally generates unity out of plurality for the purposes of political action (*contra* Hobbes), transforming collective, diverse deliberation into political decision. With regard to Schmitt's theory of legitimacy, the question becomes how he conceives the "constitution-making power" of the people (*Volk*, not *demos*) as a "unity." He does it by eliminating the independent political agency of the citizenry – without associating any notion of humanity or human rights as limiting ideas for the political exercise of power – and tacitly subordinating it to the *Furhrerprinzip*.[36]

Democratic legitimacy ... rests on the idea that the state is the political unity of a *people* ... the character of democratic legitimacy can be attributed to most constitutions in that it is based on the people's ever-present, active constitution-making power, even if that power is only tacit.[37]

The theoretical move is not surprising, as the legal pillars of legitimacy transcend democracy, or demotic authority *per se*, to include non-democratic elements of the political order. The criteria of what may count as a *legitimate* political order offer a larger umbrella than those which cover a *democratic* political order. But Schmitt's democracy makes the political agency of citizens superfluous. For "the state" that provides legitimating conditions for democracy possesses, according to Schmitt, "unity," "self-identity" (or "identity"), "similarity," and "homogeneity." And even if the state includes mechanisms of representation, they may

---

[35] Schmitt (2008 (1928)).
[36] Schmitt's dismissal of "humanity" because of its lack of a practical referent percolates throughout his works, echoing comparable criticisms of the political use of the term from the much different perspectives of Burke, Bentham, and Marx.
[37] Schmitt (2008 (1928), 138–9).

be signified by "the government, not the people."[38] Apart from "homogeneity," Schmitt's association of his other terms of art with democracy is inherently problematic, for he allows for their expression by dictatorship and discretionary power.[39] Thus, it is not surprising that Schmitt makes legality depend on sovereignty, and sovereignty on "he who defines the exception." It also differentiates Schmitt's "existential" realism from Weber's formal–legal realism and links the former's to the exaltation of personalistic, statist power over political and democratic power.

Legitimacy and legality are linked and differentiated for both Weber and Schmitt. Neither wants to associate legitimacy with an ethical norm disconnected from legality or authoritative rule and government, but neither seeks to update, say, the natural law tradition as the foundation of legitimacy. Neither wants to modernize the ethical, liberal, and democratic criteria of Locke for the conditions of the modern state – seeming to find it too unwieldy. But these versions of political realism arguably provide too much semantic and practical room for the use of legitimacy as a "just" claim for a state (Schmitt) or domination (Weber), room produced by each not clearly differentiating legitimacy as a second-best form of political rule relative to justice. This room could be occupied by unconstitutional forces that claim to provide peace and order amid domestic *stasis* by defanging democratic politics – e.g., via the Egyptian generals who overthrew Mohamed Morsi, the brutal campaign against political opponents waged by President Bashir al-Assad of Syria, or the electoral putsch of Turkey's Erdogan.

Is there a notion of legitimacy as a political virtue that might not be practically utopian or arbitrary but, instead, appropriate for typically acceptable functions of modern state power that also defines ethical limits on constitutional and governmental power in ethically pluralistic societies? Contemporary liberal political thought attempts to answer this question.

5.4   Western Liberalisms and Political Legitimacy

From Hobbes's and Locke's to Rawls's and Habermas's, Western liberal theories have mostly regarded legitimacy as a dependent concept relative to their larger political theories. Nonetheless, they define it directly or indirectly as a conjunction of ethics and power – thus centrally relevant to any consideration of democratic ethics. Early social contract theorists (e.g., Hobbes and Locke) implicitly or explicitly regard political

[38] Ibid, 240–5, 262–4.
[39] Ibid, 266.

legitimacy as a function of their imaginary partnership between "natural" human beings and the state they authorize to protect them from the travails of hypothetically natural (social) conditions. Indeed, one of the ways that liberal political theorists distinguish themselves from others is their assumption of an initial standpoint of unanimous political agreement or consensus for a political community, rather than an agentic conception of human nature (*pace* Plato, Aristotle, or Arendt) or the acceptance of conflict as a constitutive feature of political foundation (*pace* Machiavelli or Marx).

These matches between the individual and society become rhetorical and logical tools for improving the seventeenth-century English state. Ever difficult to categorize, Rousseau does not quite play the reformist game in the *ancien regime* of pre-revolutionary, eighteenth-century France. Beginning with an individualistic conception of human nature, he conceptualizes political legitimacy in purely theoretical terms, as a general will of politically virtuous citizens who coordinate their natural differences for the common good and delegate their daily management to a dutiful state. This conception of legitimacy presupposes general legislation validated by republican (or democratic) citizens (even as Rousseau despairs about representation and democratic government). This kind of liberalism projects an image of ultimate harmony as the catalyst for legitimate society, relying on an original human nature reshaped by a lawgiver.

In the twentieth century, John Rawls has, in his view, updated the social contract tradition via a combination of Kant and Bentham atop the pinnacle of the American empire in the mid-twentieth century. Jurgen Habermas has sought to modernize Kant and the best of the German Enlightenment under the aegis of the Basic Law of the Federal Republic of Germany. Yet neither directly engages contemporary versions of the political issues of *stasis* that Hobbes, Locke, Rousseau (and other political theorists we still read, from Plato to Marx) addressed. Both Rawls and Habermas are concerned with vetting disagreement while maintaining a political theory rooted in the coherence of rationality and validity. Each does so differently, but both, fundamentally, downplay the intellectual significance and practical value of democratic politics. Although the work of each has been praised or criticized extensively, both still factor in how democracy and legitimacy are related in critical discourse.

Rawls begins with an "original position," because there seems to be no other way of generating the requisite criteria (for justice as a virtue) for the "reasonable, rational" citizens who constitute the foundations of his presumptively just but only theoretically real, political order. Given this difficulty, Rawls opts for an original position that can provide the

basis for theorizing a "political" (*sic*) conception of justice "by remov-
ing from the political agenda the most divisive political issues," including "comprehensive moral doctrines."[40] Rawls is certainly correct that
identifying a conception of political virtue that could inform a modern conception of legitimacy is maddeningly difficult, but some would
say attempting to solve the problem by bracketing it comes at the
price of rendering his political theory ineffective. Moreover, epistemic
assumptions about the practical value of hypothetical reason inform his
standpoint – and that of liberalism more generally. These basically consist of the priority of theoretical over practical reason – "moral reason"
as a steering mechanism for "political power." Presumably, it guides
power and politics, now rendered as secondary considerations. The fact
that Rawls can write a theory that presumptively coordinates "moral
reason" and "democracy" stems from assumptions in liberal echelons
of Anglo-American academies about a stable meaning associated with
"moral reasonableness" and its coherent association with Western constitutional democracies that are deemed able to harness developments
in technology and capitalism.[41]

"Legitimacy," therefore, does not figure independently in Rawls's discourse about liberal justice or political liberalism. Instead, it operates as
a feature of the citizens in the original position whose expectations are
presumed to be "legitimate," for they accord with the preordained principles of justice and complementary social institutions.[42] Much like the
social contract theorists who produced a fit between their imagined citizens and just social institutions, Rawls, too, imagines a fit. The difference
is that his fit begins with hypothetical intuitions and does not seriously
challenge the extant motivations of citizens or structure of our institutions other than to rationalize them in accord with his two principles of
justice. When he takes up the idea of legitimacy in *Political Liberalism*, he
only reminds us of its dependent posture.[43] And it does not factor in his
account of an international system of fair political relations.[44]

As Jurgen Habermas moved from his Marxist origins in the Frankfurt
School to a kind of neo-Kantianism, his concerns about the problems
of Western capitalist democracies moved to the background of his

[40] Rawls (2001, 116–17).
[41] See Nagel (1987).
[42] Rawls (1971, 310–15).
[43] Rawls (1996, 136–7, 225). Cf. Rawls, "The Idea of Public Reason Revisited," 1999 (1997), 137.
[44] Rawls wrote *The Law of Peoples* to clarify the chief pillars of a moral American foreign policy.

theoretical agenda.[45] The foreground now emphasized questions of justi-fication, particularly as they touched upon questions of legitimacy in the post-war Federal Republic of Germany. But Habermas, unlike Rawls, felt the need to answer these questions with regard to universal, procedural claims about rationality and morality, "inescapable presuppositions of argumentation" (even as they are inter-subjective) in order to regulate the harmful particularity that informs historicist interpretations of polit-ical reason and ethics.[46] These preoccupied the political theory of his last major work, *Between Facts and Norms*, first published (in German) twenty-five years ago.[47] His initial intellectual catalyst for theorizing legit-imation was probably the problems he saw in the work of Max Weber.[48] He believed that Weber's conceptions of legitimacy lay mired in the var-ious habits and motives of individuals and groups. He also was unhappy with the subsequent decisionism of Schmitt. He sought to establish cri-teria of "rational validity" for legitimacy roughly grounded in a "public sphere" (substantiated by "public opinion") that would make it com-patible with modern democracy.[49] He then turned to his theory of the "immanent truth" provided by linguistic structures of communication under valid, social conditions of legitimation, aka the "ideal speech situ-ation" (a phrase that disappears in his later work).[50] Like Rawls, he turns away from politics and toward establishing the theoretical character of rational and normative validity claims for legitimacy in a hypothetically constructed idea of the public sphere and public opinion that ultimately found their ground in a "communication community" – not far removed from the community of citizens in Rawls's original position.[51] But Habermas also was dealing with serious problems close to him, namely,

---

[45] Starting with Habermas (1975 (1973)). That is not to gainsay the myriad, bracing polit-ical commentaries Habermas made about public affairs.

[46] See Habermas (1990 (1983), 43–115, at 66, 71, 88, 107–109; cf. 10). Note, more recently, Habermas (2008 (2005), 77–97, at 81–7; cf. 25). In this essay, Habermas calls attention to a previous work (87). For Habermas's ongoing efforts to adapt his theory to current history, see 2009 (2008), 138–83, 212–20.

[47] Habermas (1996 (1992)). On this book, see the collection, including an additional brief response by Habermas: Rosenfeld and Arato (1998).

[48] Habermas (1975 (1973), 97ff).

[49] Habermas states that the public sphere (*Öffentlichkeit*) is "a realm of our social life in which something approaching public opinion can be formed. Access is guaranteed to all citizens. A portion of the public sphere comes into being in every conversation in which private individuals assemble to form a public body."

[50] See Habermas (1984–5 (1981)).

[51] For an anticipation of this move, in the direction of "law" whose substantive elements are vetted by highly abstract standards of communicative rationality, see "Law as Medium and Law as Institution," in Teubner (1986, 203–20, esp. 212–14).

how to legitimate an enduring, democratic, and just political order in Germany – which previous constitutions had been unable to generate.[52]

In the wake of practical legitimation crises of Western societies (i.e., 1968–1974), these major political theorists addressed the issue of legitimation by not paying sustained attention to the political fires that manifested the crisis – the cultural revolts of post-war men and women; civil rights movements, the Vietnam War, growing social, economic, and political inequality, as well as environmental crises. Habermas was more politically critical than Rawls. He recognized and lamented "the suppression of generalizable interests," the ideological expression of which he believed his theory could identify and thereby save liberal democracy from its degradation by democratic realists.[53] But then Habermas relied on a theoretically contestable and practically ambiguous theory of linguistic truth and communication to determine (to appropriate jargon of American public officials dealing with the 2008 financial crisis) the "stress limits" of Western capitalist democracies and hence establish the conditions for democratic legitimacy.[54] Still, Habermas's theory retains historical ambitions greater than Rawls's, as he thinks that his theoretical criteria reflect the structure of human reality. The "moral basis of argumentation" stems from two human capacities: "... analytically testing the consistency of the value premises ... ; and empirically testing the realizability of goals selected from the value perspectives."[55]

Habermas's last major work, crafted out of his interpretation of the Western tradition of philosophy and political theory, reconciles his views of democracy and legitimacy.[56] From his work on the bourgeois public sphere in the nineteenth century to his final works from the 1990s and since, Habermas has been principally concerned with the idea of "legitimacy" and "legitimation." They occupy the centerpiece of his political theory – in fact "legitimacy" defines what is appropriately "between" facts (or

---

[52] See Hucko (1987). If Anglo-American theorists are dubious about the ease with which Habermas invokes "human rights," note its appearance in Article 1 of The Basic Law and absence in the American Constitution and British constitution.

[53] A noted exponent of what has been called "democratic realism" is the political perspective of Joseph Schumpeter who believed that contemporary societies which called themselves democratic needed to be ruled by managerial elites chosen in competitive elections.

[54] Habermas (1975 (1973), 143). Cf. the terminology of the American Secretary of the Treasury, Timothy Geithner, on testing the viability of American financial institutions after the Great Recession of 2008.

[55] Habermas (1975 (1973), 105–6). One can see how this binary evolves into the contrast between "validity" and "factitity" in his later works.

[56] For a more extended treatment of Habermas's late theory of democracy, see Scheuerman (2012, Part 2). (Part 1 interprets these issues in the work of Franz E. Neumann.)

factitity) and norms (or validity [*Geltung*]).[57] Why and how does it occupy such an important position in Habermas's thought? We can most efficiently address that question by looking at its use in *Between Facts and Norms*, in which he developed the discursive dimension of his democratic theory that sought complementarity between legality or legitimacy and modern democracy by means of a linguistic and proceduralist framework.[58] Here, Habermas combined his early interest in providing a post-Marxist ethics for Western constitutional democracies with concern about the cultural debates in the 1980s and 1990s about how to establish a theory of political justice and legitimacy among citizens who harbor different world-views. Like Rawls, Habermas sought to achieve consensus by limiting admissible political discourse without coercing persons – enabling one to be free by virtue of using only linguistic force – splitting the difference between radically internal subjectivity (which proliferates under a system of individual rights that validates ethically indeterminate forms of strategic action) and coercive, external objectivity (which stems from the power of law and the state to shape public ethics without relying on burdensome notions of civic virtue). As Habermas believes the former underlies the liberal tradition and the latter counts as the ultimate political effect of the republican tradition, he believes his theory has transcended the limitations of both, discursively providing an "impartial" yet democratically productive regulation and resolution of socio-political conflicts while yielding mutual implication of human rights and popular sovereignty, political ethics and democratic power.[59] Habermas acknowledges that he is trying to accommodate (*inter alia*) the political ethics of the German *Rechtstaat* and the English common law tradition, as taken up by the American Constitutional order.[60]

---

[57] "Norms" is an unsatisfactory translation of *Geltung*, for, in English, "norms" are external or preexisting constraints on social action, while "validity" refers to processes by which factual phenomena may be validated. If one asks, "validated by whom?," Habermas would answer by begging the question – for there is no "whom" worthy of note, only a "how," validated by linguistic procedures for communicative action.

[58] For *Between Facts and Norms* as the summation of Habermas's political theory, with its intellectual foundations stemming from *The Theory of Communicative Action*, see Rehg, "Translator's Introduction," to Habermas (1996 (1992), ix–x).

[59] Habermas (1996 (1992), xxv; 26–41; 87–89; 94; 108–9; 454–7).

[60] Rehg, "Translator's Introduction," to Habermas (1996 (1992), xxxiv–xxxvi). Habermas engages in critical analysis of German and American legal theorists and German and American law throughout. To be sure, no one Constitutional decision can disprove Habermas's theory – in fact, it would seem, to Habermas, that none could – but one wonders what to make of repeated Supreme Court decisions in the United States (from *Dred Scott* and *Plessy v. Ferguson* to *Citizens United*) that smack of prejudice and partisanship, namely, how a procedural framework is sufficient to explain their reasoning and outcomes, providing an effective conception of "legitimacy." For an expression by Habermas of the hypothetical validity of "the rule of law" to undergird the legitimacy of democratic procedures and deliberative politics, see Rosenfeld and Arato (1998, 395–7).

Another way of viewing Habermas's conceptual marriage of democracy and legitimacy is to understand it as an effort to correct (what he regarded as) Hannah Arendt's concept of power, which is actualized "only where word and deed have not parted company, where words are not empty and deeds not brutal." To fill the conceptual vacuum, Habermas turns to "the rule of law" as the ultimate source of legitimation – law that is not a function of practical legality.[61] For Habermas, "... law is the medium through which communicative power is translated into administrative power."[62] It comports with the autonomy of a self-legislating political community of democratic citizens – hypothetical, not actual, democratic citizens – and thereby splits the difference between the amoral norms of liberalism's adherence to the rule of law and republicanism's dependence on the political actions of citizens. He does so with an idea of procedural communitarianism rooted in a Kantian idea of law. Law, legitimately understood, guarantees democratic liberalism, for it guarantees valid (*gültig*) rights, and such (human) rights justify the law.[63] Habermas's claim that we acknowledge an "internal" relationship between popular sovereignty or democracy and human rights reflects his view that Kant's universalistic criterion of morality and legality creates the means for global standards of political community that do not fall prey to anti-democratic tradition or practices. Habermas ignores Kant's antipathy to democracy, thereby rendering it theoretically insignificant and fit for the dustbin of history. Then, Habermas goes beyond Kant's republicanism by extending his own theory of law to the action of self-legislating citizens and an international arena that lacks nations of devils.[64]

---

[61] Habermas, "Preface," *Between Facts and Norms*, xliii. Good discussions of "the rule of law" include Neumann (1986 (1923–54?)), Fine (1984), and Shapiro (1994).

[62] Habermas 1996 (1992), 150.

[63] Habermas (1996 (1992), 94, 112, 120, 124, 130–1, 296–314).

[64] Habermas (1996 (1992), 99–104, 113, 120–2). For Kant's opinion of ordinary citizens as political actors, see his essay, "Theory and Practice," in Reiss (1991 (1797), 101). In a later essay, Habermas reiterates these principles: "... law requires more than mere acceptance; besides demanding that its addressees give it *de facto* recognition, the law claims to *deserve* their recognition. Consequently, all the public justifications and constructions that are intended to redeem this claim to worthiness of recognition are part of the legitimation of government constituted through law ... Political theory [*sic*] has given a twofold answer to the question of legitimacy: popular sovereignty and human rights. The principle of popular sovereignty lays down a procedure that, because of its democratic features, justifies the presumption of legitimate outcomes. This principle is expressed in the rights of communication and participation that secure the public autonomy of politically enfranchised citizens. The classical human rights [*sic*], by contrast, ground an inherently legitimate rule of law. These rights guarantee life and private liberty – that is, scope for the pursuit of personal life-plans – of citizens. Popular sovereignty and human rights provide the two normative perspectives from which an enacted, changeable law is supposed to be legitimated as a means to secure both the private and civic autonomy of the individual." See "Remarks on Legitimation through Human Rights," in Habermas (2001 (1998), 113–16). Cf. Habermas, "The Kantian Project and the Divided West: Does the Constitution of International Law Still Have a Chance?" in 2006, 115–93.

Very nice, if you can get it. More pointedly, how does one determine the "validity" that presumably links *logos* and *ergon*? Habermas redirects us to his discourse theory of procedural political ethics. Thus:

... the *legitimacy* of statutes is measured against the discursive redeemability of their normative validity claim – in the final analysis, according to whether they have come about through a rational legislative process, or at least *could have been justified* (my italics) from pragmatic, ethical, and moral points of view.[65]

Democracy comes into play as the practical source for generating rights and law. But just as Habermas presupposes that the genesis of law does not compromise its reach, he grounds democracy in a liberal definition of equal opportunity, which we know to be an equivocal agent of democracy.[66] In his words,

In the *principle of popular sovereignty* [i.e., modern democracy], according to which all government authority derives from the people, the individual's right to an equal opportunity to participate in democratic will-formation is combined with a legally institutionalized practice of civic self-determination. (*BFN*, 169)

The question is whether the utilization of Habermas's discourse theory will avoid the same problems that have afflicted Rawls's theory, namely, a disconnect between his theoretical (albeit "post-metaphysical") grounds and individuals acting amid the dynamic of history. Linguistic procedures do not protect one against the unstable connections between *logos* and *ergon* that complicate relations between democracy and goodness.

In this vein, the question becomes, does Habermas's theoretical engine get you anywhere if you don't accept the authority of linguistic procedures for vetting admissible and productive political argument? Habermas avers that his conception of morality covers both private and public realms, both civil society and the state, democracy and law, and that his procedural requirements for morally authoritative speech have no nefarious elements. This view, however, is more assertion than argument, a reflection of intuitive assumptions shared by Habermas and Rawls, gleaned from high-level Western academic discourse from the 1950s to the 1990s, that formal notions of morality and rationality had universal and non-prejudicial critical bite. Whatever weight these assumptions had then has been lost. In addition, recalling the previous quotation from Habermas, we know that if we continue to judge the cogency of *logoi* in

---

[65] Habermas (1996 (1992), 30). This quotation makes a kindred point to the one mentioned by Williams in his posthumously published essay, "Realism and Moralism in Political Theory," (2005, 16).

[66] See, e.g., Young (1994 (1958)) and Schaar (1981 (1967)). For Habermas's invocation of liberal principles of equal concern, equal opportunity, etc., see, *inter alia*, 1990 (1983), 66 and 2008 (2005), 82.

terms of their effectiveness in *erga*, the practical legalization of the principle of equal opportunity surely has been mixed. It has increased legal opportunities of women and minorities but has also been partner to the creation of new hierarchies and increased inequality – thus not being clearly effective in fostering political equality in the society as a whole. In this respect (like equal opportunity), legitimacy checks capitalism and bigotry but doesn't diminish their power.

"Democratic procedures" are the linchpin of Habermas's democratic theory. They are designed to be liberal, purely formal and linguistic, rather than to offer substantive and practical guideposts that authoritatively direct the political judgments of citizens. But as a result, they stand prior to the deliberative drama of politics and action that join ethics and power in dynamic historical contexts. The result radically limits their rational, political cogency and practicality. While Habermas (like Rawls) does not hold to a particular view of human nature, he does believe there can and must be a prior commitment to a *procedure* that "counterfactually" validates communicative *action* (my italics) – much like Kant's categorical imperative or Rawls's original position. This produces a gap between his theory and political practice, one that he fervently wants to bridge. In his later work, he projects that bridge onto (or discovers that in) the procedures of international law.[67] If Arendt has erred on the side of unduly conjoining *logos* and *ergon*, Habermas returns by subordinating the impetus to political participation among democratic citizens to guidance from a procedural bench of professional, philosophical authority. The words of some speak louder than the actions of many. It is one thing to understand human action preceded by deliberate thought; it is another to presuppose that action can be well-guided by a meta-deliberative procedure that benefits democratic ethics.[68]

The theories of Rawls and Habermas stem from attempts by major twentieth-century political theorists, stung by totalitarianisms and racism but buoyed by post-war Western supremacy, to produce theories of justice and legitimacy that do not presuppose substantive moral and political truths. They are designed to alleviate injustices that cause harmful coercion. Yet both assume successes by modern states in their efforts to well-regulate liberalism, capitalism, and democracy. The hypothetical posture of their theories, however, diminishes their critical force,

---

[67] Habermas (2006, 115–93), and notes.
[68] For relatively favorable views of the integrity of Habermas's theoretical posture, while still recognizing the value of context and conflict in constituting political judgment, see Benhabib (1992, 73–88).

particular as complements to democracy and legitimacy. Rawls presupposes a basically just social structure that guides proper intuitions of "representative citizens." Upset by the current state of practical, political affairs, Habermas still assumes that "the force of the better argument" can move constitutional democracies out of their predicaments.[69] To be sure, one shouldn't wholly judge a theory by its most powerful interpreters – any more than we should judge Socrates by Alcibiades or Plato; Plato by Dionysius II or Aristotle; Rousseau by Robespierre, or Marx by Lenin. But readers judge theories in terms of their power to illuminate and benefit. At least with regard to the capacity of Rawls and Habermas to illuminate political legitimacy that fosters democracy, their theories fall short. Both Rawls and Habermas foreswear considerations of political virtue as a practical possibility because they regard the topic in modernity as logically impossible to parse, which leads to theories of justice that have been evacuated of history, power, and action by the blinding light of their theoretical perspectives. Are there then no roads stemming from the Western tradition that foster a concept of legitimacy as a political virtue and friend to democracy?

The French political theorist Pierre Rosanvallon has worked hard to provide an approach that happily reconciles democracy and legitimacy.[70] To what extent does his view helpfully contribute to a practical conception of democratic legitimacy as an idea adaptive to democratic ethics informed by ethics and power, linking *logos* and *ergon* so as to benefit the collectivity? At the outset of his book on the subject he stipulates the following definition of the existence of democratic legitimacy: it occurs " … when citizens believe in their own government, which cannot happen unless they have a sense of empowerment."[71] This definition cannot be understood in terms of our previous categories. It draws on the realist notion of actual belief and acceptability but goes beyond liberal notions of rights or the formalism of constitutionalist understandings

---

[69] Kuper (2004) extends "democracy" beyond borders by means of a notion of responsiveness, but his theory does not address the requirements of democratic action and accepts conventional views that the root the modern practice of politics in what he calls "liberal democracy."

[70] That said, he does not refer to "virtue" except briefly at the outset as an equivalent of legitimacy. Rosanvallon (2011 (2008), 3). Another, serious treatment of the relationship between legitimacy and democracy appears in Sadurski (2008, 1–39), advocating "democracy without values." Sadurski mostly reproduces and applies the views of procedural legitimacy and democracy forwarded by Joseph Raz and treated above via the discussions of Rawls and Habermas. See Raz (1979, Chs. 2, 11), his "Introduction" to Raz (1990, 1–19; 1994, Ch. 10). For a more substantive stipulation of a complementary relationship between legitimacy and democracy, see Brunkhorst (2010, 179–98, esp. 197–8).

[71] Rosanvallon (2011 (2008), 9).

by linking democratic legitimacy to a notion of "empowerment" (which remains undefined but correlated to political capacity). Taking his cue from the Rousseauian distinction between the general will and the will of all – legitimate, democratic government vs. majority rule by citizens who fail to demonstrate a public will – Rosanvallon believes that it has been confusingly conflated in the contemporary mind (rather than just abandoned) – so that the (also Rousseauian) assumption that governmental administration carries out the will of the people has been wrongfully delegitimized in practice.[72] He fills these lacunae with new criteria that bolster the general character of democratic legitimacy without utopianizing it; they are "impartiality," "reflexivity," and "proximity."[73] Each contributes to both democratic power and republican generality *if and only if* they are employed properly. For Rosanvallon, they are neo-Weberian ideal types designed to identify sources of democratic legitimacy, not inherently democratic ideals.[74] The sources identified are very abstract and, indeed, not inherently democratic. Impartiality, reflexivity, and proximity could be watchwords for enlightened guardians as much as democratic partisans. Rosanvallon knows this, so his justification is based on judgments about the mostly democratic effects of instituting these politically neutral principles and practices now.

To what extent is he right? As mentioned above, his claims are marked by circular reasoning, but let's leave that to one side. *Impartiality?* Bolstering democracy with this kind of "legitimacy" derives from his view that non-state organizations (various NGOs, non-profits, etc.) have become adjuncts to democratic possibility outside the state.[75] While this surely may be true – who could gainsay the democratic merits of domestic or international, do-good, charitable organizations, colleges and universities, and advocates for human rights? – one must remember that organizations not supported by tax dollars are supported by somebody's dollars, and those providing the dollars will only have a certain amount of tolerance for impartiality.[76] As for so-called independent commissions, there is (as Rosanvallon acknowledges) an infinite regress with regard to their impartiality. They may be less partisan, but they are still political. The so-called "legitimacy" of *reflexivity* expresses Rosanvallon's view

---

[72] Ibid, 4–5.

[73] Ibid, 7–8.

[74] Ibid, 11.

[75] Ibid, Chs. 4–6. Of course, one has to make distinctions here, in order to avoid having this term crown the richest man in the world as also the most democratic because of the size of his charitable contributions.

[76] The political character of NGOs and INGOs will be addressed in the next chapter.

that mostly democratic benefits stem from relating legislative and judicial power.[77]

Since ancient Athens, democratic societies have found the need to utilize courts to deal with issues of criminality and to provide an institutional check on what may be hasty legislative decisions. It is not clear, however, that the democratic benefits of judicial power are clearly greater now than they used to be. Rosanvallon does not seem to be aware, for example, of how politicized the US Supreme Court *has always been*.[78] It is mostly a countervailing source of power, properly justified by the doctrine of the separation and relative balance of powers.[79] But the exercise of its power does not automatically promote democracy and goodness. As for the legitimacy of *proximity*, this refers to the increasing importance of "the politics of presence."[80] It is not clear how much more significant this is to democracy than it was when Machiavelli referred to how the Prince could be effective and deceptive when ruling the populace because they could *see* him but not *touch* him. Social media enhance possibilities in this regard because they enable unfiltered access by citizens to semi-public realms, and the physical, political presence of "Occupy Wall Street" (2011) played a major role in focusing public attention on the issue of economic and political inequality – setting the stage for Senator Bernie Sanders' candidacy. But long before their emergence, Adolph Hitler marshaled aesthetic imagery to increase his power, and Donald Trump heavily manipulated the media in seeking the 2016 Republican Presidential nomination.[81]

Rosanvallon's wide-ranging historical and theoretical knowledge still has many gaps, and it is primarily influenced by the legacy of Rousseau's views on republics, democracy, and generality – which was dedicated to address and correct the injustices of the monarchy and aristocracy of eighteenth-century France. And it is understandable that Rosanvallon avoids questions of practical and ethical goodness as constituents of democratic legitimacy, given the historical conflation of political virtue with the Reign of Terror by the Committee of Public Safety. But the intellectual strategy of avoidance, so often used in liberal political thought, has not addressed many of the most damaging and anti-democratic effects of our time – such as increased social stratification, economic inequality, and the imperialism of executive power. Rosanvallon does not seriously

---

[77] Rosanvallon (2011 (2008), Chs. 7–9).
[78] For a critical attack on the power of judges on behalf of social ethics by a renowned judge, see Bork (2003).
[79] Cox (1977).
[80] Rosanvallon (2011 (2008), Chs. 10–12).
[81] See Tomasky (2016).

analyze these aspects of society as impediments to democratic legitimacy. Given the instability and incoherence of international law and politics amid the rivalries of states and corporations, it is hard to identify a clear, global theory of democratic and legitimacy that does not remain rooted in the ethics and politics of states.

Undaunted by these concerns, two recent theorists have generated conceptions of legitimacy that attempt to span the gap between *logos* and *ergon* more felicitously than realists and liberals by unearthing the critical potential of constitutionality as an asset of liberalism and democracy.[82] Although not conventionally liberal, the two theorists' perspectives emerged in the wake of the discussions of legitimacy offered by Rawls (indirectly) and Habermas (more directly). They offer new intellectual perspectives that emphasize how constitutionality links democracy and legitimacy so as to move the debate about their relationship forward, beyond its realist origins and extant liberal alternatives. One is that of Chris Thornhill, a British sociologist who draws on the work of Niklas Luhmann (an interlocutor with, and opponent of, Habermas) to generate a theory of constitutional legitimacy via a functionalist interpretation of historical sociology rather than critical theory. The other is reflected in the work of Hauke Brunkhorst and Jean Cohen, political theorists who have developed theories of legitimacy rooted in the idea of constitutional law and the European tradition of critical theory. For all, the value of the idea of constitutionality stems from its links to ethical and practical considerations for conceptualizing legitimacy.[83] Our question becomes: how do their ideas of legitimacy as a political virtue contribute to democratic ethics and potentially find practical traction, linking their *logos* to *ergon*?

Thornhill begins his approach with the assumption that sociology itself arose as a discipline to counter the rationally and ethical stipulative and deductive project of Enlightenment theorizing, which sociologists have regarded as unable to address adequately the complexities of the world. While building on this criticism, he wants to avoid the sociological

---

[82] Because he writes about it in a radically unfinished essay, I do not wish to discuss at any length Bernard Williams's attempt to ground a realist political theory in what he calls a "basic legitimation demand" (BLD or LEG) that combines a Hobbesian concern about collective security with liberal and modernist assumptions of the circumstances of harm. He, like Habermas, wants to get beyond Kantian formalism and Rousseauian communitarianism. And he associated the problem of a realistic account of political legitimacy in modernity as the way out. But he did not have a chance to elaborate that idea (see Williams 2005, 1–17).

[83] See Thornhill (2010, 29–56); cf. Thornhill (2011); Brunkhorst (2005 (2002)); and Cohen (2012). These authors are obviously only a few of many notables now writing, directly or indirectly, on the meanings and relationships of law, legitimacy, and constitutionality in "theory" and "practice."

positivism that grew up around it and address the "normative" character of social life, evidenced in the idea of a constitution.[84] For Thornhill, the constitutional order is a product of the political order, which itself functions as a coordinating and stabilizing mechanism for society. It is not a place of contestation; nor is it an effect of the agency of citizenship. In this respect, the "norms" that characterize and legitimize the constitutional order have an objective relationship to the social, economic, and political activities of citizens. Thornhill believes that his view of constitutionality is crucial for understanding "the sources of legitimacy," but he brackets the role of the interactions between ethics and power in the ongoing political life of society for defining what, in fact, may count as legitimate or the meaning of legitimacy. As a result, the politics of constitution-making remain outside his critical framework; they do not speak to our sense that a dynamic of *logos* and *ergon* among citizens in the public realm is needed for democratic ethics.

To be sure, working constitutions – whether the informal British constitution, the ever-changing "norm" of the American Constitution, or the evolving meaning of the Basic Law of the Federal Republic of Germany – have a special role to play in defining legitimacy. But Thornhill's functionalist model explains them relative to extant norms that are given a relatively organic structure. In his account of the making of the American Constitution, Thornhill regards "rights" primarily as agents of stabilization (rather than as tokens of political compromise or the securitization of certain practices of equal liberty) and sees the Madisonian distinction between the federal republic and democratic practice as clean-cut and unproblematic for understanding the mode of legitimation enacted by the Constitution.[85] Thornhill does not account for how the pivotal debates over the acceptance of the Federalists' Constitution were themselves practices that defined the meaning of legitimate politics and government in America; nor does he account for the various social and economic forces allied to each side of the debate. To be sure, Thornhill has demonstrated encyclopedic knowledge of the constitution-making processes in various Western societies, but one might well view his notion of legitimacy as a dependent variable, whose meaning is simply the repository of

---

[84] Using the term "norm" in political theory presupposes either a dichotomy between principles and facts, theory and empirics, or it regards facts as necessary values – as in the more traditional notion of sanctioned convention (*nomos*). Its usages typically presuppose that the normative/empirical dichotomy maintains a neutral approach to ethics, values, and goals, which I find dubious and disingenuous – something which Weber, the authoritative source of the dichotomy, knew was marked by theoretical instability and historical contingency.

[85] Thornhill (2010, 182–205).

legal processes and the constitutions used to regulate them. This makes his perspective particularly inapt for understanding the special character of legitimacy as a political virtue that might ally itself to democracy as a political order and guide views of acceptable disorder.

While Thornhill politely regards Habermas's work as a major improvement on the theoretical hegemony of Enlightenment discourse, he still finds it sorely lacking because of its implicit reliance on uncritically substantiated ideal norms.[86] That criticism certainly carries weight. But the extent to which he allies constitutionality to conventional, relatively conservative, social structures without acknowledging that his analysis sanctions that alliance compromises the utility of his sociological perspective for understanding how legitimacy might be conceptualized so as to complement, rather than automatically constrain, democracy. Unless one accepts the dicta of Hegel or the early Marx about the relationship of constitutions and democracy, the complementarity of democracy and constitutionality remains a challenge, which a notion of legitimacy needs to address. This is one of the tasks performed by Hauke Brunkhorst and Jean Cohen in their works on constitutionality, democracy, and legitimacy.

Brunkhorst's work is voluminous and extensive, but the only book of his available in English is his 2002 work, *Solidarität: Von der Bürgerfreundschaft zur gloablaen Rechtgenossenschaft*, translated in 2005 as *Solidarity: From Civic Friendship to a Global Legal Community*. In both this book and his 2010 article, "Cosmopolitan Freedom," Brunkhorst recognizes that democracy has a legitimation problem – not in terms of its procedures, which reasonably observe the principle of majority rule, but in terms of the need to promote effective democratic practice that obtains the assent of democracy's citizens.[87] Extant notions of legitimacy or "*meaning*" for democracy theoretically signify the relative success of a democratic political order. One could just as easily refer to this notion of legitimacy as a democratic political virtue. Brunkhorst, however, does not focus on more specifically defining what a notion of democratic legitimacy might mean, apart from assuring the continuation of democracy as self-government or auto-constitutionality, which begs the question. This is not a problem with Brunkhorst's theorizing, for he has not placed the notion of democratic legitimacy in the forefront of his project. It simply indicates how non-legalistic notions of legitimacy depend on codes of democratic political ethics that transcend a stipulated meaning of legitimacy.

---

[86] Thornhill (2011, 31).
[87] Brunkhorst (2005 (2002), 2010, 189).

Political theorists have grappled with the task of articulating a notion of democratic legitimacy since World War I, but it seems that little progress has occurred. The challenge is real and growing, however, as the attraction of the nation-state to its citizens has declined with the growth of global capitalism, the internet, and transnational political organizations. It is this new problematic that concerns Jean Cohen, as she attempts to articulate a place for democratic legitimacy amid globalization by means of the notion of constitutional pluralism and the hypothetical practice of a non-statist version of international federation.[88] While not declaring that federated unions of states inherently are democratic or promote democracy, Cohen argues that they are more likely both to enhance democracy in the era of globalization and to provide ethical and practical links between international legality and legitimacy. The key to her claim is belief in the democratic slant of the notion of "constitutionality," a modern, practical version of the basis for political order that splits the difference between the liberal presumption of unanimity at the foundation of social contract society and the Machiavellian–Marxist recognition that every moment of politics fundamentally exhibits an effort to alleviate conflict under a framework that would respect and overcome difference. Constitutionality aims to politicize and humanize "the rule of law" – particularly venerated in liberal political theory as the guarantee for regulated, pacific competition and conflict in civil society – by (in a Rousseauian tradition) hypothetically inserting equal political agency at the foundation of a political order. This endows the rule of law with an ethical valence potentially hospitable to democracy.[89]

As mentioned previously, however, the association of constitutionality with democracy was questioned by Marx and more recently by Sheldon Wolin, both of whom take aim at modernity and liberalism from a radically democratic point of view. Marx was taking Hegel to task (Hegel had criticized modernity and liberalism from a communitarian point of view, while not endorsing democracy). Wolin took contemporary advocates of constitutionalism to task for believing that they unquestionably benefit democracy. Neither Marx nor Wolin want to throw constitutions out, but each refuses to invest them with natural justice. For each regards constitutions as sources of regulations shaped by unjust, extant political orders that inevitably cramp the expressive authority of the *demos*.[90] Of

---

[88] Cohen (2012, 6, 84).

[89] Notable modern treatments of the rule of law include Neumann (1986 (1923–1954?)), Fine (1984), and Shapiro (1994).

[90] See Marx, "*Critique of Hegel's Philosophy of Right*," in Marx (1970 (1843)) and Wolin (1994, 29–58). Habermas believes that the tension between constitutionalism and democracy can be (theoretically) overcome. See Habermas (2001 [1998], 766–81).

course, unless the *demos* is automatically virtuous and never in doubt about how it politically ought to act in a society that brooks significant opposition to its interests, it may need some legal framework in which to operate. From the standpoint of the *demos* in need of constitutional law, it would be best if the equal authority of the law contributed to the political articulation of their better selves and constrained putatively less just opponents. That law, from a democratic point of view, would be quintessentially legitimate and a quintessential source of democratic legitimacy. But then, too, that just can express wishful thinking. How does one *ipso facto* determine the relative justice of the *demos* or a particular iteration of constitutional order?[91]

The relationship between democracy and legitimacy has acquired a new layer of complexity by European political theorists who have taken to discussing the "constituting" and "constituted" political powers in society – with the former roughly associated with the citizenry as a collective and the latter with the state, thereby naming the dual exercise of sovereignty in modernity, initially and pointedly recognized by Locke.[92] But this terminology has not clearly produced concrete advances in theoretical clarity or political productivity. Cohen implicitly recognizes this, and her route generates complementary (not consolidated) links between democracy and constitutional pluralism in an age of globalization. By providing an extensive review of efforts to theorize sovereignty and legality, from the twentieth century to the present, Cohen seeks to avoid the Charybdis of theoretical realism and the Scylla of rights-utopianism.[93] In addition, she is well aware of the limits of domestic legal institutions and their authorization of the power of the *demos* to solve problems of legitimacy in an age of globalization.[94] But because of

---

[91] On February 24, 2016, the University of Chicago Professor of Law, Geoffrey Stone, wrote in the *Huffington Post* that the Senate needed to act on President Obama's Supreme Court nominee (the soon-to-be named Federal Appellate Judge Merrick B. Garland), if America were to adhere to its traditional dedication to the rule of law. "The Supreme Court Vacancy and the Constitutional Responsibilities of the Senate." Stone was responding, in part, to the argument of Washington insiders, an ex-*Washington Post* editorial writer (now a senior fellow at the Brookings Institution) and a conservative Washington attorney, that raw power considerations within and among the federal branches of government would determine the fate of the nominee (Judge Garland). "There No Longer Are Any Rules in the Supreme Court Nominating Process," *Washington Post* (February 19, 2016). Together, these two perspectives, call them Locke's and Hobbes's in the twenty-first century, evidence the practical undecidability of the rule of law.

[92] For example, see Colon-Rios (2012).

[93] Cohen (2012, 24).

[94] See Cohen (1999, 2008).

her international focus, she avoids theorizing any notion of *democratic legitimacy* rooted in the historically local activities of various *demoi*. This is because of her respect for democracy as a political order that ought to be left to assume a plurality of sovereign, constitutional forms.[95] This means that what she calls "as good as it gets" relies on formal notions of equal political autonomy among sovereign states and a federated union of sovereign states guaranteed by a reformed (not revolutionized) United Nations system to provide practical respects for the equal and separate stations of states.[96] Why or how this would convince the permanent members of the Security Council, whose power over the General Assembly of equal and sovereign states has held sway since 1945, is not fully spelled out.

This is an interesting proposal, and one can't expect an author to address all questions raised by such an important topic in one book, but its emphasis on equality and human rights guaranteed by international legal institutions that respect the character of extant states does not recognize the radically unequal power of nation-states or how a global constitution might equalize that power in the future. As a result, it primarily invokes legitimacy and legitimation as part of a set of theoretical problems that simply possess "legitimacy" as part of their treatment of law and constitutionalism.[97] In addition, and again because of Cohen's international, legal interest in "constitutional pluralism," her theory does not extensively address how social, economic, and political power infects legal power or how the globalized exercise of political power in turn affects domestic conceptions of *democratic* legitimacy.[98] This remains an important theoretical and political task (as Cohen appreciates) because states remain the major sources of collective, demotic power, and justice needs power to resist the imperialism of capitalism.[99] As the histories of the twentieth and twenty-first century teach us, even if democracy is compromised by capitalism, capitalism needs at least low-intensity democracy to protect it against authoritarian corruption.

---

[95] Cohen (2012, 20, 56, 201–2, 325–6).

[96] Cohen (2012, 266–319).

[97] Cohen (2012); cf. Kumm (2010, 201–19) and Wahl (2010).

[98] See Cohen (2012, 25): "Efforts to contain and channel public power (at least since the onset of modernity) should be seen today as proto-democratic." Cohen's statement is not clear – at least if Germany and Italy during the inter-war period and the United States, apart from the Roosevelt era and the 1960s, serve as useful examples.

[99] This phenomenon is mostly supported rather than rebutted by nationalist reactions to the effects of capitalist globalization in the twenty-first century (see Piketty 2014). Also see Teubner (1997, 3–28, 2012).

5.5   Legitimacy and Popular Democracy in Recent Political Conflicts

Our review of different conceptions of legitimacy designed to serve "democratic societies" from the early twentieth century to the present has illustrated the conceptual landscape of efforts to identify legitimacy as an ethical and practical term mostly designed to provide criteria for assessing whether a state and its leaders are worthy of respect by democratic citizens and other states. We have noted the unwillingness of theorists to associate legitimacy with democracy except in the minimalist sense of sanctioning acquiescence by the public to state power as the most reliable source of security – nothing that views it as a complement to the widespread, active, judgment, and approval by the *demos*. This lacuna in modern political theory makes a certain amount of sense, given the bad odor of Jacobins linking democracy, virtue, and terror – even if they were acting as executive despots rather than democratic leaders – or Southern whites using their majority in state legislatures to promulgate Jim Crow law and cultural subjugation *after* President Lincoln's emancipation of African-American slaves and the victory of the Union in the American Civil War.[100] But *those* political majorities operated in emergency situations (France) or virtual caste systems that disenfranchised legitimate opponents. One might point to the election of Nazis in 1933 Germany by a minority plurality and their subsequent destruction of German political institutions, beastly belligerence, and annihilation of European Jewry. But Hitler did not come to power with a political majority and so quickly moved to terrorize anyone who did not support him. In other words, fear about a potential "tyranny of the majority" resulting from demotic political power is vastly overstated. The growth in size and power of modern states – along with the military domination of the United States as the oldest, extant, democratic republic – have been the principal agents in deflecting our attention from a conception of legitimacy that could transcend procedural equality before the law and contribute to more and better democracy in government and society.

One way of moving in this direction is to allay the fears of recent political theorists who have pursued strategies of avoidance by invoking the obsolete specter of totalitarian politics.[101] Are they "fighting the last war"? Is it possible that religiously fanatical, Jacobin, fascist, or Party-led political regimes that politicize morality – in ways that liberals from

---

[100] On how the Jim Crow South (c. 1885–1965) functioned as a country within a country, see Wilkerson (2010).

[101] For a corrective, see Wolin (2008).

Hobbes to Rosanvallon have feared – are no longer the principal threat to political activity that legitimates injustice? To be sure, political tendencies that harbor historical links to political demagoguery still exist – as evidenced in the exploitation of vulnerable citizens by leaders fanning the fiery embers of fitful economies and immigration produced by politics to which the West itself has mightily contributed. But it seems that they mostly have been pawns in the strategies of self-interested leaders. If this is the case, then liberal attempts to "level the playing field" in civil society and the state are will not only fail but also endanger democracy.

There has been informal recognition of the conceptual compatibility of democracy and legitimacy.[102] In actuality, however, the tension between the legitimacy of states and democracy, understood as a regime of active and authoritative citizenship, became more obvious after World War I. It only became more so amid the abrogations of the rule of law conducted by the regimes of Hitler and Stalin, as well as the intermittent dismantling of caste and class orders perpetuated by patriarchalism, capitalism, and colonialism after World War II, when their fabrics of rule across the globe became less legitimate, energizing the allure of "democracy" – especially since 1989. As a result, the political employment of "legitimacy" (or "illegitimacy") to designate the practical merits of states as legal collectivities has become a raw bone of contention. For legitimacy sanctions the morality of state formations that democratic citizenship renders perpetually revisable. From Kosovo to *Bush v. Gore*, to the status of the Egyptian government, to Ukraine and Crimea Ukraine and Crimea in the wake of the tumultuous events of 2014, the ongoing strife in Israel/Palestine, Syria, and Libya, and to (lest we forget) the election of Donald Trump to the American presidency, the question of what counts as an acceptable government or state has preoccupied academics and sorely disturbed citizens of seriously injurious, if not murderous, political regimes.

The words "capital," "transnational," and "cosmopolitan" have highly unstable practical referents that nonetheless populate much of contemporary political discourse and bear on our effort to understand legitimacy as a potentially democratic good. To assess their appropriate significance, it is useful to see how "legitimacy" has operated in the emergence and resolution of recent legitimation crises within and between states. By turning my focus away from critical, public discourse to more empirical material, I do not mean to reify a dichotomy between theory and practice. That

---

[102] For recognition of the tacit association of "democracy" with "legitimacy" (mostly via representation) in the twenty-first century, which then calls for a theoretical articulation of their relationship in ways different than those acknowledged by Weber, see Vieira and Runciman (2008, 124–5).

is precisely what emphasis on the *logos–ergon* nexus rejects; for it asserts that a critical notion of legitimacy in political theory must be considered as an agent of political practice. If political theory has no connection to the world as we know it, it should be catalogued in the library with short stories and novels. So the question is how the connection of theory to practice – or, less formally, *logos* to *ergon* – is understood. Providing a clear answer to that question is always vexing because of the unstable nature of the material with which one works, namely, public statements by inter- ested political actors who, knowing the positive valence of "legitimacy," automatically associate it with their political perspective – whether it be that of a politician or journalist. In addition, there are the generic limita- tions of usage and convention as an index of meaning. But they have their significance and relevance. (After all, it is not as if the historical texts of political theory are exponentially more transparent.) To be sure, there is the question of how much of the meaning of a text is illuminated by its context, as well as how that context is understood – debates which I shall not engage here but to which I am attuned. In this section, I focus on dis- course that is used by journalists and politicians to relate legitimacy and democracy, whether the locale is the United States, Iraq, Egypt, Syria, Ukraine, or the claims that stem from migrants and refugees.

My first example of a recent "legitimation crisis" comes from the 2000 close to home, namely, the 2000 Presidential Election of George W. Bush vs. Albert Gore, which was ultimately decided by the US Supreme Court in *Bush v. Gore*. It is of particular interest because the resolution was most successful while the rational grounds for it were quintessentially arbitrary – which speaks to the character of political legitimacy, if not the justice, of the American political system. Where there certainly were irregularities in many voting locales across the country, the most significant ones occurred in Florida, where thousands of votes cast for Al Gore were problematically cast because of imperfect voting machines and incompetent voting mon- itors in Miami's Dade County – a Democratic stronghold – and so not counted, and tens of thousands of African-Americans – who typically vote 90 percent Democratic in Florida – either had their votes discounted or were prevented from voting on apparently partisan grounds.[103] There was a call for a recount. It was initially rejected by Florida's Secretary of State,

---

[103] See United States Civil Rights Commission Report on Voting Irregularities in the 2000 Presidential Election (June 2001). See www.usccr.gov/pubs/vote2000/report/main.htm. According to Gallup Poll findings, African-Americans felt particularly cheated by this election, but once the Supreme Court made its decision were not about to take to the streets. See www.gallup.com/poll/2188/Black-Americans-Feel-Cheated-Election-2000. aspx?utm_source=email-a-friend&utm_medium=email&utm_campaign=shar- ing&utm_content=morelink.

Kathryn Harris, who had worked for the Bush campaign; then, her decision was overturned by Florida's Court of Appeals, whose membership was dominated by Democrats, which in turn was appealed to the US Supreme Court. By a 5–4 margin, split along ideological lines, the Court decided against a recount and thereby upheld Florida's electoral votes going to George W. Bush – and hence the election (despite Al Gore's advantage in the national popular vote). Interestingly, the Court stipulated that its decision had no precedential value – that is, it was unique to this case. Sovereignty was decided by the exception; the rule of law became a function of political domination of the judiciary, and many political commentators went up in arms.[104]

Taking the major senses of legitimacy into account, the legitimacy of George W. Bush's election to the American presidency in November–December, 2000 was not clear. Most Americans, however, responded passively (albeit unhappily, in many instances) to the decision. Despite the relatively obvious disenfranchisement of Black and Jewish voters for Al Gore by the decision of the Supreme Court, it was not contested. Americans were split on who deserved to win Florida before the Supreme Court's decision, but they went along with the Supreme Court's final decision and accepted George W. Bush as the new President of the United States.[105] As time went on, the legitimacy of this presidency no longer was vocally doubted. The decision conformed to legal procedures and was accepted by the politically effective populace – even if the legal basis for legitimation was itself primarily evidence of political power exercised in the Schmittian vein.[106] After this decision, the prestige of the Supreme Court as an institution that remains relatively above the partisan fray of politics continued to decline (a movement that began a few years before 2000 and then continued over the next thirteen years).[107] Its decisions

---

[104] For an example of commentary, along with the legal decisions, see Dionne and Kristol (2001). For a sound account of the Republicans' sabotage of the rule of law in the adjudication of the controversy prior to the decision by the US Supreme Court, see Boies (2004, 355–459).

[105] *The New York Times*, December 14, 2000; *The New York Times*: "Posner v. Dershowitz," July 15, 2001.

[106] Major legal scholars – Alan Dershowitz (Harvard) and Richard Posner (Chicago) – immediately debated and wrote about the merits of the decision. Bruce Ackerman (Yale) weighed in soon after. But there was no more consensus among them than among members of the Supreme Court. Notably, the grounds of their arguments were different. Dershowitz argued the merits of the decision; Posner argued for the decision as, pragmatically speaking, the best possible outcome (Dershowitz 2001; Posner 2001). Ackerman directly raises the question (not the meaning) of legitimacy (see Ackerman 2002). For a historical perspective, see Zelden (2008).

[107] See data from the Pew Research Center on "Supreme Court": www.people-press .org/2013/03/25/supreme-courts-favorable-rating-still-at-historic-low/.

continued to be followed, and so the institution continues to be "legitimate," but the decision – along with the deceptively sold invasion in Iraq; the bank bailouts of 2008, and the US Supreme Court's endorsement of big money as a principal actor in electoral politics – surely contributed to the decline in general confidence in the American political system over the past fifteen years. Coupled to the federal government's televised disdain for the black people of New Orleans in relation to Hurricane Katrina, acceptance of the torture systematically applied to Iraqis in the Abu Ghraib prison, and the Republican refusal to share power with the President after the election of 2010, seeds of doubt in the legitimacy of governmental institutions grew (evidenced, perhaps, by the success of the insurgent presidential candidacies of Senator Bernie Sanders and businessman Donald J. Trump).[108]

The question of legitimacy has mostly gained prominence of late in new political thinking in relation to international affairs.[109] Without the approval of the United Nations and arguably against international law, NATO invaded the Serbian province of Kosovo to back the insurrection of the Kosovo Liberation Army and its attempt to gain independence from a dangerous Serbia led by the now-deceased indicted international law suspect Slobodan Milosevic. After warning in 1998 that a military intervention in Kosovo would not be "legitimate," The Independent International Commission on Kosovo supported by UN Secretary-General Kofi Annan called NATO's military intervention two years later, *post-hoc*, "illegal but legitimate."[110] This embarrassing statement led the United Nations to authorize a commission to provide a linguistic framework to legitimize the seemingly humanitarian intervention in Kosovo that would also legitimize a humanitarian intervention in conditions that closely resembled the situation of Rwanda in 1994. The result was a document and a doctrine, "the responsibility to protect" (R2P), which justifies armed intervention on behalf of humanitarian concerns. Its rationale transcends the UN Charter's exclusive, statutory justification of the use of force (Article 51): to be used only against sovereign states that use force against other sovereign states and jeopardize "regional stability." (This was relied on to authorize UN forces to combat North

---

[108] See data from the Pew Research Center, "Beyond Distrust: How Americans View Their Government," November 23, 2015. From 2002 to 2015, after the brief uptick following the attacks on September 11, 2001, the decline has been steady. For a relevant judgment of the US Supreme Court, see the opinion of Justice Kennedy in *Citizens United* (2010).

[109] See the work of Clark (2005, 2007). Clark (2005, 165) notes that Annan, post 9/11/2001, believed that international legitimacy needed to become a function of the global war against terror (also see Hirschl 2010). On the conflicted features of legitimacy in relatively recent times, see Fraser (2009, 76–99).

[110] See the Executive Summary in *The Kosovo Report*. 4. However, in 1998, Annan generally resisted the idea of any intervention without the official backing of the Security Council.

Korea's invasion of South Korea in 1950.) Soon after its publication by an UN-sponsored report in 2001, however, this preliminary attempt to link inter-state and intra-state issues was seriously undermined by one of its principal backers, the United States, with an invasion of Iraq that lacked support from the United Nations Nonetheless, the General Assembly sanctioned the doctrine in 2005, and it was used by President Obama to authorize air strikes designed to save Libyan civilians and undermine the regime of Muhammar Gaddafi in 2011.[111] More recently, the meaning of legitimacy has been contestably invoked in both domestic and international conflicts – the civil strife of Egypt, Syria, the Russian annexation of Crimea and interference in eastern Ukraine, and Donald Trump's contacts with Russians intent on interfering with the American presidential election on Mr. Trump's behalf. To be sure, legitimacy functions as a "hurrah" word (i.e., a felicitous performative utterance) – everyone wants it, as it immediately sanctions the power of those who (or that which) has it or wants it via its ethical tone, but its content and purpose vary widely.[112] Less significantly for us, it is used as a tool of rhetoric and propaganda to *obtain* (unsuccessfully) military aid and political support, e.g., by various opposition groups to the rule of Bashar al-Assad in Syria.[113] This makes sense, indeed is "legitimate," because "legitimacy" functions as a speech-act designed to secure practical assent rooted in ethical agreement. It operates liminally, on the border of *logos* and *ergon*, seeking to make its discursive claims hold in practice. But the range of denotations of legitimacy in public discourse is not limitless; it is not merely one of many rhetorical tools. It reflects the dependency of "legitimacy" on an implicit conception of lawful, just order in a particular society, and "we" are inclined to accept a diversity of conceptions – whether as realists, liberals, or those dedicated to more ethically oriented notions of legitimacy.[114] This wide use illuminates the contemporary significance of theoretical conceptions previously treated

---

[111] The issue of humanitarian intervention in relation to democracy will be discussed in the next chapter.

[112] Quentin Skinner long ago noticed this dimension of the use of "legitimacy" as well as "democracy." See Skinner (1973, 287–306; 1974, 277–303, at 299–301). For its deceptive usage by the US government in supporting groups that sought to replace Muhammar Gaddafi, which NATO had just overthrown, see the two-part article by Jo Becker and Scott Shane, "Clinton, 'Smart Power' and a Dictator's Fall" and "After Revolt, a New Libya 'With Very Little Time Left'," *The New York Times*, February 28–9, 2016.

[113] See, for example, Steven Erlanger and Rick Gladstone, "France Grants Its Recognition to Syria Rebels," *The New York Times*, November 13, 2012 (also see Hurd, 2007).

[114] Aristotle argued for flexibility in the use of criteria for determining constitutional and ethical support for an authoritative government. See his *Politics*, III–IV.

in this book and thus sheds light on the limited critical bite of legitimacy as a political term of art. Without ethical standards for legitimate, authoritative cooperation, language itself loses its meaning – today just as was the case (according to Thucydides) in Corcyra under its conditions of *stasis* nearly 2,445 years ago.[115]

Three other contested political concepts and practices infuse contemporary uses of the notion of legitimacy: constitutional authority, human rights, and democracy. Constitutional authority and the correlative presumptions of political order and an effective rule of law – in conjunction with a monopoly on the use of force – comprise the minimal conditions of publicly accepted meanings of legitimacy. Thus, the rebellious secessionists in eastern Ukraine may claim authority over cities and swaths of Ukrainian territory, but no-one currently ascribes legitimacy to the basis of their exercise of political power, particularly after they shot down a civilian airliner flying at 33,000 feet. It is not simply the case that they have not had elections. In Egypt, the recently elected President (and General) el-Sisi was, most would agree, inaugurated under conditions of electoral illegitimacy – since he had removed the previous democratically elected President of Egypt, President, Mohammed Morsi (who had curtailed civil liberties) by the use of force; precluded any serious political contestation of his candidacy for president, and has suppressed political opposition from civil society while in office.[116] Nonetheless, the United States, Europe, and, it seems, a majority of the Egyptian people regard him as the legitimate leader of the Egyptian state. This is the case because of the long-standing authority the military has been able to exercise in Egypt – under Nassar, Mubarak, and now el-Sisi. Most Egyptians were exhilarated by having forced Mubarak out of office and out of town during "the Arab Spring." Yet they became disenchanted by the economic instability, constraints on the political rights of opponents, and overall discontent with the political rule of Morsi and the Muslim Brotherhood – itself undermined by the army and, probably, the United States and Israel. This left most Egyptians little choice other than accepting el-Sisi as their "legitimate" head of state.[117]

---

[115] See Keith A. Darden, "The War on Truth in Ukraine," *The New York Times*, Op-Ed, April 27, 2014; Thucydides, III.81–82.

[116] See Stevenson (2015).

[117] See the columns about, and coverage of, events in Egypt in *The New York Times*, from 2012 to 2014 – e.g., Joshua Stacher, "How Egypt's Army Won," Op-Ed, June 29, 2012; David D. Kirkpatrick and Mayy el Sheikh, "Voting Opens in Egyptian Election Lacking Suspense," May 26, 2014. The United States' backing of Sisi for the sake of its foreign policy, particularly with regard to Israel and Islamists, certainly fortified Sisi as a legitimate, albeit not clearly legal or democratically elected, leader of Egypt.

In a political order with stronger constitutional and democratic traditions, the requirements of legitimacy are stronger, as departures from
the reigning legitimate political standard would not have to go as far as
autocracy in order to violate the constitutional order. As Montesquieu
and Rousseau noted, the political order that requires the greatest extent
of virtue among the citizenry is democracy.[118] But these are affirmations
of theoretical ideals. As we have seen in the United States with *Bush
v. Gore*, the issue is more adherence to constitutional procedures and
political institutions than to democracy *per se*. That is probably because
the bar for what counts as a democratic country these days is so low.
"Free and fair elections" of leaders who function under term limits
seem to be all that is necessary, with "freedom" and "fairness" themselves dependent on contestable criteria and subject to distortion. Such
criteria were used to recognize the government of Nouri al-Maliki in
Iraq, before the underlying "legitimacy" of his authority and power was
undercut by Sunni opposition; the successful takeover in short order of
one-third of his country by foreign forces, and the collapse of his officer
corps when attacked by the self-authorized Islamic State of Iraq and
Syria (ISIS – or ISIL [Islamic State of Iraq and the Levant]). However,
if the government is not regarded as legitimate by significant international powers – such as the Hamas government in Gaza by Israel and
the United States – meeting procedural rules for elections will not satisfy
criteria for legitimacy. There are practical tipping points for what counts
as legitimate political action – often shaped by demagogic politicians and
fueled by populist resentment.

Legitimacy is a necessary condition for political virtue in society, but
it certainly is not sufficient, and the discursive authority of states to
determine its meaning in ways that satisfy their practical interests makes
its complementarity to democracy in contemporary political discourse
suspect. Sufficiency is attained only if the preponderance of informed,
effective, and publicly and demotically articulated opinion in the country approves of the government as the best possible arrangement for
the exercise of political power. *International* legitimacy has even stiffer
requirements. The People's Republic of China was legitimate in the eyes
of the Chinese people and most of the world for a long time before the
United States decided the PRC could replace the Republic of China
(Taiwan), on the Security Council of the United Nations as the legitimate representative of the Chinese state. And Hamas seems to have
the support of the Gazans even if no other government besides those

---

[118] See Montesquieu, *The Spirit of the Laws*, II.2; III.3. Rousseau, *The Social Contract*, I.7–8;
II.3–4, 6, 11; III.4.

of Turkey and Qatar sympathizes with its policies (even as most of the civilized world sympathizes with the plight of Gazan civilians suffering from the firepower of the Israeli army and air force). The importance of legitimacy as a political term today stems from the social fact that, girded by law and military force, it occupies conceptual space between constitutional democracy and despotism.

The notion of legitimacy typically sanctions state power as good, or good enough, but, drawing on its ethical roots, it also can be a demotic tool for criticizing the modern state. As a result, legitimacy now functions ambiguously and contingently as a term of political art in relation to democracy. The relationship of legitimacy as a kind of sanction for political goodness and democracy – whether its Rousseauian or Weberian sense ought to prevail – must account for the contingent dramas of political life. One may allow legitimacy to be defined by nation-states, thereby invariably sanctioning injustice, or elevate legitimacy to such a high ethical plane that one's critical perspective becomes disengaged from actual battles for justice within or between states.[119]

5.6   Conclusion – Democratic Legitimacy in a Digital Age

Democracy is not self-legitimating, because democracy only immediately defines a particular way of exercising power – one that puts the *demos* front and center but must draw on other sources of ethics and power to make it a legitimate political order. Moreover, the *demos* never acts as an undifferentiated unit. Citizens act as individuals but also as groups and in blocs – much more so than in Athenian democracy. They need they need to reach out to citizens who don't share their political ethic. It needs some ethic of legitimacy for a democratic constitution if it would continue to enlist the support of the citizenry. If democracy and legitimacy were to become complementary, one would need, therefore, to have a working conception of democratic legitimacy – that is, a notion of legitimacy which sanctioned a political order that compatibly linked the practical ethos of leaders and citizens, which served as a guidepost for evaluating the relative democracy and goodness of a government and social order. It would have to denote a political virtue rooted in

---

[119] On global constitutionalism and global democracy, see the opening editorial statement of the journal *Global Constitutionalism*, Vol. 1, No. 1 (March 2012), 1–15: "Global Constitutionalism: Human Rights, Democracy, and the Rule of Law," co-written by Antje Wiener, Anthony F. Lang, Jr., James Tully, Miguel Poiares Maduro, and *Mattias Kumm*, along with the collection of articles in Archibugi et al. (2012). For more practical (but still theoretical) discussions of the problems facing the European Union, see Weiler and Wind (2003).

action that expressed a connection between *logos* and *ergon* that bene-
fited the collectivity. Realists assert that such justification is primarily
a spin-off of power relations; liberals believe it should emerge from a
politically neutral and rational process that accommodates differences in
ethical outlook and presupposes basic features of modern capitalism and
bureaucracy. Yet neither of these approaches can authoritatively evaluate
modern states that would combine democracy and legitimacy. Indeed,
"democracy" has assumed such an ideological cast that it is nearly mean-
ingless to use it as a guide for determining legitimacy. Moreover, in the
world of social media, where tweets help elect American presidents, few
have a grasp of what the public realm for demotic action consists of. And
in practical, political discourse, democracy is used rhetorically as a *tool*
for legitimating states that have only a marginal relationship to democracy cogently understood.

We have noted that solidifying a concept of democratic legitimacy may
be a fruitless enterprise, but pursuing it as a political goal certainly contributes to a coherent understanding of democratic ethics today – the
potential complementarity of democracy and goodness in contemporary political life. This is a major, current challenge for theoretical analysis, given that the modern state is a dubious friend of democracy that
nonetheless offers the most viable public arenas for democratic action.
No comparable political authority in the transnational, international, or
compounded local realms can come close to offering the capacity for
concerted, effective, demotic action. The wide array of personal connections that can produce political effects with the digitalization of knowledge and social media weakens the authority of borders that can foster
democratic community even as it enlarges the potential for democratic
action.[120] Seeking contingent but continuing partnerships between democratic ethics and state power is about the best one can hope for as a criterion nowadays for democratic legitimacy. It needs to operate at the level
of personal commitment; neighborly associations; regional and national
governments; and international organizations. It stands for an institution
that is generally acceptable to a collectivity that has the power to change it.
As such, it evokes more of a realist than a liberal or ethical conception
of legitimacy, as it denotes legitimacy as a virtue in *ergon*, if not in *logos*.
But it stands as a revocable agreement that requires support from a
discourse about ethical and practical values that cuts across practical

---

[120] A recent collection of essays on the contemporary landscape of democratic citizenship
articulates the mark of the digital age on the action of citizenship as a flow between
"influence" and "voice" (see Allen and Light 2015).

differences – something that has characterized political and democratic discourse for 2,700 years.

Part of the problem we have found in discussing "democratic legitimacy" today is the inevitably circular character of the argument. One seeks a definition of legitimacy that is democratic, but (1) legitimacy often remains undefined (even by Rosanvallon) and (2) the meaning of "democratic," the *explicans* (the "meaning") derives from assumptions about the *explicandum* (what counts as democratic). Can the problems of existing democracies be solved by more democracy (adopting the beguiling mantra of John Dewey) or, as claimed here, by increasing the authoritative power of democratic citizenship?[121] The standard answer is, "no." But then we should ask, why? Skeptics say that more democracy is impractical; critics of democracy suspect that more democratic activity will be uninformed and unethical. If we are convinced by these claims, then democracy and legitimacy will be irreconcilable. But what is the evidence for these claims? In the United States, is any greater regulation of financial capitalism on behalf of the *demos* impractical? Most Americans don't think so. Would greater democratic control result in unethical politics, potentially a tyranny of the majority? One should recall that contemporary majorities of citizens exercise only marginal political power. Whatever power they have is filtered through numerous institutional inequalities that preselect political candidates, direct media outlets that still dominate demotic access to political information, and produce differentiated starting lines from the moment of birth. In the United States, the Founders feared democratic majorities – but this mostly took the form of the power of the states. To be sure, states still are often sources of offensive political sentiments, but today's conflicts between state power and federal power are not between states' power and minimal federal power, *pace* 1787, but between federal and state power as agents of the *demos* or of established privilege. One might say that we still are trying to reconcile democracy and goodness in ways that do not blindly presuppose the virtue of the *demos* or of established conceptions of ethics and power. As for presupposing the lack of political potential among the *demos*, the only certainty connected to that view is disbelief in the potential for demotic political action and tacit acceptance of national and transnational inequalities that favor a few at the expense of many.

---

[121] See Dewey (1946 (1927), 146). The full quote from which this phrase is taken is as follows: "... whatever changes may take place in existing democratic machinery, they will be of a sort to make the interest of the public a more supreme guide and criterion of governmental activity, and to enable the public to form and manifest its purposes still more authoritatively. In this sense, the cure for the ailments of democracy is more democracy."

Indeed, unless we think about ethical criteria of legitimacy which promote democracy in relation to a *demos* that can achieve a kind of political virtue by willingly and rationally participating in the operation of political institutions, legitimacy will just be a political term that has little substantive meaning other than the practical recognition of state power and those who manage to maintain a monopoly on the use of force over the citizenry. In these circumstances, legitimacy as a political virtue does not complement democracy as a political regime or social order. It relates to democracy as the price of social order and the hope for political change. As a kind of political goodness, its meaning is moot.

What does this say about legitimacy as a political virtue, excellence, or good for democracy? Imagining a properly *democratic* definition of legitimacy today, in line with the definition of democracy used in this book, would not cut much ground. The legitimacy of a democratic order will be greater to the extent that it simultaneously observes the rule of law and extends the reach of democratic power so as to maintain and promote it for all citizens and to sanction their leaders with "trust and confidence."[122] When this occurs, and it probably will be more an exception than a rule, democracy and legitimacy correspond. The exceptions result not only from the absence of inherent bonds among citizens whom we might associate with a contemporary *demos* but also from the necessary tension between demotic interests and ethics and those of the modern state – let alone the difficulties of identifying *demoi* in transnational political contexts.

Authoritative claims of legitimacy – like declarations of constitutionality – by their very nature in modernity delimit democratic politics or contestations of authority. But this does not render either of them automatically anti-democratic. There may be times when democratic societies need Ulysses' instructions to his crew to bind him to the ship mast while he was subjected to sirenic enchantments.[123] But today we should keep in mind that Ulysses will be viewed either as a shackled *demos* or a besieged state, depending on one's political perspective. As we have noted, while "democracy" has become more widely accepted as the term of art that characterizes lawful or legitimate governments or states in the last century, and equal rights have become more widespread, the extent of the power of the *demos* over the machinery of government remains debatable. Once citizens accepted the modern state as

---

[122] Jack M. Balkin emphasizes the importance of "trust and confidence" as supplements to procedural legitimacy and crucial for democratic legitimacy in "Legitimacy and the 2000 Election," in Ackerman (2002, 210–28).
[123] Cf. Elster (1979).

the appropriate mechanism for regulating politics, theories and practices of the state, sovereignty, and, later, legitimacy operated as immediate constraints on the political freedom of democracy. As a result, "democratic legitimacy" is mostly an oxymoron nowadays.[124] Inevitably, modern usages of legitimacy in relation to governments and institutions immediately raise questions about their effects – particularly whether or not they are democratic. The result of this practical circumstance points to the manner in which the meaning of legitimacy is dependent, not any more self-evident than other terms of political art. Their meanings do not descend from heaven nor are they shackled to the sky. What justice means is not radically relative, but it is inherently changeable. As a result, what promotes beneficial, legitimate democratic politics that reconciles the integrity of law and the active articulation of interests and values by various incarnations of the *demos* cannot be specified in advance. It is resolved in the ongoing discussions and polemics that inform our political lives.

---

[124] This is the way Robert C. Post conforms democracy and sovereignty, in Post (2000, 209–23).

6   Human Rights and Democracy

6.1   Introduction

"Human rights" articulates a political discourse that is ratified in current legal documents, marked with a storied history, fitfully honored by international institutions, and widely respected as a global ethic of legitimacy – even if it is known more for being violated than enacted.[1] Its different dimensions in the world partner with widely different meanings – e.g., by the US Department of State's Bureau of Human Rights, Democracy, and Labor or Amnesty International or its diverse incarnations by academics – not unusual for political concepts, but, interestingly, for all of these human rights is allied with democracy. Indeed, the founding documents of modern meanings of human rights – the liberal revolutions of the United States and France as well as the Universal Declaration of Human Rights (UDHR) signed without opposition (albeit eight abstentions) on December 10, 1948 at the United Nations – ally their principles with democracy, understood more or less as officially exhibited by those who have informally earned membership in "the international community."[2] Established at the end of World War II, this discourse now would apply to nearly all nations after the lightning-like decimation in 1989 of the pitched opposition in power and human rights rhetoric between the power blocs of NATO and the Warsaw Pact. Human rights play a pivotal role for understanding democratic ethics on a transnational scale. But how do human rights and democracy relate to one another? A massive number of books and articles have discussed aspects of human rights, especially since the 1980s, but few have

---

[1] Portions of this chapter have been published in Wallach (2005, 2011a).
[2] There were seven abstentions, and two countries were absent for the vote. On how the idea of "the international community" functions, or could function, in relation to human rights, see Beitz (2009).

discussed how human rights work in relation to democracy. Do human rights foster, impair, or just contingently partner with democracy?[3]

The standard view is that democracy harbors the potential for the abuse of power, which human rights does not – elevating the value of human rights above corrosive conflict and democracy. But that is because human rights are designed as supra-political standards of human flourishing. In themselves, human rights have no political authority even if their meaning constrains political actors. But human rights are better understood as worldly meanings and practical phenomena, best if they are *not* treated as transpolitical, standing for a universal human ideal that can be, for better or worse, realized in democratic practice. For human rights are human creations and inherently political, reflecting various combinations of ethics and power.[4] It is impossible to imagine the simultaneous political complementarity or practical enforcement of all thirty-one human articles in the UDHR. Given the conceptual allure of human rights and its extensive practical usage for intentionally good ends, how should we understand the meaning and promotion of human rights as a potential agent of goodness for democracy as an order of power with an ethical discourse that enables it to function – in single nations or globally?

Given the contemporary anarchy over the meaning and priorities among human rights, as well as the project undertaken here, we need to recount briefly the history that informs the perplexing character of human rights as a contemporary term of conceptual and political art, particularly in relation to democracy.[5] The informal (not literal) association of rights with humanity or human beings in general became intellectually and politically significant in the tumultuous seventeenth and eighteenth centuries of Europe, which involved a distinct major minority of the human race – not antiquity (at least, not ancient Greece).[6] In relation to these tumults, Hobbes, Locke, and Rousseau identified "natural rights" of human beings as the foundation for the political rights

---

[3] For human rights as the moral regulator for democracy, see books and essays by Jurgen Habermas beginning in the 1990s. Also see Goodhart (2005) and Gould (2004, 2014).

[4] From this perspective, one can bracket epistemological questions about the universal, relativist, phantasmagoric, or strictly ideological character of human rights. These questions cannot be firmly answered, and focusing on them inhibits understanding their meaning and role as linguistic candidates for a global political ethic of legitimacy beyond the nation-state, germane for democratic ethics in the twenty-first century. Below, its discursive and practical uses are understood in terms of whether or not they enhance the goodness of democracy.

[5] There are numerous good histories of human rights. The historicist treatment of human rights here focuses on its relationship to democracy (see Hunt 2008; Lauren 1998/2003; Morsink 1999; Moyn 2010). From the perspective (*sic*) of the United Nations, see Normand and Zaidi (2008).

[6] See Burnyeat (1994).

of legitimate governments (surely drawing on previous iterations), replacing the previous acceptance of a single conception of *Ius* or *Recht* as the basic integument for society as a whole. The effort to derive freedom and equality for human beings from a natural state meant that such natural rights were tantamount to human rights. One cannot know whether these assertions were made in good faith – that is, whether they operated as props for states, rhetorical support for new political orders, or springboards for colonialist, imperialist, and racist ventures.[7] Of more significance for the idea of human rights was its enunciation in three later historical moments that evidenced crises of political legitimation.

The first occurred in the liberal revolutions of the late eighteenth century. In the Declaration of Independence, the United States (via Thomas Jefferson) claimed that all men are created equal and endowed by their Creator with basic, unalienable rights. France's 1789 *Declaration of the Rights of Man and Citizen* associated human rights with the rights of the civilized (male) citizens of France, thereby providing crucial bulwarks for a new French nation. Yet the potential of this moment did not fulfill the pretensions of its name as a practical, political injunction designed to better the condition of *all* human beings, and the next 175 years involved major struggles for the emancipation of slaves, women, and wage-earning men. Only in the second moment – the passage on December 10, 1948 by the UN General Assembly of the *Universal Declaration of Human Rights* – did "human rights" become a widespread, affirmative, political ethic and ideal. It took hold in the wake of a desire for a new ethical discourse in a world transformed by the horrific killings of millions of persons during World War I and particularly World War II, and the prospects of the end of Jim Crow legislation in the United States and decolonization abroad. This universalized political idea gained much greater global traction in the wake of the third moment, when the ideological politics and interpretive divides that separated NATO and Soviet views of human rights lost their moorings, and the victimization of humanity by terrorist attacks caught the attention of governments and the media. The idea of human rights has been politically contested over a long period of political time, particularly in Western history. This is not to say, however, that "human rights" need be seen as an exclusively "Western" idea. The practices to which human rights refer, whether in the Declaration of the Rights of Man and Citizen or the UDHR, have plausible equivalents in many other societies – just as is the case with democracy, which, though born in ancient Athens

---

[7] To be sure, the idea of human right, if not human rights, appears in the work of Thomas Aquinas (see Finnis 1998, 135–8).

as a political practice, resonates with social practices in non-Western societies.[8]

Despite this variegated history, many want to view "human rights" – as articulated by the French National Assembly, Franklin D. Roosevelt,[9] or the UN General Assembly, or elaborated in subsequent official, international documents – not as an ethical and political tool but as a conceptually coherent, substantive entity, a *thing* (or a bundle of *things*) to be honored as a trump card in politics, a universal code for moral and political conduct the violation of which should trigger immediate and widespread opprobrium, if not political action. Even as it has the weakest of all practical supports among claims by human beings for political rights, it has the loudest moral resonance. Who opposes human rights? Therefore, we should take human rights discourse "off the shelf" and use it as a moral guide and template for political practice – in the words of the Samantha Power – an "inspiration" for "impact." If we are good, the "realization" of human rights should be at the front and center of our practical agendas.[10]

This advice, however, is misguided. We know that the range of human rights to be realized surely will differ depending upon whom one consults. Only civil and political rights are typically regarded as "core" human rights, and they appear at the beginning of the UDHR. However, that document also includes economic, social, and cultural rights, not to mention the rights encoded in various international conventions – such as the right to be protected from torture, racial discrimination, discrimination against women, unjust treatment as a refugee or member of an indigenous people, or, the most popular of human rights, the rights of the child, and so on – and all of these are embraced by many as mutually entailed human rights. Apart from human rights *minimalists* (such as John Rawls and Michael Ignatieff), who only provide political endorsement for civil and political kinds of human rights, and maximalists (often post-Marxists

---

[8] Besides, Athens was not "Western." That geographical and cultural term stemmed from the schism in the Christian church between Rome and Constantinople. For the non-Western reach of both democracy and human rights, see Sen (2009, esp. 321–87).

[9] For example, see Roosevelt's "Four Freedoms" speech (January 6, 1941) and his articulation of a second Bill of Rights to complement the US Constitution of 1789 and the attending Bill of Rights of 1791 (State of the Union Address, January 4, 1944).

[10] Power and Allison (2006). *Realizing Human Rights*. Cf. Balfour and Cadava (2004, 293), Wilson and Brown (2006), and Habermas (2010). Habermas extensively discussed the idea of human rights in his earlier works. See Habermas (1996 (1992), esp. 3.1), which reappears in slightly modified forms in Habermas (1998 (1996), esp. Pt. IV), "Human Rights: Global and Internal." Also see Habermas (2001 (1998)), reprinted as "On Legitimation Through Human Rights" in De Greiff and Cronin, eds. (2002, 197–214).

who envision the interdependency of human rights), there are liberal human rights agency theorists, such as Amartya Sen (discussed previously and later in this chapter), as well as human rights *normativists*, who argue that human rights "norms" should be enforced wherever possible.[11] My simple point is that "human rights" are typically regarded as good, whatever "they" are, and the political setting for their realization is taken to be bad – as it were, on the wrong side of morality. Practice is incorrigible or backward and needs enlightening and improving by the idea and practice of human rights – whether the tools for implementation are persuasion or ammunition – so as to elevate the "human" over the "political," assuming that efforts to draw on human rights discourse to shape political discourse are unproblematic.[12] The problem with this political agenda is that "rights" present a defensive, minority-oriented political agenda. While "human rights" surely are necessary to protect against the ruthless behavior of authoritarian regimes and the wrongful behavior of democratic governments, they typically do not fuel political power that directly benefits the majority of human beings in various political contexts. Instead, they mark, after the fact, grievous political injuries in order to mobilize efforts to condemn and disempower the guilty perpetrators – worthy efforts, to be sure, but as they become salient in the wake of these harms they potentially distract public attention from the sources of the problems.

"Human rights" today provide an ethical aspiration with weak political moorings that would complement "democracy." We are led to believe that human rights articulate the other side of democracy, and the UDHR presupposes a friendly kinship between them. Human rights and democracy *can* be complementary (as they are designated as being in Article 29 of the UDHR); human rights can be used to enhance democratic virtue.[13] But their semantic references do not map onto one another, which raises the question of whether, and if so how, discourses of human rights can promote democracy and goodness in particular societies. Indeed, human rights are a political wish list that cannot be made practically coherent. As a result, they cannot offer a framework for enhancing democracy.

---

[11] Risse et al. (1999, esp. 1–38; 2013).

[12] There is no clear boundary between the human and the political as the relative protection of "sub-human" animals results from political judgments, and the "nature" of humanity is constructed out of political decisions that favor the lives of some kinds of persons rather than others. And, need it be said these days, "nature" itself is often a political construction given the effects of human activity on the physical environment.

[13] On how human rights and democracy may complement each other in critical discourse and practice, see Tully (2014). For a merger of human rights and democracy, see Goodhart (2005). Also see Benhabib (2011).

The reverse is the proper view. Democracy must be the primary conduit through which human rights are realized.

To justify this claim, I need to clarify the irreducibly problematic character – or *logos* – of human rights, in history and the present. In Section 6.2.1, I shall elucidate two, familiar paradoxes that constitute the very idea of human rights. In Section 6.2.2, I shall interpret how these paradoxes are (and are not) overcome in the dominant theoretical framework for human rights, that of liberal democracy. These two parts of Section 6.2 clarify human rights as a contemporary *logos*. Then, I shall turn in Section 6.3 to well-known historical events – or *erga* – in which human rights discourse has played and may continue to play a significant role. Section 6.3.1 concerns the intersection of human rights discourse and cultural practices that seemingly flout its ethical requirements – namely, female genital cutting and the right of Muslim women, whether young students or teachers, to wear headscarves in public schools (viz., in France, Germany, and the United Kingdom). Section 6.3.2 considers the use of human rights as a justification of military intervention by an external power to address human rights abuses in another country – often known as the question of "humanitarian intervention," recently encoded in an UN-sanctioned policy known as "*the responsibility to protect.*"[14] These two domains of practical usage of human rights discourse enable us to understand best the way it operates in relation to democratic ethics – and should shed light on the meaning of the events themselves. The chapter closes in Section 6.4 with arguments about how to complement efforts to enhance both human rights and democracy. These discussions enable us to see how human rights functions as an asset or drawback to democratic virtue and the complementarity of goodness and democracy.

---

[14] *Responsibility to Protect* [R2P]: *Report of the International Commission on Intervention and State Sovereignty* (Ottawa: International Development Research Centre, 2001). The United Nations adopted the principles of R2P as its own in 2005, in the following terms: "Prevention requires apportioning responsibility to and promoting collaboration between concerned States and 'the international community.' The duty to prevent and halt genocide and mass atrocities lies first and foremost with the State, but the international community has a role that cannot be blocked by the invocation of sovereignty. Sovereignty no longer exclusively protects States from foreign interference; it is a charge of responsibility where States are accountable for the welfare of their people. This principle is enshrined in article 1 of the Genocide Convention and embodied in the principle of 'sovereignty as responsibility' and in the concept of the Responsibility to Protect. The three pillars of the responsibility to protect, as stipulated in the Outcome Document of the 2005 United Nations World Summit (A/RES/60/1, para. 138–40), [are] formulated in the Secretary-General's 2009 Report (A/63/677) on Implementing the Responsibility to Protect."

6.2   The *Logos* of Human Rights and Democracy

6.2.1   *The Constitutive Paradoxes of Human Rights*

Two paradoxes inform and problematize every discursive and practical employment of "human rights." The first is *substantive* and directly *political*; it concerns the relation between "the human" and "the political," and belongs to the domain of political ethics in general. The other is more nearly *epistemological* and *moral*; it addresses the issue of how one understands and practices the relationship between idea and actuality, or moral universality and cultural relativity. Each stems from the fact that human rights cobbles together two kinds of concepts and practical relations that are not innately friendly and treats them as one, ignoring the inherent absence of complementarity in their relationship. Thus, the discourse of human rights synthesizes and occludes paradoxical features of the origins, history, and character of human rights as an idea and a practice, making it far from self-evident as a conceptual "thing" or guide to moral and political practice.

Paradox has always marked the invocation of human rights. Since their discursive inception, the initial paradoxes have not been solved so much as layered by new iterations of them – namely, that initiated in the UDHR, which identifies governments as the promissories for enforcing human rights, even as they are the agents which most notably violate human rights. Joining the paradoxes is an overarching feature that articulates human rights as both a transpolitical phenomenon, acceptable to everyone and thereby not a divisive practical agent, and a political phenomenon, designed to uplift (and thereby disrupt) all human societies. The fluid semantics of human rights might suggest that any theoretical analysis designed to advance a general understanding of the concept amounts to a fool's errand: leave it for use by metaphysicians, rhetoricians, activists, or ethnographers.[15] However, that leaves a significant realm of public discourse to the effects of either detached academic observations or the instrumental deployment of practical actors.[16] While such projects often constitute and benefit our understanding

---

[15] See Geuss (2001, 138–46, 152). Criticisms of "rights talk" go back three centuries. See its treatment by Edmund Burke, Jeremy Bentham, Karl Marx, and anti-secular natural law theorists. Aspects of these criticisms appear in their own right or recast by deconstructionist, pragmatist, poststructuralist, postcolonial, feminist, or simply realist thought. On this subject, also see Hart (1984 (1955)). For an imaginary of how to fulfill all of the different kinds of human rights – social and economic rights no less than civil and political rights – see Fukuda-Parr et al. (2015).

[16] See the work of Jurgen Habermas and John Rawls (discussed below). For ethnographies of human rights discourse, see *American Anthropologist* 2006 and Goodale (2009). Cf. Douzinas and Gearty (2014).

of human rights in political discourse, they do not exhaust its meaning. And despite the radically contestable, diverse usages, and questionable cogency of the notion of human rights, the term retains primacy as the principal currency for the realm of international political ethics; it would seem to harbor potential as a lever for improving the human condition. For the foreseeable future, the paradoxical but practical relationship between the human and the political will continue to exist. Philosophical analysis cannot argue the paradox away, and yet the troubling instabilities that belong to human rights will remain – causing more consternation than "essentially contestable concepts."[17] For example, the numbers of displaced persons and refugees have grown in recent years amid the instabilities of global politics (despite the growing linguistic currency of "human rights"). While these persons are political objects generated by conflicts among elites and states, their actual condition remains external to that of political subjects or full members of states – such that addressing their plight in terms of "human rights" still confuses the issue of their human and political status.

These paradoxes have been noted by others besides myself.[18] My effort to move the debate forward here is designed to achieve three objects: *to describe how* two paradoxical elements *unavoidably constitute* human rights theory and practice, and have done so from the beginning of their usage in political discourse; *to note that* the *effect* of these paradoxes tends to marginalize human rights ideals in political practice; and *to argue that* if we do not fully appreciate these paradoxes, the ethical and political well-being signified by various projects currently and potentially associated with human rights will not fare well in the world. After so doing, I shall offer some preliminary suggestions about what should be thought and done about human rights in light of its constitutive paradoxes. Ultimately, human rights should be understood *not* as a first-order philosophical or moral concern but a second-order political construction which, in order to function effectively, must be construed in terms of related discursive, ethical, and practical realities that form the historical context of its operation.

To reiterate, the *first* paradox stems directly from the diverging, substantive parts of human rights, namely, "*the human*" as a fact, value, norm, or ideal and "*rights*," which belong to subjectively asserted and objectively protected domains of political power and ethics. At first

---

[17] See Gallie (1955–6) and Connolly (1983/74).
[18] See Arendt (1951), "The Decline of the Nation-State and the End of the Rights of Man," 267–302; Benhabib (n. 57); Douzinas, 2000); Baxi (n. 19 below). Cf. Hunt (2007) and Wallach (2005).

glance, the couple of the human and the political looks fairly glamorous. The "human" (at least *qua Homo sapiens*) is a relative constant across historical time, providing a link between our past, present, and future.[19] Across the centuries and in every language, the number of genes belonging to *Homo sapiens* have remained constant, and we continue to make many of the same mistakes we always have. By contrast, the "rights" of humans are seen to signify a progressively better and wider set of goods for human beings. First articulated in Roman times to *differentiate* status (and coordinated with another oxymoronic Roman neologism, "natural law"), they subsequently became associated with *natural* human traits that transcended status and rank (though not gender in theory, and certainly not wealth in practice) – particularly in seventeenth-century Europe, even as they marked an egalitarian *achievement* of status and rank for many citizens.[20] This democratization of the idea of human dignity reformulated the rhetorical democratization of political virtue that marked that establishment of Athenian democracy.

When this occurred, the political rights of citizens of various states – particularly those of England, the United States, and France – began to be seen as *ipso facto* human or "natural" to human beings, in the form of *natural* rights. However, these justified rights of citizens in particular states – necessarily shy of universally human rights. So the next step in a progressively understood march of history was to dispense with the political identity that guaranteed rights and simply refer to *human rights* possessed by *human beings* regardless of their political affiliation – or lack thereof. The problematic political character of the human as a subject of "human rights" was mostly ignored. Now, the challenge simply became that of *realizing* human rights, over and potentially against the states that enabled and would guarantee human rights. This illustrated an incoherent linkage between the *logos* and *ergon* of the new order of international human rights. The institutionalization of the United Nations and the rhetorical force of the UDHR were to overcome the particularistic ideas and practices of human rights of the past so as to enact their promise. But here, too, the tension between the human and the political is denied, and the need for potentially cooperative rather than necessarily hierarchical relations between the idea of human rights and social practices is ignored. Indeed, recent attempts (in Kosovo, Libya) to couple the human and the political as "humanitarian intervention," with

---

[19] Upendra Baxi has called our current environment "post-human" (see Baxi 2000, 2007).
[20] On early modern notions of natural rights, see Tuck (1979, 2001); cf. Tuck (2016). For ethical and political aspirations associated with "human rights" in major documents written in pre-Roman or non-Western times, see Ishay (2004).

minor regard for the harm or good for its purported beneficiaries caused by its enactment, have used the peaceable idea of human rights as an instrument of military violence.

This first paradox ineluctably leads to the *second*, namely, that the justification of human rights has to be universal while their "realization" has to be relative and particular – which is another way of saying that human rights are necessarily *both* universal and monological *as well as* particular, plural, and relative – even as logically it cannot have all of these characteristics at once. Human rights are supposed to be *both* universal *and* particular – even as the secular logic that supposedly informs human rights says that they cannot be so except in the mode of "application" or "realization." To an important extent, however, recent anthropological literature has transcended this debate as a problem for human rights practice, by recognizing (1) the multivocality of culture, not to mention its reflections and disjunctures of power and (2) the effects of globalization.[21] But human rights is then shorn of its substantive content and viewed as a tool, while the paradoxical tension between the *idea* and the *practice* of human rights remains typically denied or ignored.

These conceptual paradoxes existed at the beginnings of the invocation of human rights in political discourse. The cultural historian Lynn Hunt has noted what she called "the paradoxical origins of human rights."[22] By this she refers to the oft-noted paradox that accompanied the dramatic invocation of human rights in political discourse in the late eighteenth century – namely, its use in justifying the democratic overcoming of privilege and illegitimate authority in two discrete countries, the United States and France. She combines features of my two "constitutive" paradoxes when she states that universality was invoked as "self-evident" in order to overcome a recalcitrant opposition to human rights generated by imperial or feudal regimes. In my terms, the so-called *universal* and *political* morality of *the human* was realized as a *particular practical* intervention in singular states. These political efforts were surely warranted and typically justified through the language of the Enlightenment. Reformist or even revolutionary politics marked the exercise of human reason; human reason was good; and its practical exercise would yield historical progress. Kant felt able to claim in the wake of the French Revolution that historical progress would result from the mere instantiation of law – even in a "nation of devils."[23] Good ideas deserved imminent enactment – aspiration, impact.

---

[21] See Wilson (1997, 2003) and Cowan et al. (2001).
[22] Hunt (2000, 3–18).
[23] "Perpetual Peace: A Philosophical Sketch," in Kant (1991, 112).

But the notion of self-evidence in political documents is partly ironic – a feature whose seriousness Hunt only lightly acknowledges. For the invocation of "self-evidence" in political discourse implies either the need for persuasion or intolerant presumption. On behalf of human rights, political opposition was killed, banished, or subordinated in revolutionary upheavals. In other words, the political invocation of self-evidence not only undermines the universality implicit in its claim but also transforms a presumed fact of nature into a value on the march, such that theory aspires to rule or emancipate practice. Meanwhile, the new political language of human rights obscures the damage produced by the resulting domination. Interestingly, in her more recent, award-winning book, Lynn Hunt does not emphasize the paradoxical character of the origins of human rights but simply invokes their "self-evidence." She regards them as a natural efflorescence of Western culture in the second half of the eighteenth century, echoing previous claims made by the Argentinian jurist Eduardo Rabossi and the American pragmatist Richard Rorty that human rights are best regarded not as a philosophy or moral theory but as a Western cultural practice that ought to be extended by engaging the sympathies of others.[24]

This activity of sympathetic and empathetic connection with distant others emerged as a broad-based sociological phenomenon in the nineteenth century, in the wake of the political assertion of "human rights." It came to be called "humanitarianism" and was designed to reach out to those left out by the human rights framework, which we know only applied to citizens of particular countries. Ironically, the limits of human rights generated the humanitarian movement, a movement rooted in emotional more than political connection, insofar as humanitarian agencies from the Red Cross to the International Rescue Organization gain their distinctive status from being officially regarded as non-political – even less "political" than human rights (partly because they do not discriminate between the injured or displaced persons they assist).[25] The emergence of the humanitarian movement was doubly ironic given its initial appearance amid the advent of Western imperialism, colonialism, mass warfare, and slavery, which fostered much of the suffering it sought to alleviate, and in the wake of the incarnation of human rights by the liberal revolutions.[26] In this vein, two major differences between human

---

[24] Rabossi and Rorty, in Rorty (1993, 111–34).
[25] See Wilson and Brown (2009) and Rieff (2002).
[26] One should note, however, that Clare Barton's humanitarian efforts and the birth of the Red Cross during the American Civil War did not result from slavery – although that was the radical basis for the outbreak, longevity, and devastation of that deadly war.

rights and humanitarianism deserve note: the former ethically and politically addresses states on behalf of egalitarian claims of all human beings, which the latter does not, while the latter assumes a non-political but inegalitarian pose, linking the care-giver and the care-receiver. Humanitarianism emerged in the nineteenth century but gained much more energy (and money) in the twentieth and twenty-first centuries. It legitimated a new kind of compassionate and sympathetic inequality, replacing the coercive inequality sanctioned by aristocratic rule.[27] Of course, one might note that its focus on visible human horrors lends itself to sensational coverage and may distract attention from their political sources.

Both human rights and humanitarian movements produced internal conflicts between the human and the political. But of course this was not the first occasion in which this occurred. It just assumed a new cast. For Aristotle had elided the contrast, if not conflict, between the human and the political when he identified "man" (*ho anthropos*) as a political animal (*politike zoon*) – that is, as an individual (man) whose (male) potential only could be fully realized in the life of a *polis*.[28] Aristotle's notion of a natural, human, and political *telos* enabled him to conceptualize notions of the common good that elided the potential for enduring conflict between the human and the political while naturalizing unequal statuses for categories of human beings.

At the dawn of modernity, Thomas Hobbes drew energy for his own theories of human freedom and equality, ethics and politics, by disintegrating the *telos* of Aristotle's conception of the natural character of political man and the ethical–political character of natural man. In so doing, he eliminated the natural differentiation of status that belonged to Aristotle's metaphysical teleology. But Hobbes's critique of Aristotle rendered ineffective and incoherent any notion of the common good as a practical challenge to the power of the state as sovereign. The political

---

[27] One of the interesting linguistic denotations of the inegalitarian nature of this kind of humanitarianism is the double meaning of the word, "help." References to "the help" designated servants (not slaves) who attended to the needs of the virtual masters, while "help" referred to services from those who have to those in need, an extension of charitable aid.

[28] The radical contrast between *zoe* – a natural function – and *bios* – a human creation – is put to interesting use by the Italian theorist Giorgio Agamben. But while he draws it from Aristotle, Aristotle's texts and theories do not warrant the categorical division between the two that Agamben finds so crucial for his theory of *Homo sacer* and the post-totalitarian politics of the camp (see Agamben 1998 (1995)). While the Aristotelian synthesis was central in the late twentieth-century revival of theoretical interest in political as well as legal citizenship, it's important to recall that Aristotle's world-view entwined hierarchies between master and slave, men and women, proper male citizens and male wage-laborers – not to mention Greeks and barbarians.

emergence of rights discourse in the liberal revolutions of the late eighteenth century regenerated the Aristotelian elision of the difference between "the human" and "the political" on the bases of Hobbesian metaphysics. This historical conflation made possible the first paradox of human rights.

In the United States, for example, subsequent to the declaration of the unalienable [human] rights of life, liberty, and the pursuit of happiness, a Constitution was written only on the condition that citizens possessed certain civil rights that would protect them from the government which they had just authorized. Similarly, the first Republic of France relied on a Declaration of the Rights of Man and Citizen – recognizing the difference between the human and the political but denying the prospect of conflict between them. Man, or more ecumenically, human beings, were natural creatures marked by differences but also equal moral faculties. These human characteristics would be fulfilled in their rights as citizens. Thus, republican rights *were* human rights, and republican France *ipso facto* promoted the interests of humanity. But the danger of not acknowledging the constitutive gap between theory and practice that belongs to human rights now clearly emerged. Robespierre and Napoleon believed they understood this, but their projects of republican virtue as terror and civilization as imperial rule undermined the positive potential of their ideologies and paved the way for moralistic imperialism in the nineteenth century. If conducted by states, such as the United States, the United Kingdom, and France, guns were often its agents. If conducted by groups seeking membership within the cherished circle of citizens, it occurred through protests against slavery, the subordination of women as second-class citizens, imperialism, and the legal domination of wealth in legal determinations of citizenship. Eventually, these protests achieved success. Sometimes they employed the vernacular of human rights; sometimes, civil rights; sometimes, human dignity or equality. In each case, a universal claim was invoked as part of a particular political struggle. No international covenants or institutions sanctioned these struggles, but history saw progress on behalf of "human rights."[29] Alas, for many, it often was wise to get out of its way.

Given that the harsh features mentioned above occurred prior to the official invocation in the UDHR of human rights as a binding norm on all states, one might think that the global scope of the UDHR could, in theory if not practice, in aspiration if not impact, claim to eliminate the constitutive paradoxes between the human and the political, on the one

---

[29] See Ishay (2004).

hand, and the universal or moral and the particular or cultural, on the other. As the opening words of the Preamble in the UDHR states, this document champions "the inherent dignity of the equal and inalienable rights of all members of the human family [as] the foundation of freedom, justice, and peace in the world."[30] The first paradox would be overcome if the norms were to apply to all states equally – but this masked differences in political power; the second would be diluted because the UDHR presumes that distinctions or major conflicts between human beings and citizenship – indeed, between universal human rights and the particularity of democracy – are remediable. Yet the UDHR displayed a bit too much by way of wishful thinking. Because the UDHR did not acknowledge the constitutive paradoxes – between human rights as a virtuous human norm and power-driven mechanisms for its enforcement, as well as between putatively universal moral standards and the differentiated cultures in which they would become real – its persuasive appeal was politically limited.

Hannah Arendt anticipated these difficulties when she noted that human rights became fully revealed only when human beings had been stripped of their dignity, becoming bare, or barely human, during the period of the Minority Treaties between the two World Wars and the Holocaust. Only when *human* beings could act and be effectively heard within discrete *political* communities that differentiate them from other human beings could their human rights become something more than signs of the dispossessed. And, indeed, the discourse of human rights has gained the most traction when it is cited as a radical loss of humanity – through the torture, arbitrary imprisonment, or genocidal attack on individuals and peoples. But this entails a peculiar result: that which should be most cherished by us becomes an effective part of politics only when it has been lost. And so Arendt claimed that human rights must amount to, in what has now become a poster-phrase in much academic discourse (although Arendt notably did not elaborate its specific meaning), namely, "the right to have rights," or, "the right of every individual to belong to humanity, [which] should be guaranteed by humanity itself." This implies a shared human characteristic that enables human beings to make universal claims against and for particular, political authorities.[31] But this phrase doesn't dissolve the paradox. For

---

[30] Connecting "dignity" to human rights has been championed by Habermas, on Kantian grounds (above n. 2), and Jeremy Waldron, on utilitarian grounds (see Waldron 2007).

[31] For Arendt's formulation of the phrase, see Arendt (1951), "The Decline of the Nation-State and the End of the Rights of Man," 296–99, at 298. On which, see Isaac (1996, 61–84); Michelman (1996, 200–9); and Ingram, "What is a 'Right to Have Rights'? Three Images of the Politics of Human Rights," 2008, 401–16; cf. Gundogku (2015).

the previous question about *where* is the human whose rights will be protected simply becomes another: *who* or *what* enforces "the right to have rights"? What does its substance consist of? How does one connect the *logos* and *ergon* of human rights? One could say that the UDHR and attending covenants amount to its basic substance and mechanisms of enforcement. But, as mentioned previously, those covenants are enforced fitfully – according to relatively arbitrary criteria – even if the effects may be beneficent. And after all, the UDHR was an aspirational document, not a legally binding document, and subsequent human rights conventions still are not enforced (although this is marginally changing with the creation and slowly strengthening International Criminal Court). And as previously noted, these rights are enforced by governments – one of the many agents of power that jeopardize, if not abuse, the norms and practices associated with human rights. The assumption is that the moral standard of human rights, adhered to by signatories of the UDHR, will be smoothly, albeit imperfectly, politically enforced by the states which that standard would bind, aka "the international community."

We ignore these paradoxes, if not contradictions, because there often seems to be no better alternative. For no-one wants a world state, nor do we want to allow the sovereignty of states over their citizens and residents to result in egregious, systematic, violent acts against their people. Some would solve these paradoxes by redefining human rights as democracy and democracy in terms of human rights. But this just begs the question or reduces even further the intellectual scope of our political vocabulary. At this point, then, we need now to move from conventional political discourse to critical, political theory about human rights, particularly in relation to democracy (most particularly its dominant, liberal–capitalist version), so as to raise once again the question of how to think about human rights, as *logoi and erga*, and use them to accommodate goodness and democracy.

6.2.2 *Human Rights and Liberal Democracy*

Liberal democracy inherently imparts constraints on the exercise of democracy – such as the rights of private property, free speech and assembly, the superiority of the power of representatives to the power of the *demos*, privacy, equality of political status among all human natures, and constitutional sovereignty. These qualifications, however, are taken for granted as part of what counts today as "democracy." Altogether, the biggest qualification is that of legal rights for citizens to protect them against the power of a sovereign state. There is also the general question of the relationship of "rights" to democracy. While the idea of political rights in the *Magna Carta* limited the power of kings and subsequent political rights articulated in the natural rights tradition and the liberal revolutions of the late eighteenth century established realms of protected power for citizens, other justifications of liberal rights, e.g., by the Federalists, Tocqueville, and John Stuart Mill, aimed to protect individuals and minorities from the purported danger of tyrannical majorities – even though evidence of the *demos* directly acting as a tyrannical majority was virtually non-existent.[32] These justifications of rights posed a conflict between democracy and rights so as to limit democratic activity engineered from below. Liberal democracy established via political representation sought protection from demotic democracy.

The protection of individual rights does not automatically benefit democracy, because what individuals do with their rights is explicitly not, *ipso facto*, subject to review. Rights-holders can do what they want with their right as long as that action counts, according to a court, as a proper exercise of that right. In other words, the relative virtue of rights depends on their political use and judicial acceptance. Their value for democracy depends on whether they are used virtuously in ways that enhance democracy. Rights offer legal protections for individuals; democracy describes a kind of political action. Whether or not they complement each other only can be answered contingently and contextually. The question therefore becomes: how should one go about assessing these contingencies and contexts? The critical discourse of liberal democracy provides an anchor for harmonizing human rights and democracy, and we shall engage it by addressing the works of John Rawls and Charles Beitz, Amartya Sen and Martha Nussbaum, and Seyla Benhabib,[33] all of whom deal with the constitutive paradoxes of human rights.

---

[32] One might point to Shay's Rebellion, an effort by small-scale New England farmers to protect their properties from foreclosures initiated by large banks under the aegis of the Commonwealth of Massachusetts – a crucial catalyst for the movement to generate the strong federal government legitimated by the Constitution of the United States. But, given the economic straits experienced by the farmers that arguably warranted governmental aid rather than punishment, there were serious questions of justice at stake. Mob rule was not the issue. Indeed, "mob rule" has never threatened constitutional governments or even their colonial or aristocratic predecessors. The phrase is a tool of political rhetoric more than a description of political reality – even though there was an implicit pact between lynch mobs and state governments in the Jim Crow South, and it surely would be worrisome if a democratic government acted like a crowd. While it surely erred in convicting and executing the ten generals and Socrates, the Athenian *demos* never politically acted more like an irrational mob than other governments in history. For a good record of reconstructed historical misjudgments of democracies, see Roberts (1994).

[33] See Donnelly (1990).

A liberal democratic embrace of human rights does not equally embrace all elements of the UDHR; instead, it favors those that reinforce liberal political ethics – namely, civil and political rights that protect the moral conscience, property, and physical security of the individual. This is not because liberal democrats dislike the political promise associated with economic, social, and cultural rights; they simply regard them as difficult to support without jeopardizing the exercise of liberal rights – just like domestic liberal democrats (in the academic sense) are loathe to infringe on the economic liberties of citizens. As a result, the liberal democratic understanding of human rights, relative to the UDHR, shrinks the practical content of the UDHR to protecting the security rights of individuals that are commonly understood and protected by judicial institutions of the state. As Marx noted in his 1843 essay, "On the Jewish Question," human rights ultimately amount to liberal rights. This has been the tack taken by liberal champions of human rights, who emphasize the priority of rights or capacities of *individuals* – who are the legatees of unequal social orders – in the general articulation of ethical political discourse. In so doing, they effectively marginalize the value of demotic power in the conception and constitution of human rights.[34] How so?

In *The Law of Peoples*, Rawls frankly states that his conceptualization of this law is not itself a theory of global justice but rather a theory "which extends the idea of a social contract to a Society of Peoples" – thereby making the world peaceful and safe for liberal democracies.[35] Indeed, Rawls states explicitly that in his "Law of Peoples ... we work out the ideals and principles of the *foreign policy* of a reasonably just *liberal* people" (Rawls's italics).[36] Human rights play a relatively minimal role in the theory as a whole, even as Rawls also designed the theory to protect and promote "basic human rights" across the globe.[37] He primarily regards human rights as restrictions on state sovereignty that protect the state's citizens, particularly the restrictions that have gained international acceptance since World War II. They apply to non-liberal, as well as liberal, states. But not all states observe them – in particular, states that fall under his category of "outlaw states" (the leaders of which *do not* observe obligations to their citizens or other states) and "burdened societies" (states which *cannot* observe obligations to their citizens or other states). However, "benevolent absolutist" (i.e., anti-democratic)

---

[34] Thus see, e.g., Berlin (1969 (1958)), Cranston (1962), Rawls (1999), and Ignatieff (2000).
[35] Rawls (1999, vi).
[36] Ibid, 10.
[37] Ibid, 93.

states that are not "decent" or "well-ordered" are regarded as observers of "human rights."[38] The so-called well-ordered societies of liberal and decent peoples (i.e., non-democratic, potentially theocratic, but consultative societies) have a "duty to assist" the burdened, but how to exercise that duty is a matter of political statesmanship rather than legal obligation – what Kant called "imperfect obligations."

Rawls associates his definition of human rights with those identified in Articles 3–18 of the UDHR. He also defines their political role as follows: It (1) is necessary but not sufficient for the social conditions of decent peoples; (2) prohibits intervention in societies that uphold human rights; and (3) limits the pluralism of peoples – i.e., nonviolently establishes a floor upon which acceptable cultural diversity could develop.[39] As a result, economic, social, and cultural rights are, as they have been in the past, subordinated to the civil rights and some of the political rights guaranteed in the UDHR. In addition, democracy is not understood as a basic human right. For Rawls, this is the price one has to pay for generating a useful and coherent political theory that does not encourage military adventurism. He calls it a "realistic utopia" – something that he does not associate with the UDHR. But it also interestingly reveals how a Rawlsian theory of human rights that could inform American foreign policy ultimately regards human rights as different from democracy and not requiring democracy (while the United States articulates "human rights and democracy" as conjoint ideals of American foreign policy). Indeed, Rawls's political theory of human rights suggests that human rights informed by his theory should guide public policy at the expense of promoting: democracy worldwide; systematic attempts to redress economic inequality on a global scale, or other forms of injustice.[40] Nonetheless, the influence of this, Rawls's last, book is considerable.[41]

More recently, Charles Beitz has analyzed international relations from a Rawlsian perspective in order to elaborate Rawls's insufficiently spelled-out conception of human rights. Rather than defining it from the normative position of Rawls's liberalism-inspired "realistic utopia" of *The Law of Peoples*, Beitz offers an analytical examination of "the idea of human rights" as an "emergent … normative … practice." He believes it helps to view human rights through the lens of a theory of justice or

---

[38] Ibid, 27, 65, 78–81.
[39] Ibid, 80.
[40] Cf. Brown (2004, 461–2).
[41] See Martin and Reidy (2005). Rawlsians have tried to extend the economic egalitarianism of *A Theory of Justice* to a global scale. See Pogge and Caney in Pogge (2001, 6–23, 123–44) and Brock (2009, 58–63).

comprehensive moral value.[42] And yet Beitz regards human rights primarily as practices to be protected by states. While recognizing the state-centric paradigm through which human rights function as a practice, Beitz does not acknowledge the extent to which this framework may privilege institutionalized, rather than aspirational and agency-based, conceptions or practices of human rights.[43] Ironically, "the idea of human rights" is understood primarily in legitimating, rather than critical, terms. To put it another way, the constitutive paradoxes of human rights – namely, the tension between the facticity of being human and the socially constructed nature of the individual as a rights-bearing creature and the more practical paradox of the UDHR (in which the institutionalization of rights as protection against states is carried out by states) – become acceptable by accepting the extant normativity of "human rights" while making its primary interpretation the responsibility of powerful states. Like Rawls, Beitz does not believe that human rights (as a practice) should be a tool of states, but the only constraint on states stems from a discursive medium backed by powerful international institutions, aka "the international community." As a result, human rights in *logos* signify protections for individuals against states but in *ergon* identify abuses in weak postcolonial states – typically invoked after the fact to protect individuals who pose no threat to the major political powers. In other words, the paradoxes that have bedeviled the discourse of human rights have been suppressed. Beitz's analytical explanation of "the idea of human rights" surely has clarified the discursive and critical terrain of human rights as a practice, but its political effect mostly reinforces and clarifies conventional conceptions of human rights.

Another adaptation of liberal conceptions of human rights to contemporary issues occurs in the work of Michael Ignatieff and other "liberal hawks" who endorsed the Bush administration's invasion of Iraq in 2003 (such as Thomas Friedman, Peter Beinart, and Paul Berman). Ignatieff linked human rights and the use of military force to justify NATO's effort to protect threatened Albanians in Kosovo from the potential of ethnic violence (which violated international law) and, later, the American government's invasions of Afghanistan and Iraq as responses to terrorism. Ignatieff only allows human rights to signify the non-derogable security

---

[42] Beitz (2009, 7–12, 96–102).

[43] In Beitz's (2009, 128) words, "… a practice of human rights … might be described as 'statist' in at least two senses: its standards apply in the first instance to states, and they rely on states, individually and collectively, as their principal guarantors … The practice of human rights as it has been developed so far can only be understood as a revisionist appurtenance of world order of independent, territorial states."

rights – rights that states have been uniquely created to protect.[44] More boldly than Rawls, who wants his "Law of Peoples" to constrain the power politics of states, Ignatieff only assigns "negative rights" (i.e., "negative liberties," a term invented by his mentor, Isaiah Berlin) to mark genuine human rights. Since such rights require protection by states to exist, the ground rules for protection and the nature of what is to be protected ("values") are determined principally by states and their national interests. Constraints upon states that stem from the political agency of ordinary citizens or democracy more generally disappear.

But even liberal theorists who are more critical of state power and the status quo have shaped their views of human rights by their liberal theories rather than propose distinctively new ethical and political standards for human rights. This is the case with the work of Amartya Sen. To begin with, Sen's effort to chart a theory of human rights is slightly ironic. After all, his contribution to political theory principally involves showing how the affirmation of "rights" is insufficient for the protection and promotion of human freedom(s). One should rather think in terms of the language of "capabilities" and "opportunities." Thus, in tune with the UDHR, Martha Nussbaum (who has worked with Sen on "the capability approach") has developed a list of human capacities whose development ensures the fullest expression of human freedom (though Sen disagrees with the strategy of constructing lists).[45] But the capabilities approach does not stray far from rights-based liberalism. Sen notes that the protection of many individual "rights" are crucial for the development of the central human capabilities and that an enormous difference separates the individuals who do or do not have the capacity to eat but may experience the same physical condition (e.g., Gandhi on a hunger strike and inescapably hungry Indians). An increase in capacities to exercise rights and obtain primary goods is measured by an increase in individual "opportunities" to develop them rather than their actual achievement.[46]

Similar to the UDHR, the capabilities approach identifies political aspirations without a political mechanism to develop them. As a result, Sen's theory of human rights, like Rawls's, operates primarily as a moral minimum for measuring physical conditions rather than as a critical tool for identifying pathways toward the global development of justice.[47]

---

[44] See Ignatieff (2000, 2004). Cf. Wallach (2005, 136). Samantha Power, a previous colleague of Ignatieff's at Harvard's Carr Center for Human Rights and ambassador to the United Nations in the Obama administration, vigorously advocated American military intervention to avoid humanitarian catastrophes, e.g., in Sudan and Libya.
[45] Nussbaum and Sen (2002, 117–49, 2011).
[46] Sen (2009, 228–38).
[47] Sen (2004).

We are to think of human development without a developer or without recognizing the implicit connection between any strategy of development and
political goals.[48] Sen's focus on capabilities justifies more attention to economic and social rights than they are given by Rawls and Beitz. However,
he still assigns a subordinate status to them under the Kantian category of
"imperfect obligations" (i.e., obligations that are not legally enforceable) –
bolstering them only by insisting that such obligations warrant wide-ranging
public discussion and deserve assent only if sanctioned by "global public
reason" and his theory of human rights.[49] One might recall liberal critics of
greater equal opportunity, who castigate the more ambitious political goal
of necessarily imposing egalitarian outcomes and fail to attend to the political consequences of girding politics in a luminous phrase.

Sen states contentedly, "there is ... no great deficit in the balance
of trade between theory and practice" with his conception of human
rights.[50] But I have my doubts. Sen wants us to focus on building human
capacities as a way of protecting human rights, but he also finds no
inherent conflict between capacities and rights or between public reasoning and political power. Failing to respect this tension has bedeviled important strands in Western political thought – Marxists as well as
liberals.[51] Both Marx and Sen wave away the first constitutive paradox of
the human and the political.[52] The problematic politics of communism
are well-known. For Sen, development is a social and economic process that does not produce serious political conflict. In this respect, both
he and Nussbaum reflect their intellectual debt to Aristotle (as well as
Adam Smith, Wollstonecraft, and Kant). For they have modernized and
liberalized the Aristotelian process that "naturally" and smoothly (in theory if not in practice) moves between potentiality and actuality. Sen and
Nussbaum make this move in order to avoid the gaps in human well-
being tolerated by protection of core human rights in the liberal tradition.
Sen seeks to overcome these limitations by integrating cultural diversity

---

[48] Sen (1999).
[49] Sen's contributions to the development of the UNDP's Human Development Index
have provided highly useful analytical tools.
[50] Sen (2004, 356).
[51] Recall Marx's famous vision at the end of the first part of "On the Jewish Question":
"Human emancipation will only be complete when the real, individual man has absorbed
into himself the abstract citizen; when, as an individual man, in his everyday life, in his
work, and in his relationships, he has become a species-being; and when he has recognized and organized his own powers (*forces propres*) as social powers so that he no longer
separates this social power from himself as *political* power." Karl Marx, "On the Jewish
Question," in R. Tucker, ed. *The Marx–Engels Reader*, 2nd ed. (New York: W. W. Norton,
1978), 46.
[52] Sen (1999, 2004, 2009).

and human rights. But this effort simply stipulates a harmony between "rights" and "virtues," stating how "rights" can be shorn of their individ- ualistic roots and "virtue" can lose its potential for corrosive collectivism, promoting cultural diversity without sanctioning unjust inequalities.[53]

Sen's confidence in his theory of human rights stems from his con- sideration of them solely from concern with the logical coherence of his definition. Attention to the practical coherence of instantiating it does not concern him – or only concerns him through the process of "public reasoning" as a practical procedure for constituting the substantive reali- zation of human opportunities and capacities. Structural limitations that impede the development of public reasoning are relegated to the level of practical resistance to his theory. Similarly, when he conceptualizes democracy as "a universal value," a political order that can develop from any of the world's cultural traditions, he primarily considers democracy as a form of ethics rather than a form of power.[54] As examples of his con- ception of democracy as a universal value vindicated as government by discussion, Sen invokes John Stuart Mill – fairly radical in the domestic politics of his own country, to be sure, but also a good civil servant for the British East India Company and its colonial ventures.[55] Moreover, two of the examples Sen cites to demonstrate the central value of "government by discussion" as the key to both democracy and human rights – those of the Bengali famine and the Great Leap Forward – surely occurred in countries where the government did not operate through public discus- sion. Moreover, that avoids a prior question: why did they have govern- ments which avoided public discussion? Fulsome, diverse public debates certainly can improve public policy. But their energy and success depend on collective conditions of ethics and power which foster mutual respect, economic well-being for the many, and political equality for all – none of which immediately arise from public reasoning.

Tough political questions about the manner in which one is to relate ethics and power in particular collectivities are precisely those that Sen's capabilities approach avoids because its *telos* of freedom is understood as self and social development rather than the exercise of collective power by ordinary citizens – i.e., by a contemporary version of the *demos*. Sen translates his capabilities into actualities, as Rawls translates his rights into realities, by means of procedural reasoning that does not address the constitutive role played by politics in the determination of human goods. Ironically, while Sen and Nussbaum found historical and philosophical

---

[53] Cf. Brighouse and Robeyns (2010).
[54] Sen (1999b, 3–17, 2009, 324–8).
[55] See Doyle (2015).

roots for their theory of capabilities in Aristotle, both minimize the manner in which human capacity for Aristotle was measured against the bar of exercising *both* political power *and* political ethics. Anyone unable to participate practically in actually and effectively determining the political good for society had only partially achieved the development of his (*sic*) virtue and freedom. One must attend to the means for achieving human virtues as the precondition for achieving human rights. In practical terms, this must involve contestation, not just protection. In this vein, Sen's theory of human rights, like that of all liberal democrats, highlights the rights or virtues of individuals in words but practically defaults to the power and authority of the state in deeds.

The last perspective addressed in the vein of liberal democracy that addresses human rights is Seyla Benhabib's. Developed over two decades, her work begins from Habermas's discourse ethics (see Chapter 5) and Benhabib's own notion of "justificatory universalism" to use human rights as a framework for improving democracy, through "democratic iterations."[56] How does Benhabib establish the connection between human rights and democracy? She defines "democratic iterations" as "complex processes of public argument, deliberation, and learning through which universalist right (*sic*) claims are contested and contextualized, invoked, and revoked, throughout legal and political institutions as well as in the public sphere of liberal democracies."[57] My discussion of her work will proceed by unpacking this notion in order to appreciate its contributions to understanding human rights as a democratic virtue. The principal difference is that, following the view of democratic ethics articulated argued herein, I hold that such ethics have to begin from an actual *demos* and then endeavor to foster maximal, practical goodness wherever one can in that democratic polity. Benhabib, along with other liberal democrats, begin from a rational conception of liberties and rights and seek to expand the hold of those on the activities of individual citizens. The rational hold of such claims, *pace* Habermas, is a universal extension of a formal, legal constraint on justifiable political arguments.[58] While Habermas argues that this implies a mutually nourishing relationship between human rights and popular sovereignty, as well as law and democracy, Benhabib argues for the integrated relationship between human rights and democracy – in theory as a guide to practice – to deal with the paradox of "democratic closure," i.e., the way in which every democracy

---

[56] See Benhabib (2002, 2004, 12ff., 2006, esp., 2011). Cf. Benhabib (1992, 23–67).

[57] Benhabib (2004, 19–21, 171–212, Cf. 2006, 45–80, 2011, 15–16, 75–6, 112–13, 129–31, 151–3, 181–2). On the meaning of "iteration," see Derrida (1988, 1–23, esp. 7–9).

[58] Habermas (1996 (1992), Ch. 3, cf. 1998 (1996), 137, 191).

presupposes that citizens are both author and subject of its laws while affecting those who are not full members.

In relation to the meaning of democracy used in this book, which stays close to its semantic meaning as the authoritative exercise of political power by citizens as a *demos* in a collectivity, Benhabib, instead, accepts the modern equivalence of democracy and representative government. This enables her to label constitutional governments with various degrees of political partici-pation by citizens in electing public officials as sources of "democratic legit-imacy" whereby citizens are both the authors of legal rights and subjects of governmental actions – even though they are only authors in words, not deeds – other than the weakly binding force of elections. Alternatively, she asserts that a feature of current democratic governments is that they express "self-legislation as self-constitution" via democratic iterations.[59]

Reading these discursive formulae in relation to political reality reveals a logical disconnection. For Benhabib's (and Habermas's) invocation of popular sovereignty is hypothetical, not practical, since the state – not the people – is practically sovereign in modernity. The notion of "we the people" is rhetorical, not practical, a matter of *logos* not *ergon*, as practical power is lodged with public officials with nebulous ties to the citizenry and the binding parts of constitutional law. And whether or not public officials enact their constitutional authority in order to promote human rights is an open question – not a foundation of action. Well aware of this, Benhabib emphasizes the political entitlement of membership for individuals – the free and equal right to have rights – as the principal, human, and political guidepost for democratic iterations that constantly redraw the boundaries between insiders and outsiders. What citizens do with their political membership is not her principal concern.

The issue that compromises this theoretically attractive perspective is the constitutive gap between properly procedural argumentation and practical politics, between state sovereignty and popular sovereignty, between democratic theory as a universalist ideal and democratic virtue as a political achievement.[60] Using human rights as a norm for politics presupposes the hold of universality on human and political activity, in

---

[59] Benhabib (2004, 43–8).

[60] From Benhabib (2004, 44): "The tension between universal human rights claims, and particularistic cultural and national identities, is constitutive of democratic legitimacy. Modern democracies act in the name of universal principles which are then circum-scribed within a particular civic community." Cf. 47: "The paradox [of democratic legit-imacy] is that the republican sovereign should undertake to bind its will by a series of precommitments to a set of formal and substantive norms, usually referred to as 'human rights.'" Similarly, the authority of cosmopolitanism or international law is contingent, not necessary, but Benhabib claims the contrary: "... cosmopolitan rights create a net-work of obligations and imbrications around sovereignty."

a Kantian vein. But, to recall, that universality *ipso facto* distinguishes between the different ways in which people act politically – generally looking down on the historicity of political action, and hence looking down on the merits of democracy. The assumption is that the universal norm is good while the practical iteration needs correction. Thus, Benhabib's "democratic iteration" may be theoretically appealing without being clearly democratic in practice or adequately sensitive to the obstacles to democracy. For its procedural character puts in abeyance a political question – namely, democracy for what? How does one promote human rights as a democratic asset? We know how, throughout the political history of human rights, its universality has been more rhetorical than real, such that its exercise depends very much on who controls its meaning – e.g., John Yoo and President George W. Bush or Human Rights Watch and Amnesty International.[61] Raising this question does not imply dedication to a kind of political realism that abjures the interconnection of ethical purpose and political action. Gestures toward a global political ethic that would enhance everyone's "human" potential can helpfully affect transnational and international politics. But once "human rights" achieves a *normative* status in politics, it becomes ideological – for good or ill – since it effectively acts as partial politics masquerading as universal politics. The resulting disempowered discourse of democracy leads to the practical subordination of her conception of democracy under the conceptual umbrella of human rights. This renders political injustices in daily life as secondary deformations of ideal philosophical reality; it means that the powerful and constitutively political character of injustices appear as surprising rather than basic. Benhabib understandably embraces human rights as protections from majoritarian power associated with democratic government. But democratic *government* is *always* a danger to the *demos* as well as minorities, intellectual or ethical, whose sense of political virtue is jeopardized.

Given the constitutive paradoxes of human rights, therefore, the critical identity of "democratic iterations" amounts to having one's cake while eating it, for it endorses democratic procedures without endorsing the political outcomes that stem from the use of these procedures, as long as it conforms to human rights norms. In the political realm and generally

---

[61] For John Yoo's interpretation of international law and human rights as authorizations for the American invasion of Iraq and unconventional punishments of individuals labeled as associates of Al Qaeda and the Taliban – such as waterboarding, sleep-deprivation, indefinite detention in solitary confinement and other practices generally viewed as torture, in violation of the Geneva Convention, Article 3, to which the United States is a signatory – see his Memorandum for William J. Haynes II, General Counsel, Department of Defense (January 9, 2002), available online, and Yoo 2003.

speaking, more democracy is better than less. But the question of "democracy for what?" does not engage Benhabib. There are no democratic ethics, apart from the stipulated meaning of human rights as *the* ethical framework within which democracies ought to operate. Democracy and human rights are *indeterminately* interrelated – one is both for democracy and against it – which undermines the critical coherence of "democratic iterations." This is not a problem as long as the *demos* has not been corrupted and practical renditions of human rights cohere. But without having a sense of *how* these phenomena are practically manifest in relation to political power, the notion of "democratic iterations" mostly fogs efforts to conceptualize human rights as an agent that enhances democracy, reconciling democracy and goodness. The priority of democratic power over individual rights as a precondition of political goodness distinguishes the position articulated here from Benhabib's notion of "democratic iterations" – a procedure that has no ethical compass besides an overly indeterminate embrace of human rights and democracy.

The drafters of the UDHR, who operated as an arm of the member states of the United Nations, never imagined that they actually were drafting a constitution of global ethics; rather, they saw it as an aspirational framework for the future construction of a global political ethics.[62] They hoped it would motivate states to move in the directions sanctioned by that document. They believed that it could generate a progressively higher bar for political legitimation on a global scale. It has generated attention to human rights as a language of legitimation, but its unique utility is hard to evaluate although it is difficult to imagine that we would do worse without their good efforts.[63] Among the various reasons that might account for this state of affairs is the manner in which human rights discourse has been shaped by the liberal ideologies of large and powerful nation-states and the Western funding of most human rights organizations – which may deflect pressure on Western governments. But the problem is not unique to liberalism or nation-states. For the constitutive paradoxes that belong to "human rights" tend to marginalize *both* the "human" in relation to the "rights" of their citizens (see Arendt) *and* the active exercise of the rights of their citizens in relation to the power of their states (see realist critiques of rights). As for those who continue to champion human rights as an international practice or as vindicated by the UDHR as a whole, one marvels at treatments of human rights as transpolitical phenomena; they sublimate the paradoxes that constitute the heart of modern versions of human rights and therefore fail to

---

[62] See Morsink (1999); cf. Glendon (2001).
[63] For differing views, see Mertus (2005, 317–33).

acknowledge the dangers (along with the virtues) of human rights as a practical, political discourse. To be sure, these arguments will not settle the matter. Deviations from the *logos* of rights discourse are typically excused by liberals as problems of politics, not liberalism. Moreover, there always will be disagreement about whether the gap between the *logos* of rights and the *ergon* of their practicality reflects incidental deviations or systematic, avoidable problems with rights discourse itself. The argument will be resolved politically, and should be, with arguments based on accounts of ethical dispositions, structures of power, and politics.

6.3   The *Ergon* of Human Rights and Democracy

Exasperated by the failure of states to live up to their commitments to the UDHR or attending covenants, human rights organizations, humanitarian agencies and non-governmental organizations have stepped into the breach – either identifying and potentially saving individuals suffering at the hands of their governments or naming and shaming those engaged in human rights abuses of various kinds. These organizations – such as *Medicins Sans Frontieres*, Amnesty International, and Human Rights Watch, not to mention the thousands of other NGOs in the global East, West, North, and South – surely have good intentions and do good work. They seek to alter the behavior of governments for the better, and often do so. They have been constructive agents of change, trying to make governments end their most abusive policies and respect international human rights. They highlight human rights as a major concern in and for the United Nations.[64] They aid those who experience extreme suffering that results from political forces beyond their control. We have seen much of this lately in concern about the treatment of women in non-Western cultures (or parts of those cultures), whether it be in the areas of education or health, as well as efforts of humanitarian organizations to care for refugees from the Syrian war or the ongoing border war in Somalia and Kenya.[65] At the same time, the principal *modus operandi* of NGOs typically takes the form of cultural or military intervention to address a seemingly abnormal condition – in the form of parachuting Westerners or UN-funded local organizations into a country's troublesome, if not violent, cultural or political situation. As a result, human rights campaigns or humanitarian aid may exhibit paternalism, depoliticization of the causes of the unhappy situation, or catastrophe, and *either*

---

[64] See Korey (1998) and Kuper (2004, 2005). Cf. Scholte (2011).
[65] For a recent narrative account of the disastrous conditions of the Dadaab refugee camp, which holds 400,000 persons from Kenya, Ethiopia, and Somalia, see Rawlence (2016).

provide indirect support for regimes that have instigated the suffering they would alleviate *or* disempower political partisans whose ultimate success a country needs.[66] In this respect, the responses of NGOs to various political crises exhibit the practical complement of the theoretical subordination of politics and democracy to human rights. From the perspective of their worldview, because of its roots ion universalism, every violation of human rights appears as a violation of a moral principle, with the result that injustices appear to be singular, surprising, accidental, epiphenomenal, readily avoidable, and remediable – assaults on individuals as victims rather than extreme manifestations of tensions and conflicts that finally have surfaced. Here, too, there is a disconnect between the explicit rationale of humanitarian or human rights NGOs and the political consequences of their actions. Because they are reactive, rather than proactive, their work may distract attention from the wounds they would heal.

In the last decade, the unintended consequences of cultural or military interventionism have been noted. Thus, policy analysts Marina Ottaway and Thomas Carothers, of the Washington, D.C.-based Carnegie Endowment for International Peace, became skeptical of efforts by NGOs to democratize civil society in authoritarian or post-authoritarian societies. The NGOs were radically limited by their narrow political basis and dependence on funding from foreign sources.[67] For these authors, "nation-building" as an international enterprise of promoting "democracy" and "human rights" does not receive "two thumbs up."[68] Correlatively, the journalist David Rieff offered a bitter critique of humanitarianism after having noted that, in Serbia, humanitarian relief efforts unintentionally propped up or protected agents of violent regimes.[69] Harvard Law School professor David Kennedy also noted the inherently political and contextual character of humanitarian relief efforts. Imposing international law may well have unwanted, unintentional consequences; a more pragmatic and political approach is needed.[70]

But does this mean that the immediate practical impact of human rights should be presumptively nil until a thorough investigation of facts on the ground is made? What if that is not possible? How long does one wait? Jews could have used more than a little outside help in dealing with the Nazis during the 1930s and early 1940s, but it is hard to gainsay President Roosevelt's decision not to liberate the camps until

---

[66] This political conundrum severely divided the humanitarian organization *Medicins Sans Frontieres*.

[67] Ottaway and Carothers (2000).

[68] See Bush (2015).

[69] Rieff (2002).

[70] Kennedy (2004).

the Nazis had unconditionally surrendered. Since a twenty-first-century Third Reich is not likely to emerge, we shall pursue these issues within extant discursive and practical frameworks, in terms of cultural and military intervention on behalf of human rights.

6.3.1   *Human Rights, Cultural Ethics, and Democracy*

When articulated in the UDHR, human rights were not questioned by many as potential threats to cultural norms of particular societies. The main challenge was to uplift apparently backward states to the human rights empyrean. Not long after, but particularly in the wake of the end of the Cold War, human rights norms came into conflict with cultural practices traditionally accepted and adhered to in many societies. The most famous conflict concerned the practice of female genital cutting (FGC). It has been endorsed by women as well as a society's traditional male leaders, even considered as an empowering practice for women. Others have regarded it as simply archaic and vestigial, likely to disappear as fast as the foot-binding of women in early twentieth-century China. However, many in the countries where it is practiced, as well as in the West, it is viewed as severely damaging to women's sexual and physical health – such FGC could be outlawed without threatening the cultural habits supported by the rite.[71] To be sure, certain non-Western practices involving women play upon Western, colonialist sensibilities that regard, e.g., certain African practices as "savage," such that those practicing them are "victims" who need to be "saved" or rescued, but that may not be simply true.[72] Other gendered, cultural norms enforced by, e.g., the Taliban in Afghanistan or patriarchal Nigerian tribes keep girls from receiving the same educational opportunities as boys and prevent women from owning land (as was the case in nineteenth-century Britain). They are justified as necessary for sustaining "the family," but these arguments have been used in the West, too, against gay marriage. Who defines what counts as a family, and at what cost?[73] This is a difficult issue, and the experience of non-Western societies parallels the economic inequalities fostered by Western societies – which also have a racial and gendered component, even as capitalist firms typically don't offer major opposition to formal equal opportunities for women, African-Americans, or trans- individuals. And it doesn't mean that one should forgo egalitarian economic policies

---

[71] See Shell-Duncan and Hernlund (2000), especially the articles by Gruenbaum, Mackie, and Ahmadu.
[72] See Mutua (2002, 2016, esp. 165–83, 212–15).
[73] See An-Na'im (2011 (1992)).

for women just because their addition to the labor force has enabled firms to keep wages lower than they might be.

These cultural and economic issues that concern the relative power and opportunities of races, sexes, and genders are not readily resolved on the smooth conceptual plane of "human rights." After all: (1) cultures no longer have clear boundaries, if they ever did; (2) what counts as "the culture" within a culture is politically contested; and (3) globalization has meant that cultural material and identity are widely disseminated, preventing them from easy capture by legal categories – a problem evidenced in *l'affaire foulard* (discussed below). Moreover, cultural relativism does not imply moral relativism; nor does it imply an *a priori* dominance of cultural meaning and value over other sources of meaning and value (although it does imply the constitutive role of culture in the construction of human meaning).[74]

The residents of Darfur have needed outside help, along with the people of Bahrain, Congo, North Korea, Saudi Arabia, Yemen, Kenya, Somalia, and Haiti (even though the latter may be said to have received too much outside help).[75] So do the citizens of Iran, Iraq, and Afghanistan – not to mention the stateless Palestinians – principally because democracy in their countries has been weakened by corrupt and/or dictatorial rule or domination that may or may not be sanctioned by Western, Middle Eastern, or Asian powers. Most recently, NATO member Turkey and its president have sanctioned attacks on free political speech by ordinary citizens as well as professional academics.[76] Should, or does, money simply follow strategic interests? Are NGOs businesses of good Samaritans and the flag-bearers of human rights acting in the context of a weak United Nations? Or, are powerful and self-interested, if not overtly terrible, states the preferred destination for our political energy and money? The problem is vexed because NGOs and INGOs are legally non-partisan, officially non-political organizations.[77] But they obviously operate in a highly political context. Even if their internal operation is democratic and political, they should affect the broader political environment in which they work in order to avoid simply being reactive. But for them to address this issue systematically undermines the nominally apolitical character of their mission. That is, their officially non-political status harms their full appreciation of the political environment in which they operate and

---

[74] See the work of Wilson (1997) and Cowan et al. (2001).
[75] Schuller (2012). Cf. INCITE! Women of Color Against Violence, 2007.
[76] See "Turkey: Detention of academics intensifies crackdown on freedom of expression," Amnesty International, January 15, 2016 (available online).
[77] For an analysis of this problem, see Rubenstein (2015).

which they, presumably, want to bend toward democracy and justice. Perhaps social movements should become the locus of our human rights energies, but then that amounts to significant and dangerous political intervention, which human rights discourse is not supposed to endorse.

One must face the question of whether these organizations and movement, too, are side-stepping, and not addressing, the sources of hegemonic *power* and *injustice* that ravage the lives of millions of human beings – phenomena that inevitably involve interactions of individuals and institutions and making judgments about them. But doing so is politically difficult even in a relatively open society – see the obstacles the mainstream media and the Democratic Party placed before the Presidential campaign of Senator Bernie Sanders – let alone a human rights or humanitarian organization working in contemporary Russia, Egypt, Afghanistan, China, or Saudi Arabia. That said, such organizations typically have an easier go of it than funneling resources to demotic and dissident movements. In any event, a political overview of the situations in which external aid from human rights or humanitarian organizations indicates that the historical dynamic of politics does not observe the practical boundaries between human rights norms, which are supposed to apply prior to the outbreak of war, and those of humanitarian law, which apply during or immediately after war.[78]

Scholars have tried to bridge the gap between universalistic human rights norms and locally enforced cultural norms by means of aspirational language – such as the notion of "universal cultural legitimacy."[79]

---

[78] See Chandler (2001, 678–700).

[79] Abdullahi Ahmed An-Na'im coordinates human rights and cultural difference. For example: "I would make the existing [International Bill of Human Rights] the foundation of future efforts to establish cultural legitimacy for human rights by interpreting the current provisions and developing an appropriate literature, sensitive to the need for cultural legitimacy. For example, it would be useful to contrast the values and institutions of various cultural traditions with the values underlying the International Bill of Human Rights and the specific implications of those values. Processes of internal cultural dynamics and change may then be used to reconcile and resolve any conflicts and tensions that exist between the values and institutions of a given cultural tradition and those envisaged by the current standards of human rights." The term "universal cultural legitimacy" may have been coined by An-Na'im, initially in "Islam, Islamic Law, and the Dilemma of Cultural Legitimacy for Universal Human Rights," in Welch and Leary, eds. (1990a, 31–54), and other articles he penned about the same time, e.g., "Problems of Universal Cultural Legitimacy for Human Rights," in An-Na'im and Deng, eds. (1990b), and An-Na'im (1992). Updated versions of the latter two appear in An Na'im (2011 (1992), 65–96, 97–117). The quotation comes from the book, 85–6. A more explicit definition of cultural legitimacy begins with the following (69): "The prime feature underlying cultural legitimacy is the authority and reverence derived from internal validity. A culturally legitimate norm or value is respected and observed by the members of a particular culture, presumably because it is assumed to bring satisfaction to those members. Because there may be conflicts and tensions between various competing conceptions of

But a harmonious middle ground is more hypothetical than real, as it requires an ideal negotiation that satisfies international human rights criteria and virtually all segments of the local culture. It begs the questions, insofar as the devil will be in the details.

This discussion suggests that "human rights" may not be invariably a talisman for good – or for democracy. One notable example stems from the democratic protests of Chiapas, Mexico that were thwarted by the federal government relying on human rights law.[80] That may not be the rule, but the political languages of human rights and democracy may be practically confusing. Another example comes from the French issue of Islamic garb for women in public schools or public places. In this instance, the French state, which has institutionalized the ban on headscarves in public schools and niqabs in public spaces, justifies its politics on the basis of equality and human rights – even if the ban clearly buttresses a particular sense of French culture and national solidarity. Yet Islamic women who prefer to wear religious garb believe that the state now inhibits their freedom of religion and cultural expression (which also are guaranteed in the UDHR as human rights), even as some have migrated to France from countries that grant them fewer political rights than those allowed them in France. Given the different ways in which European and American countries treat the legitimacy of the public display of religious garb, the matter is clearly an issue of political negotiation as well as human rights – with each country considering its history as well as the present.[81] It is not a resignification of the politically artificial "liberals–communitarians" debate of the 1980s and 1990s, since self-proclaimed liberals are proclaiming communitarian views – and vice versa – in various countries.[82]

Action on behalf of human rights usually addresses extreme and obvious injustices but not the larger political problems they symptomize. These more readily arise as one addresses the impediments to democracy. In this respect, therefore, one might think of identifying human rights as protections for minorities, while democracy protects majorities (along with the quasi-dependent notion of goodness as illuminated

---

individual and collective satisfaction [not to mention about the boundaries and contents of a culture], there is in any culture constant change and adjustment of the norms or values that are accorded respect and observance. Such change and adjustment appears related to prevailing perceptions of whether a specific normative behavior does or does not bring *sufficient satisfaction* [my italics] to warrant its continuation."

[80] See Collier (2001).

[81] The issue recalls the contrary justifications provided by German and American courts for different legal postures toward the public parading of Nazi slogans and paraphernalia.

[82] Korteweg and Yurdakul (2014), Elver (2012), Amer (2014), Joppke (2009), Laborde (2008), and Scott (2007).

so far). Certainly economic and social rights for most citizens of a society are most likely to result from a democratic political order more than a judicial protection of individual rights.[83] From our earlier investigations, it seems that protecting rights for a majority, as in the right to private property, may have anti-democratic consequences under the aegis of capitalism. In turn, freedom of religion and freedom of speech are typically injured by a dominant government threatened by dissident minorities whose campaigns would practically benefit the majority in society. So the question becomes whether attention to the most desperate circumstances that gain attraction from major international rights organizations and the media actually undermine long-term political change, which tends to require more power for democratic political movements and challenges to institutional power. But this question should be answered not in the legislation of theory (*logos*) but in relation to the historical dynamic at work (*ergon*) in political situations. This does not imply moral relativism or tacit acceptance of majority domination. Rather, it calls for the invocation of astute political judgment, with relatively greater dedication to the well-being of the *demos* than to the rights of individuals – although such rights warrant protection as constituents of demotic power. This is due not to favoritism toward the group over the individual but to practical considerations about how to shape political power so as, ultimately, to benefit most human beings. It is not about sacrificing individuals to abstract norms but rather fidelity to political consequences as well as ethical norms.

6.3.2   *Human Rights as Engines of Political Charity*

We have just addressed the debate about the practical conflicts arising from the constitutive paradoxes of human rights in cultural, relatively non-violent, ways. The issues emerged prior to the UDHR, in the dire situation of European Jewry between the wars and during World War II and the statement by the American Anthropological Association that noted the social constitution of rights and the potential within human rights doctrine to impose universalistic norms which failed to respect legitimate

---

[83] India allows citizens to petition its Supreme Court directly on behalf of deprivations of their basic civil, political, economic, social, and cultural rights. This constitutional empowerment of ordinary citizens is remarkable and valuable. But most cases take years to litigate and, after being resolved, are not followed up by significant political redress – because the Indian state does not demonstrate the political willingness to seriously address the problems.

local practices.[84] Now, we turn to justifications of hostile intervention to curtail or forestall gross abuses of human rights and doubts about its virtue and efficacy. They come in two forms, one resulting from the use of violence by major powers; the other illustrated in the plight of refugees fleeing from war seeking refuge in countries that (rightly or wrongly) deny their entry. The first is familiarly known as "humanitarian intervention." The second could be so named in a counter-intuitive, unnerving mode.

The doctrine presently embraced by "the international community," which stipulates criteria for legitimate, violent intervention to bolster human rights and alleviate humanitarian suffering, is known as "the responsibility to protect" (R2P). First publicly articulated in 2001, it directly grew out of a project funded by the United Nations in 1999, in line with Kofi Annan's statement of regret about the way the United Nations was hampered from properly intervening in Rwanda in 1994 and circumvented in Kosovo in 1998 by NATO, such that "the international community" should operate with two conceptions of sovereignty, not one.[85] It quickly gained currency in the midst of the agony of many nations and those concerned about the power of the United Nations and international law in the face of the unilateral decision by the United States to invade Iraq. R2P was adopted becoming a policy adopted by the UN General Assembly in 2005 and sustained by the Secretary-General in 2009.[86] It was also used by President Obama to justify American bombing in Libya in 2011, a venture that officially was designed to protect civilians but ultimately led to the overthrow of Muhammar Gaddafi and the destabilization of Libya.[87] Does this new

---

[84] Statement by the American Anthropological Association, *Statement on Human Rights*, Vol. 49, Pt. 4 (October–December 1947), 539–43. Since then, the AAA has modified its position to transcend any opposition between human rights and culture (1999).

[85] Kofi Annan, "Two Concepts of Sovereignty," *The Economist*, September 16, 1999. Yet Annan was wary of how humanitarian intervention might become a dangerous tool used by the powerful against the weak. See *Secretary General Presents his Annual Report to General Assembly*, UN Press Release SG/SM/7136 GA/9596, September 20, 1999 (Annan 1999b), cited in Orford (2003, 41). For a contrary view, see Marks (2000).

[86] (A/RES/60/1, para. 138–140) and formulated in the Secretary-General's 2009 Report (A/63/677) on Implementing the Responsibility to Protect.

[87] President Obama actually used the phrase, "responsibility to protect" in his letter to Congress of March 21, 2011 declaring his authority to intervene militarily in Libya: "Qadhafi has forfeited his responsibility to protect his own citizens and created a serious need for immediate humanitarian assistance and protection, with any delay only putting more civilians at risk." He further defended his decision to intervene militarily in Libya in a speech to the National Defense University on March 28, 2011: www .npr.org/2011/03/28/134935452/obamas-speech-on-libya-a-responsibility-to-act. In the wake of the disastrous use of force against the Gaddafi regime, the website for the R2P project now separates its "principles" from its "implementation," inadvertently supporting the critique offered here stemming from the need for greater attention to the logos– ergon dynamic. See http://responsibilitytoprotect.org/index.php/crises/crisis-in-libya, uploaded March 23, 2016.

doctrine prevent or instigate violence?[88] Does it mimic what Third World countries feared as covers for intervention by First World countries, or does it provide an appropriate justification for armed intervention for human rights violations and humanitarian catastrophes wherever they occur?

The question has been debated for the past fifteen years, so that most of the possible answers to the question have been posed and have many intellectual supporters. Not fully appreciated, however, are the reasons for the opposing positions and the historical provenance of the doctrine itself. As has been recently pointed out, the doctrine of R2P grew out of not only the political and humanitarian disasters of Rwanda and the Balkan wars of the 1990s but a general concern about the need to protect internally displaced persons (acronymed as IDPs) – initially articulated in the phrase, "sovereignty as responsibility."[89] Opposition to it also has significant antecedents, in the fear of small nations of the use of international law and institutions to provide cover for the political ambitions of large, more powerful nations – i.e., fear of neocolonialism or imperialism.[90] The most striking aspect of discussions about R2P has been the relative absence of discussion of "the day after." The initial document, *The Responsibility to Protect*, mentions "the responsibility to prevent," "the responsibility to protect," and "the responsibility to rebuild," but learned discussions of the doctrine have concerned the ethics of intervening and generally ignored any critical assessment of its consequences.[91] A historical understanding of both human rights and humanitarian intervention provided needed perspective on the politics and ethics of intervention, debunking *both* the notion of "Westphalian sovereignty" prior to the late twentieth century *and* the unique character of R2P as a practice, if not a doctrine.[92]

The need for this discussion of consequences is analytical as well as political. Analytically, the dominant discussion of humanitarian intervention reads it on the model of domestic fire-fighting. A fire breaks out. Those suffering and endangered call 911. The fire department roars

---

[88] See *Responsibility to Protect: Report of the International Commission on Intervention and State Sovereignty* (Ottawa: International Development Research Centre, 2001). See Evans (2009) and Weiss (2007), both of whom contributed to the initial report. This project has its supporters and critics. For examples of the former, see Cooper and Kohler (2009), Bellamy (2015), and, now Thakur and Maley (2015). Cf. Genser and Cotler (2012). For the latter, see Pattison (2010); cf. Mehta (2006). Cf. Sharma and Welsh (2015).

[89] See Glanville (2014, esp. 171–212), and references to the work of Francis Deng; cf. Holzgrefe and Keohane (2003).

[90] See Anghie (2005, 196–272). Cf. Glendon (2001, 20).

[91] For an exception, see Doyle on "Postbellum Peacebuilding," Doyle (2015, 147–85).

[92] See Simms and Trim, *Humanitarian Intervention: A History*, 2011, 1–24, 365–401, and *passim*.

in; firefighters put out the fire; then, they leave, as heroes. The presumption is that the family or business whose building has been damaged has fire insurance to finance the rebuilding, so that the injured persons need no institutional follow-up to recover from their devastating experience.

In humanitarian intervention, however, there is no insurance company. The people of the country that experiences the intervention suffer from some disaster, but that disaster has political antecedents not captured in the analogue of the fuel, spark, and flammable material that make for a fire. They also suffer extensively – not just a day, week, or month – from the invasion and its consequences. In the aftermath of World War II, the United States poured billions of dollars into Western Europe to restore political and economic institutions that had been in place. In countries that don't have previously strong institutions and in which invading powers are not inclined to stay for long, the *consequences* of intervention may be just as devastating as the *rationale* justifying the initial intervention. And inevitably so. For *either* the invaders – typically major world powers – invade and stay, compromising the political autonomy of the country whose fire they have put out. *Or* they don't or can't take full responsibility for what they have wrought and leave the country they have saved in tatters – Iraq and Libya are two, well-known, recent examples.

This is not a question of the Powell doctrine, namely, "If you break it, you own it," because humanitarian intervention supposedly is not about conquest or an excuse for the intervener's expansion of state power. Nor is it about dedication to humanitarian principles versus self-interested calculations of *realpolitik*. It's about the *politics* of humanitarian intervention. Focus on justifications of intervention should be coupled to a policy that can make good on the likely consequences, more than an "exit strategy." It has to comprehend the consequences of using military power for "humanitarian intervention" and reject the rescue idiom of R2P. It would seem that no-one with authoritative power made these calculations prior to the American invasion of Iraq or the American/NATO intervention and bombing of Libya.[93]

The second, relatively new, dimension of "humanitarian intervention" has been the disastrous European and American response to the refugee crisis spawned by the war in Syria that broke out in 2011. Now, Syrian and Iraqi citizens, fleeing the civil war in Syria and the horrors of ISIL, have become non-state agents of humanitarianism performing a kind of reverse intervention into whatever safe havens they can find. They remain depoliticized and stateless, all because of wars that have

---

[93] See Todorov and Glanville in Scheid, ed. (2014, 46–58, 148–65). America's rush to judgment in Libya is well documented in *The New York Times*, February 28–9, 2016.

their roots in the American invasions of Iraq and Libya as well as the demonic policies of Assad. The refugees are intervening without weapons into states that could have helped.[94] Given the recent histories of Iraq and Libya, it would seem that Europeans and Americans are much more comfortable bombing those countries so as to generate refugees than they are willing to accept the consequences of their military campaigns. The extent of the unwelcoming response of many European states and the United States reveals the incoherence of their official dedication to humanitarian concerns, as well as the disconnect between the place of refuge sought by refugees and the source of their need for asylum. Article 14 (1) of the UDHR grants "everyone ... the right to seek and to enjoy in other countries asylum from persecution," while the country that provides temporary asylum has no legal obligation to grant them permanent residency – illustrating the conflict between the human and the political – only not to return them to the state from which they fled if that would put them in physical danger (*refoulement*).[95]

But that analytical incoherence has another political corollary due to the manner in which the effects of capitalist-induced globalization affects its human subjects differently. The *demos* in advanced, Western, capitalist countries have been steadily abandoned by their political leaders, such that their sense of collective power, in turn, has diminished. And this conditions their susceptibility to displacing their anger on others and expressing prejudicial sentiments of one sort or another. Which suggests that attention to human rights ought to promote the exercise of demotic power.

Perhaps the problems human rights and humanitarian organizations address are best understood when their more traditional definitions remain in place – when human rights count modestly as guideposts for, rather than the principled expression of, justice, and humanitarianism is regarded not as an activist project but as a secondary remedy for suffering caused by political agents. Indeed, how does one use the discourse of human rights to identify and comparatively evaluate the injustices experienced by Iranians under an authoritarian regime; Iraqis suffering from the aftermath of the regime of Saddam Hussein and the invasion of the Americans; Afghans who have to choose between a corrupt government, a

---

[94] The humanitarian crisis most directly spawned by the civil war in Syria has led some humanitarian agencies to become political, by declaring their unwillingness to facilitate policies of European states that reject refugees seeking asylum and place them in detention camps. See www.commondreams.org/news/2016/03/24/humanitarian-groups-refuse-partake-mass-expulsion-refugees.

[95] See the 1951 Convention on Refugees (responding to World War II) and the 1967 Protocol Relating to the Status of Refugees. On the international law on asylum seekers and refugees, see Weissbrodt (2008, Chs. 5–7).

zealously militant, religious, and patriarchal guerrilla network, and an army of Westerners that would benefit them even as they bomb them – not to mention the experiences of the Palestinians as people under Israeli occupation, who are ruled by manipulating politicians and have been caught in the crossfire of neighboring Arab states? Is the problem whether their experience of abuse can or cannot be found under one the articles of human rights law *or* whether there can be agents for the amelioration of their indignant conditions? Moreover, we know that R2P will not be used against the five permanent members of the Security Council. These questions do not have easy answers, but *not* asking or addressing them assures unnecessary harm and destruction in the light of which assertions of human rights mostly function as rhetorical guises – when they are more than that. Again, it is important to acknowledge the primacy of democracy over human rights, as a way of recognizing when considering a military intervention how much more time and care goes into fostering a democratic society than using courts to protect individual human rights.

6.4   Complementing Human Rights and Democracy

Although the idea of "human rights" suggests that it is an umbrella under which all other rights are covered, the practice is inverted. One need not adopt T. H. Marshall's optimistic, progressive, Western, and canonical description of the evolution of rights discourse – from civil to political to welfare rights – to recognize that "human rights" as a practical political idea emerged *after* nearly every other kind of right took hold in human societies.[96] In other words, human rights as an idea lags far behind human rights as a practice, reflecting a major disconnect between human rights as a *logos* and human rights as an *ergon*. To be sure, the challenge always has been how to relate the *logos* and *ergon* of human rights, human rights as "aspiration" and human rights as political reality. Moreover, the notion of human rights retains moral and political appeal, for millions of human beings as well as thousands of academics who study its nature and effects. It can serve as a phrase whose violation is attached to the commission of atrocities and to global sympathy. Overall, this is a good thing. But it is not so good if it distracts attention from the economic, social, and political agents that have fueled the atrocities.

If the political advance of human rights may not be understood coherently as an end in itself but as an instrument of democratic agency, is

---

[96] See Marshall (1964 (1949)).

there a way to make it more politically effective for the individuals on whose behalf the UDHR was designed? In particular, is there a way for human rights to become a complement to democracy, given that the institutionalization of "rights" does not form a general, widespread political agenda and inherently restricts democratic agency, replacing it with the authority of relatively non-democratic courts and judicial authorities?[97] I think there is, and in a manner that draws on, even as it departs from, the UDHR and human rights as a practice. It must proceed in a way that, at a minimum, forestalls use of the idea of human rights as a supplement to the work of an occupying army actually engaged in the commission of human rights abuses (at least arguably so from a different interpretation of human rights), as was tried for a few weeks by the US Army in its first year occupying Iraq and later by the Iraqi police, or serves as an adjunct to invasion.[98] It also ought not to be grounded in the premises of liberal democracy. One of the differences between devotion to liberal, or limited, democracy and democracy as a political aspiration is that liberal democrats typically begin by stipulating presumptively rational or moral boundaries to democratic action, by way of rights, without critically considering the practical dimensions of politically and forcibly implementing those boundaries. The problem becomes evident when liberal democrats relate human rights to democracy. They embrace the UDHR endorsement of democracy as a natural political complement to human rights but enforce it without regard to the comparative value of various rights or regard derogation in the enforcements of the rights as incidental, accidental, or collateral damage. The perspective offered here does not presume the sufficiency of democracy as a political virtue

---

[97] See Tamanaha (2004, 102–41).

[98] Humanitarian organizations began to enhance their capacity for helping the people of Iraq *before* the American invasion of March 2003. See *The New York Times*. Also note the efforts on behalf of "human rights" by Paul Bremer, the first leader of the American occupation of Iraq after the invasion (May 11–June 26, 2003). He sought to improve the behavior of American soldiers, who already had been reported to be engaged in human rights abuses by Human Rights Watch, Amnesty International, and *The New York Times* (July–August 2003), years before the widely reported acts of torture committed by US Army personnel in the Abu Ghraib prison from 2003 to 2006. But only a few weeks after their introduction, the US Army ended use of such guides to military conduct. After supporting the Iraqi Interior Minister and serving under the Governing Council (which replaced the Coalition Provisional Authority after July 13, 2003), Bremer turned his focus away from the US Army and argued that civil violence in Iraq lay with "the police" and urged that the police "receive some basic human and civil rights training before being deployed." See Bremer (2006, 154–5; cf. 203, 213). For documentation by the US Army of human rights abuses in Abu Ghraib, as early as 2004, see The Taguba Report, excerpted in Ehrenberg et al. (2010, 422–5). For the efforts of humanitarian organizations to pick up the predictable human pieces shattered by the American invasion of Iraq, see McGinty (2003).

of democracy – the premise of the book is that democracies are not self-legitimating. Rather, it puts democracy front and center as the major agent for promoting human rights – not just condemning its abuses. Democracies will be improved by respect for human rights, but the latter should not be viewed as authoritative sources for regulating the former. After all, who will be regulating the regulators?

Complementarity is possible; human rights can function as a democratic virtue. The *first* step in promoting this condition is to recognize that the constitutive paradoxes of the UDHR characterize any version of human rights that would aspire to be a beacon for international or global political ethics and democracy.

The *second* is to recollect the motivation of the UDHR as a restraint on the power of states. But rather than immediately identifying states as the primary agents for defining the extent of such restraint, one should relate human rights to democracy in ways that determine the manner in which demotic power in different societies can become more effective as levers of state behavior. That is, do not associate "democracy" with states that call themselves democratic but foster the democratic agency of their citizens.

Third, one must appreciate how the power of humanity is still principally actualized through the power of states and their citizens, so that the realization of human rights depends on the ongoing activities of political membership. Given that such rights amount to claims that such activities are goods for most citizens, they amount to calls for *political virtues* as much as human rights – unrealized virtues that need to complement politically calls for rights that human beings currently do not exercise.

Fourth, a working conception of human rights that protects and promotes human well-being must recognize that they only will flourish in democratic political orders – just as the UDHR asserts. But such democracies will only enhance and effect human rights if the power they exercise primarily derives from the many rather than the few. Because such power cannot be responsibly exercised in a unified, global manner, it has to be rooted in a plurality of *demoi* asserting a plurality of virtues rather than the ascendance of a few whose official roles are to protect the law, order, and the Gross Domestic Product of nation-states. Collective power that enhances the well-being of most persons draws on local, practical roots – not global, universalistic ideals pitched by officialdom. This mandate may seem overly optimistic, particularly because these states heavily depend upon receipts from capitalist economies. But the state is more than a business enterprise, and, despite practical efforts to the contrary, fellow citizens treat one another as more and better than consumers. One might associate the agenda of such *demoi* with protecting the environment and decreasing the gap between rich and poor.

These conditions for generating greater coherence for a contemporary conception of human rights are practically steep but rooted in political realities. They indicate that it must not be understood primarily as the civil and political rights officially upheld by liberal democratic states – crucial as they are to protect in equitable and coherent ways. For example, refugees occupy conditions of relative statelessness that put them at a relative disadvantage to citizens. This must be acknowledged and remedied, since their condition was not chosen but generated by states whose leaders opt for war as their means of politics. But we also cannot dismiss the tensions refugees may generate in states into which they seek entry and whose prerogatives to enforce their boundaries and conditions of membership are protected by the UDHR. Not to acknowledge such considerations dismisses demotic power and needs, and so cuts off one's nose to spite one's face. Simply referring to the rights of refugees sanctioned by international human rights covenants will not be sufficient. Instead, one ought to defend the persons whose well-being is safeguarded in the UDHR and deserve care. Their needs warrant attention as citizens who authoritatively constitute the power of the state in which they are or were members – at the political limit, states directed by the *demos* rather than in deference to elites – and put maximal pressure on the political agents who catalyzed their political homelessness. The rights to which human beings the world over should aspire cannot be limited to the security rights fitfully protected by the institutions of state power. The only way to harness the power of the state for good rather than ill is to understand "human rights" as virtues that require manifold material and cultural conditions for their achievement – lest human discourses be misused.

Despite the supportive armor of international human rights law – not to mention the attractive character of human rights as a principal banner for myriad political actors – we have seen that human rights functions mostly as a dependent, rather than independent, concept in political ethics. If human rights are to occupy a unique and valuable position in a political discourse that promotes the well-being of most human persons, if not humanity, then it ought *not* to be understood primarily in the grandiose terms offered by official documents and authorized agents of political legitimation or philosophical justification – via, for example, the dominant discourses of liberal rights, human capacities, or "global responsibilities."[99] Despite the pretensions of much human

---

[99] See Kuper (2005), esp. the article by Pogge (3–35), extrapolating global responsibilities from Article 28 of the UDHR.

rights discourse to define what human beings universally ought to have as their protected, normal condition, I argue that it is best rendered in a more limited vein – not in terms of civil and political rights versus economic, social, and cultural rights but as an adjunct to democracy. Rather than pretending to perform the role of the major global political ethic, "human rights" should be understood as a form of politically engaged ethical criticism that attempts to inform the public realms and the agendas of political actors as a discourse to identify unjust political extremes and endangered minorities. In other words, "human rights" cannot be "enforced" and should not serve as a global political ethic. Whatever good can come from human rights mostly arises from the concerted action of democratic publics and states. Well-meaning NGOs cannot come close to matching their power and money.

In this role, human rights can fulfill their potential as a variegated standard of virtue for transnational political ethics in a world whose code word for political legitimacy is democracy. Human rights have served as a principal locus for significant political debates about democracy and political virtue in the post-1948 world of international politics and transnational cultures. It is an ethical and political concept whose usage contributes to local, national, and global practices; as such, it warrants critical analysis and theoretical exposition. But whether this conception warrants practical support depends on the appreciation of its paradoxical conceptual character and savvy, political judgments of how it might be productively employed. In this way, my argument seeks *both* to deconstruct the popular, policy-driven, state-sponsored linkage of democracy and human rights that occurs frequently in the discourse of governmental officials *and* to reconstruct it in a way that strengthens its utility – more as a tool of ethical criticism than legitimation – while noting the myriad ways in which human rights function as signs of pluralized global virtue in the discourses of contemporary political democracies.

These conditions do not forecast an easy path for practically articulating or actualizing the promise of human rights. But at least they preserve human rights as a critical tool that benefits ordinary human beings rather than an ideological tool that legitimizes the power of deceptive, inegalitarian ideologies and dominant state power. They define human rights as a paradoxical, political concern, in which a productive linkage between human rights as words and deeds depends on, rather than constrains, demotic power. If human rights depend upon and express these critical virtues, they can foster democratic ethics and exhibit democratic virtue. They can begin to accommodate democratic political boundaries and moral horizons. These are civil, political, economic, social, non-discriminatory, egalitarian, and cultural rights as practices that shape the realities and prospects of President Roosevelt's Four Freedoms as "the highest aspiration of the common people" and bestow genuine political meaning on the UDHR as "a common standard of achievement for all peoples and all nations."[100] Politics and democracy may defy human rights in some respect, but defy human rights to some degree, often with good reason, but understanding rightly how human rights can provide ethical complements to democratic thought and action can promote justice in our increasingly interconnected world.

[100] From the Preamble to the UDHR.

Conclusion: Political Action and Retrospection

This book has tried to accomplish two tasks at once: to provide an account of the principal features of democratic ethics, as a set of dispositions that inform political action, and to identify the major features of those dispositions by interpreting the sources of their historical dynamic and role in the political present. In so doing, it not only has provided analysis and information but has made a larger claim for the importance of this approach for enhancing democratic ethics and action. I have done this not because of finding inherent intellectual fault with more strictly analytical or structural/theoretical approaches to understanding democracy but because of my beliefs that (1) today's cultures, so deeply shaped by the anti-historical presentism of technology, capitalism, and screen-life mask the well-springs of coherent and successful *political* life and action and (2) the best way to strip away these masks is to attend to the power and historical dynamism that enables democratic ethics to take hold, in arguments that possesses both narrative and logical features. We then have a view of action *in* theory, rather than as an application *of* theory. Need it be said, the book's historicist turn does not articulate a new view of the power of history. History is always with us, and its power and character depend on how *we* – that ever elusive entity – read it. This historicism reflects my view that democratic ethics is best understood in a constitutive relationship to the exercise of political power – not as a function, by-product, or instrument of power but as a component that gives it meaning in the present and direction for the future. The focus of democratic ethics has to be *action* if democracy is to flourish.

The connections between historicity, power, and action in this book do not reduce the need or value of critical thought. Nor does this approach imply a template for accommodating democracy and goodness. Which is not to say that I would have nothing to say about how to be the mayor of Poughkeepsie or the governor of or United States senator from New York, etc., or that these posts have easy demands to meet. Rather, it is designed to offer an approach to democratic action that depends on political actors for its fulfillment – perhaps in the way that teachers hope that their students will derive the proper implications from their teachings, as Socrates was generally unable to impart in the *ergon* of his life but Plato had him do in writing (with the interactive acceptance of a listener) in the *logos* of the *Republic* (518c–d). These lessons attend to the value of democracy as the fulfillment of active citizenship – more than as rights, principles, or practical norms.

I have carried out this enterprise by focusing on five conceptual practices that have arisen and endured over time as constitutive features of democratic ethics. They belong to goodness as a phenomenon of morals and practical power which facilitates democracy when it cannot be self-legitimating. The five central elements – virtue, representation, civil rightness, legitimacy, and human rights – emerged in distinctive eras of democracy's incarnation, when their basic meaning was and is poignantly at play. But this has not been with the aim of downplaying one feature of democratic ethics with regard to another. Furthermore, comparing their relative significance, value, and meaning is a political judgment that only can be made well by knowing possible and practical alternatives for action.

In reading these dimensions of goodness in relation to democracy, we have found, somewhat ironically, that each idea is best understood if not treated as a good in itself in relation to democracy but rather as a double-edged asset. Although necessary for democracy, they have been most helpful to democracy if neither is wholly determined by current configurations of democratic power nor elevated to the status of a principle to which democracy should submit. Thus, when *virtue* blends with democracy, that democratic society becomes arrogant; when virtue immediately qualifies democratic action it degrades the dignity of the *demos*. *Representation* is a necessary feature of modern democracies, and is useful because of the time for political concentration and expertise it allows for representatives to do good political work. But it also is dangerous when it encourages the presumption that representatives are adequate substitutes for the ongoing political voices, interests, beliefs, and actions of citizens. *Civil rightness* addresses the reality of a social realm not wholly under the direction of democratic government. Acknowledging this social realm from the standpoint of democracy means allowing considerations of merit and opportunity to operate under the rule of law and play important social functions that cannot be well done by all. But the meanings of these terms should not indulge *a priori* practical determinations of their meaning and use, for that undermines the freedom and equality for all upon worthy rule of law depends. When appended to a modern government, *legitimacy* tends to announce the value of the state, since it overrides any one of its ethical conceptions. In effect, it secures the possibility of democratic action. Yet by virtue of its status *above* the people, particularly amid the power of the modern state and the instabilities of globalization, the notion of legitimacy undermines that feature of democracy which requires that it also be secured *by* the people. Finally, the idea of *human rights* reminds us every day of how unequal are the situations of human beings born into this world under contingent and (from the view of the newborn) arbitrary conditions, as well as unequal and unjust practices sanctioned by governments. A myriad of actions call out to be done to address the injustices signaled by human rights abuses. But human rights also misleadingly tend to signify universal justice, yet human rights advocates than do little more than undertake rescue missions, unable either to identify or provide what societies need to address the abuses. The fulfillment of human rights depends on democracy, not democracy on human rights. The allure of universal justice only can be approached through demotic power lodged in particular collectivities, not humanity as a whole.

While the aim of this book throughout has been to present scholarly, historicist, and analytical arguments that will pass the bar for professionals and the reading public, it also has had in view some of the major political problems of our time. They are not directly those of capitalism, social inequality, environmental degradation, racism, sexism, or political chauvinism – even though their power and injustices dwarf the issues this book engages. But its arguments have practical aspirations. They would allow us to address the problems generated by major injustices enabling us to listen more carefully to ethically driven and power-laden arguments about them, thus catalyzing more political participation by citizens. The book has sought to avoid sterile castigations of opponents from different intellectual stalls who complain about the other for not being sufficiently abstract (*pace* Rawls) or concrete (*pace* journalists) or from different practical stalls for being insensitive to morality (e.g., religious tenets or ancient virtues) or power (e.g., military security).

These days, democracy is constantly under siege by the powerful who would enthral the emotions of citizens to stockholders, rage, resentment, or by relative outsiders who do not acknowledge the genuine dilemmas of political judgment and choice. Democracy thrives when presupposes and addresses its insufficiencies, its need for a complementary paradigm of goodness but also is willing its insufficiencies, needing a horizon of goodness, but always willing to accept the authority of its basic membership, the *demos*, as the principal political power of the best possible social orders.

An abiding aim of these claims is recognition of the historical troubles of an effective *demos*. In antiquity, the *demos* was exclusive in ways that are rightfully forbidden today. In modernity, its power is truncated by representation, capitalism, individualized subjectivity and consumerism, as well as the modern state. Today, political motivations for conceptions of goodness that could motivate an actual *demos* have little traction. We only need to focus on how many citizens, willingly and via direct inducement, are drawn to demagogues as well as progressives, while few know how to reconcile political differences without ignoring injustices. Good societies, truly just societies, do not inhabit our world. Thus, while the arguments presented here are designed to turn the attention of those interested in democratic ethics to its historical roots for the sake of democratic futures, the complementarity of democracy and goodness today, not unlike in the past, occurs more on the horizon than the immediacy of political action. Yet the alternatives to more democracy in today's constitutional republics are worse. My hope is that my historicist analyses of democratic ethics will allow us to see those horizons more clearly from where we are and where we have been so that we can better cast our futures.

Bibliography

(Secondary Sources and Primary Sources Post-Antiquity)

Abdullah, H. J. 2002. "Religious Revivalism, Human Rights Activism and the Struggle for Women's Rights in Nigeria," in A. A. An-Na'im, ed., *Cultural Transformation and Human Rights in Africa* (London: Zed Books), 151–91.

Ackerman, B. A., ed. 2002. *Bush v Gore: The Question of Legitimacy* (New Haven: Yale University Press).

Adkins, A. W. H. 1960. *Merit and Responsibility: A Study in Greek Moral Values* (Chicago: University of Chicago Press).

Agamben, G. 1998 (1995). *Homo Sacer: Sovereign Power and Bare Life*, trans. D. Heller-Roaze (Stanford: Stanford University Press).

Allen, D. and J. S. Light, eds. 2015. *From Voice to Influence: Understanding Citizenship in a Digital Age* (Chicago: University of Chicago Press).

Almeida, J. A. 2003. *Justice as an Aspect of the Polis Idea in Solon's Political Poems: A Reading of the Fragments in Light of the Researches of the New Classical Archaeology* (Leiden: Brill).

Alonso, S., J. Keane, and W. Merkel, eds. 2011. *The Future of Representative Democracy* (Cambridge: Cambridge University Press).

Amer, S. 2014. *What Is Veiling?* (Chapel Hill: University of North Carolina Press).

American Anthropological Association. 1947. "Statement on Human Rights," *American Anthropologist*, Vol. 49, Pt. 4, 539–43.

American Anthropological Association. 1999. Adopted by the membership – June. www.americananthro.org/ConnectWithAAA/Content.aspx?ItemNumber =1880.

Andrew, E. R. 1989. "Equal Opportunity as a Noble Lie," *History of Political Thought*, Vol. 10, No. 4, 577–95.

Andrewes, A. 1956. *The Greek Tyrants* (London: Hutchinson's University Library).

Anghie, A. 2005. *Imperialism, Sovereignty and the Making of International Law* (Cambridge: Cambridge University Press), 196–272.

Angier, T. 2012. *Techne in Aristotle's Ethics: Crafting the Moral Life* (London: Bloomsbury Academic).

2016. "Aristotle on Work," *Revue Internationale de Philosophie*, 435–49.

Ankersmit, F. R. 2002. *Political Representation* (Stanford: Stanford University Press).

An-Na'im, A. A. 1990a. "Islam, Islamic Law, and the Dilemma of Cultural Legitimacy for Universal Human Rights," in C. E. Welch, Jr. and V. A. Leary, eds., *Asian Perspectives on Human Rights* (Boulder: Westview Press), 31–54.

    1990b. "Problems of Universal Cultural Legitimacy for Human Rights," in A. Ahmed An-Na'im and F. Deng, eds., *Human Rights in Africa: Cross-Cultural Perspectives* (Washington, D.C.: Brookings), 331–67.

    1992. "Toward a Cross-Cultural Approach to Defining International Standards of Human Rights: The Meaning of Cruel, Inhuman, or Degrading Punishment," in *Human Rights in Cross-Cultural Perspectives: The Quest for Consensus* (Washington, D.C.: Brookings), 19–43.

    2011 (1992). *Muslims and Global Justice* (Philadelphia: University of Pennsylvania Press), 65–96, 97–117.

Annan, K. 1999a. "Two Concepts of Sovereignty," *The Economist*, September 16.

    1999b. Secretary General Presents his Annual Report to General Assembly, UN Press Release SG/SM/7136 GA/9596, 20 September 1999, cited in Orford, A. 2003. *Reading Humanitarian Intervention* (Cambridge: Cambridge University Press), 41.

Aquinas, T. 2002. In R. W. Dyson, ed., *Political Writings* (Cambridge: Cambridge University Press).

Archibugi, D., M. Koenig, and R. Marchetti, eds. 2012. *Global Democracy: Normative and Empirical Perspectives* (Cambridge: Cambridge University Press).

Arendt, H. 1951. *The Origins of Totalitarianism* (New York: Harcourt Brace Jovanovich).

    1958. *The Human Condition* (Chicago: University of Chicago Press).

    1963. *On Revolution* (New York: The Viking Press).

    1968. "Tradition in the Modern Age," in *Between Past and Future: Eight Exercises in Political Thought* (New York: Viking Press).

    1972 (1970). "Civil Disobedience," in *Crises of the Republic* (New York: Harcourt Brace Jovanovich, Inc.).

    1973. *On Revolution* (New York: Viking Press).

Ashcraft, R. 1986. *Revolutionary Politics and Locke's Two Treatises of Government* (Princeton: Princeton University Press).

Bailyn, B. 1967. *The Ideological Origins of the American Revolution* (Cambridge, MA: Harvard University Press).

    1968 (1965). *The Origins of American Politics: The Charles K. Culver Lectures, Brown University* (New York: Knopf).

Baker, K. M. 1987. "Representation," in K. M. Baker, ed., *The French Revolution and the Creation of Modern Political Culture, Vol. 1 – The Political Culture of the Old Regime* (Oxford: Pergamon Press), 469–92.

    1990. *Inventing the French Revolution: Essays on French Political Culture in the Eighteenth Century* (Cambridge: Cambridge University Press).

    ed. 1994. *The Terror, Volume 4 of the French Revolution and the Creation of Modern Political Culture* (Oxford: Pergamon).

Balfour, I. and E. Cadava. 2004. "The Claims of Human Rights: An Introduction," *South Atlantic Quarterly* Vol. 103, No. 2/3 (Spring/Summer), 277–96.

Balkin, J. M. 2002. "Legitimacy and the 2000 Election," in Ackerman, ed., *Bush v. Gore: The Question of Legitimacy* (New Haven: Yale University Press), 210–28.

Ball, T., ed. 2003. *The Federalist Papers, with Letters of 'Brutus'* (Cambridge: Cambridge University Press).

Balot, R. 2001. *Greek and Injustice in Classical Athens* (Princeton: Princeton University Press).

2009. "The Virtue Politics of Democratic Athens," in Salkever, ed., *The Cambridge Companion to Ancient Greek Political Thought* (Cambridge: Cambridge University Press).

2014. *Courage in the Democratic Polis: Ideology and Critique in Classical Athens* (Oxford: Oxford University Press).

2017. "Was Thucydides a Political Philosopher?" in S. Forsdyke, R. Balot, and E. Foster, eds. *The Oxford Handbook to Thucydides* (Oxford: Oxford University Press).

Baxi, U. 2000. *The Future of Human Rights* (New Delhi: Oxford University Press).

2007. *Human Rights in a Post-Human World* (New Delhi: Oxford University Press).

Beard, M. A. 2015. *SPQR: A History of Ancient Rome* (New York: Liveright).

Bedau, H. 1970. *Civil Disobedience: Theory and Practice* (New York: Macmillan), essays by Henry David Thoreau, "Civil Disobedience" (1849) and Martin Luther King, Jr., "Letter From Birmingham City Jail" (1963).

Beiser, F. C. 2011. *The German Historicist Tradition* (Oxford: Oxford University Press).

Beitz, C. R. 2009. *The Idea of Human Rights* (Oxford: Oxford University Press).

Bellamy, A. J. 2015. *The Responsibility to Protect: A Defense* (Oxford: Oxford University Press).

Benhabib, S. 1992a. "In the Shadow of Aristotle and Hegel: Communicative Ethics and Current Controversies in Practical Philosophy," in S. Benhabib, ed., *Situating the Self: Gender, Community, and Postmodernism in Contemporary Ethics* (New York: Routledge).

1992b. "Models of Public Space: Hannah Arendt, the Liberal Tradition, and Jurgen Habermas," in C. Calhoun, ed., *Habermas and the Public Sphere* (Cambridge, MA: MIT Press), 73–88.

ed. 1996. *Democracy and Difference: Contesting the Boundaries of the Political* (Princeton: Princeton University Press).

2002. *The Claims of Culture: Equality and Diversity in the Global Era* (Princeton: Princeton University Press).

2004. *The Rights of Others: Aliens, Residents, and Citizens* (Cambridge: Cambridge University Press).

2006. *Another Cosmopolitanism*, with contributions by J. Waldron, B. Honig, and W. Kymlicka, edited and introduced by R. Post (New York: Oxford University Press).

2011. *Dignity in Adversity: Human Rights in Hard Times* (Cambridge: Polity, 2011).

Bentham, J. 1983. In F. Rosen and J. H. Burns, ed., *Constitutional Code Volume I* (Oxford: Clarendon Press).

1988. *A Fragment on Government* (Cambridge: Cambridge University Press).

1996. In J. H. Burns and H. L. A. Hart, eds., with intro. F. Rosen, *An Introduction to the Principles of Morals and Legislation* (Oxford: Oxford University Press).

2002. "Nonsense Upon Stilts ...," in P. Schofield, C. Pease-Watkin, and C. Blamires, eds., *The Collected Works of Jeremy Bentham: Rights, Representation, and Reform – Nonsense Upon Stilts and Other Writings on the French Revolution* (Oxford: Clarendon Press).

Berlin, I. 1969. "Two Concepts of Liberty" (1958), in *Four Concepts of Liberty* (New York: Oxford University Press).

Berman, A. 2015. *Give Us the Ballot: The Modern Struggle for Voting Rights in America* (New York: Farrar, Straus and Giroux).

Blok, J. H. and A. P. M. H. Lardinous, eds. 2006. *Solon of Athens: New Historical and Philological Approaches* (Leiden: Brill).

Bobonich, C. 2002. *Plato's Utopia Recast: His Later Ethics and Politics* (Oxford: Oxford University Press).

2015. "Aristotle, Political Decision-making, and the Many," in T. Lockwood and T. Samarasf, eds., *Aristotle's Politics a Critical Guide* (Cambridge: Cambridge University Press), 142–62.

Bohman, J. 2007. *Democracy across Borders: From Demos to Demoi* (Cambridge, MA: MIT Press).

Boies, D. 2004. *Courting Justice* (New York: Hyperion).

Bok, D. 1993. *The Cost of Talent: How Executives and Professionals are Paid and How It Affects America* (New York: The Free Press).

Bork, R. 2003. *Coercing Virtue: The Worldwide Rule of Judges* (Washington: The American Enterprise Institute).

Bowen, W. G. and D. Bok. 1998. *The Shape of the River: Long-Term Consequences of Considering Race in College and University Admissions* (Princeton: Princeton University Press).

Bremer, L. P. 2006. *My Year in Iraq: The Struggle to Build a Future of Hope* (New York: Touchstone).

Brett, A., J. Tully, and H. Hamilton-Bleakley, eds. 2006. *Rethinking the* Foundations of Modern Political Thought (Cambridge: Cambridge University Press).

Brock, G. 2009. *Global Justice: A Cosmopolitan Account* (Oxford: Oxford University Press).

Brooks, D. 2015. *The Road to Character* (New York: Random House).

Brown, W. 2004. "'The Most We Can Hope For': Human Rights and the Politics of Fatalism," *South Atlantic Quarterly*, Vol. 103, 461–2.

2015. *Undoing the Demos: Neoliberalism's Stealth Revolution* (New York: Zone Books).

Brunkhorst, H. 2005 (2002). *Solidarity: From Civic Friendship to a Global Legal Community*, trans. J. Flynn (Cambridge, MA: MIT Press).

2010. "Constitutionalism and Democracy in the World Society," in P. Dobner and M. Loughlin, eds., *The Twilight of Constitutionalism*.

Burnyeat, M. 1994. "Did the Ancient Greeks Have a Concept of Human Rights?" *Polis*, Vol. 13, No. 1–2, 1–11.

Bush, S. S. 2015. *The Taming of Democracy Assistance: Why Democracy Promotion Does Not Confront Dictators* (Cambridge: Cambridge University Press).

Camp, D. A. and D. C. Campbell, eds. 1982. *Greek Lyric Poetry: A Selection of Early Greek Lyric, Elegiac, and Iambic Poetry* (Bristol: Bristol Classical Press).

Campbell, D. A. 1967. *Greek Lyric Poetry: A Selection of Early Greek Lyric, Elegiac and Iambic Poetry* (New York: St Martin's Press).

Carr, E. H. 1951 (1939). *The Twenty Years' Crisis, 1919–1939; an Introduction to the Study of International Relations*, 2nd ed. (London: Macmillan & Co.).

Cartledge, P. 2000. "Greek Political Thought: The Historical Context," in C. Rowe and M. Schofield, eds., *The Cambridge History of Greek and Roman Political Thought* (Cambridge: Cambridge University Press).

  2013. "Introduction," in Herodotus: *The Histories*, trans. T. Holland (New York: Penguin).

Cassirer, E. 1963. *The Question of Jean-Jacques Rousseau* (Bloomington: Indiana University Press).

Chandler, D. 2001. "The Road to Military Humanitarianism – How the Human Rights NGOs Shaped a New Humanitarian Agenda," *Human Rights Quarterly*, Vol. 23, No. 3, 678–700.

Chhibber, P. and S. L. Ostermann. 2013. "A Democratic Balance: Bureaucracy, Political Parties, and Political Representation," in J. H. Nagel and R. M. Smith, eds., *Representation: Elections and Beyond* (Philadelphia: University of Pennsylvania Press), 166–91.

Clark, I. 2005. *Legitimacy in International Society* (Oxford: Oxford University Press).

  2007. *International Legitimacy and World Society* (Oxford: Oxford University Press).

Clarke, M. V. 1936. *Medieval Representation and Consent: A Study of Early Parliaments in England and Ireland* (London: Longmans).

Cohen, J. L. 1999. "Changing Paradigms of Citizenship and the Exclusiveness of the Demos," *International Sociology*, Vol. 14, No. 3, 245–68.

  2008. "Rethinking Human Rights, Democracy, and Sovereignty," *Political Theory*, Vol. 36, No. 4, 578–606.

  2012. *Globalization and Sovereignty: Rethinking Legality, Legitimacy, and Constitutionalism* (Cambridge: Cambridge University Press).

Collier, J. F. 2001. "Durkheim Revisited: Human Rights as the Moral Discourse for the Post-colonial, Post-Cold War world," in A. Sarat and T. R. Kearns, eds., *Human Rights: Concepts, Contests, Contingencies* (Ann Arbor: University of Michigan Press), 63–88.

Collingwood, R. G. 1939. *Autobiography* (Oxford: Clarendon Press).

Colon-Rios, J. I. 2012. *Democratic Legitimacy and the Question of Constituent Power* (New York: Routledge).

Connolly, J. 2013. *The State of Speech: Rhetoric and Political Thought in Ancient Rome* (Princeton: Princeton University Press).

Connolly, W. 1983/74. *The Terms of Political Discourse*, 2nd ed. (Princeton: Princeton University Press).

  1995. *The Ethos of Pluralization* (Minneapolis: University of Minnesota Press).

Constant, B. 1988 (1819). "The Liberty of the Ancients Compared With That of the/Moderns," in B. Fontana, ed. and trans., *Constant, Political Writings* (Cambridge: Cambridge University Press), 307–28 and "Principles of Politics Applicable to All Representative Government," in *Constant, Political Writings*.

Cooper, A. A. 1699/1711. In P. Ayres, ed., *An Inquiry Concerning Virtue, or Merit, in Characteristicks of Men, Manners, Opinions, Times,* Vol. 1 (Oxford: Clarendon Press, 1999), 189ff.

Cooper, R. H. and V. Kohler, eds. 2009. *The Responsibility to Protect: Global Moral Compact for the Twenty-First Century* (New York: Palgrave Macmillan).

Cornford, F. M. 1971 (1907). *Thucydides Mythistoricus* (Philadelphia: University of Pennsylvania Press).

Cover, R. 1983–4. "The Supreme Court, 1982 Term – Foreword: Nomos and Narrative," *Harvard Law Review,* Vol. 97, 1–68.

Cowan, Jane K., M-B. Dembour, and R. A. Wilson, eds. 2001. *Culture and Rights: Anthropological Perspectives* (Cambridge: Cambridge University Press).

Cox, A. 1977. *The Role of the Supreme Court in American Government* (New York: Oxford University Press).

Cranston, M. 1962. *Human Rights To-day* (London: Ampersand).

Cremin, L. A. 1957, *The Republic and the School: Horace Mann on the Education of the Free Man* (New York: Teachers College Press/Columbia University).

Crisp, R. and M. Slote, eds. 1997. *Virtue Ethics* (Oxford: Oxford University Press).

Dahl, R. A. 1956. *A Preface to Democratic Theory* (Chicago: University of Chicago Press).

    1961. *Who Governs?* (New Haven: Yale University Press).

    2008 (1998) *On Democracy* (New Haven: Yale University Press).

Dahrendorf, R. 1979. *Life Chances: Approaches to Social and Political Theory* (Chicago: University of Chicago Press).

De Greiff, P. and C. Cronin, eds. 2002. *Global Justice and Transnational Politics* (Cambridge, MA: MIT Press).

Derrida, J. 1988. "Signature, Event, Context," in *Limited Inc* (Evanston: Northwestern University Press), 1–23.

Dershowitz, A. 2001. *Supreme Injustice: How the Court Hijacked Election 2000* (New York: Oxford University Press).

Dewey, J. 1946 (1927). *The Public and Its Problems* (New York: Swallow Press).

    1957 (1922). *Human Nature in Conduct: An Introduction to Social Psychology* (New York: The Modern Library).

    1969 (1888) "The Ethics of Democracy," in J. Dewey and J. A. Boydston, eds., *The Early Works of John Dewey, Vol. 1: 1882–1888* (Carbondale: Southern Illinois University Press), 227–49.

    1985 (1939). "Creative Democracy: The Task Before Us," in J. A. Boydston, ed., *The Later Works, 1925–1953, Vol. 14: 1939–1941* (Carbondale: Southern Illinois University Press).

Dilthey, W. 2002 (1910). In R. A. Makkreel and F. Rodi, eds. with intro., *The Formation of the Historical World in the Human Sciences* (Princeton: Princeton University Press).

Dionne, E. J. 2012. *Our Divided Heart: The Battle for the American Idea in an Age of Discontent* (New York: Bloomsbury).

Dionne, E. J., Jr. and W. Kristol, eds. 2001. *Bush v Gore: The Court Cases and Commentary* (Washington: Brookings Institution).

Dobner, P. and M. Loughlin, eds. 2010. *The Twilight of Constitutionalism?* (Oxford: Oxford University Press).

Donlan, W. 1999 (1980) *The Aristocratic Ideal and Selected Papers* (Wauconda: Boldazzi and Carducci).

Donnelly, J. 1990. "Human Rights and Western Liberalism," in A. An-Na'im and F. Deng, eds., *Human Rights in Africa* (Washington, D.C.: Brookings Institution), 31–55.

Douglass, R. B., G. R. Mara, and H. S. Richardson, eds. 1990. *Liberalism and the Good* (New York: Routledge).

Douzinas, D. 2000. *The End of Human Rights: Critical Legal Thought at the Turn of the Century* (Oxford: Hart).

Douzinas, D. and Gearty, C., eds. 2014. *The Meanings of Rights: The Philosophy and Social Theory of Human Rights* (Cambridge: Cambridge University Press).

Downs, R. B. 1974. *Horace Mann: Champion of Public Schools* (New York: Twayne).

Doyle, M. W. 2015. *The Question of Intervention: John Stuart Mill and the Responsibility to Protect* (New Haven: Yale University Press).

Dunn, J. 1988. "Rights and Political Conflict," in L. Gostin, ed., *Civil Liberties in Conflict* (London: Routledge).

1990. *Interpreting Political Responsibility: Essays 1981–89* (Princeton: Princeton University Press).

1996. "The History of Political Theory," in *The History of Political Theory and Other Essays* (Cambridge: Cambridge University Press), 11–38.

2005. *Democracy: A History* (New York: Atlantic Monthly Press, 2005).

Dworkin, D. 2000. *Sovereign Virtue: The Theory and Practice of Equality* (Cambridge, MA: Harvard University Press).

Ehrenberg, J., J. P. McSherry, J. R. Sanchez, and C. M. Sayej, eds. 2010. *The Iraq Papers* (New York: Oxford University Press).

Ehrenberg, J., J. P. McSherry, J. R. Sanchez, C. M. Sayej, and J. Elster. 1984. *Ulysses and the Sirens: Studies in Rationality and Irrationality* (Cambridge: Cambridge University Press).

Elster, J. 1979. *Ulysses and the Sirens: Studies in Rationality and Irrationality* (Cambridge: Cambridge University Press).

Elster, J. and R. Slagstad, eds. 1988. *Constitutional Democracy* (Cambridge: Cambridge University Press).

Elver, H. 2012. *The Headscarf Controversy: Secularism and Freedom of Religion* (Oxford: Oxford University Press).

Esquith, S. L. and S. Gifford, eds. 2010. *Capabilities, Power, and Institutions: Toward a More Critical Development Ethics* (University Park: Pennsylvania State University Press).

Euben, J. P. 1977. "Creatures of a Day: Thought an Action in Thucydides," in T. Ball, ed., *Political Theory and Praxis: New Perspectives* (Minneapolis: University of Minnesota Press).

1990. *The Tragedy of Political Theory* (Princeton: Princeton University Press).

Evans, G. 2009. *The Responsibility to Protect: Ending Mass Atrocity* (Washington, D.C.: Brookings Institution Press).

Ferry, L. 1990. *Rights: The New Quarrel between the Ancients and the Moderns*, trans. F. Philip (Chicago: University of Chicago Press).

Figueira, T. and G. Nagy, eds. 1985. *Theognis of Megara: Poetry and the Polis* (Baltimore: Johns Hopkins University Press).

Fine, B. 1984. *Democracy and the Rule of Law: Liberal Ideals and Marxist Critiques* (London: Pluto Press).

Finkelberg, M. 1998. "TIME and ARETE in Homer," *Classical Quarterly*, N.S. 48, 14–28.

　2002. "Virtue and Circumstances: On the City-State Concept of ARETE," *American Journal of Philology*, Vol. 123, 35–49.

Finley, M. I. 1978. "The Athenian Empire: A Balance Sheet," in *Economy and Society in Ancient Greece* (New York: Viking Press), 41–61.

　1978 (1965). *The World of Odysseus*, revised ed. (New York: The Viking Press).

　1984. *Politics in the Ancient World* (Cambridge: Cambridge University Press).

　1985 (1978). *Democracy Ancient and Modern*, 2nd ed. (New Brunswick: Rutgers University Press).

Finnis, J. 1998. *Aquinas: Moral, Political, and Legal Theory* (Oxford: Oxford University Press).

Fisher, N. R. E. 1982. *Hybris: A Study in the Values of Honour and Shame in Ancient Greece* (Warminster: Aris and Phillips).

Fishkin, J. 1983. *Justice, Equal Opportunity, and the Family* (New Haven: Yale University Press).

Fitzsimmons, M. T. 1994. *The Remaking of France: The National Assembly and the Constitution of 1791* (Cambridge: Cambridge University Press).

Floyd, J. and M. Stears, eds. 2011. *Political Philosophy versus History? Contextualism and Real Politics in Contemporary Political Thought* (Cambridge: Cambridge University Press).

Forrest, W. G. 1966. *The Emergence of Greek Democracy: The Character of Greek Politics* (London: Weidenfeld & Nicolson).

Forsdyke, S. 2017. "Thucydides' Historical Method," in S. Forsdyke, R. Balot, and E. Foster, eds., *The Oxford Handbook to Thucydides* (Oxford: Oxford University Press).

Foucault, M. 1980 (1977). In C. Gordon, ed., *Power/Knowledge: Selected Interviews, 1972–1977* (New York: Pantheon).

Fralin, R. 1978. *Rousseau and Representation: A Study of the Development of His Concept of Political Institutions* (New York: Columbia University Press).

Frank, J. 2005. *A Democracy of Distinction: Aristotle and the Work of Politics* (Princeton: Princeton University Press).

Frankel, H. 1975 (initial version published in 1951). *Early Greek Poetry and Philosophy – A History of Greek Epic, Lyric, and Prose to the Middle of the Fifth Century*, trans. M. Hadas and J. Willis (Oxford: Basil Blackwell), 532–3.

Fraser, N. 2009. "Transnationalizing the Public Sphere: On the Legitimacy and Efficacy of Public Opinion in a Postwestphalian World," in *Scales of Justice: Reimagining Political Space in a Globalizing World* (New York: Columbia University Press).

Freeman, R. B. and J. Rogers. 2007. "The Promise of Progressive Federalism," in J. Soss, J. S. Hacker, and S. Mettler, eds., *Remaking America: Democracy and Public Policy in an Age of Inequality* (New York: Russell Sage Foundation), 205–27.

French, P. A., T. E. Uehling, Jr., H. K. French, eds. 1988. *Midwest Studies in Philosophy – Volume XIII, Ethical Theory: Character and Virtue* (Notre Dame: University of Notre Dame Press).

Fritz, C. D. 2008. *American Sovereigns: The People and America's Constitutional Tradition before the Civil War* (Cambridge: Cambridge University Press).

Fukuda-Parr, S., T. Lawson-Remer, and S. Randolph, eds. 2015. *Fulfilling Social and Economic Rights* (Oxford: Oxford University Press).

Gadamer, H.-G. 1975 (1960). *Truth and Method* (New York: The Seabury Press).

Galston, W. 1986. "Equality of Opportunity and Liberal Theory," in F. S. Lucash, ed., *Justice and Equality Here and Now* (Ithaca: Cornell University Press).

Gardiner, P. 1996. "Interpretation in History: Collingwood and Historical Understanding," in A. O'Hear, ed., *Verstehen and Humane Understanding: Royal Institute of Philosophy Supplement 41* (Cambridge: Cambridge University Press), 109–20.

Genser, J. and I. Cotler, eds. 2012. *The Responsibility to Protect: The Promise of Stopping Mass Atrocities in Our Time* (Oxford: Oxford University Press).

Gentili, B. 1988 (1985). *Poetry and Its Public in Ancient Greece: From Homer to the Fifth Century*, trans. with intro. A. Thomas Cole (Baltimore: Johns Hopkins University Press).

Geuss, R. 1981. *The Idea of a Critical Theory: Habermas and the Frankfurt School* (Cambridge: Cambridge University Press).

  2001. *History and Illusion in Politics* (Cambridge: Cambridge University Press).

  2004. "Dialectics and the Revolutionary Impulse," in F. Rush, ed., *The Cambridge Companion to Critical Theory* (Cambridge: Cambridge University Press).

  2008. *Philosophy and Real Politics* (Princeton: Princeton University Press).

Glanville, L. 2014a. "Armed Humanitarian Intervention and the Problem of Abuse after Libya," in D. E. Scheid, ed., *The Ethics of Armed Humanitarian Intervention* (Cambridge: Cambridge University Press).

  2014b. *Sovereignty and the Responsibility to Protect: A New History* (Chicago: University of Chicago Press.

Glazer, N. 1978. "Affirmative Action in Employment: From Equal Opportunity to Statistical Parity," in *Affirmative Discrimination: Ethnic Inequality and Public Policy* (New York: Basic Books), 33–76.

Glendon, M. A. 2001. *A World Made New: Eleanor Roosevelt and the Universal Declaration of Human Rights* (New York: Random House).

Goldstene, C. 2014. *The Struggle for America's Promise: Equal Opportunity at the Dawn of Corporate Capitalism* (Biloxi: University Press of Mississippi).

Goodale, M., ed. 2006. American Anthropologist, Vol. 108, 1–83. M. Goodale, ed., includes articles by Cowan, Goodale, Merry, Riles, and Wilson.

  2009. *Human Rights: An Anthropological Reader* (Malden: Wiley-Blackwell).

Goodhart, M. 2005. *Democracy as Human Rights: Freedom and Equality in the Age of Globalization* (New York: Routledge).

Gough, H. 1998/2010. *The Terror in the French Revolution*, 2nd ed. (London: PalgraveMacMillan).

Gould, C. C. 2004. *Globalizing Democracy and Human Rights* (Cambridge: Cambridge University Press).

2014, "Is There a Human Right to Democracy?," in *Interactive Democracy: The Social Roots of Global Justice* (Cambridge: Cambridge University Press).

Guarini, E. F. 1990. "Machiavelli and the Crisis of the Italian Republics," in G. Bok, Q. Skinner, and M. Viroli, eds., *Machiavelli and Republicanism* (Cambridge: Cambridge University Press).

Guinier, L. 1995. *Tyranny of the Majority: Fundamental Fairness and Representative Democracy* (New York: The Free Press).

2015. *The Tyranny of the Meritocracy: Democratizing Higher Education in America* (Boston: Beacon Press).

Gundogku, A. 2015. *Rightlessness in an Age of Rights: Hannah Arendt and the Contemporary Struggle of Migrants* (Oxford: Oxford University Press).

Habermas, J. 1975 (1973). *Legitimation Crisis* (Boston: Beacon Press).

1984–5 (1981). *The Theory of Communicative Action*, 2 vols., trans. T. McCarthy (Boston: Beacon Press).

1990 (1983). "Discourse Ethics: Notes on a Program of Philosophical Justification," in *Moral Consciousness and Communicative Action*, trans. C. Lehnhardt and S. W. Nicholson (Cambridge, MA: MIT Press).

1996 (1992). *Between Facts and Norms: Contributions to a Discourse Theory of Law and Democracy*, trans. W. Rehg (Cambridge, MA: MIT Press).

2001 (1998). "Remarks on Legitimation Through Human Rights," in *The Postnational Constellation: Political Essays*, trans. M. Pensky, P. De Greiff, and C. Cronin, eds., *Global Justice and Transnational Politics* (Cambridge, MA: MIT Press, 2002).

2006. "The Kantian Project and the Divided West: Does the Constitution of International Law Still Have a Chance?," in *The Divided West* (Cambridge: Polity Press).

2008 (2005). "On the Architectonics of Discursive Differentiation: A Brief Response to a Major Controversy," in *Between Naturalism and Religions: Philosophical Essays*, trans. C. Cronin (Cambridge, MA: Polity Press).

2009 (2008). "Political Communication in Media Society: Does Democracy Still Have an Epistemic Dimension? The Impact of Normative Theory on Empirical Research," in *Europe: The Faltering Project*, trans. C. Cronin (Cambridge: Polity Press).

2010. "Human Dignity and the Realistic Utopia of Human Rights," in *Metaphilosophy*, Vol. 41, No. 4 (July), 464–80.

Hacker, J. S. and P. Pierson. 2005. *Off Center: The Republican Revolution and the Erosion of American Democracy* (New Haven: Yale University Press).

Halberstam, D. 1992 (1972). *The Best and the Brightest* (New York: Ballantine).

Halevy, E. 1972 (1928). *The Growth of Philosophic Radicalism*, trans. M. Morris (London: Faber & Faber Limited).

Hammer, D. 2002. *The Iliad as Politics: The Performance of Political Thought* (Norman: University of Oklahoma Press).

Handlin, O. 1966. The popular sources of political authority; documents on the Massachusetts constitution of 1780. Edited with an introduction by Oscar and Mary Handlin (Cambridge, MA: Harvard University Press).

Hansen, M. H. 1990. *Athenian Democracy in the Age of Demosthenes* (Oxford: Blackwell).

　　2005. *The Tradition of Ancient Greek Democracy and Its Importance for Modern Democracy* (Copenhagen).

Hanson, R. H. 1985. *The Democratic Imagination in America* (Princeton: Princeton University Press).

　　1989. "Democracy," in T. Ball, J. Farr, and R. L. Hanson, eds., *Political Innovation and Conceptual Change* (Cambridge: Cambridge University Press), 68–89.

Hare, R. M. 1967. "The Lawful Government," in P. Laslett and W. G. Runciman, *Philosophy, Politics, and Society, Third Series* (Oxford: Basil Blackwell), 157–72.

Hart, H. L. A. 1984 (1955) "Are There Any Natural Rights," reprinted in J. Waldron, ed., *Theories of Rights* (New York: Oxford University Press).

Hartz, L. 1955. *The Liberal Tradition in America: An Interpretation of American Political Thought Since the Revolution* (New York: Harcourt Brace Jovanovich).

Haubold, J. 2000. *Homer's People: Epic Poetry and Social Formation* (Cambridge: Cambridge University Press).

Hawthorn, G. 2012. "Receiving Thucydides Politically," in K. Harloe and N. Morley, eds., *Thucydides and the Modern World: Reception, Reinterpretation and Influence from the Renaissance to the Present* (Cambridge: Cambridge University Press), 212–28.

Henderson, J. 2002. "Demos, Demagogue, Tyrant in Attic Old Comedy, in K. A. Morgan, ed., *Popular Tyranny: Sovereignty and Its Discontents in Ancient Greece* (Austin: University of Texas Press), 117–54 and 155–79.

Hill, C. 1975. *Change and Continuity in 17th Century England* (Cambridge, MA: Harvard University Press).

Hirschl, R. 2010. *Constitutional Theocracy* (Cambridge, MA: Harvard University Press).

Hirschman, A. O. 1982. *Shifting Involvements: Private Interest and Public Action* (Princeton: Princeton University Press).

Hobbes, T. 1991 (1651). In R. Tuck, ed., *Leviathan* (Cambridge: Cambridge University Press).

Hochschild, J. 1995. *Facing Up to the American Dream: Race, Class, and the Soul of the Nation* (Princeton: Princeton University Press).

Honig, B. 1993. *Political Theory and the Displacement of Politics* (Ithaca: Cornell University Press).

Holzgrefe, J. L. and R. O. Keohane, eds. 2003. *Humanitarian Intervention: Ethical, Legal, and Political Dilemmas* (Cambridge: Cambridge University Press).

Hucko, E. M. 1987. *The Democratic Tradition: Four German Constitutions* (Oxford: Berg Publishers).

Hunt, L. 2000. "The Paradoxical Origins of Human Rights," in J. N. Wasserstrom, L. Hunt, and M. B. Young, eds., *Human Rights and Revolutions* (Lanham: Rowman & Littlefield), 3–18.

　　2007. *Inventing Human Rights: A History* (New York: W. W. Norton).

Hurd, I. 2007. *After Anarchy: Legitimacy and Power in the United Nations National Security Council* (Princeton: Princeton University Press).

Hutcheson, F. 2008 (1725). In W. Leidhold, ed., *An Inquiry into the Original of Our Ideas of Beauty and Virtue*, revised ed. (Indianapolis: Liberty Fund).

Ignatieff, M. 2000. *Human Rights as Politics and Idolatry* (Princeton: Princeton University Press).

2004. *The Lesser Evil: Political Ethics in an Age of Terror* (Princeton: Princeton University Press).

Ingram, J. D. 2008. "What is a 'Right to Have Rights'? Three Images of the Politics of Human Rights," *American Political Science Review*, Vol. 102, No. 4, 401–16.

Irwin, E. 2005. *Solon and Early Greek Poetry: The Politics of Exhortation* (Cambridge: Cambridge University Press).

Isaac, J. 1996. "A New Guarantee On Earth: Hannah Arendt on Human Dignity and the Politics of Human Rights," *American Political Science Review*, Vol. 90, No. 1, 61–84.

Ishay, M. 2004. *The History of Human Rights: From Ancient Times to the Globalization Era* (Berkeley: University of California Press).

Issacharoff, S. 2011. "On Political Corruption," in M. Youn, ed., *Money, Politics, and the Constitution: Beyond Citizens United* (New York: The Century Foundation), 119–34.

Jaeger, W. 1939–1945. *Paideia: The Ideals of Greek Culture: Vol. I*, 2nd ed. (New York: Oxford University Press).

Jaspers, K. 1958. *The Idea of the University* (Boston: Beacon Press).

Jefferson, T. 1999. In J. Appleby and T. Ball, eds., *Political Writings* (Cambridge: Cambridge University Press).

Jencks, C. 1984. "What Must Be Equal for Opportunity to be Equal?," in N. Bowie, ed., *Equal Opportunity* (Boulder: Westview Press).

Jones, A. H. M. 1957. *Athenian Democracy* (Oxford: Basil Blackwell).

Joppke, C. 2009. *The Veil: Mirror of Identity* (Cambridge: Polity).

Judis, J. B. 2016. *The Populist Explosion: How the Great Recession Transformed American and European Politics* (New York: Columbia Global Reports).

Kallet, L. 2002. "Demos Tyrannos: Wealth, Power, and Economic Patronage" in K. A. Morgan, ed., *Popular Tyranny: Sovereignty and Its Discontents in Ancient Greece* (Austin: University of Texas Press).

Kalyvas, A. 2008. *Democracy and the Politics of the Extraordinary: Max Weber, Carl Schmitt, and Hannah Arendt* (Cambridge: Cambridge University Press).

Kalyvas, A. and I. Katznelson. 2008. *Liberal Beginnings: A Republic for the Moderns* (Cambridge: Cambridge University Press).

Kammen, M. 1986. *The Origins of the American Constitution* (New York: Penguin).

1991. *Mystic Chords of Memory: The Transformation of Tradition in American Culture* (New York: Alfred A. Knopf).

Kane, J. and Patapan, H. 2012. *The Democratic Leader: How Democracy Defines, Empowers, and Limits Its Leaders* (Oxford: Oxford University Press).

Kane, J. and H. Patapan, eds. 2014. *Good Democratic Leadership: On Prudence and Judgment in Modern Democracies* (Oxford: Oxford University Press).

Kant, I. 1929/33 (1781/7). *Critique of Pure Reason*, trans. N. K. Smith (London: Macmillan).

1991 (1784–95). In H. S. Reiss, ed., *Political Writings*, 2nd ed. (Cambridge: Cambridge University Press).

Kantorowicz, E. 1957. *The King's Two Bodies* (Princeton: Princeton University Press).

Karlan, P. S. 2014. "Citizens Deflected: Electoral Integrity and Political Reform," in R. C. Post, ed., *Citizens Divided: Campaign Finance Reform and the Constitution.*

Karst, K. 1989. *Belonging to America: Equal Citizenship and the Constitution* (New Haven: Yale University Press).

Keedus, L. 2015. *The Crisis of Historicism: The Early Political Thought of Hannah Arendt and Leo Strauss* (Cambridge: Cambridge University Press).

Kelly, D. 2003. *The State of the Political: Conceptions of Politics and the State in the Thought of Max Weber, Carl Schmitt, and Franz Neumann* (Oxford: Oxford University Press).

Kelly, P. 2011. "Rescuing Political Theory from the Tyranny of History," in Floyd and Stears, eds., *Political Philosophy versus History* (Cambridge: Cambridge University Press), 13–37.

Kennedy, D. 2004. *The Dark Sides of Virtue: Reassessing International Humanitarianism* (Princeton: Princeton University Press).

Keohane, N. 2010. *Thinking about Leadership* (Princeton: Princeton University Press).

Keuth, H. 2005. *The Philosophy of Karl Popper* (Cambridge: Cambridge University Press).

Keyssar, A. 2000/9. *The Right to Vote: The Contested History of Democracy in the United States*, revised ed. (New York: Basic Books).

Kloppenberg, J. T. 2000 (1991). "Virtue," in J. P. Greene and J. R. Pole, eds., *A Companion to the American Revolution* (Malden: Blackwell).

Koppelman, A. 1996. *Antidiscrimination Law and Social Inequality* (New Haven: Yale University Press).

Korey, W. 1998. *NGOs and the Universal Declaration of Human Rights: A Curious Grapevine* (New York: St. Martin's Press).

Korsgaard, C. 1996. *Creating the Kingdom of Ends* (Cambridge: Cambridge University Press).

Korteweg, A. C. and G. Yurdakul, eds. 2014. *The Headscarf Debates: Conflicts of National Belonging* (Stanford: Stanford University Press).

2000. *The Kosovo Report* (Oxford: Oxford University Press).

Kramnick, I., ed. 1999. *The Portable Edmund Burke* (New York: Penguin).

Krueger, A. B. 2007. *What Makes a Terrorist* (Princeton: Princeton University Press).

Kumm, M. 2010. "The Best of Times and the Worst of Times: Between Constitutional Triumphalism and Nostalgia," in P. Dobner and M. Loughlin, eds., *The Twilight of Constitutionalism* (Oxford: Oxford University Press).

Kuper, A. 2004. *Democracy beyond Borders: Justice and Representation in Global Institutions* (Oxford: Oxford University Press).

ed. 2005. *Global Responsibilities: Who Must Deliver on Human Rights?* (New York: Routledge).

Laborde, C. 2008. *Critical Republicanism: The Hijab Controversy and Political Philosophy* (Oxford: Oxford University Press).

Lane, M. 2011. "Constraint, Freedom, and Exemplar," in J. Floyd and M. Stears, eds., *Political Philosophy vs. History* (Cambridge: Cambridge University Press).

2013. "Claims to Rule: The Case of the Multitude," in M. Deslauriers and P. Destree, eds., *Cambridge Companion to Aristotle's Politics* (New York: Cambridge University Press), 247–74.

Lauren, P. G. 1998/2003. *The Evolution of International Human Rights: Visions Seen* (Philadelphia: University of Pennsylvania Press).

Lemann, N. 1999. *The Big Test: The Secret History of the American Meritocracy* (New York: Farrar, Straus and Giroux).

Lessig, L. 2011. *Republic, Lost: How Money Corrupts Congress – And a Plan to Stop It* (New York: Twelve).

Leveque, P. and P. Vidal-Naquet. 1992 (1964). In D. A. Curtis, trans. and ed., *Cleisthenes the Athenian: An Essay on the Representation of Space and Time in Greek Political Thought from the End of the Sixth Century to the Death of Plato, With a New Discussion of the Invention of Democracy by Pierre Vidal-Naquet, Cornelius Castoriadis, and Pierre Leveque* (Atlantic Highlands: Humanities Press).

Levin, R. 2013. *The Worth of the University* (New Haven: Yale University Press).

Lewis, J. 2006. *Solon the Thinker: Political Thought in Archaic Athens* (London: Duckworth).

Lichtheim, G. 1967 (1965). "The Concept of Ideology," in *The Concept of Ideology and Other Essays* (New York: Vintage Books), 3–46.

Lintott, A. 1999. *The Constitution of the Roman Republic* (Oxford: Oxford University Press).

Lloyd-Jones, H. 1971. *The Justice of Zeus* (Berkeley: University of California Press).

Locke, J. 1988 (1690). In P. Laslett, ed., *Two Treatises of Government* (Cambridge: Cambridge University Press).

Long, A. A. 1970. "Morals and Values in Homer," *The Journal of Hellenic Studies*, 90, 121–39, followed by Adkins's response, "Homeric Values and Homeric Society," *The Journal of Hellenic Studies*, 91 (1971), 1–14.

Loraux, N. 1986 (1981). *The Invention of Athens: The Funeral Oration in the Classical City*, trans. A. Sheridan (Cambridge, MA: Harvard University Press).

2009. "Thucydides and Sedition among Words," in J. S. Rusten, ed., *Oxford Readings in Classical Studies: Thucydides* (Oxford: Oxford University Press), 261–292.

MacIntyre, A. 1981. *After Virtue: A Study in Moral Theory* (Notre Dame: University of Notre Dame Press).

Manin, B. 1997. *The Principles of Representative Government* (Cambridge: Cambridge University Press).

Manville, P. M. 1990. *The Origins of Citizenship in Ancient Athens* (Princeton: Princeton University Press).

Marks, S. 2000. *The Riddle of All Constitutions: International Law, Democracy, and the Critique of Ideology* (Oxford: Oxford University Press).

Marshall, T. H. 1964 (1949). "Citizenship and Social Class," in T. H. Marshall, ed., *Class, Citizenship and Social Development* (Cambridge: Cambridge University Press).

Martin, R. and D. A. Reidy, eds. 2005. *Rawls's Law of Peoples: A Realistic Utopia?* (Oxford: Blackwell).

Marx, K. 1970 (1843). In J. O'Malley, ed., *Critique of Hegel's Philosophy of Right* (Cambridge: Cambridge University Press).

1978 (1843). "On the Jewish Question," in R. Tucker, ed., *The Marx-Engels Reader*, 2nd ed. (New York: W. W. Norton).

Marx, L. 2000 (1964). *The Machine in the Garden: Technology and the Pastoral Ideal in America* (New York: Oxford University Press).

Mason, A. T. 1965. *Free Government in the Making: Readings in American Political Thought*, 3rd ed. (New York: Oxford University Press).

McCormick, J. 2011. *Machiavellian Democracy* (Cambridge: Cambridge University Press).

McGinty, R. 2003. "The Pre-war Reconstruction of Post-war Iraq," *Third World Quarterly*, Vol. 24, 601–17.

Mehta, P. B. 2006. "From State Sovereignty to Human Security (via Institutions?)," in T. Nardin and M. S. Williams, eds., *Humanitarian Intervention – NOMOS XLVII* (New York: New York University Press), 259–85.

Mehta, U. 1999. *Liberalism and Empire: A Study in Nineteenth-Century British Liberal Thought* (Chicago: University of Chicago Press).

Meier, C. 1990 (1980). *The Greek Discovery of Politics*, trans. D. McClintock (Cambridge, MA: Harvard University Press).

Meiklejohn, A. 1913. *Freedom and the College* (New York: Century).

1920. *The Liberal College* (Boston: Marshall Jones).

1948. *Free Speech and Its Relation to Self-Government* (New York: Harper).

Merquior, J. G. 1980. *Rousseau and Weber: Two Studies in the Theory of Legitimacy* (London: Routledge & Kegan Paul).

Mertus, J. A. 2005. "Human Rights and Civil Society, in R. A. Wilson, ed., *Human Rights in the "War on Terror"* (Cambridge: Cambridge University Press), 317–33.

Mhire, J. J. and B. P. Frost, eds. 2014. *The Political Theory of Aristophanes: Explorations in Poetic Wisdom* (Albany: SUNY Press).

Michelman, F. 1996. "Parsing 'A Right to Have Rights,'" *Constellations*, Vol. 3, No. 2 (October), 200–9.

Mill, J. S. 1991 (1861). "Considerations of Representative Government," in J. Stuart Mill, ed., *On Liberty and Other Essays* (Oxford: Oxford University Press).

Miller, M. A. 2013. *The Foundations of Modern Terrorism: State, Society and the Dynamics of Political Violence* (Cambridge: Cambridge University Press).

Morgan, E. 1989. *Inventing the People: The Rise of Popular Sovereignty in England and America* (New York: W. W. Norton).

Morris, I. 1996. "The Strong Principle of Equality," in J. Ober and C. Hedrick, eds., *Demokratia: A Conversation on Democracies, Ancient and Modern* (Princeton: Princeton University Press), 19–48.

Morsink, J. 1999. *The Universal Declaration of Human Rights: Origins, Drafting, Intent* (Philadelphia: University of Pennsylvania Press).

Mosse, C. 2013. "The Demos's Participation in Decision-Making: Principles and Realities," in J. P. Arnason, K. A. Raaflaub, and P. Wagner, eds., *The Greek Polis and the Invention of Democracy* (West Sussex: John Wiley & Sons).

Mousourakis, G. 2003. *The Historical and Institutional Context of Roman Law* (Aldershot: Ashgate).

Moyn, S. 2010. *The Last Utopia: Human Rights in History* (Cambridge, MA: Harvard University Press).

Mueller, J.-W. 2016. *What Is Populism?* (Philadelphia: University of Pennsylvania Press).

Mutua, M. 2002. *Human Rights: A Political and Cultural Critique* (Philadelphia: University of Pennsylvania Press).

2016. *Human Rights Standards: Hegemony, Law, and Politics* (Albany: SUNY Press).

Nagel, T. 1987. "Moral Conflict and Political Legitimacy," *Philosophy and Public Affairs*, Vol. 16, No. 3, 215–40.

Nagy, G. 1999. *The Best of the Achaeans: Concepts of the Hero in Archaic Greek Poetry*, revised ed. (Baltimore: Johns Hopkins University Press).

Neumann, F. 1986 (1923–1954?). *The Rule of Law: Political Theory and the Legal System in Modern Society* (Leamington Spa: Berg).

Neustadt, R. E. and E. R. May. 1986. *Thinking in Time: The Uses of History for Decision-Makers* (New York: The Free Press).

Nietzsche, F. 1997 (1876), "On the Uses and Disadvantages of History for Life," in R. J. Hollingdale, ed. and trans., *Untimely Meditations* (Cambridge: Cambridge University Press), 57–123.

1986 (1886) *Human, All Too Human*, trans. R. J. Hollingdale (Cambridge: Cambridge University Press).

Normand, R. and S. Zaidi, 2008. *Human Rights at the UN: The Political History of Universal Justice*, United Nations Intellectual History Project (Bloomington: Indiana University Press).

Noussia-Fantuzzi, M. 2010. *Solon the Athenian, the Poetic Fragments* (Leiden: Brill).

Nussbaum, M. and A. Sen, eds. 1993. *The Quality of Life* (Oxford: Clarendon Press).

2002. "Capabilities and Human Rights," in C. Cronin and P. De Greiff, eds., *Global Justice and Transnational Politics* (Cambridge, MA: MIT Press), 117–49.

. 2011. *Creating Capabilities: The Human Development Approach* (Cambridge, MA: Harvard University Press).

Ober, J. 1989. *Mass and Elite in Democratic Athens* (Princeton: Princeton University Press).

1996 (1993). "The Athenian Revolution of 508/7 B.C.: Violence, Authority, and the Origins of Democracy," in *The Athenian Revolution: Essays in Ancient Greek Democracy and Political Theory* (Princeton: Princeton University Press), 32–52.

1998. *Political Dissent in Democratic Athens: Intellectual Critics of Popular Rule* (Princeton: Princeton University Press).

2005. "Aristotle's Natural Democracy," in R. Kraut and S. Skultety, eds., *Aristotle's Politics: Critical Essays* (Lanham: Rowman & Littlefield).

2007. "Natural Capacities and Democracy as a Good-in-Itself," *Philosophical Studies*, Vol. 132, 59–73.

2008. "The Original Meaning of 'Democracy': Capacity to Do Things, Not Majority Rule," *Constellations*, Vol. 15, No. 1, 1–9.

Orfield, G. and S. E. Eaton. 2016. *Dismantling Desegregation: The Quiet Reversal of Brown v. Board of Education* (New York: The New Press).

Orwell, G. 1952 (1938). *Homage to Catalonia* (Boston: Beacon Press).

1983 (1939). *1984: A Novel* (New York: New American Library).

Ottaway, M. and T. Carothers, 2000. *Funding Virtue: Civil Society and Democracy Promotion* (Washington, D.C.: Carnegie Endowment for International Peace).

Parker, R. 1996. *Athenian Religion: A History* (Oxford: Oxford University Press).

Parry, A. M. 1981 (1957). *Logos and Ergon in Thucydides* (New York: Arno Press).

Patterson, C. 1981. *Pericles' Citizenship Law of 451–50 B.C.* (New York: Arno Press, 1981).

Pattison, J. 2010. *Humanitarian Intervention and the Responsibility to Protect: Who Should Intervene?* (New York: Oxford University Press).

Paul, E. F., F. D. Miller, Jr., and J. Paul, eds. 1988. *Virtue and Vice* (New York: Cambridge University Press).

Pepperman, B. T. 2010. *Horace Mann's Troubling Legacy: The Education of Democratic Citizens* (Lawrence: University of Kansas Press).

Pettit, P. 1997. *Republicanism: A Theory of Freedom and Government* (Oxford: Oxford University Press).

Piketty, T. 2014. *Capital in the Twenty-First Century* (Cambridge, MA: Harvard University Press).

Pitkin, H. F. 1972. *The Concept of Representation* (Berkeley: University of California Press).

1989. "Representation," in T. Ball, J. Farr, and R. Hanson, eds., *Political Innovation and Conceptual Change* (Cambridge: Cambridge University Press), 132–54.

2004. "Representation and Democracy: Uneasy Alliance," *Scandinavian Political Studies*, Vol. 27, 335–42.

Pogge, T. 2001. *Global Justice* (Oxford: Blackwell).

Pole, J. R. 1966. *Political Representation in England and the Origins of the American Republic* (New York: MacMillan).

1993. rev. & exp. (1978). *The Pursuit of Equality in American History* (Berkeley: University of California Press).

1983. *The Gift of Government: Political Responsibility from the English Restoration to American Independence* (Athens: The University of Georgia Press).

Popper, K. R. 1957 (1936). *The Poverty of Historicism* (New York: Harper & Row).

Posner, R. A. 2001. *Breaking the Deadlock: The 2000 Election, the Constitution, and the Courts* (Princeton: Princeton University Press).

Post, L. F. 1916 (1903). *The Ethics of Democracy: A Series of Optimistic Essays on the Natural Laws of Human Society*, 3rd ed. (Indianapolis: Bobbs-Merrill).

Post, R. C. 2000. "Between Philosophy and Law: Sovereignty and the Design of Democratic Institutions," in I. Shapiro and S. Macedo, eds., *Designing Democratic Institutions – NOMOS XLII* (New York: New York University Press), 209–23.

2015. *Citizens Divided: Campaign Finance Reform and the Constitution* – The Tanner Lectures on Human Values, with commentary by P. S. Karlan, L. Lessig, F. Michelman, and N. Urbinati (Cambridge, MA: Harvard University Press, 2014).

Power, S. and Allison, G., eds. 2006. *Realizing Human Rights: Moving From Inspiration to Impact* (Palgrave MacMillan).

Raaflaub, K. 1989. "Contemporary Perceptions of Democracy in Fifth-Century Athens," *Classica et Mediaevalia,* Vol. XL, 33–70.

1994. "Democracy, Power, and Imperialism in Fifth-Century Athens," in J. P. Euben, J. R. Wallach, and J. Ober, eds., *Athenian Political Thought and the Reconstruction of American Democracy* (Ithaca: Cornell University Press).

1998. "The Transformation of Athens in the Fifth Century," in D. Boedeker and K. A. Raaflaub, eds., *Democracy, Empire, and the Arts* (Cambridge, MA: Harvard University Press).

2013a. "Perfecting the 'Political Creature': Equality and 'the Political' in the Evolution of Greek Democracy," in J. Arneson, K. A. Raaflaub, and P. Wagner, eds., *The Greek Polis and the Invention of Democracy: A Politico-cultural Transformation and Its Interpretations* (Chichester: Wiley-Blackwell).

2013b. "*Ktema es aiei*: Thucydides' Concept of 'Learning through History' and Its Realization in His Work," in A. Tsakmakis and M. Tramiolaki, eds., *Thucydides between History and Literature* (Berlin: Walter de Gruyter), 3–22.

Raaflaub, K., J. Ober, R. W. Wallace, w/ P. Cartledge, and C. Farrar. 2005. *The Origins of Democracy in Ancient Greece* (Berkley: University of California Press).

Rabinow, P., ed. 1984. *The Foucault Reader* (New York: Pantheon).

Radkau, J. 2011. *Max Weber: A Biography* (Cambridge: Polity).

Ranciere, J. 2006 (2005). *Hatred of Democracy*, trans. S. Corcoran (London: Verso).

2010. In S. Corcoran, ed. and trans., *Dissensus: On Politics and Aesthetics* (London: Continuum).

Rawlence, B. 2016. *City of Thorns: Nine Lives in the World's Largest Refugee Camp* (New York: Picador).

Rawls, J. 1971. *A Theory of Justice* (Cambridge, MA: Harvard University Press).

1996. *Political Liberalism* (New York: Columbia University Press).

1994. *Ethics in the Public Domain* (Oxford: Oxford University Press), Ch. 10.

1999 (1997). *The Law of Peoples, with "The Idea of Public Reason Revisited"* (Cambridge, MA: Harvard University Press).

1999a (1985). "Justice as Fairness: Political, not Metaphysical," in S. Freeman, ed., *Collected Papers* (Cambridge, MA: Harvard University Press).

1999b (1987). "The Idea of an Overlapping Consensus," in S. Freeman, ed., *Collected Papers* (Cambridge, MA: Harvard University Press).

2001. *Justice as Fairness: A Restatement* (Cambridge, MA: Harvard University Press).

Raz, J. 1979. "'The Claims of Law' and 'The Rule of Law and Its Virtue'," in *The Authority of Law* (Oxford: Clarendon Press).

ed. 1990. "Introduction," in J. Raz, ed., *Authority* (New York: New York University Press), 1–19.

1994. *Ethics in the Public Domain: Essays in the Morality of Law and Politics* (Oxford: Clarendon Press).

Reich, R. 2015. *Saving Capitalism: For the Many, Not the Few* (New York: Alfred A. Knopf).

Reid, J. P. 1989. *The Concept of Representation in the Age of the American Revolution* (Chicago: University of Chicago Press).

Reill, P. H. 1975. *The German Enlightenment and the Rise of Historicism* (Berkeley: University of California Press).

Reiss, H., ed. 1991. *Kant: Political Writings* (Cambridge: Cambridge University Press).

Responsibility to Protect: Report of the International Commission on Intervention and State Sovereignty. (Ottawa: International Development Research Centre, 2001).

Rieff, D. 2002. *A Bed for the Night: Humanitarianism in Crisis* (New York: Simon & Schuster).

Risse, T., S. C. Ropp, and K. Sikkink, eds. 1999. *The Power of Human Rights: International Norms and Domestic Change* (Cambridge: Cambridge University Press).

2013. *The Persistent Power of Human Rights: From Commitment to Compliance* (Cambridge: Cambridge University Press).

Risse, T. and K. Sikkink, *The Power of Principles: The Socialization of Human Rights Norms in Domestic Practice*.

Roberts, J. T. 1994. *Athens on Trial: The Anti-Democratic Tradition in Western Political Thought* (Princeton: Princeton University Press).

Robinson, E. W. 1997. *The First Democracies: Early Popular Government Outside Athens* (Stuttgart: Franz Steiner Verlag).

2011. *Democracy beyond Athens: Popular Government in the Greek Classical Age* (Cambridge: Cambridge University Press).

Rorty, R. 1979. *Philosophy and the Mirror of Nature* (Princeton: Princeton University Press).

1993. "Human Rights, Rationality, and Sentimentality," in S. Shute, ed., *On Human Rights, Oxford Amnesty Lectures* (New York: Basic Books), 111–31.

Rosanvallon, P. 2011 (2008). *Democratic Legitimacy: Impartiality, Reflexivity, Proximity*, trans. A. Goldhammer (Princeton: Princeton University Press).

Rosen, F. (1983). *Jeremy Bentham and Representative Democracy: A Study of the Constitutional Code* (Oxford: Clarendon Press).

Rosenblatt, H. 1997. *Rousseau and Geneva: From the First Discourse to the Social Contract, 1749–1762* (Cambridge: Cambridge University Press).

Rosenblum, N., ed. 1991. *Liberalism and the Moral Life* (Cambridge, MA: Harvard University Press).

Rosenfeld, M. and A. Arato, eds. 1998. *Habermas on Law and Democracy: Critical Exchanges* (Berkeley: University of California Press).

Rousseau, J.-J. 1973 (1754). In G. D. H. Cole, ed. and trans., *The Social Contract and Discourses* (New York: E. P. Dutton).

1986 (1953). *Political Writings* (Madison: University of Wisconsin Press).

Rowe, C. J. 1983. "The Nature of Homeric Morality," in C. A. Rubino and C. W. Shelmerdine, eds., *Approaches to Homer* (Austin: University of Texas Press), 248–75.

Rowe, C. J., M. Schofield, w/ S. Harrison, and M. Lane, eds. 2000. *The Cambridge History of Greek and Roman Political Thought* (Cambridge: Cambridge University Press).

Rubenstein, J. C. 2015. *Between Samaritans and States: The Political Ethics of Humanitarian INGOs* (Oxford: Oxford University Press).

Sadurski, W. 2008. *Equality and Legitimacy* (Oxford: Oxford University Press).

Salkever, S., ed. 2009. *The Cambridge Companion to Ancient Greek Political Thought* (Cambridge: Cambridge University Press).

Samuel, L. R. 2012. *The American Dream: A Cultural History* (Syracuse: Syracuse University Press).

Sandel, M. J. 1996 (1982). *Liberalism and the Limits of Justice* (Cambridge: Cambridge University Press).

Schaar, J. H. 1981 (1967). "Equality of Opportunity and Beyond," in his collection of essays, *Legitimacy in the Modern State* (New Brunswick: Transaction Publishers), 193–210.

Scheuerman, W. E. 2012. *Frankfurt School Perspectives on Globalization, Democracy, and the Law* (New York: Routledge).

Schmitt, C. 1996 (1932a). *The Concept of the Political*, trans. G. Schwab (Chicago: University of | Chicago Press).

  2004 (1932b). *Legality and Legitimacy*, trans. J. Seitzer (Durham: Duke University Press).

  2006 (1922). *Political Theology: Four Chapters on the Concept of Sovereignty* (Chicago: University of Chicago Press).

  2008 (1928). *Constitutional Theory*, trans. J. Seitzer (Durham: Duke University Press), 2.

  2014 (1921). *Dictatorship: From the Origin of the Modern Concept of Sovereignty to the Class Struggle*, trans. M. Hoelzl and G. Ward (Cambridge: Polity Press).

Schofield, P. 2006. *Utility and Democracy: The Political Thought of Jeremy Bentham* (Oxford: Oxford University Press).

Scholte, J. A., ed. 2011. *Building Global Democracy? Civil Society and Accountable Global Governance.* (Cambridge: Cambridge University Press).

Schuller, M. 2012. *Killing with Kindness: Haiti, International Aid, and NGOs* (New Brunswick: Rutgers University Press, 2012).

Schumpeter, J. 1950 (1942). *Capitalism, Socialism and Democracy*, 3rd ed. (New York: Harper & Row).

Scott, J. C. 1990. *Domination and the Arts of Resistance: Hidden Transcripts* (New Haven: Yale University Press).

Scott, A. 2010. *Talking to the Enemy: Religion, Brotherhood, and the (Un)Making of Terrorists* (New York: HarperCollins).

Scott, J. W. 2007. *The Politics of the Veil* (Princeton: Princeton University Press).

Scurr, R. 2006. *Fatal Purity: Robespierre and the French Revolution* (New York: Henry Holt).

Sen, A. 1985. "Rights and Capabilities," in T. Honderich, ed., *Morality and Objectivity* (London: Routledge), 130–48.

  1999a. *Development as Freedom* (New York: Alfred A. Knopf).

  1999b. "Democracy as a Universal Value," *Journal of Democracy*, Vol. 10, No. 3, 3–17.

  2004. "Elements for a Theory of Human Rights," *Philosophy and Public Affairs*, Vol. 32, No. 4, 315–56.

  2005. "Merit and Justice," in S. Bowles and S. Durlauf, eds., *Meritocracy and Economic Inequality* (Princeton: Princeton University Press).

  2009. *The Idea of Justice* (Cambridge, MA: Harvard University Press).

Sennett, R. 1998. *The Corrosion of Character: The Personal Consequences of Work in the New Capitalism* (New York: W. W. Norton).

Shapiro, I. 1982. "Realism in the Study of the History of Ideas," *History of Political Thought*, Vol. VIII, No. 3, 535–78.

ed. 1994. *The Rule of Law – NOMOS* (New York: New York University Press).

1999. *Democratic Justice* (New Haven: Yale University Press).

2003a. *The Moral Foundations of Politics* (New Haven: Yale University Press).

2003b. "John Locke's Democratic Theory" in I. Shapiro, ed., *Two Treatises of Government and A Letter Concerning Toleration* (New Haven: Yale University Press).

2005 (1992). "The Difference That Realism Makes: Social Science and the Politics of Consent" (with Alexander Wendt), in *The Flight From Reality in the Human Sciences* (Princeton: Princeton University Press).

2009. *Political Representation*, S. C. Stokes, E. J. Wood, and A. S. Kirshner, eds. (Cambridge: Cambridge University Press).

2010. *The Real World of Democratic Theory* (Princeton: Princeton University Press).

2016. *Politics against Domination* (Cambridge, MA: Harvard University Press).

Sharma, S. K. and J. M. Welsh. 2015. *The Responsibility to Prevent: Overcoming the Challenges of Atrocity Prevention* (Oxford: Oxford University Press).

Sharp, A., ed. 1998. *The English Levellers* (Cambridge: Cambridge University Press).

Shay, J. 1994. *Achilles in Vietnam: Combat Trauma and the Undoing of Character* (New York: Scribner).

2002. *Odysseus in America: Combat Trauma and the Trials of Homecoming* (New York: Scribner).

Shell-Duncan, B. and Y. Hernlund, eds. 2000. *Female "Circumcision" in Africa* (Boulder: Lynne Rienner).

Siegel, R. 2012. "Equality Divided," *Harvard Law Review*, Vol. 1, 127.

Sieyés, E. J. 2003. In M. Sonenscher, ed. and trans., *Political Writings, Including the Debate between Sieyes and Tom Paine in 1791* (Indianapolis: Hackett).

Simms, B. and D. J. B. Trim. 2011. *Humanitarian Intervention: A History* (Cambridge: Cambridge University Press).

Skinner, Q. 1969 (1989). "Meaning and Understanding in the History of Ideas," in J. Tully, ed., *Meaning and Context: Quentin Skinner and His Critics* (Princeton: Princeton University Press).

1973. "The Empirical Theorists of Democracy and Their Critics: A Plague on Both Their Houses," *Political Theory*, Vol. 1, No. 3, 287–306.

1974. "Some Problems in the Analysis of Thought and Action," *Political Theory* Vol. 2, No. 3, 277–303.

1989. "A Reply to My Critics," in J. Tully, ed., *Meaning and Context: Quentin Skinner and His Critics* (Princeton: Princeton University Press), 255–58.

1996. *Reason and Rhetoric in the Philosophy of Hobbes* (Cambridge: Cambridge University Press).

2002 (1972, rev.) "Conquest and Consent: Hobbes and the Engagement Controversy," in Q. Skinner, ed., *Visions of Politics – Volume III: Hobbes and Civil Science* (Cambridge: Cambridge University Press).

2005. "Hobbes on Representation," *European Journal of Philosophy*, Vol. 13, No. 2, 155–84.

2010. "On Trusting the Judgement of Our Rulers," in R. Bourke and R. Geuss, eds., *Political Judgement: Essays for John Dunn* (Cambridge: Cambridge University Press).

Smelser, N. J. 2007. *The Faces of Terrorism* (Princeton: Princeton University Press).

Sourvinou-Inwood, C. 1990. "What is Polis-Religion?" in O. Murray and S. Price, eds., *The Greek City from Homer to Alexander* (Oxford: Oxford University Press).

Starr, P. 1984. *The Social Transformation of American Medicine: The Rise of a Sovereign Profession and the Making of a Vast Industry* (New York: Basic Books).

Ste. Croix, G. E. M. de. 1953/4. "The Character of the Athenian Empire," *Historia*, Vol. 3, 1–41.

2004. *Athenian Democratic Origins* (Oxford: Oxford University Press).

Stevenson, T. 2015. "Sisi's Way," *London Review of Books*, Vol. 37, No. 4 (February 19), 3–7.

Strauss, L. 1953. *Natural Right and History* (Chicago: The University of Chicago Press).

1959 (1949). "Political Philosophy and History," in *What is Political Philosophy and Other Essays* (Glencoe: The Free Press), 56–77.

1964. *The City and Man* (Chicago: University of Chicago Press).

Stein, R. 2010. *For Love of the Father: A Psychoanalytic Study of Religious Terrorism* (Stanford: Stanford University Press).

Talmon, J. L. 1952. *The Origins of Totalitarian Democracy* (London: Secker & Warburg).

Tamanaha, B. Z. 2004. *On the Rule of Law: History, Politics, Theory* (Cambridge: Cambridge University Press).

Tandy, D. W. and W. C. Neale, eds. 1996. *Hesiod's Works and Days – A Translation and Commentary for the Social Sciences* (Berkeley: University of California).

Taylor, B. P. 2010. *Horace Mann's Troubling Legacy: The Education of Democratic Citizens* (Lawrence: University of Kansas Press).

Tawney, R. H. 1931–51. In R. Titmuss, ed., *Equality* (London: Allen & Unwin).

Teachout, Z. 2014. *Corruption in America* (Cambridge, MA: Harvard University Press).

Teubner, G., ed. 1986. *Dilemmas of Law in the Welfare State* (Berlin: Walter de Gruyter).

ed. 1997. "'Global Bukowina': Legal Pluralism in the World Society," in G. Teubner, ed., *Global Law without a State* (Aldershot: Dartmouth), 3–28.

2012. *Constitutional Fragments: Societal Constitutionalism and Globalization*, trans. G. Norbury (Oxford: Oxford University Press).

Thakur, R. and W. Maley, eds. 2015. *Theorising the Responsibility to Protect* (Cambridge: Cambridge University Press).

Thompson, D. F. 1976. *John Stuart Mill and Representative Government* (Princeton: Princeton University Press).

Thornhill, C. 2010. "Legality, Legitimacy and the Constitution: A Historical-functionalist Approach," in C. Thornhill, and S. Ashenden, eds., *Legality and Legitimacy: Normative and Sociological Approaches* (Baden-Baden: Nomos).

2011. *A Sociology of Constitutions: Constitutions and State Legitimacy in Historical-Sociological Perspective* (Cambridge: Cambridge University Press).

Tocqueville, A. 1969 (1835, 1840). In J. P. Mayer, ed., *Democracy in America*, trans. G. Lawrence (New York: Doubleday).

1955 (1856). *The Old Regime and the French Revolution*, trans. S. Gilbert (New York: Vintage).

Todorov, T. 2014. "The Responsibility to Protect and the War in Libya," in D. E. Scheid, ed., *The Ethics of Armed Humanitarian Intervention* (Cambridge: Cambridge University Press).

Tomasky, M. J. 2016. "Trump and the Media," *The New York Review of Books*, April 21.

Tuchman, B. 1962. *The Guns of August* (New York: Macmillan).

Tuck, R. 1979. *Natural Rights Theories* (Cambridge: Cambridge University Press).

2001. *The Rights of War and Peace: Political Thought and the International Order from Grotius to Kant*, revised ed. (Oxford: Oxford University Press).

2006. In A. Brett, J. Tully, and H. Hamilton-Bleakley, eds., *And Rethinking [Quentin Skinner's] the Foundations of Modern Political Thought* (Cambridge: Cambridge University Press), 171–98 and 191–218.

2016. *The Sleeping Sovereign: The Invention of Modern Democracy* (Cambridge: Cambridge University Press).

Tucker, R. C. 1978. *The Marx-Engels Reader*, 2nd ed. (New York: W. W. Norton).

Tully, J., ed. 1988. *Meaning and Context: Quentin Skinner and His Critics* (Princeton: Princeton University Press).

2014. "Two Traditions of Human Rights," in M. Lutz-Bachmann and A. Nascimento, eds., *Human Rights, Human Dignity, and Cosmopolitan Ideals: Essays on Critical Theory and Human Rights* (Surrey: Ashgate), 139–57.

Tully, J. and J. Locke, eds. 1983 (1690). *A Letter Concerning Toleration* (Indianapolis: Hackett).

Ullmann, W. 1975. *Law and Politics in the Middle Ages: An Introduction to Medieval Political Ideas* (Ithaca: Cornell University Press).

Urbinati, N. 2006. *Representative Democracy: Principles and Genealogy* (Chicago: University of Chicago Press).

2011. "Representative Democracy and Its Critics," in S. Alonso, J. Keane, and W. Merkel, eds., *The Future of Representative Democracy* (Cambridge: Cambridge University Press).

Vieira, M. B. and D. Runciman. 2008. *Representation* (Cambridge: Polity Press).

Vlastos, S. 1995 (1946). "Solonian Justice," *Classical Philology*, Vol. 41, reprinted in *Studies in Greek Philosophy – Vol. I: The Presocratics*, D. W. Graham, eds., (Princeton: Princeton University Press), 32–56.

Wahl, R. 2010. "In Defence of 'Constitution'," in P. Dobner and M. Loughlin, eds., *The Twilight of Constitutionalism* (Oxford: Oxford University Press), 220–42.

Waldron, J. 1995. "The Wisdom of the Multitude: Some Reflections on Book 3, Chapter 11 of Aristotle's Politics," *Political Theory*, Vol. 23, 563–84.

2007. "Dignity and Rank," *European Journal of Sociology*, Vol. XLVIII, 201–37.

Wallach, J. R. 1983. "Review of *After Virtue: An Essay in Moral Theory*, by Alasdair MacIntyre," *Telos*, Vol. 57, 233–40.

1987. "Liberals, Communitarians, and the Tasks of Political Theory," *Political Theory*, Vol. 15, No. 4, 581–611.

1992. "Contemporary Aristotelianism," *Political Theory*, Vol. 20, No. 4, 613–41.

1994. "Two Democracies and Virtue," in J. P. Euben, J. R. Wallach, and J. Ober, eds., *Athenian Political Thought and the Reconstruction of Athenian Democracy* (Ithaca: Cornell University Press).

1997. "Review of W. Connolly, The Ethos of Pluralization," *Political Theory*, Vol. 25, No. 6, 886–93.

2000. "Can Liberalism Be Virtuous?" in *Polity*, Vol. 32, No. 1, 163–74.

2001. *The Platonic Political Art: A Study of Critical Reason and Democracy* (University Park: The Pennsylvania State University Press).

2003. "American Constitutionalism and Democratic Virtue," in *Ratio Juris*, Vol. 15, No. 3, 219–41.

2005. "Human Rights as an Ethics of Power," in R. A. Wilson, ed., *Human Rights in the 'War on Terror'* (Cambridge: Cambridge University Press), 108–36.

2011a. "Constitutive Paradoxes of Human Rights: An Interpretation in History and Political Theory," in A. Sarat, ed., *Studies in Law, Politics and Society, Vol. 56–Human Rights: New Possibilities/New Problems* (Emerald), 37–66.

2011b. "*Demokratia* and *Arete* in Ancient Greek Political Thought," *POLIS: The Journal for Ancient Greek Political Thought,* Vol. 28, No. 2, 181–215.

2016a. Review of Alasdair MacIntyre's *After Virtue*, in J. Levy, ed., *Oxford Handbook of Classics in Contemporary Political Thought* (Oxford: Oxford University Press), www.oxfordhandbooks.com/view/10.1093/oxfordhb/9780198717133.001.0001/oxfordhb-9780198717133-e-52.

2016b. "Deconstructing the Ancients-Moderns Trope in Historical Reception," *Polis: The Journal of Ancient Greek Political Thought*, Vol. 33, No. 2, 265–90.

Waltz, K. 1959. *Man, The State, and War: A Theoretical Analysis* (New York: Columbia University Press).

Walzer, M. 1983. *Spheres of Justice* (New York: Basic Books).

Weber, M. 1958a (1904). *The Protestant Ethic and the Spirit of Capitalism*, trans. T. Parsons (New York: Charles Scribner's Sons).

1958b. "The Social Psychology of the World's Religions," in H. H. Gerth and C. Wright Mills, eds., *From Max Weber: Essays in Sociology* (New York: Oxford University Press), 267–301.

1968. In G. Roth and C. Wittich, eds., *Economy and Society: An Outline of Interpretive Sociology* (Berkeley: University of California Press).

1994. In R. Speirs, ed., *Political Writings* (Cambridge: Cambridge University Press).

1975 (1926, 1950). In trans. from the German and H. Zohn, ed., *Max Weber: A Biography* (New York: John Wiley & Sons).

Weiler, J. H. H. and M. Wind, eds. 2003. *European Constitutionalism beyond the State* (Cambridge: Cambridge University Press).

Weiss, T. 2007. *Humanitarian Intervention – Ideas in Action*, w/ foreword by G. Evans (Cambridge: Polity Press).

Weissbrodt, D. 2008. *The Human Rights of Non-Citizens* (Oxford: Oxford University Press).

Westen, D. 2007. *The Political Brain: The Role of Emotion in Deciding the Fate of the Nation* (New York: PublicAffairs).

Wilkerson, I. 2010. *The Warmth of Other Suns: The Epic Story of America's Great Migration* (New York: Random House).

Williams, B. 1962. "The Idea of Equality," in P. Laslett and W. G. Runciman, eds., *Philosophy, Politics, and Society*, 2nd series (Oxford: Basil Blackwell), 110–31.

　　1985. *Ethics and the Limits of Philosophy* (Cambridge, MA: Harvard University Press).

　　1993. *Shame and Necessity* (Berkeley: University of California Press).

　　2005. *In the Beginning Was the Deed: Realism and Moralism in Political Argument* (Princeton: Princeton University Press).

Wilson, R. A., ed. 1997. *Human Rights, Culture & Context: Anthropological Perspectives* (London: Pluto Press).

　　ed. 2003. *Human Rights in a Global Perspective* (Cambridge: Cambridge University Press).

Wilson, R. A. and R. Brown, eds. 2006. *Humanitarianism and Suffering* (Cambridge: Cambridge University Press).

Wilson, R. A. and R. D. Brown, eds. 2009. *Humanitarianism and Suffering: The Mobilization of Empathy* (Cambridge: Cambridge University Press).

Wolff, E. N. 2002. *Top Heavy: The Increasing Inequality of Wealth in American and What Can Be Done About It* (New York: The New Press).

Wolin, S. 1960/2004. *Politics and Vision: Continuity and Innovation in Western Political Thought*, expanded ed. (Princeton: Princeton University Press).

　　1989. *The Presence of the Past: Essays on the State and the Constitution* (Baltimore: Johns Hopkins University Press).

　　1994. "Norm and Form: The Constitutionalizing of Democracy," in J. P. Euben, J. R. Wallach, and J. Ober, eds., *Athenian Political Thought and the Reconstruction of American Democracy* (Ithaca: Cornell University Press).

　　2008. *Democracy Incorporated: Managed Democracy and the Specter of Inverted Totalitarianism* (Princeton: Princeton University Press).

　　2016. In N. Xenos, ed., *Fugitive Democracy and Other Essays* (Princeton: Princeton University Press).

Woloch, I. 1994. "The Contraction and Expansion of Democratic Space during the Period of the Terror," in *The French Revolution and the Creation of Modern Political Culture, Volume 4: The Terror* (Oxford: Pergamon Press).

Women of Color Against Violence, ed. 2007. *The Revolution Will Not Be Funded: Beyond the Non-profit Industrial Complex* (Cambridge: South End Press).

Wood, G. S. 1969. *The Creation of the American Republic, 1776–1787* (New York: W. W. Norton).

Wood, D. 2016. *What Have We Done* (New York: Little Brown).

Wright, E. O. and J. Rogers. 2011. *American Society: How It Really Works* (New York: W. W. Norton).

Yack, B. 1993. *The Problems of a Political Animal: Community, Justice, and Conflict in Aristotelian Political Thought* (Berkeley: University of California Press).

Yoo, J. 2003. "International Law and the War in Iraq," *American Journal of Int'l Law*, Vol. 97, 563.

Young, M. 1994 (1958). *The Rise of the Meritocracy 1870–2033* (New Brunswick: Transaction Books).

Young, I. M. 2000. *Inclusion and Democracy* (Oxford: Oxford University Press).

Zelden, C. 2008. *Bush v. Gore: Exposing the Hidden Crisis in American Democracy* (Lawrence: University of Kansas Press).

Index

action, 17
  arete as, 63
  centrality of, 12–17, 24, 44, 205–6,
    273–4, 275–6
  civil rightness and, 183–5
  dangers of episodic, 132
  democratic ethics as, 48
  demotic agency, 51–2
  as essential to democracy, 3–4
  human rights, 255–7, 266–71
  instability of political, 23
  materialist-individualist, 44–5
  political cooperation, 45–6
  political participation, 56
  realist view, 29–31
  representation and, 140–2
affirmative action, 147, 170, 171–4
African Americans, 106, 170–6.
  See also civil rightness; equal
  opportunity
After Virtue: a study in moral theory
  (MacIntyre), 27
Alito, Samuel, 172
American dream, 146–7
Anti-Federalism, 124–8
Apology of Socrates (Plato), 77–9
Aquinas, Thomas, 108
Arendt, Hannah, 16, 45, 52, 242
arete, 6, 18, 58
  as action, 63
  as aristocratic trait, 79
  Aristotle on, 81–91
  challenges to, 67–73
  with *demokratia*, 73–7
  legitimacy and, 188–9
  in modern representative democracy,
    98–9
  modern separation from democracy,
    91–3
  origins, 53, 56–60
  Plato on, 80–1
  political dimension, 60–6

secondary views, 57–8
  Socratic, 77–9
aristocracy. *See also* classes, social
  in ancient Greece, 60, 65, 67, 71,
    87–9
  claims to *arete*, 79
  modern economic elites, 138–45
  oligarchy, 71–2, 77, 87–9
  shifts in power, 151
Aristophanes
  Clouds, 79
Aristotle, 60
  on *arete*, 81–91
  historicism of, 32
  Nicomachean Ethics, 84
  on Plato, 83–4
  Politics, 84–90
  telos, 240
Athenian democracy, 9, 12
  arete in, 56–8
  in concert with *arete*, 73–7
  demos, 95
  emergence, 67
  exercise of power in, 102–3
  features of *arete*, 59–60
  idealized by Mill, 121–3
  legitimacy and, 188–9
  modern views, 58–9
  overview, 53–60
  separation from *arete*, 81–91
  tension with *arete*, 80–1

*Bakke v. Regents of the University of
  California*, 171
Beitz, Charles, 246–7
Benhabib, Seyla, 251–4
Bennett, William J., 54
Bentham, Jeremy, 107, 119–21, 160
Between Facts and Norms (Habermas),
  201, 203–6
Brooks, David
  Road to Character, The, 54